THE CHINESE SHADOW ON INDIA'S EASTWARD ENGAGEMENT

India, one of the largest importers of oil in the world, has been diversifying its energy resource options and moving towards greater energy security. This book analyses India's potential for building energy ties in the Asia-Pacific considering the global and regional power politics. Facing China's growing influence in Asia, India's eastward engagement with its extended neighbours has been entrenched in its Act East Policy and institutional commitments towards Southeast Asia.

This volume focuses on diverse facets of energy security beyond the traditional understanding of demand and supply and price and stability. It examines India's energy sector, its dependence on hydrocarbons, and the push towards renewable and alternate energy resources. It further looks at the strategic importance of the Indian Ocean and South China Sea regions in geopolitical negotiations from an energy perspective and how China's influence in the region will affect India's moves towards greater energy cooperation with the countries of East Asia.

With contributions by leading experts, the volume seeks to fill a major void in this theme and cater to the needs of a variety of audiences including academics, policymakers and experts in international relations, geopolitics and geoeconomics, and professionals in the field of energy studies.

Sanjay K. Bhardwaj is Professor of South Asian Studies and the Energy Studies Programme at the School of International Studies, Jawaharlal Nehru University, New Delhi. He was Chairperson at the Centre for South Asian Studies and Director of the Energy Studies Programme at SIS, JNU. He specialises in India's foreign policy, energy security, politico-security and economic issues of India and South Asia, Southeast Asia and East Asia.

Routledge Critical Perspectives on India and China

India and China together are home to more than one-third of the world's population. Two of the fastest growing economies today, these two nations will be key to the world's future.

This unique collaborative series between the Routledge India and China publishing programmes aims to bring cutting-edge, interdisciplinary research from and on these two global powers. The books in this series will focus on topical and emergent issues in contemporary India and China, presenting new perspectives on politics, society, economy, environment, and culture.

India and China
Economics and Soft Power Diplomacy
Edited by Geeta Kochhar and Snehal Ajit Ulman

The Rise of India and China
Social, Economic and Environmental Impacts
Edited by Kala S Sridhar and Li Jingfeng

The Chinese Shadow on India's Eastward Engagement
The Energy Security Dimension
Edited by Sanjay K. Bhardwaj

For more information about this series, please visit:
www.routledge.com/Routledge-Critical-Perspectives-on-India-and-China/book-series/RCPIC

THE CHINESE SHADOW ON INDIA'S EASTWARD ENGAGEMENT

The Energy Security Dimension

Edited by Sanjay K. Bhardwaj

Routledge
Taylor & Francis Group
LONDON AND NEW YORK

First published 2022
by Routledge
2 Park Square, Milton Park, Abingdon, Oxon OX14 4RN

and by Routledge
605 Third Avenue, New York, NY 10158

Routledge is an imprint of the Taylor & Francis Group, an informa business

British Library Cataloguing-in-Publication Data
A catalogue record for this book is available from the British Library

Library of Congress Cataloging-in-Publication Data
A catalog record has been requested for this book

ISBN: 978-0-367-75268-2 (hbk)
ISBN: 978-0-367-76000-7 (pbk)
ISBN: 978-1-003-16506-4 (ebk)

Typeset in Bembo
by SPi Global, India

Dedicated to my
mother

नास्ति मातृसमा छाया नास्ति मातृसमा गतिः।

नास्ति मातृसमं त्राणं नास्ति मातृसमा प्रपा ॥
---वेदव्यास, (महाभारत, शान्तिपर्वI २६६/३१)

There is no shade like a mother, no resort like a mother, no security like a mother, no other ever-giving foundation of life!

(*Veda Vyasa, Mahabharata, Shantiparva, 266/31*)

CONTENTS

List of figures *x*
List of tables *xii*
List of contributors *xiv*
List of abbreviations *xx*
Acknowledgements *xxvii*

Introduction 1
Sanjay K. Bhardwaj

PART I
Energy security policy: Debates in India **13**

1 India's energy security contours 15
Sanjay K. Bhardwaj

2 India's energy security in the era of global energy transition 32
Girijesh Pant

3 Challenges and strategy for an energy secure India 52
Shebonti Ray Dadwal

4 Energy efficiency and clean energy transitions in India: What do these mean for climate change mitigation? 67
Meeta Keswani Mehra and Deepti Kohli

5 Low-carbon energy security for India: Exploring Asia-Pacific cooperation 99
Sacchidananda Mukherjee

PART II
India's Act East policy and energy cooperation 125

6 India's energy cooperation with Southeast Asia under Act East policy 127
S.D. Muni

7 India's Act East policy: The energy dimension 139
G.V.C. Naidu

8 India's energy trade with Southeast Asia: Opportunities and challenges 157
Amita Batra and Priyanshi Chauhan

9 ASEAN–India energy cooperation: Current status and future scope of cooperation 180
Prabir De and Durairaj Kumarasamy

PART III
India–China: Geo-politics of energy cooperation 201

10 Deconstruction of regions: Emerging role of subregional cooperation in Asia 203
Takaaki Oiwa

11 China's energy cooperation with Southeast and South Asia 217
Srikanth Kondapalli

12 Factoring Northeast Asia in India's energy security 230
Sharad K. Soni

13 The 'Belt and Road Initiative' and India–China energy cooperation and competition 248
B.R. Deepak

14 Geo-politics of the South China Sea: The energy perspective 262
Sanjay K. Bhardwaj and Md. Obaidur Rahaman

Index *283*

FIGURES

1.1	Energy security's 4A inter linkage with sustainability indicators	17
1.2	Various perspectives of energy security	18
1.3	Elements of energy transition: Energy system and drivers for change	20
1.4	Basic aspects of energy security	20
4.1	Share of energy consumption	68
4.2	Primary energy consumption trends	69
4.3	Growth rate of energy consumption	70
4.4	Sector-wise use of natural gas in India during 2016–2017	74
4.5	Sectoral consumption of petroleum products in India during 2016–2017	74
4.6	Sector-wise consumption of electricity in India during 2016–2017	75
4.7	CO_2 emissions in India during 1990–2015 (million tons)	81
4.8	Per-capita CO_2 emissions in India and the world for 1990–2015	82
4.9	CO_2/total primary energy supply (TPES) for India and the world	82
5.1	Compound average annual growth rate of TPED (%) (IEA's New Policies Scenario)	102
5.2	Energy intensity of GDP (kg of oil equivalent per $1,000 GDP at constant 2011 PPP)	107
5.3	CO_2 emission intensity of GDP (kg per 2011 PPP $ of GDP)	107
5.4	Compound average annual growth rate of energy-related CO_2 emission (IEA's New Policies Scenario)	109
5.5	Present and future energy demand by fuel in Indian the power sector	110
5.6	India's demand for TPED in alternative scenarios	110
5.7	India's energy-related CO_2 emissions in alternative scenarios	111
5.8	Prospects for electricity import (GWh) for India	114

5.9 Prospects for electricity export (GW) from India 114
7.1 India–ASEAN trade 144
7.2 China–ASEAN trade 145
8.1 Energy mix (MW) 159
8.2 Net energy imports as a percentage of energy use (2014) 160
8.3 Net energy imports as a percentage of energy use 2000–2014 161
8.4 Per capita electric power consumption (KWh) 2014 162
8.5 Access to electricity (percentage of population) 2016 162
8.6 India's export and import of fuel with Bangladesh 2006–18 164
8.7 India's export and import of fuel with Myanmar 2006–18 164
8.8 India's export and import of fuels with Vietnam 2006–18 164
8.9 India's trade in fuels with Indonesia 2006–2018 165
8.10 India's trade in fuels with Malaysia 2006–2018 165
8.11 India's trade in fuels with Thailand 2006–2018 166
8.12 China's net energy imports (as a percentage of energy use): 1999–2014 169
8.13 Import of crude oil through the South China Sea 169
8.14 Comparison of region-wise fuel imports: 2018 171
8.15 Comparison of fuel imports of India and China from selected Southeast Asian countries: 2018 171
9.1 Interconnection Projects of ASEAN Power Grid. ASEAN Centre for Energy (ACE) 190
9.2 ASEAN Renewable Energy Targets. Authors' own based on ASEAN Centre for Energy (ACE) 192
9.3 SDG 7 and India SDG 7 and India United Nations, 2020 195
9.4 ASEAN–India Energy Cooperation Outline Authors' own 196
10.1 Economic corridors in the Greater Mekong subregion 205
10.2 Achievement of the highest growth rates by CLMVs in the ASEAN region 206
10.3 Economic corridors proposed by BRI 207
10.4 Depiction of China as the upper riparian country of many transboundary rivers 209
14.1 Strategic significance of South China Sea 267
14.2 Exporters (2016) 268
14.3 Importers (2016) 268

TABLES

1.1	Share of different sources in primary energy mix	16
4.1	Primary energy consumption across different regions of the world (Mtoe)	69
4.2	Primary energy consumption across Asia Pacific countries (Mtoe)	70
4.3	Key energy indicators across select countries for 2016	72
4.4	Energy demand by end-use sectors	75
4.5	Contribution of individual fuel supplies in total primary energy supply	77
4.6	Trends of foreign trade in India for 2016–2017 (in million tons)	78
4.7	Projections of total primary energy supply and total final consumption under the two scenarios	79
4.8	Share of global emissions and population for major emitters, 2010	81
4.9	GHG emissions inventory (in CO_2 equiv terms) and key contributing sectors	83
4.10	Aggregate CO_2 emissions in India under the alternative IEA scenarios	83
4.11	Overall energy intensity of India and world from 1990 to 2030	85
4.12	Sectoral energy intensity for India (thousand Indian rupees (INR))	85
4.13	Energy saving by end-use based on efficiency scenario (in per cent)	86
4.14	Energy saving in building sector based on the efficiency scenario	89
4.15	Energy saving in residential sector based on efficiency scenario	90
4.16	Cumulative energy saving, avoided generation capacity and GHG reduction	91
5.1	Source-wise projection of India's total primary energy demand (TPED) (IEA's new policies scenario)	101
5.2	Coal balance of India for 2016–2017 (provisional)	103

5.3 Crude oil and petroleum products balances of India for 2016–2017 (provisional) 104
5.4 Selected indicators for 2016 106
5.5 India's energy-related CO_2 emission (IEA's new policies scenario) 108
5.6 Net energy imports of selected countries in Asia Pacific region (Mtoe) 112
5.7 Export and import of electricity, 2016 113
5.8 Cost of electricity from renewable sources 116
5.9 Cost assumptions for high-voltage DC (HVDC) cables in AUD 117
7.1 India's trade balance with ASEAN members (USD million) 144
7.2 India's imports from select ASEAN countries ($mn) 145
7.3 India's exports to select ASEAN countries ($mn) 145
7.4 FDI in ASEAN 146
7.5 Indian energy investments in Southeast Asia 146
7.6 Natural resources exploration 147
7.7 Indian FDI in ASEAN (000s US$) 147
8.1 Exports and imports of fuel by India (US thousand $) 163
9.1 Targets for SDG 7 181
9.2 Energy resource potential in South Asia 182
9.3 Renewable energy potential in South Asia 182
9.4 India's export of HSD to South Asian countries (US$ million) 183
9.5 India's export of high-speed diesel, top ten destinations 185
9.6 Major Indian firms invested in energy sector in ASEAN: 2008–19 186
11.1 China's energy forecasts, 1995–2020 218
14.1 Estimated hydrocarbon production in SCS (2011) 265
14.2 Estimated proved and probable reserves in SCS (2011) 266

CONTRIBUTORS

Amita Batra is Professor of Economics and currently Chairperson at the Centre for South Asian Studies, School of International Studies, Jawaharlal Nehru University (JNU). She has also been Senior Visiting Fellow at the Department of Political Economy, Faculty of Arts and Social Sciences at the University of Sydney in October 2018 and the first holder, in January–May 2013, of the ICCR Professorial Chair in Contemporary Indian Studies at the Centre for South Asian Studies & Edinburgh-India Institute, University of Edinburgh.

Sanjay K. Bhardwaj is Professor of South Asian Studies and the Energy Studies Programme at the School of International Studies, Jawaharlal Nehru University, New Delhi. He was Chairperson at the Centre for South Asian Studies and Director, of the Energy Studies Programme at SIS, JNU. He specialises in India's foreign policy, energy security, politico-security and economic issues of India and South Asia, Southeast Asia and East Asia. He is recipient of the Sir Ratan Tata Fellow Award 2009–10, London School of Economics and Political Science, London, UK, ASIA Fellows Awards 2010–11, ASIA Scholarship Foundation, Bangkok, Chinese Academy of Social Science – ICSSR Fellow – 2013, Beijing, China, and SUSI Fellow 2018 National Security Policy Making at University of Delaware, USA. He has completed major projects on 'India's Energy Security: Inter-regional Cooperation to Energy Security Society' and 'India's Neighbourhood Policy: Small and Big Neighbours in South Asia'. He has authored a number of books/monographs and over three dozen articles and research papers. He has successfully supervised more than 30 PhD scholars and 40 MPhils on many contemporary issues viz. water, energy, connectivity, border, domestic and foreign policy issues.

Priyanshi Chauhan is Senior Research scholar, pursuing a PhD degree and obtained MPhil in Energy Studies at the Centre for South Asian Studies, School of International Studies, Jawaharlal Nehru University, New Delhi. She holds a MA degree in International Relations and is an Economics graduate from the University of Delhi. Her research interests include energy trade, energy security, economic integration and foreign policy in South Asia.

Prabir De is Professor at the Research and Information System for Developing Countries (RIS), New Delhi. He is also the Head of ASEAN-India Centre (AIC), RIS. He is also an Adjunct Fellow of the National Maritime Foundation (NMF), New Delhi; Institute of Chinese Studies (ICS, New Delhi and South Asia Network of Economic Modelling (SANEM), Dhaka. Dr De works in the field of international economics and has research interests in international trade and development. He was a Visiting Fellow of the Institute of Developing Economies (IDE-JETRO), Japan; Asian Development Bank Institute (ADBI), Tokyo; and Visiting Senior Fellow of United Nations Economic and Social Commission for Asia and the Pacific (UNESCAP), Bangkok. He obtained an MSc in Economics from Calcutta University and PhD in Economics from Jadavpur University, Kolkata. He has contributed several research papers in international journals and written books on trade and development. His recent work includes *Act East to Act Indo-Pacific: India's Expanding Neighbourhood* (2020), and he edited a volume (with Selim Raihan), *Trade and Regional Integration in South Asia: A Tribute to Saman Kelegama.* He is the Founding Editor of the *Journal of Asian Economic Integration*, published by Sage.

B.R. Deepak is Professor at the Centre for Chinese and South East Asian Studies, Jawaharlal Nehru University, New Delhi. He was trained in Chinese history and India–China relations at the Peking University and Chinese Academy of Social Sciences, Beijing, at Jawaharlal Nehru University, New Delhi and University of Edinburgh, UK. He has been the Nehru and Asia Fellow at the Chinese Academy of Social Sciences, Beijing. His publications include *India and China 1904–2004: A Century of Peace and Conflict* (2005); *India–China Relations in First Half of the Twentieth Century* (2001); *India–China Relations: Future Perspectives* (co ed. 2012); *India–China Relations: Civilizational Perspective* (2012) *China: Agriculture, Countryside and Peasants* (2010); *Cheeni Kavita: Gayarvin Shatavdi se Chuahdvin Shatavdi Tak* (*Chinese Poetry: 1100 BC to 1400 AD*) (2011), a translation of 88 selected classical poems for which he was awarded the 2011 'Special Book Prize of China', the first Indian to receive the highest literary award from China. The author has been a visiting professor at the Chinese Academy of Social Sciences, Tianjin Foreign Studies University, China, Doon University, Dehradun India, and Teaching Fellow at the Scottish Centre of Chinese Studies in the University of Edinburgh, UK.

Deepti Kohli holds an MSc Economics degree (with specialization in Environmental and Resource Economics) from The Energy Resource Institute (TERI) School of Advanced Studies (SAS), New Delhi. She has obtained an MPhil, and submitted a PhD degree at the Centre for International Trade and Development, School of International Studies, JNU. As a visiting faculty at TERI SAS, she has taught a course on Economics of Climate Change to post-graduate students. Her research and teaching interests include environmental and energy economics, climate change, political economy, international trade and microeconomics.

Srikanth Kondapalli is Professor in Chinese Studies at Jawaharlal Nehru University. He was Chairman of the Centre for East Asian Studies, SIS, JNU. He is also an Honorary Fellow at Institute of Chinese Studies, Delhi and Research Associate at Centre for Chinese Studies, University of Stellenbosch, South Africa. He served at the Institute for Defence Studies & Analyses, New Delhi for nearly 12 years. He is educated in Chinese Studies Division of School of International Studies, Jawaharlal Nehru University, New Delhi. He learnt Chinese language at Beijing Language and Culture University and was a post-Doctoral Visiting Fellow at People's University, Beijing from 1996–1998. He was a Visiting Professor at National Chengchi University, Taipei, in 2004 and a Visiting Fellow at China Institute of Contemporary International Relations, Beijing, in May 2007. He was Honorary Professor at Shandong University in 2008. He has published two books, two monographs, co-edited a volume and several articles in edited books and in national and international journals and newspapers.

Durairaj Kumarasamy, is a consultant at ASEAN India Centre (AIC), Research and Information System for Developing Countries (RIS), New Delhi. He was 'Think Tank Initiative Fellow' at the Institute of Economic Growth, New Delhi. He also worked as a Consultant at Institute of Economic Growth, New Delhi. He has also served as a Consultant to the UNESCAP. He is the Assistant Editor of the *Journal of Asian Economic Integration*, published by Sage. He obtained his PhD in Economics from Department of Economics, Pondicherry University (Central University), Puducherry, India. His research broadly covers topics in International Trade, Regional Integration, Foreign Direct Investment and Applied Econometrics. He published his research in referred international and national journals, working papers, edited volumes and research reports.

Meeta Keswani Mehra is Professor of Economics at the Centre for International Trade and Development (CITD), School of International Studies, Jawaharlal Nehru University (JNU). Meeta has also held the position of Chairperson of the Centre during December 2013–December 2015 and January 2018–January 2020. She obtained her PhD degree in Economics from the Economics and Planning Unit, Indian Statistical Institute, Delhi Centre, after which she joined the Jawaharlal Nehru University in 2004, where she teaches macroeconomics, open-economy macroeconomics, environmental economics and regulatory economics to post-graduate students. Her research lies in the interface of growth theory, international trade, energy economics, environment and climate economics, politics of regulation and political business cycles. She has published papers in journals such as *Environmental and Resource Economics, Research in Economics, International Economic Journal, Indian Growth and Development Review* among others.

Sacchidananda Mukherjee is Associate Professor at the National Institute of Public Finance and Policy (NIPFP), New Delhi. He works in the field of public finance and environmental economics. He has been conducting policy research for the federal and provincial governments in India for more than a decade. He has a PhD in Economics from the University of Madras (Madras School of Economics), Chennai. His recent books include *Evolution of Goods and Services Tax in India* (co-authored, 2019), *Environmental Challenges and Governance: Diverse Perspectives from Asia* (co-edited, 2017) and *Environmental Scenario in India: Successes and Predicaments* (co-edited, 2012).

S.D. Muni is Professor Emeritus at the School of International Studies, Jawaharlal Nehru University (JNU), New Delhi. He is also a member of the Executive Council of the Institute for Defence and Strategic Analyses, New Delhi. He taught and conducted/guided research at JNU, New Delhi; National University of Singapore, Singapore; Banaras Hindu University, Varanasi; and Rajasthan University, Jaipur. He was India's Special Envoy for Southeast Asian Countries for the UN Security Council Reforms (2005–2006) and also served as India's Ambassador (1997–1999) to Lao People's Democratic Republic. He was nominated to the first-ever constituted National Security Advisory Board of India in 1990–1991. Professor Muni also addressed the UN Special Committee on Indian Ocean in Socci (former Soviet Union). In 2005, the Sri Lankan president bestowed him with the 'Sri Lanka Ratna', the country's highest national award for a foreigner. Sri Venkateswara University, Tirupati (Andhra Pradesh), honoured him in 2014 with the 'Life Time Achievement Award' in South and Southeast Asian Studies. Author and editor of about 30 books and monographs, he has published nearly 250 articles and research papers in Indian and international journals. He has extensively travelled on academic assignments and has had associations with several international think tanks and research centres in Europe, the Americas and Asia.

G.V.C. Naidu is Retired Professor and the former founder–chairperson of the Centre for Indo-Pacific Studies, Jawaharlal Nehru University, New Delhi. He specializes in Indo-Pacific affairs, including political economy, maritime security and India's engagement with this region. His visiting appointments include Research Fellow at the Institute of Southeast Asian Studies, Singapore; Japan Foundation Visiting Professor at the Daito Bunka University and Gakushuin University, Tokyo; Visiting Fellow at the East-West Center, Honolulu; Visiting Fellow at the Japan Institute of International Affairs, Visiting Professor at National Chengchi University, Taipei and Visiting Professor at National Chung Hsing Univesity, Taichung, Taiwan.

He has to his credit five books, five monographs and a large number of articles, chapters in books, and research papers published in India and abroad.

Girijesh Pant is National Fellow ICSSR, Symbiosis International University Pune. He was Dean and Professor in the School of International Studies at Jawaharlal Nehru University (JNU) and former Vice Chancellor of Doon University. Having obtained his PhD from JNU, he started his career with the Federation of Indian Chambers of Commerce and Industry (FICCI), New Delhi (India). He then joined JNU, where he has been teaching for the last three decades. His areas of research interest include political economy of development, West Asian economies, international energy affairs, India's energy security, and corporate social responsibility. He has contributed more than 70 research papers and authored/edited 10 books. He has been the senior Fulbright visiting fellow at the University of Illinois and has travelled extensively delivering lectures and participating in conferences and seminars at various international and national universities.

Md. Obaidur Rahaman has obtained his PhD degree on 'India's Maritime Strategic Interests in South China Sea: A Geopolitical Analysis' at the Centre for International Politics, Organisation and Disarmament, School of International Studies, Jawaharlal Nehru University, New Delhi, India.

Takaaki Oiwa is an author, currently positioned as Research Fellow at the Japan International Cooperation Agency (JICA) Ogata Research Institute. Before coming to this position, he was Professor of the Faculty of Economics and Graduate School of Economics of Yamaguchi University in Japan, Senior Research Fellow of Lee Kuan Yew School of Public Policy at the National University of Singapore and several other academic positions in Japan. His research interests are political economy of Indo-Pacific, critical developmental geopolitics, and de-territorialization and re-territorialization of regional framework.

Shebonti Ray Dadwal is an independent energy, resources and climate change consultant, with a wide range of experience in media, government and academia. Prior to April 2019, she worked in IDSA, now known as MP-IDSA, where as Senior Fellow, she headed the Non Traditional Security (NTS) Centre for several years. She was also a member of the Institute's flagship journal *Strategic Analyses'* Editorial Board. She also worked in *The Financial Express* from 2002–2005 as Senior Editor. She served as Deputy Secretary at the National Security Council Secretariat from 2000–2001. Her research focus is on energy security and she published her second book *The Geopolitics of Gas: Common Problems, Disparate Strategies* in 2017. Her other published work includes a monograph on *The Geopolitics of America's Energy Independence: Implications for China, India and the Global Energy Market* and a book, *Rethinking Energy Security in India*, which was published in 2002. She has also co-edited two books – *Asian Strategic Review 2018: Energy Security in Times of Uncertainty* and *Non-Traditional Security Challenges in Asia: Approaches and Responses,* published by Routledge in 2015. She has co-authored the IDSA Report on *Security Implications of Climate Change for India* (2009). In April 2009, Ray Dadwal was awarded a Chevening Fellowship by the Foreign and Commonwealth Office of the UK on completion of a course in Economics of Energy at the Institute for Energy Research and Policy, University of Birmingham, UK. She has also written several peer-reviewed articles and papers focusing on energy security as well as on international geo-economic and strategic issues.

Sharad K. Soni is Professor and Chairperson of Centre for Inner Asian Studies, School of International Studies and Director, International Collaboration at Jawaharlal Nehru University in New Delhi. His research interests lie in Inner Asian/ Eurasian Studies with a focus on great power politics in a historical and geopolitical context, foreign policy and security issues, identity and migration, as well as society, culture and politics in Mongolia and Mongol culture areas of Asiatic Russia, Central Asia and China's Inner Mongolia. He has to his credit six books, including *Mongolia Today: Internal Changes and External Linkages* (2016). In 2015, he was conferred with Order of *Nairamdal* by a decree of the President of Mongolia in recognition of his contribution to Mongolian Studies.

ABBREVIATIONS

AEP	Act East Policy
ADB	Asian Development Bank
AEC	ASEAN Economic Community
AECA	ASEAN Energy Cooperation Agreement
AEPSS	ASEAN Emergency Petroleum Sharing Scheme
AFOC	ASEAN Forum on Coal
AIIB	Asia Infrastructure Investment bank
AMEM	ASEAN Ministers on Energy Meeting
AMG	AktobeMunaiGas
AMS	ASEAN Member States
APAEC	ASEAN Plan of Action for Energy Cooperation
APEC	Asia-Pacific Economic Cooperation
APG	ASEAN Power Grid
APSA	ASEAN Petroleum Security Agreement
AREH	Asian Renewable Energy Hub
ASCOPE	ASEAN Council for Petroleum
ASEAN	Association of South East Asian Nations
ATF	Air tribune fuel
B2B	Business to business
BBIN	Bangladesh, Bhutan, India and Nepal
BCF	Billion cubic feet
BCIM	Bangladesh–China–India–Myanmar
BCIMEC	Bangladesh–China–India–Myanmar economic corridor
BCM	Billion cubic metres
BEE	Bureau of Energy Efficiency
BIMP	Brunei, Indonesia, Malaysia, Philippines

BIMSTEC	Bay of Bengal Initiative for Multi-Sectoral Technical and Economic Cooperation
BOT	Build–operate–transfer
BP	British Petroleum
BPCL	Bharat Petroleum Corp Ltd
BRI	Belt and Road Initiative
BRICS	Brazil, Russia, India, China, South Africa
BSCFD	Billion standard cubic feet per day
BTU	British thermal unit
CA	Central Asia
CAAGR	Compound average annual growth rate
CADP	Comprehensive Asia Development Plan
CAGR	Compound annual growth rate
CAR	Central Asian Republics
CBET	Cross border electricity trade
CBM	Coal bed methane
CBTA	Cross-Border Transport Agreement
CCGT	Combined cycle gas turbines
CCT	Clean coal technologies
CCWAEC	China–Central-West Asia Economic Corridor
CGD	City gas distribution
CIS	Commonwealth of Independent States
CLMV	Cambodia, Laos, Myanmar, Vietnam
CMREC	China–Mongolia–Russia Economic Corridor
CNG	Compressed natural gas
CNOOC	China National Offshore Oil Corporation
CNPC	China National Petroleum Company
CO_2	Carbon dioxide
COC	Code of conduct
COP	Conference of parties
CPCC	China Petroleum and Chemical Corporation
CPEC	China–Pakistan economic corridor
CPP	China Petroleum Pipeline Bureau
CPS	Current policies scenario
CPSES	Central Public Sector Enterprises
CPTPP	Comprehensive and Progressive Trans-Pacific Partnership
DBT	Direct benefit transfer
DC	Direct current
DCOC	Declaration of code of conduct
DDUGJY	Deen Dayal Upadhyay Gram Jyoti Yojna
DGPC	Druk Green Power Corporation Ltd.
DIG	Director General of Hydrocarbons
DMO	Domestic market obligations
DMU	Decision making units

DoNER	Development of North-East Region
DRE	Decentralised renewable energy
DRI	Direct reduced iron
DSFA	Discovered small field awards
E&P	Exploration and production
EAGA	East Asia Growth area
ECBC	Energy Conservation Building Code
ECBC-R	Energy Conservation Building Code for Residential Buildings
EE&C-SSN	Energy Efficiency and Conservation Sub-sector Network
EEF	Eastern Economic Forum
EEZ	Exclusive economic zone
EIA	Energy Information Administration
EOI	Expression of interest
EOR	Enhanced oil recovery
EPD	Energy planning department
ERIA	Economic Research Institute for ASEAN and East Asia
EU	European Union
EV	Electric vehicles
EVN	Vietnam Electricity
FAME	Faster Adoption and Manufacturing of Hybrid and Electric Vehicles
FDI	Foreign Direct Investment
FIT	Feed-in-tariffs
FTA	Free Trade Agreement
G20	Group of 20
G2G	Government to government
GAIL	Gas Authority of India Ltd
GBI	Generation-based incentives
GBS	General budget support
GDP	Gross domestic product
GHG	Greenhouse gas
GMS	Greater Mekong Subregion
GOI	Government of India
GSI	Geological Survey of India
GW	Gigawatt
GWH	Gigawatt hour
HAPUA	Heads of ASEAN Public Utilities Authorities
HELP	Hydrocarbon Exploration Licensing Policy
HFO	Heavy fuel oil
HPCL	Hindustan Oil Corp Ltd
HSD	High speed diesel
HSDO	High speed diesel oil
HVDC	High voltage direct current
IAEA	International Atomic Energy Agency
IAF	Indian Air Force

IAFS	India–Africa Forum Summits
ICE	Internal combustion engineered
IDP	Internally displaced persons
IEA	International Energy Agency
IEF	International Energy Forum
IEO	International Energy Outlook
IGEF	Indo-German Energy Forum
IMF	International Monetary Fund
INDCs	Intended nationally determined contributions
IOCL	Indian Oil Corporation Limited
IOCS	International oil companies
IORA	Indian Ocean Rim Association
IPI	Iran, Pakistan, India
IPP	Independent power producers
IPS	Indo-Pacific strategy
IREDA	Indian Renewable Energy Development Agency
IRENA	International Renewable Energy Agency
ISA	International Seabed Authority
ISTS	Inter-State Transmission System
JICA	Japan International Cooperation Agency
JOC	Joint operating company
JSG	Joint study group
KG	Kilogram
LED	Light emitting diode
LEP	Look East Policy
LMC	Lancang–Mekong Cooperation
LNG	Liquefied natural gas
LPG	Liquified petroleum gas
MEMR	Ministry of Energy and Mineral Resources
MGC	Mekong Ganga Cooperation
MIB	Myanmar, India, Bangladesh
MIGA	Multilateral Investment Guarantee Agency
MJ	Mega joules
MMSCM	Million standard cubic meters
MMTPA	Million metric tonne per annum
MNRE	Ministry of New and Renewable Energy
MOE	Ministry of Energy
MOGE	Myanmar Oil and Gas Enterprise
MoPNG	Ministry of Petroleum and Natural Gas
MoSPI	Ministry of Statistical Planning and Implementation
MOU	Memorandum of understanding
MPE	Myanmar Petroleum Enterprise
MPPE	Myanmar Petroleum Products Enterprise
MSR	Maritime Silk Road

MT	Million tonnes
MTOE	Million tonnes of oil equivalent
MW	Megawatt
MWH	Megawatt hour
NAM	Non-aligned movement
NAPCC	National Action Plan on Climate Change
NDA	National Democratic Alliance
NDR	National Data Repository
NDRC	National Development and Reform Commission
NEC-SSN	Nuclear Energy Cooperation Sub Sector Network
NEEPCO	North Eastern Electric Power Corporation
NELP	New Exploration Licensing Policy
NEMC	National Energy Management Committee
NEP	National Economic Policy
NER	North East Region
NITI	National Institution for Transforming India
NIO	National Institute of Oceanography
NMP	National Mineral Policy
NOC	Nepal Oil Corporation
NOCs	National oil companies
NOX	Nitrogen oxides
NPP	Nuclear power plants
NPS	New Policies Scenario
NRL	Numaligarh Refinery Limited
NSM	National solar mission
NTPC Ltd.	National Thermal Power Corporation Limited
OALP	Open Acreage Licensing Policy
OBOR	One Belt One Road
OECD	Organisation for Economic Cooperation and Development
OMCs	Oil marketing companies
ONGC	Oil and Natural Gas Corporation
OPEC	Organisation of Petroleum Exporting Countries
OVL	ONGC Videsh Limited
PAT	Perform, achieve, trade
PBC	Bangladesh Petroleum Corporation
PELS	Petroleum exploration licenses
PETRONAS	Petroliam National Berhad
PFC	Power Finance Coroporation
PM	Particulate Matter
PMUY	Pradhan Mantri Ujjwala Yojana
PPA	Power purchase agreement
PPP	Purchasing power parity
PSC	Production sharing contract
PSCs	Public sector companies

PSUs	Public sector units
PVEP	Petrovietnam Exploration Production Company
PVN	Petrovietnam Vietnam Oil and Gas Group
R&D	Research and development
RCEP	Regional Comprehensive Economic Partnership
RE	Renewable energy
REPP	Regional Energy Policy and Planning
RE-SSN	Renewable Energy Sub-sector Network
RGT	Regasifiation Terminals
RIC	Russia–India–China
RIL	Reliance Industries Limited
RPO	Renewable purchase obligation
RSC	Revenue sharing contract
S&L	Standard and labelling
SA	South Asia
SAARC	South Asian Association for Regional Cooperation
SAGAR	Security and Growth for All in the Region
SCS	South China Sea
SCO	Shanghai Cooperation Organization
SDG	Sustainable development goals
SDS	Sustainable development scenario
SEA	Southeast Asia
SEAP	Super-efficient equipment program
SEC	South Asian Energy Centre
SEDS	Socio-economic development strategies
SEFA	Sustainable energy for all
SERC	State Electricity Regulatory Commission
SEZ	Special economic zone
SINOPEC	China Petroleum and Chemical Corporation
SKO	Superior kerosene oil
SLOC	Sea lines of communication
SMES	Small and medium enterprises
SMMEs	Small, medium and mini enterprises
SMS	Seafloor massive sulphides
SOx	Sulphur oxides
SPR	Strategic petroleum reserves
SREB	Silk Road Economic Belt
TAGP	Trans-ASEAN Gas Pipeline
TAPI	Turkmenistan, Afghanistan, Pakistan, India
TAR	Trans-Asia Railway
TCF	Trillion cubic feet
TERI	The Energy Resource Institute
THDC	Tehri Hydro Development Corporation
Toe.	Tonne of oil equivalent

TPED	Total primary energy demand
TPES	Total primary energy supply
UJALA	Unnat Jyoti by Affordable LEDs for All
UN	United Nations
UNCLOS	United Nations Convention for the Law of the Sea
UNEP	United Nations Environment Programme
UNFC	United Nations Framework Classification for Fossil Energy and Mineral Reserves and Resources
VAT	Value added tax
VINACOMIN	Vietnam National Coal and mineral Industries Group
WB	World Bank

ACKNOWLEDGEMENTS

A work of this endeavour can be accomplished only by the grace of almighty and support from individuals around. As I am about to reach the final milestone, retrospection reminds me to be indebted to each one, who helped me in achieving this.

At the onset, I extend my deepest gratitude to all the authors for their valuable contribution to this volume. I acknowledge the venerated support from the Ministry of Oil and Natural Gas as well as the national and international oil companies under its aegis. I would like to show my greatest appreciation to Shri Dharmendra Pradhan, the Union Minister of Oil and Natural Gas for his nonpareil encouragement to take this facet of India's energy security studies. Mr Binay Pradhan, a promising officer of Indian Foreign Service has been instrumental to impression this study with ideas and vision on India's energy engagement. Mr Sunjay Sudhir, Joint Secretary, Minister of Petroleum and Natural Gas, extended valuable official support to complete this study. I am also thankful to Dr R.K. Malhotra, Director General and Mr N.K. Bansal, Mr S. Rath, Director, Federation of Indian Petroleum Industry, New Delhi, for their unwavering succour in form of empirical inputs emanating from their long standing experience in the field.

Initial subject understanding on India's energy scenario, debates and dialogues on energy mix and energy transition, policy and societal perspectives of India, South Asia and Southeast Asia were garnered through a series of conferences on India's Energy Security and Cooperation held at School of International Studies, Jawaharlal Nehru University, New Delhi and abroad. The conferences were graced by eminent national and international panellists and scholars, which included H.E. Syed Muazzem Ali, former High Commissioner of Bangladesh to India, New Delhi, H.E. Moe Kyaw Aung, Ambassador Extraordinary and Plenipotentiary, Embassy of the Republic of the Union of Myanmar, New Delhi, Prof. Takaaki Oiwa, Professor, Faculty of Economics, Yamaguchi University, Yamaguchi, Japan, Prof S.D. Muni, Professor Emeritus, JNU and Former Ambassador, Prof Priyankar Upadhyaya and

Anjoo Sharan Upadhyaya, Prof. Muchkund Dubey, Former Foreign Secretary, Dr P.C. Maithani, Adviser, Ministry of New and Renewable Energy, former Foreign Secretary of Bangladesh Amb. Farooq Shoban, Amb. Wali-ur Rhaman, Tezpur University, Vice Chancellor Prof. V.K. Jain, Prof. Zhu Cuiping, Deputy Director, Research Institute for Indian Ocean Economics, Yunnan University of Economics and Finance, Kunming, China, Dr Li Yanfeng, Research Institute for Indian Ocean Economics, Yunnan University of Economics and Finance, Kunming, China, Prof. Zhang Jiadong, Deputy Director, Indian and Gandhian Studies, Fudan University, Shanghai, China, Dr Liu Peng, Associate Professor, Research Institute for Indian Ocean Economics, Yunnan University of Economics and Finance, Kunming, China, Dr Ijaz Hossain, Professor, Department of Chemical Engineering, BUET, Dhaka, Professor Mohammad Tamin, Pro-Vice Chancellor, BRAC University, Former Special Assistant to Chief Advisor of the Caretaker Government of Bangladesh, Mr Rafiqul Islam, Director, Training, Bangladesh Power Management Institute, Power division, Ministry of Power, Energy & Mineral Resources, Bangladesh, Prof. Badrul Imam, Professor, Department of Geology, University of Dhaka, Bangladesh.

The study would not have taken its true dimension and scale without the research inputs from scholars, industry experts, trainers, and contractors of NOCs and IOCs, other international organizations, and also policy makers. In pursuit of first-hand experience, I visited institutions in India and abroad like Numaligarh Refinery, Morangi, Department of Energy, Tejpur University, Assam, Vietnam National University, Diplomatic Academy of Vietnam, Institute for Foreign Policy and Strategic Studies, Centre for Energy Studies, Gadjah Madah University, Indonesia, Indonesian Institute for Energy Economics, Jakarta and Energy Institute Malaysia (EI Malaysia), Department of Energy and the environment, University of Delaware, USA, the CATO Institute, Washington DC, Department of Geology, BUET, Petro-Bangla, Bangladesh Enterprise Institute and Bangladesh Heritage Foundation, Bangladesh Institute of International and Strategic Studies, Dhaka, Jahangir Nagar University, Dhaka, Australian National University, South Asian University New Delhi and the World Bank, (India Head).

I am truly grateful to all the faculty members of School of International Studies, specially Energy Studies Programme, JNU for their constant support. Finally, I would also like to express my overarching appreciation for the indispensable support in making this research study a success. Specially, Prof. S.D. Muni, Prof. Amita Batra, Prof. Sharad K. Soni, Dr Saurabh, Prof. Shahab Enam Khan, Ms Priyanshi Chauhan.

Last but not least, these acknowledgements would remain imperfect without a mention of my fellow team members Dr Vivek Soni, Ms Pooja Sharma, Mr Oliver Gonsalves, Dr P. Marshal and Dr Prashant Trivedi, Dr Abhinav Mishra, Mr Manish Pujari and all others to whom I stand ever grateful.

I am also indebted to my wife, Dr Pavitra Bhardwaj, for being a strong pillar of support during all phases of this work. Her contribution is highly valued.

Prof. Sanjay K. Bhardwaj
14 January 2021

INTRODUCTION

Sanjay K. Bhardwaj

The energy security discourse

Energy security has become a critical factor for India in terms of its national security, development agenda, and, of course, human security. As such the energy security complex has become a complicated phenomenon beyond the traditional understanding of demand and supply and price and stability. The dependence on fossil fuel frequently afflicts national security decision-making and is hardly a new issue. However, the evolving geopolitics during the post-COVID world systems will have significant implications on the energy framework across the world. With the US having a high agenda of shifting dependency from the Middle Eastern fossil fuel, China increasingly becoming a dominant factor in the Gulf and the Persian belts, and the Russian–EU geopolitical tussles over energy pipelines, developing economies in the Asia-Pacific region are likely to occupy almost two-thirds of global energy demand between 2020 and 2040. The evolving geostrategic competition to secure the maritime transport supply lines is also critical for India in its pursuit for energy sufficiency.

Being mindful of the paradigm-altering COVID pandemic that originated in China in November 2019, there has been a significant fluctuation in demand for electricity and supply of energy products. The International Energy Agency (IEA) has identified that the COVID-19 pandemic represents the largest plunge in the world's energy system in more than 70 years. Like the impact on the economy and public finances, the pandemic has reduced energy demand that led to an 8 per cent decrease in demand in 2020. Nonetheless, in the post-COVID world the demand is expected to rise in which the issues of ensuring security, clean and affordable energy policies and compliances will feature the most. Perhaps, the commitments pledged in the Paris Agreement to ensure clean energy and environmental security will be the top priorities for the global leaders. Henceforth, energy security will dominate the heart of energy policy, sustainable development, and global and regional cooperation leading to more resilient societies.

Post-2019, popularly known as the post-COVID world, Asia will remain the catalyst for global economic stability and energy consumption. India and China will continue to be the largest energy-consuming countries due to their vast populations, while Japan, South Korea, and Saudi Arabia will continue to be other top countries with high energy consumption. All these high-growth markets will be challenged by the upcoming or existing climate change issues; hence renewable energy sources and a cleaner energy mix will become the central agenda in the energy security policy and discourse. That certainly indicates that India's immediate neighbourhood will remain susceptible to the geopolitics of energy supply, and the policy framework for energy security will change. India will need to cooperate with Southeast and Northeast Asia to ensure energy security through cooperation and collaboration.

As India rises economically, the global centre of gravity is inexorably shifting to this region, and it will not be an exaggeration to contend that what happens in this region will have enormous implications for the rest of the world. Undoubtedly, intra and inter-regional energy cooperation will have a snowballing effect that would lead to greater economic cooperation to further strengthen economic resilience against energy and social shocks. India has also been among the fastest emerging markets and most resilient economies in the world over the last two decades. India's economic dynamism has been accompanied by rapid urbanisation and consequent consumption and lifestyle changes. The demographic dividend, along with the considerable size of the aspiring youth and the middle class is fetching significant economic returns for the country. However, a little less than one-fourth of its population lives below the poverty line.[1] India has emerged as a reliable nuclear power – both military and civil usage – which is buttressed by its accomplishments in space, missile and dual-use technologies. As a growing economic power, India is no longer an aid-receiving country; in fact, it provides technical, developmental and humanitarian assistance to many countries in Asia and beyond. This is denoting India as an essential player on the world stage in the twenty-first century.

However, India's sustainable economic growth significantly depends on the long-term and uninterrupted supply of energy from multiple sources at a reasonable price. India was the third-largest crude oil importer in the world in 2018 after the US and China.[2] Its import profile includes Iraq, Saudi Arabia, Iran, Nigeria, UAE, Venezuela, Kuwait, Mexico, Angola, US, Malaysia, Oman, Brazil, Qatar, and Russia. That means India imports its oil from a diverse source of suppliers spanning from North and South to Southeast Asia. India's energy connection makes it a global state in terms of energy diplomacy and diversity. At the same time, India's fast-paced economic growth and growing energy market status have reaped India some benefits vis-à-vis energy producers and suppliers as a huge and growing energy market. Since the 1990s, India has been exploring multiple energy policy options (domestic and overseas), multiple fuels, and multiple suppliers. Among the other options, the country is strategising to tap and explore participation in trans-national oil and natural gas and pipeline projects. In 2019, India and Nepal inaugurated South Asia's first cross-border oil pipeline, allowing the landlocked Himalayan nation of Nepal to receive an uninterrupted supply.[3]

India has been exploring possibilities to tap gas from Iran and from Turkmenistan for which negotiations have been in progress for the last 20 years. It is a part of transnational projects such as the Iran–Pakistan–India (IPI) and Turkmenistan–Afghanistan–Pakistan–India (TAPI) gas pipelines, and Iran–India as well as India, Bangladesh, and Myanmar gas pipelines have been in the policy agenda. One should note that these projects have been stalled for multiple interlinked reasons, including geopolitics, economic viability, and political stalemates. The post-COVID economic needs and reconstructions will allow India to invigorate these processes. As natural gas is a clean fuel and will be increasingly used by power and fertiliser industries, the demand for natural gas is expected to rise in the country at present and in the future as well.

As the global search for solutions to energy demands, depletion in natural resources, and state and market-centric geopolitics have intensified, these challenges to energy cooperation have often emerged as barriers to collective energy security. Undoubtedly, India faces uncertainty in its energy discourse, as well as its neighbours in the East. Because of the growing political ambiguities in many oil-producing countries (Gulf) and aggravating conflicts over offshore (South China Sea) and onshore natural resources, coupled with domestic politics, geographical constraints and economic reasons, many projects have not yielded the desired outcomes to the energy users, especially those from Asia. Indian companies have been investing in Bangladesh, Myanmar, Vietnam, Mongolia, Russia, and elsewhere to meet the country's ever-growing energy needs as well as to foster regional and trans-regional economic cooperation through energy connectivity and investments.

The Government of India's Act East policy expanded the scope of Look East from just economic to politico-strategic and cultural dimensions. Apart from Southeast Asia, the countries of Northeast Asia and Far East Asia were also taken under its ambit. The repeated enunciation that the regional organisation ASEAN is at the heart of India's policy is a testimony to this. The Indian government linked the development of Northeastern Indian States to the success of the Act East policy. The objective of the Act East policy is to promote economic cooperation, cultural ties, and develop a strategic relationship with countries in the Asia-Pacific region through continuous engagement at bilateral, regional and multilateral levels thereby providing enhanced connectivity to the states of the Northeastern region including Arunachal Pradesh.[4] The erstwhile Look East policy had initially ignored the development of this region as it was focused on advancing trade and investment cooperation with the ASEAN. However, with the constitution of the DoNER (Development of North-East region) as a separate department in 2001 and then upgrading it to a full-fledged ministry in 2004, this gap was filled up. With the initiation of India's Act East policy, emphasis on the development of the Northeast region has been stepped up. This region has become critical for establishing connectivity – both physical and energy-related – with the ASEAN countries.

A look at the statistics on the increasing economic relationship between India and ASEAN depicts this aptly. The ASEAN constitutes home for 649.1 million people with the combined estimated GDP of US$ 3.0 trillion. Investment from ASEAN to India has been over US$72 billion in the last 17 years, accounting for more than 17 per cent of India's total Foreign Direct Investment (FDI). India's investment in ASEAN during the same period has been more than US$40 billion.[5] India's economic engagement in Southeast Asia can also be understood in perspective if viewed relative to other major economies of East Asia. The Japan–ASEAN trade stood at US$218 billion in 2017; however, Japan's biggest strength is its substantial investible capital reserve. It has invested more than $400 billion in Southeast Asia, which makes it the topmost investor in Southeast Asia. In the case of India's trade, it went up from $56 billion in 2010 to about $72 billion in 2017. China's trade with ASEAN has gone up from US$213 billion in 2010 to $570 billion in 2018.

All these challenges and windows of opportunities, as mentioned in this introductory chapter, highlight the need for reform, innovation, and deeper engagement between India and its neighbours in the East. Hence, this book has been commissioned to make intellectual and policy inquiries into the ongoing energy security debates linking India with its Eastern neighbours. In this debate, China features significantly due to its sheer economy, consumption patterns, and geostrategic presence. The Southeast Asian countries feature equally prominently given the geopolitics and geoeconomics of energy security in which India is an important part.

The premise of the book

The subject of *Energy Security* necessitates reflections from many dimensions. Demand and supply are, perhaps, the two essential aspects of any study related to energy security. Many studies have been carried out that highlight the dependence of long-term and uninterrupted supply of energy on sustainable economic growth with a focus on both policy and social inclusions. The first five chapters discuss all these aspects of energy security, energy transition, and national, regional and global factors in scripting the national energy policy in detail.

Part I Energy security policy: Debates in India

The first part of the book reveals that to achieve energy security as well as reduce the current account deficit, it will be necessary for India to gradually reduce imports of high-value primary energy sources like crude petroleum and natural gas, which are used for power generation. In the long run, India needs to reduce its dependence on imported coal for power generation. This aspect of energy security has been discussed in detail in the first chapter of this book. The chapter discusses the emerging scenario in which India's energy security policy has to be embedded. The chapter argues that since climate change activists and advocates are demanding that India should cut its carbon emissions, challenges for a sustainable energy transition have economic and political implications. The chapter provides that some of the Indian cities are the most polluted in the world and according to a projection by the Global Carbon Project, India is the fourth highest emitter of carbon dioxide (CO_2) in the world, accounting for 7 per cent of global emissions in 2017, behind China at 27 per cent, the US at 15 per cent, and the European Union at 10 per cent.[6] The cause of the growth in emissions is attributed to India's rapid economic growth and the use of coal.

The second chapter argues that at the onset of the global energy transition, the countries across the globe are engaged in redefining their energy mix in favour of renewable energy. Pant points out the factors that are likely to shape India's energy security doctrine in coming times. It is critically linked to its capacity to mediate and negotiate between competing and conflicting orientations of global and domestic energy regimes. It is conflicting because, to meet its energy needs, India will continue to depend heavily on hydrocarbons, including coal, therefore deviating from the global goal of moving away from fossil fuels. It is competing because in its drive to change its energy mix in favour of renewable in a targeted way, it relies on the import of technology and equipment, which in turn has been adversely impacting the local renewable industry, thereby impeding the possibilities of technological breakthroughs at the national level. Pant also argues that energy security is no longer confined to the supply or demand security of hydrocarbons. It means energy security is not only accounts for availability but accessibility and affordability as well.

Dadwal, in the third chapter, argues that India's energy sector has undergone a massive transformation, in terms of energy access, delivery, infrastructure enhancement, and, more importantly, a considerable increase in the use of cleaner fuels. But several challenges remain and will need to be addressed before India can be deemed not only an energy secure country that can ensure access to clean and sustainable energy to all its citizens but also considered as a responsible member of the global energy community.

In the fourth chapter, Keswani and Kohli emphasise redefining India's energy security doctrine and points out the importance of energy-efficiency and cleaner technologies as instruments for climate change mitigation. It is defining its pathway in consonance with its commitment to the Paris Agreement. Having committed to reducing its carbon emissions by 30–35 per cent by 2030, from the base year of 2005, under the Paris Agreement in 2015, India has come under mounting international pressure to meet its commitments. India is also playing a leadership role in defining global solar regime as well. Hence, both the global compulsions and the domestic imperatives are becoming drivers in its scripting.

Mukherjee, in the fifth chapter, highlights that India's energy security is significantly dependent on imports of primary energy sources. Recognising the criticality of hydrocarbon in its energy needs, it is repositioning itself in the global hydrocarbon market by diversifying its bilateral and multilateral engagements, scaling up at strategic level. However, its dependence on fossil fuels has also invited the attention of climate change activists. A large part of India's imported energy sources is used – either directly and/or after refinement – for the generation of electricity. Earlier the geographical proximity and India's robust engagement have not sufficiently enthused New Delhi to pay greater attention to the energy dimension of cooperation with the extended eastern neighbours. As Mukherjee explores in his chapter, in future it would be necessary for India to explore the Asia-Pacific region in mobilising finance to invest in inter-regional electricity transmission infrastructure to facilitate cross border electricity trade (CBET).

The quest for energy security has led India to find ways to ensure that the country's energy requirements are met uninterruptedly. Whereas energy denotes diverse dimensions, the primary focus has been on oil and gas since India is critically dependent on imported sources. India is experiencing an increasing demand for energy owing to its economic dynamism, urbanisation and the need for socio-economic development. One of the ways to address the challenge of rising energy demand is through energy trade and collaboration opportunities within the region and beyond. In light of the looming concerns of climate change, India has evolved an extensive policy framework to reduce greenhouse gas (GHG) emissions by emphasising deployment of energy-efficient technologies and promoting the share of renewables in the energy mix under the ambit of the National Action Plan on Climate Change (NAPCC).

To this end India, being a rapidly growing economy, with significant dependence on its natural resource base and predominantly climate-sensitive sectors, has displayed steady efforts to chart ecologically sustainable growth pathways in the face of local pollution and climate change. In support of these, India has put in place various financial, economic and cooperation instruments towards energy efficiency and cooperation, such as the Perform, Achieve, Trade (PAT), a market-based instrument for energy-saving and trade, and incentives for the dissemination of renewable energy technologies through cuts in subsidy on fossil fuels, taxing carbon, feed-in-tariffs (FiT), renewable purchase obligations (RPOs), and generation-based incentives (GBIs) for renewable energy.

Part II India's Act East policy and energy cooperation

The Middle East, East Asia, and, more recently, Africa have been principal suppliers to India; however, India's energy link with Southeast Asia remains less explored. As options on India's western and northern fronts are limited due to its hostile political relations with Pakistan and China, Southeast Asian countries including Vietnam, Malaysia, Indonesia, and Myanmar provide opportunities for expansion of India's energy engagement. The eastern corridors, Bangladesh including India's Northeast states are alternative prospects in energy trade, particularly in hydrocarbons resources.

The sixth chapter highlights the necessity for India–Southeast Asia cooperation in the energy sector. Muni highlights that the significance of this region in India's Look East policy had only begun to be realised in economic and energy areas in recent decades. He identifies that a robust push to India's energy cooperation was provided by Mani Shankar Aiyar, during 2005–2006, as a Union Minister of Petroleum and Natural Gas. He initiated a policy to set up firm and cooperative network of oil and gas pipelines with all the neighbours including Bangladesh, Pakistan, and China. One can argue that Mr Aiyar's energy cooperation policy was not conceived strictly within the framework of the Look East policy. However, it was bound to have a significant impact there. He was conscious of the energy needs of the fast-growing economies like Japan, South Korea, India, and China, the four largest energy importers, as well as of energy suppliers like Myanmar, Malaysia, Indonesia, and Papua New Guinea, among India's eastern neighbours. He made a strong plea for energy cooperation among all to build an 'Asian Century'. This approach included laying down oil and gas pipelines with the Southeast Asian countries via Bangladesh and India's Northeastern region.

However, Aiyar's approach came into conflict with the priorities of the Ministry of External Affairs and India's security establishments. Accordingly, this approach could not be pursued after his exit from the Petroleum Ministry. After Mr Dharmendra Pradhan took over the ministry in 2014, he gave a new dimension to energy cooperation. India's Act East policy has pursued enhanced energy cooperation with its extended eastern neighbours at regional and bilateral levels. Moreover, Muni's chapter discusses that the challenge for India to synergise and streamline its Act East policy in the energy sector remains formidable due to multiple factors. It means stronger energy links can immensely contribute to the success of the Act East policy. Nevertheless, India's objectives to achieve its energy security and environment sustainability need to be integrated.

Naidu, in the seventh chapter, discusses that New Delhi needs to look at energy cooperation with this region in the larger geo-economic and geo-political dynamics. Naidu identifies that not enough resources have been allocated to the projects for exploring renewable and alternate energy resources in the Eastern countries. India's ASEAN Fund for Science and Technology supported these programmes, but that is not enough to enhance the desired cooperation. India has invested more than US$10 billion in improving its renewable energy sources like solar, wind and biogas. ASEAN is collaborating with more resourceful countries like Germany, Japan, and Canada, and perhaps India does not fit into its priorities in this sector. This could be one of the reasons for encouraging the private sector to come forward and contribute as was underlined in the 2016–2020 Plan of Action. Similarly, Batra and Chauhan, in the eighth chapter, identify the opportunities for energy cooperation in the form of interconnected power transmission grids and natural gas pipelines. However, they also discuss the challenges to such energy cooperation, which include the increasing competition for scarce energy resources and the strategic implications of increasing Chinese presence in these countries, economic challenges of limited sector reforms and high investment requirements, and also the environmental and humanitarian concerns.

ASEAN and India have huge potentials and complementarities in terms of access to conventional and renewable energy resources. In the ninth chapter, De and Kumarasamy identify that ASEAN and India are the fastest growing economies in the world and have been looking for more energy to drive growth. Both ASEAN and India are also committed to Sustainable Development Goals (SDG) to ensure access to affordable, reliable, sustainable and modern energy for all by 2030 apart from moving towards low-carbon growth path through promoting different means of renewable energy sources.

Part III India–China: Geopolitics of energy cooperation

This part of the book highlights the geopolitics of energy cooperation in which China's geostrategic and geopolitical presence need in-depth analysis. The increasing Chinese shadow on India's eastward engagement has become an essential factor in its energy security discourse. Historically, the Indian Ocean is also considered as a critical corridor for both trade and energy resources from the oil-rich West Asia to the big economies of East Asia. In terms of economy, the Indian Ocean Region (IOR) has become more critical now with a growing volume of trade and the simultaneous rise of threats from non-state actors along the traditional trade routes and choke points.[7] Far more crucial is the brewing naval rivalry among the major Indian Ocean powers. Underlining the strategic importance of the Indian Ocean, the US Navy strategist Rear Admiral Alfred Thayer Mahan (1840–1914) once said, 'Whoever controls the Indian Ocean dominates Asia. This Ocean is the key to the seven seas in the twenty-first century, the destiny of the world will be decided in these waters'.

The global powers are using economic might such as infrastructural development and naval presence in the littoral and island countries of the region. The Indian Ocean sealines of communication (maritime highways) have become the central conveyor belt for international trade and energy supply, therefore emerging as a significant global intersection for geopolitics. It is also important to note that being the largest trading nation in the region, maritime security in the Indo-Pacific is more important for China. China's interest in the Indian Ocean is 'commercial'; however, it took into account the possibility of conflict. Conversely, India too perceives the Chinese initiatives as inauspicious to its interests, which is why India refuses to take part in the Chinese BRI initiative.

The vital strategic importance of the IOR is from the perspective of energy security. Many Asian countries, including India and China, depend on oil imports from West Asia. Almost 50 per cent of the world's tanker and more than 80 per cent of oil transportation from West Asia to East Asia pass through this region.[8] This makes the security of these energy and trade corridors around the Straits of Hormuz, the Mozambique Channel, and the Malacca Straits highly significant. About 90 per cent of China's trade is carried out by the sea. The BRI, while setting up a geopolitical and geoeconomic Silk Road Economic Belt (SREB) and the twenty-first century Maritime Silk Road (MSR) connecting China to Africa and Europe by land and sea, is thus deepening reforms inside China by enabling the Chinese overcapacity, capital, and technology to go global. China has identified the seventh major economic corridor, i.e. China–Myanmar Economic Corridor (CMEC), which was added in 2018. This would be the second bilateral economic corridor after the China–Pakistan Economic Corridor (CPEC) and perhaps another flagship as far as connectivity in Southeast Asia and South Asia is concerned. These new transit routes will avoid the choke points in the Indian Ocean. Highlighting the crucial role of the Indian Ocean, a recent report in Chinese official media stated that about 'four-fifths of China's oil' transit through the choke points in the Indian Ocean. Thus, China is investing in the Belt and Road project to avoid these chokepoints for an uninterrupted supply of energy from various sources.

Oiwa, in the tenth chapter, identifies that the superimposition of other sub-regional cooperation schemes on GMS will generate new insights into broader regional frameworks, such as ASEAN, inter-region across East Asia and South Asia, Belt and Road Initiative, and Indo-Pacific vision. A sub-region for energy collaboration may also be considered a subgrouping of countries either within a region or across regions. Oiwa's chapter focuses on the subgrouping of countries across regions and reveals the deficiencies of broad regional frameworks, irrespective of whether they are regional, interregional, or super-regional.

Kondapalli, in the eleventh chapter, points out that as China has been rising to the second-largest economy in the world, and its appetite for energy resources has also increased by leaps and bounds. It presently accounts for 12 per cent of global energy demand, and its rate of growth is four to five times that of the world figure. China's demand for oil has doubled from 3.4 to 6.8 mb/d in a decade, and the figure is expected to go up to 11 mb/d by 2030. For energy security, China has also adopted various measures like securing energy resources through investments and diversification, making efforts for a smooth transfer of these resources through land and maritime areas. While China is heavily dependent on West Asia and Africa for such resources, the role of Southeast and South Asia cannot be entirely ignored in the China energy matrix, especially the regional power market and energy infrastructure. Kondapalli further specifies that China has been making comprehensive inroads in the region through long-term arrangements and has been making efforts to diversify the energy mix in order to bring in its comparative advantages.

Northeast Asia is a subregion of East Asia, which has been one of the fastest-growing energy markets for over past 30 years or so. Soni, in the twelfth chapter, points out that Northeast Asia is positioned at a crucial juncture of the energy supply chain. China, Japan and the two Koreas are the top ten world oil-consuming countries. At the same time, Russia and Mongolia are now represented as a new source of energy suppliers making the region a critical entity connecting a network of growing supplies and markets. The chapter argues that the Russian Far East and Mongolia, being components of Northeast Asia, reserve a significant source of energy supply, which may provide an extra edge to India in fulfilling the gaps in its growing energy demands through cooperative mechanisms. Moreover, with all these countries belonging to Northeast Asia accounting for almost one-fifth of the world economy, this subregion is a key unexplored energy-reserve region. India, for quite some time now, has been trying to intellectually invest in and take part in multilateral cooperation initiatives to enhance its Northeast Asia outreach in its quest for energy security.

While Mongolia–Russia joint ventures are currently gaining much attention, Mongolia is diversifying investment partners in its nuclear industry sector to avoid over-reliance on any single party. Given India's status as Mongolia's 'Third Neighbour' as well as post-Modi's 2015 visit thaw in bilateral relations, particularly in uranium and renewable energy sector, there is much scope for energy cooperation between the two sides in particular and Northeast Asia in general. Bringing a unique 'North' component to India's East Asia campaigning now appears to have started paying a dividend in New Delhi's eastward engagement for its energy security. However, external hurdles in the face of growing Chinese influence in the region has to be faced in exploring energy cooperation with other stakeholders.

Deepak, in the thirteenth chapter, highlights that India and China should cooperate in the international energy markets to curb the crude oil prices, bring down the prices of the bids, transportation, and share their experience and technologies to overcome their dependence on developed countries. Furthermore, building sizeable oil reserves would be too expensive for both, and, hence, it would be sensible to consider co-financing an oil reserve system for mitigating the risks in the international energy market. Also, since some of the institutions such as the Asian Infrastructure Investment Bank promote North–South financial cooperation under the BRI, it would make sense if India makes use of such institutions. Cooperation between India and China in the energy sector in third countries is not only eminently desirable but also entirely feasible.

The last part of the book identifies that directly or indirectly China has influenced India's energy engagement, particularly with Myanmar and Vietnam. The existing energy cooperation is relatively lesser than the considerable potential. This has been due to various politico-economic factors like lack of funding for the energy projects, absence of a strong political will, and varying energy needs, and infrastructure capabilities. China has been hugely resourceful and efficient in competing with India in the third countries for accessing its energy resources.

In fact, India's efforts to forge energy cooperation with China, both bilaterally and in third countries, have not succeeded because of strategic hiatus between the two Asian giants, which are now increasingly becoming sharper. India's primary challenge in the Indo-Pacific region is of competition and rivalry with China in the field of energy and trade. China has raised serious objections to Indian company ONGC Videsh's investment in exploration for hydrocarbons in the South China Sea of Vietnam's territorial waters.[9] Despite limited success, however, it remains involved. India has also developed a strategic partnership with Vietnam. As Bhardwaj and Rahaman highlight in the fourteenth chapter, the South China Sea has become one of the most contested and disputed maritime zones over its territorial rights and maritime sovereignty claims.

The presence of abundant natural resources and its strategic significance motivated China to redefine territorial rights. To control the islands, water, marine resources, the oil and natural gas, fisheries, and other hydrocarbon deposits and strategic positions of the South China Sea, both the littoral states and China are intensifying their naval and military activities in the region. As a result, the South

China Sea has become a new 'flash point' in the Asia-Pacific region. In this context, India's navigational rights and engagement with the littoral states has become a point of contestation in the South China Sea. Since India occupies an important position in Asia for strategic development, it has been noticed that a country's economic progress is closely linked with the progress and development of its energy sector, and India is not an exception.

However, the idea of broader cooperation with China in the energy sector has emerged. The present Petroleum Minister in Modi regime, Mr Dharmendra Pradhan has proposed that India and China should join hands in coping with the challenge of 'crude volatility', i.e. fluctuating prices of crude oil in the global market. In fact, he has gone to the extent of proposing a block of Asia's four highest oil consumers and importers to form a 'buyers' block' to negotiate with the oil exporters. Since transporting Russian oil to India is uneconomical, India has also proposed to swap this oil with China in return of oil and gas that China is extracting from other third countries like Myanmar. These are innovative proposals and will transform the nature of India's energy relations with its eastern neighbours. However, there is a significant strategic hurdle hampering these proposals in transforming to reality. It may be kept in mind that it was the strategic factors that had blocked the innovative ideas from being pursued.

Concluding remarks

China's role in the ASEAN has further become an essential component in Indian national security discourses. China perceives India's attempt to counter the pre-eminence of the former in the region by entering a strategic and economic relationship with the countries of the Indo-Pacific region with a sense of unease. An initiative for Quad is one of the recent examples of this multi-alignment. While the significant surge in the trade between China and ASEAN countries is being appreciated, the increasing influence and assertiveness of China in territorial matters of South China Sea is causing concern for most of the Southeast Asian countries. This is pushing them towards Quad nations. In many ways, this also provides an opportunity for India, as closer connections with the ASEAN will help her counter-pressure China as and when required. For instance, Delhi's naval exercises, the port of calls, SAGAR project and maritime security dialogues with littoral countries in the South China Sea serve to remind Beijing of India's ability and willingness to increase the cost of Chinese unilateralism in the region.[10]

Henceforth, this book on India's energy security analyses the inter-regional cooperation and policy issues in India's Eastward approach. It attempts and estimates the type and quantity of energy reserves, apart from examining the opportunities for investment and partnership, which have been analysed in the context of Chinese shadow. It also explores the existing institutional mechanism, bilateralism, resource nationalism and role of the state in energy cooperation. Overall, the book paints a large multi-layered canvas of India's energy security issues and approaches. All the 14 chapters contributed by eminent academicians and practitioners create a complete landscape encompassing the number of energy reserves, opportunities for investment and partnership, institutional mechanisms and the role of the state in energy cooperation. This may prove to help garner a holistic perspective on issues of internal and external hurdles, extra-regional players, and competition in energy cooperation with India.

Notes

1 World Bank. India. 2018. Accessed 14 November 2020. https://data.worldbank.org/country/india.
2 *BP Statistical Review of World Energy*. BP. 2019. Accessed 14 November 2020. www.bp.com/content/dam/bp/business-sites/en/global/corporate/pdfs/energy-economics/statistical-review/bp-stats-review-2019-full-report.pdf.
3 Adhikari, D. 'India, Nepal open region's first transnational pipe.' Anadolu Agency. 10 September 2019. Accessed 14 November 2020. www.aa.com.tr/en/asia-pacific/india-nepal-open-region-s-first-transnational-pipeline/1577865.
4 *Act East Policy*. Press Information Bureau. December 23, 2015. Accessed 14 November 2020. http://pib.nic.in/newsite/PrintRelease.aspx?relid=133837.
5 Chakravarty, P. R. *India's Changing Global Priorities and the Role of the Act East Policy*. ORF. 25 April 2018. Accessed 14 November 2020. www.orfonline.org/research/indias-changing-global-priorities-and-the-role-of-the-act-east-policy/.
6 'Record carbon emissions seen as energy use grows most in decade.' *Business Line*, 26 March 2019 Accessed 14 November 2020. www.thehindubusinessline.com/news/science/record-carbon-emissions-seen-as-energy-use-grew-most-in-decade/article26641235.ece.
7 Pillai, Rajagopal Rajeswari, Biswas Arka. *Military Build-Up in the Indian Ocean: Implications for Regional Stability*. ORF Occasional Paper, 74, October 2015.
8 Ibid. Also see endnote 5.
9 Joint Statements issued at the end of the visits of India's President in November 2018 and the Vice-President in May 2019, to Vietnam. Ministry of External Affairs, Government of India. 2019. Accessed 14 November 2020. www.mea.gov.in.
10 Mukherjee, Sacchidananda. *Exploring Low-Carbon Energy Security Path for India*. NIPFP working paper No. 259, 2019. Accessed 14 November 2020. www.nipfp.org.in/publication/working-paper.

PART I

Energy security policy

Debates in India

1

INDIA'S ENERGY SECURITY CONTOURS

Sanjay K. Bhardwaj

Background

Energy is an essential element for any state to grow and prosper. By nature, there exist so many forms of energy in the natural resources. Primitive humans first began to use fire from easily accessible timber, thus giving a way for energy to become a basic element to humankind. With technological advances in coal mining, coal, which has higher energy density, came to be widely used. Further, progress in the geological system, and drilling, completion and refining technologies drove oil and natural gas production to increase substantially. These energy resources replaced coal as the largest energy in the world, leading to the second transformation – from coal to oil and natural gas.[1]

In the last quarter of the twentieth century, due to the population explosion, sustained increase in the economic and social demand has pushed rapid utilisation of energy resources. In fact, ecological and environmental problems caused by the use of coal, oil and other high-carbon energy resources have become increasingly prominent. Hence, with the advent of a low-carbon society, the third major transformation from traditional fossil fuel to non-fossil new energy has become inevitable.[2] On expanding the above context of energy, in the past few decades, especially since the post economic liberalisation, energy from conventional (such as coal, gas, hydro), non-conventional (wind, solar, biomass) and also from tidal and oceans types of sources have gained more focus on securing energy needs (Table 1.1).

Subsequently, in this ever-growing world economy, the global energy scenario is changing fast: new technologies are emerging; the energy mix is diversifying; global energy demand is rising; and cooperation for resources is intensifying. In today's world, energy security has been at the top of the global development agenda.[3] This has also appeared as a standalone goal in the 'Agenda: 2030 of UN Sustainable Development Goals', which is to 'Ensure access to affordable, reliable, sustainable

TABLE 1.1 Share of different sources in primary energy mix

Primary energy supply	*2012*	*2022*	*2030*	*2047*
Coal	47	52	51	52
Oil	27	28	29	28
Gas	8	9	9	8
Nuclear, hydro and renewable	3	6	6	8
Others	14	6	5	5

Source: Based on report on India's energy security scenario by NITI Aayog, Government of India

and modern energy for all'. Thus, the availability of the energy mix at affordable prices[4] is an emerging issue of discourse in various socio-economic and political aspects of societal construct.

Moreover, given that natural resources are unevenly distributed across the globe, energy security surfaces as a predominant concern for states along with the national security. Consequently, both economic and strategic interests coupled with emerging competition over scarce resources inhibit the resolution of security concerns in the long run. There exist a number of contesting peripheral energy security constructions, which generate a more 'positive' discourse on energy security with major stress on sustainability of the economy and human welfare. However, it is worth noting that the concept of 'energy security' as an emerging field of social science research is still in its nuance stage, particularly in the Global South. In this context, energy security discourse and practice in India is also constructed largely as a national security issue, emphasising the need to secure the state in terms of economic and/or strategic interests by providing secure energy supplies at stable prices.[5] Hence, the country needs an extensive contextual review of its energy policy.

In order to develop a more 'positive' discourse on energy security, it is vital to gain an insight on the framework of energy security in the Indian context. This chapter aims at combining multiple perspectives on (energy) security and raises pertinent questions regarding the significance of context for realising the value of security. While dealing with this aspect in detail, first of all the concept of energy security needs to be understood.

Concepts of energy security

The concept of energy security is understood through different perspectives. Cherp and Jewell cited that

> It is a common observation that energy security means different things in different situations and to different people. There are natural explanations for this variation. First, energy systems vary from one place to another which gives rise to different energy security problems. Secondly, the 'energy security'

term is sometimes extended to other energy policy issues ranging from energy poverty to climate change.[6]

Definition

Energy security is a widely discussed concept that has found a place in the literature of social science and sciences. Therefore, despite the high importance of 'energy security' in policy, several authors have pointed out that the term is not clearly defined. As in the words of Löschel, 'the concept of 'security of energy supply', or in short form 'energy security', seems to be rather blurred'.[7] Others echoed that there is no common interpretation of energy security. According to Checchi, Behrens, and Egenhofer,[8] the concept of energy security is 'elusive', 'slippery' or 'difficult' to define.[9]

Nevertheless, many believe that due to basic characteristics and its central position in the economy, the term 'energy security' has been recognised as element of strategic development. One of the most frequently quoted definitions of Yergin on energy security is 'availability of sufficient supplies at affordable prices'.[10] The European Commission has also defined it as 'uninterrupted physical availability on the market of energy products and services on the market, at a price which is affordable for all consumers'.[11] As per Bohi and Toman, 'the loss of economic welfare that may occur as a result of a change in the price or availability of energy',[12] and sometimes energy security has also been defined on physical, economic dimensions and, geopolitical aspects.

In a study, Cherp and Jewell (2011) described the concept of energy security as indicated in Figures 1.1 and 1.2 on its 4A's perspectives, i.e., availability, affordability, accessibility and acceptability, resources allocation across the nations to consume energy at customer level.[13]

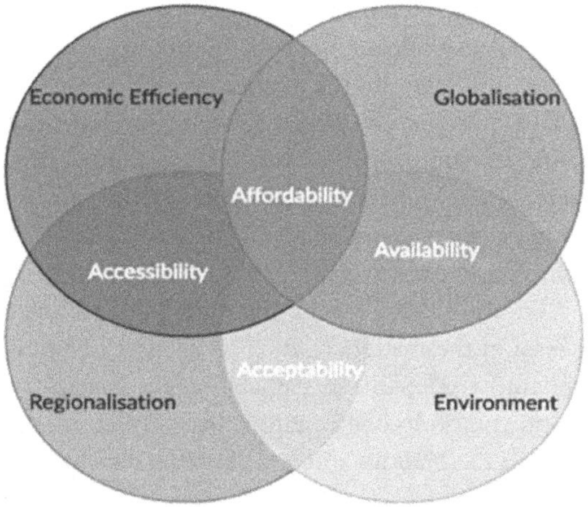

FIGURE 1.1 Energy security's 4A inter linkage with sustainability indicators. Authors, based on the figure in Bert Kruyt, D.P. van Vuuren, H.J.M. de Vries, H. Groenenberg, 'Indicators for energy security.' *Energy Policy*, 37, no. 6 (2009), pp. 2166–2181.

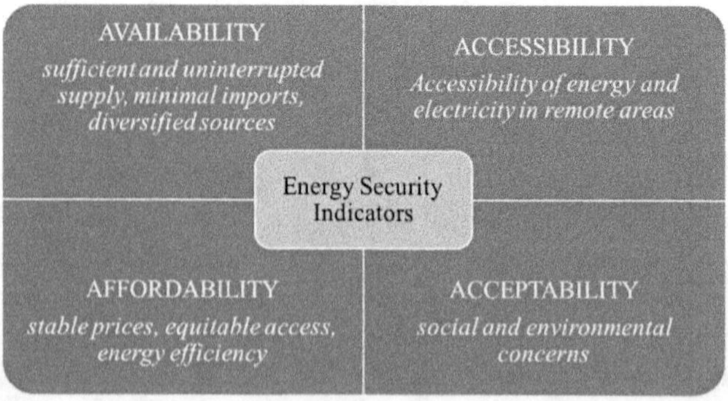

FIGURE 1.2 Various perspectives of energy security. Authors, based on A. Cherp and J. Jewell. 'Measuring energy security: from universal indicators to contextualized frameworks.' In *The Routledge Handbook of Energy Security*, edited by B. K. Sovacool, UK and New York: Routledge, 2011, pp. 330–355.

Policy framework

Energy policies find a significant place in the national policy as energy security attains a substantial forte in the form of energy strategy, which eventually becomes a part of national strategy. In fact, energy security can be viewed as a sub-set of national security. Considering the broader horizons of energy security including accessibility, political economy, environmental concerns, energy policies are plausible to reflect all the challenges and concerns to be able to construct an effective and favourable national policy agenda. Energy policy as part of national policy will then play a larger role in international policy while formulating the agendas of international cooperation.

In fact, the possible, efficient and sustainable utilisation of energy has never been possible without having a systematic policy structure in societies and also without international cooperation. While in the matters of foreign affairs related to energy security, many authors recognised energy as strategic element and presented its nexus not only with development of sector but also mutual growth with economies asking for inter-state cooperation[14]. In the nexus, Madan talked about foreign policy on energy security series, specifically studied India's concern.[15] Ebinger shows that the asymmetric growth pattern often leads to spurring political insurgence and social dislocation that compels the states to think through the prism of national security even in the matters relating to energy[16]. That means, the current national energy picture argues that sustainable energy security can be achieved through bilateral and multirole collaboration besides expanding the meaning of energy security beyond the traditional scope of national security in many countries including India.

Theoretically, the contemporary approaches to energy security are still accompanied by conventional understandings of the notions of energy and security. Henceforth, fossil fuels have been the pivotal point and their state remains the central concern. However, with the growth of new technologies and new economic architectures, this understanding of energy security is not only becoming outdated, but also impractical. Energy can no more be perceived as an exclusive idea in isolation, it has been generally agreed upon to be closely associated with climate and human security. As global systems are becoming deeply interconnected and economies far more interdependent, the environmental degradation caused by climate change is causing spillover effects on security. As a result, the traditional approach to security has become a contested concept. As Dalby asserts, there is a need for 'immediate action to drastically curtail greenhouse gas emissions for everyone's security… this is not security understood as preparing for war with rival states…environmental change now makes the necessity of rethinking security unavoidable'[17].

In fact, the countries are diversified on various fronts, *viz*. resource availability, climate zones and social slabs. Region specific load pattern, industrial demand of energy intensifies next level of challenges to security of supply across all states in the region. But each of available energy source and technological options, have their advantages over the others, also reflect their limitations on use due to their locations. Additionally, due to climate change and disturbance in natural ecosystem, adoptions of increased prices on energy and technology by consumer becomes unacceptable, and have also shown resource limitations and utilization barriers for socio-economic developments.

Since climate change and environment are now in the frontrunners of global agenda for sustainable development and resource management, rethinking about natural resources has become a critical trend. This has profound implication for security thinking too. This change of approach will require states to forego the conventional premises of security thinking that revolved around the notions of geopolitics and securing oneself at any price to be paid for. Sustainability is the key idea to be put at focal point in all security strategy deliberations[18]. The deepening ties between economy and environment along with new manifestations of threats have compelled the states to remodel their behaviour and prioritise their responses. The idea of securing oneself at the cost of others has been long challenged and highly contested. As Burke stresses, 'to secure nations, states must ensure that the world is secured'[19].

In fact, there are five key elements in (Figure 1.3) energy system transition. The energy systems composed of three parts: demand, supply, and the institutional context in which these operate and come together. The two main macro-drivers of energy system transitions: economic development and climate change, also encompass other important drivers, including local pollution and energy security. There are continuous interactions between all these five elements. Economic development and climate change goals influence each other, and the different parts of the energy system interact. In addition, there is pressure from the two macro-drivers on the energy system, and the energy system itself also affects economic development and climate goals.[20] Overcoming such limitation cannot be a simple task of achieving higher levels of 'energy security' without having cooperation and setting mutual policy dialogues within and among the country (Figure 1.4).

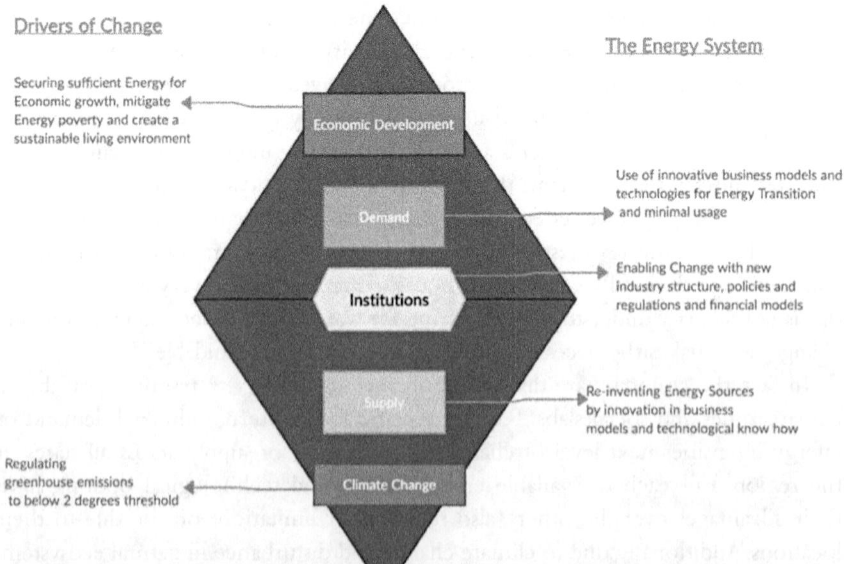

FIGURE 1.3 Elements of Energy Transition: Energy System and Drivers for Change. Authors, based on data from the Energy Transition Commission, 2019.

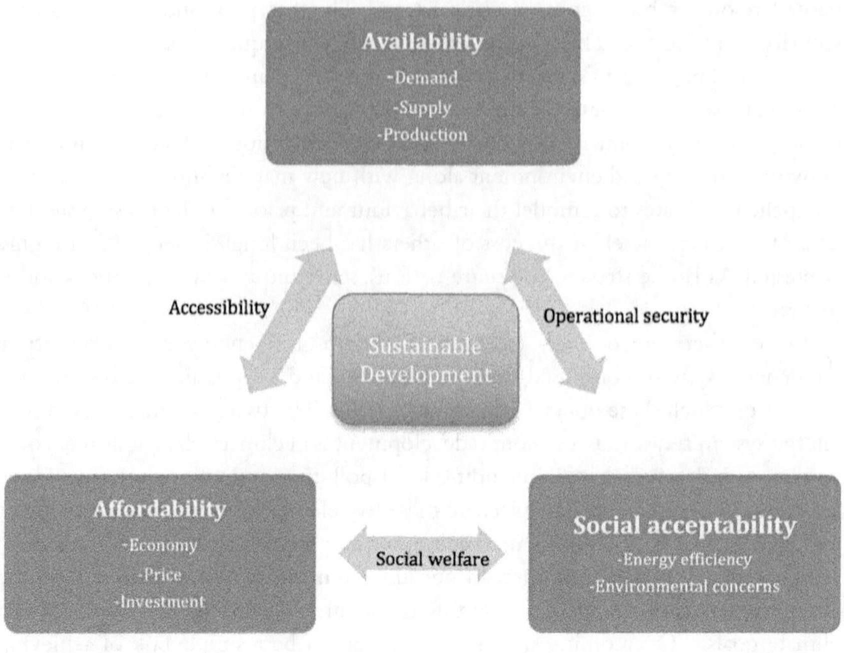

FIGURE 1.4 Basic Aspects of Energy Security. Authors, based on data from Energy Transition Commission, 2019.

Thus, energy security has been understood from many dimensions. To begin with, 'demand' and 'supply' are the two basic aspects of any study related to energy security. Many studies have been carried out that highlight the dependence of long-term and uninterrupted supply of energy on sustainable economic growth and focused on both policy and social inclusions. This idea of energy security creates a framework of 'zero-sum competition' between states over fossil fuels to stabilize or even maximize their own supply by increasing the demand. In turn, this provides a breeding ground for inter-state conflict and creates a space for mistrust and insecurity. In fact, conventional energy resources instead of being a part of the 'global commons', are deemed to be the property of the state where they occur naturally and are also finite, which makes it an intrinsically geopolitical issue.[21] The competing perspectives on energy supply-price factors largely dominate the existing debates on energy security. That shows the deliberation is focused on how best to ensure secured energy supplies at stable prices.

The traditional forms of security, therefore, enable the state to view energy as a national security concern that focuses on gaining access to the fossil fuel supplies, even at the outlay of future of climate and human security. Paradoxically, state dependency on fossil fuel to ensure 'national (energy) security' has direct implication on climate change, which, if allowed to continue as per the current trend, will become a major cause of insecurity for the population and topography over the years to come. Henceforth, the conundrum lies in the mismatch between the state's responses to the climate change and the embedded reliance on traditional approach to security.

Energy security dimensions

The energy security debate has two theoretical dimensions – realism and liberalism. The realist or 'geo-strategic' theorists argue that anarchic and open world order is bound to incite competition over finite resources. They advocate interventions through controlling supplies, either by investment or politico-institutional links with exporting states or by gaining energy independence. But, the liberal dimension undertakes more of a market-based approach to energy security. The market-based approach suggests that cooperation on energy is attainable and advocates for liberalisation of energy markets and for greater integration on energy issues. The struggle for controlling the coal, natural gas reserves, and electricity supply has made the states take a political approach rather than a purely market and public-driven approach. Cho identified that 'in order to ensure energy security along with maintaining economic growth, it is necessary for India to establish energy cooperation, enhance regional connectivity, and invest in adequate infrastructure'.[22]

However, in both the domains, the meaning of energy security is rarely questioned. The domain of energy is, therefore, 'saturated with the language of security', and a closer exposition into the energy-security debates implies that 'there simply is no need to debate what energy security is, because we know both that energy is a security issue and what security is'.[23] Nguyen identified that vulnerable supplies and unstable prices of energy could be seen as consequences of the dependence on imported energy. Energy consumption of other regions in the world tends to stabilize or even decrease, while the demand for energy in emerging Asian economies increases sharply.[24] This has further complicated the meaning of energy security. This steep rise or fluctuation in energy prices continues due to growth in energy demand and dependence on fossil fuels. This results in complex security approach to energy security, which reinforces the state's monopoly. Nguyen further identified that

> energy security must face more obstacles than before. Countries in Asia and the Pacific have owned the majority of fossil and non-fossil energy resources, and these are net exporters of coal, natural gas (through the pipeline), and electricity, but net importers of oil and Liquefied Natural Gas (LNG).[25]

The ever-increasing energy demand and rapidly depleting resources have pushed the states into a 'resource race' with apprehensions of a looming conflict among states.[26] Hence, the factor of 'high politics' has put the energy security agenda into the framework of geopolitics in the region and beyond.

As a result, the strategic actors influence hardline and non-hardline foreign policy beliefs among the national (energy) policymakers. The complex trade-off between economic development and the transition from conventional to renewable energy, with a significant focus on ecological considerations, dominates the decision-making structure in which the regional security complex plays a significant role. Within the mould of the existing international system, renewable and nuclear energy seems to be exploited in a way that is wasteful economically and potentially poses checks on the development and delivery of utilities in the long run.[27] From an economic viewpoint, the rapid expansion of the multilateral agencies and the international oil companies in Asia shows that the future transformations of the energy market will be dominated by the prosumers public–private partnership. Thus, the importance of understanding the subject becomes crucial in the case of India, as India is one of the diverse and pluralistic states that has shown well proven potential of energy resources and occupies an important position in Asian region for strategic development.

India's energy security discourse

India, being a fast-growing economic and strategic power, is facing a shifting world order characterised by not only of geo-politics of 'military' but a 'new geo-politics of energy'.[28] However, this politics of resources is grounded in the foreign policy or security discourse in an assertive form as one would observe, in the case of the United States, Germany, France or China. India is not only a large energy consumer; it is also one of the largest net oil importers. This makes it particularly vulnerable to the changing global energy dynamics, which can be a potential threat to economic and political stability.

Apart from the conceptual part, the energy security literature in India tends to focus on approaches for accomplishing energy security through market or strategic terms. In the Indian context, energy security borrows heavily from a traditional, state-centric notion of security where state aims to attempt to maximize its security to protect itself from external threats – supply instability and price volatility.[29] Thus, the energy security discourse in India is emphatically linked with the regional security complex in which the country emphasises multiple forms of security, which are influenced by the multidimensional interest of the actors ranging from internal to strategic, and external to technological.

The international relations, and perhaps the bilateral relationship between India and external world undertakes energy security as a critical feature in which supply and demand and securing the resources for national security dominate the discourse. The country pursues policies to strengthen its influence over the regional energy framework in which its national security interests interplay with the interests of the extra-regional and international powers. Buzan mentioned, 'the regional level is likely to increase in importance compared with the global one, and that India's problem is how to position itself within this change'.[30] The U.S., Russia and China are focusing more on the region through multiple initiatives such as the Indo-Pacific strategy (IPS), Belt and Road Initiative (BRI), Brazil, Russia, India, China, South Africa (BRICS) initiative, Shanghai Cooperation Organization (SCO), Mekong-Ganges Cooperation (MGC), Indian Ocean Rim Association (IORA), and the Indo-Pacific Quad and Quad plus. In these initiatives, India is a direct and indirect party.

The energy discourses in India highlight that in international and regional relations, two alarming tendencies have emerged. On the one hand, the U.S.-centric unipolar system is deteriorating, and at the same time, the U.S. and its allies continue to undermine the international security regimes and multilateral organisations causing more insecurity to the existing international security architecture. The politics of energy supply and routes, predominantly aiming at the Chinese economic and security interests, has intensified. U.S.–Russia relations are now animatedly influenced by political pressure from Washington to make Moscow reduce and eventually stop Russian energy exports to Europe in order to clear the market for the U.S. products. On the other hand, the U.S.–China trade war, and U.S.–Iran or U.S.–North Korea are increasingly expanding space for the China-led alliance to gain prominence in the energy security framework, pursued through OPEC and the evolving Middle Eastern and African geopolitical equations[31].

India, with its maximum energy needs and economic development, is not the only recipient of external influences, its energy policies, efficiency, and development output effects global energy and regional development. A study conducted by Ma, Hsieh and Chiu shows that the decision-making units (DMU) are significant weak in the South Asian countries. While there are 16 DMUs in Europe and the Americas, only three exist in Asia. This indicates significant regional differences in energy efficiency for the directional, non-directional, and wrong inputs and outputs. This is more so given the current state of the global economy and energy production and consumption in which China and India are the more prominent players with poor energy performance of 0.5964 and 0.6603, respectively.[32] DMU as an indicator further highlights that the energy decision-making remains inefficient compared to the European or American cases.

State-energy security discourse and practice in India is constructed mainly as a national security issue, emphasising the need to secure the state in terms of economic and strategic interests by providing guaranteed energy supplies at a stable price. This energy supply discourse is discussed through the prisms of national security, as the government believes that the natural resources are inadequate. The economic growth has placed it as one of the economic powerhouses in the contemporary global economic architecture, and it is increasingly becoming integrated with global economy. The country would require a stable and secured energy supply to continue the growth momentum. However, stability of supply and price is found to be problematic and 'negative', as encouraging competition over finite sources of energy resources and production perpetuates insecurity for states and often fails in securing human security, the environment and climate.[33] Consequently, both economic and strategic interests coupled with emerging competition over scarce resources inhibits in resolving security concerns in the long run.

India's energy scenario and policy initiatives

Maximal resource utilisation helps India in achieving its objectives of universal access to energy from the grass-root level to supporting the country's overall progress through industrial development. This has also supported an increase in the balance of payments on one side and enhanced bilateral trade and commodity exchange (various types of energy products) in the region.

India's energy scenario in BP's Energy Outlook 2019 reflects that the country's share of global demand will rise to 11 per cent in 2040 from 5 per cent in 2016, while its energy demand growth would be around 165 per cent. The energy consumption would grow by 4.2 per cent, faster than all major economies in the world. The report also highlighted that India's power consumption is expected to treble – by 241 per cent – with coal remaining the dominant fuel source, although its share of generation is expected to drop from 77 per cent in 2016 to 64 per cent in 2040. Nevertheless, the share of renewable energy is expected to rise from 5 per cent to 23 per cent.[34] Oil imports have also been indicated to increase by 175 per cent and account for 65 per cent of the increase in energy imports, followed by increase in gas by (+291 per cent) and coal by (+79 per cent). The report mainly observed a decline in oil (−24 per cent) production is offset by increases in coal (+154 per cent), gas (+99 per cent), and non-fossil fuels by 544 per cent, which raise a concern to manage existing oil and gas capacity and add new capacity.[35]

The demand for coal will see the biggest growth, expanding by 132 per cent, followed by renewable energy by 409 per cent, natural gas by 85 per cent and oil by 129 per cent. With demand for energy in the transport sector growing by 4.4 per cent annually, oil will remain the dominant fuel source with a 96 per cent market share in

2040, despite the focus on electric vehicles.[36] The country will remain dependent on imports of energy resources, mainly fossil fuels and particularly oil and gas as India's indigenous production of fossil fuels is, and will continue to be, inadequate to meet the country's escalating demand, Currently, the import dependency for oil, natural gas and coal are 83 per cent,[37] 45 per cent (LNG),[38] and 35 per cent,[39] respectively, as its domestic crude oil production has been declining. In fact, in the financial year (2018–2019), it has registered the lowest output recorded in the past nine years.[40]

The highest output recorded in the gas sector in the past three years as compared with previous years presents a more optimistic picture in India. The natural gas output in the financial year 2018–2019 was at 30,057 million standard cubic meters (mmscm).[41] However, any reduction in gas imports is unlikely. The LNG import will go up substantially as the country is gradually moving to a 'gas-based economy'. In the process to import a substantial amount of gas some 11 LNG terminals are being planned over the next seven years in addition to the existing four.[42]

The outlook released by BP estimates that India's current energy mix is growing very slowly with fossil fuels meeting 82 per cent of demand in 2040, down from 93 per cent in 2016.[43] As the energy sector has significant linkages with gross domestic product (GDP), it is also seen that the country's energy sector must typically grow by a 2–3 per cent rate, as part of the GDP to sustain the economy.

Economic growth and the ever-expanding population have put energy security in a perilous state in India, which is evident through sustained energy and power shortages that impede development and growth. The energy interaction and policies are dominated by transactions such as production (export and consumption), purchasing (import and diversification) and transit of energy. Thus, the current energy security debate highlights gaps in terms of policy between national security and energy transition, supply source and demand patterns, political interests and consumption trends, and dependency syndrome and diversification costs in the long term that require investment and reforms. However, due to a change of economical and infrastructure paths of developments for creating a cleaner and safer environment, India started focusing on both conventional (coal, gas, hydro, nuclear-based capacity addition) and non-conventional (solar, wind, biomass etc.) resources. In the last two decades, renewable energy captured attractiveness and cost-effective solutions to energy security without putting much effort into inter-regional cooperation and policy inclusion, perhaps due to clean environmental concerns. India has undertaken multiple rounds of energy sector reform. The Indian energy sector reform shows unbundling, the establishment of an independent regulatory commission, removal of price controls, the licensing of power generation, introduction of power trading and the establishment of multiple forms of power exchanges.

In the context of current global challenges, India has also signed the Paris Climate Agreement COP21 intending to take various measures to save the world from disastrous consequences of climate change. This compels policymakers to rethink the energy policies of the country. Energy subsidies remain a critical factor in economic policymaking, which has strong political and social connotations. Given the context of energy security, the contemporary literature on politics, economics, trade and energy often substantiates the need for cross-border energy initiatives by emphasizing the intrinsic link between energy and economic development.

Trans-national cooperation

India is energy poor and suffers from energy deficits and multiple energy security issues. The country tends to exploit country-specific resources complementarities and demand characteristics, yet the approaches and modalities of inter-regional cooperation vary.[44] The regional cooperation and bilateral energy agreements have been a trade-creating initiative; the bureaucratic and political barriers largely stifled the benefits of energy trade. Efficient cooperation regimes can enhance energy trade, which would require enhancing the relative balance in the potential trade between the partners and the agreements as well as the default enhanced protection rather than reduced protection.[45] The potential for further strengthening of India's energy security relationship needs to have a mapping of the horizontal and thematic issues that could be useful. India is concerned about climate change, depletion of fossil fuel resources, changing consumption patterns due to population growth and economic development and expansion, distribution and use of energy, and limitations in diversification and transition.

However, the idea of protectionism is dominated by the monopolisation of energy distribution, developing domestic infrastructure and capabilities in both traditional and renewable energy sectors, and imports and exports under the rationale of energy security and national interests. India has also introduced non-tariff measures and barriers in energy trading, which comes in the form of resource protectionism and policies such as the Cross-border Trade of Electricity Guideline 2016 (later 2018).[46] However, India has revised its Cross Border Trade of Electricity Regulations 2019 to ease the energy trade.[47] The revised regulation, to a large extent, complements the SAARC Framework Agreement on Energy Cooperation (Electricity).[48] The Framework Agreement has significantly emphasised the need to promote regional power trade within the spirit of SAARC, which seeks to promote and facilitate collective growth and welfare in South Asia.[49]

Apart from the bilateral, sub-regional and SAARC Energy initiatives, India has expressed an intention to work on energy security through BIMSTEC. The discourse of energy security in India highlighted that the challenges to universal electricity access and the limited availability of indigenous hydrocarbon resources are common phenomena. That essentially prompts India to initiate, lately though, hydrocarbon exploration and production in the Bay of Bengal. The Indian north-eastern region has hydro resources that can be viable for energy trade between the eastern neighbours of India to ensure collective energy security. The region has the potential of about 58971 MW electricity generation, almost 40 per cent of the country's total hydro potential, out of which only 1427 MW are being harnessed.[50] In addition, 151.68 bcm natural gas is available in the region. However, the region is strategically located between Bangladesh, Myanmar and China.[51] Hence, the energy resources and trade involvements merit national security attention rather than economic attention. In terms of its sheer geographic location, India retains the key position for trade facilitation and energy connectivity within SAARC and, to a large extent, within BIMSTEC.

The geopolitics of the energy supply route

The geopolitics of the energy supply route dominates in the energy security complex across the regions. As Kaplan mentioned,

> Geopolitics is the battle for space and power played out in a geographical setting. Just as there are military geopolitics, diplomatic geopolitics and economic geopolitics, there is also energy geopolitics. For natural resources and the trade routes that bring those resources to consumers is central to the study of geography.[52]

Perhaps the increasing role of the transit states for energy trading becomes another important dimension in energy trade, configuring in the global network of energy supplies.[53] The control over the energy supply routes and the transit states is now at the core of IPS and BRI agenda. Most of the oil and LNG projects are dependent on the maritime route, which causes new geopolitical problems directly linked with energy transport, logistics and storage. Hence, political and foreign policy risks are exacerbated by the chokepoints for energy transit routes. According to OPEC estimates, '79.4 per cent of the world's proven oil reserves are located in OPEC member countries with the bulk of OPEC oil reserves in the Middle East amounting to 64.5 per cent of the OPEC total'.[54] Nearly two thirds of the world's oil trade is made through maritime routes, whereas there are four global chokepoints for the trade of this commodity.

The Strait of Hormuz is highly linked with India's energy supply. This Strait is a 21- mile wide passage between Oman and Iran, connecting the Persian Gulf, the Gulf of Oman and the Arabian Sea, and predominantly used for oil and LNG exports from Iraq, Kuwait, Bahrain, Qatar, UAE and Saudi Arabia.[55] India is politically linked with these countries for human resources export, which earns a significant amount of remittances and energy trade. The Strait of Malacca is considered as the second most crucial oil trading chokepoint, located between Indonesia and Malaysia, through which 30 per cent of global maritime crude oil trade, equivalent to 15 million barrels per day, is done.[56] This Strait is of vital interest to China since 90 per cent of crude oil volumes flowing through the South China Sea is transited through the Strait of Malacca. This Strait is located between Africa and the Persian Gulf to connect the Asian markets with the Middle Eastern and African oil producers. This is the shortest sea route for the East Asian energy importers. Even the Suez Canal, combined with the SUMED Pipeline, is a strategic trade route that connects the Mediterranean to the Red Sea for oil, petroleum products and LNG shipments to Europe and North America. The southbound crude oil shipments through the Canal connect Singapore, China and India with the Middle Eastern,

Russian and African oil producers. The Strait of Bab el-Mandeb is increasingly becoming a geostrategic chokepoint for the U.S. and China as it is a narrow passage located between the Horn of Africa and the Middle East, precisely between Djibouti and Yemen. China's first overseas military base, costing US$590 million, was set up in Djibouti, which significantly demonstrates the Chinese People's Liberation Army's (PLA) power projection capabilities in the Horn of Africa and the Indian Ocean.

Conclusion

Multiple factors have played a critical role in the energy security domain of India which includes political, economic and strategic interests not only of the regional countries but also of the extra regional countries such as China, the United States and Russia. Even the geopolitics of energy trading routes have significant influence on the economic domain of India. Paradoxically, the inter-regional energy discourse cannot be seen in isolation of these three regional and global actors simultaneously involved in the geo-political and geo-economic dimensions of energy. The energy politics will continue to unfold in which India's overseas engagement for energy security will carry on with dictating bilateral relations and political rhetoric. Hence, the indigenous capacity to shift to alternative energy sources will determine the limits of interdependence and independence in the energy politics.

India's energy security is determined through national security prisms in which defence and conventional security play critical roles. The discourses clearly demonstrate that India's main counter-balance against China lies in a closer relationship with the U.S., Europe and Japan. The risks of the U.S.–China rivalry have provided India with opportunities to maximise national and energy securities by forming direct and indirect alliances with the U.S. bloc. The U.S.–China rivalry can entrap development discourses by over-emphasising the strategic priorities. This can lead to compromising the process of self-reliance on indigenous sources of energy, viz. renewable energy, and make India more dependent on the geopolitical interests of the global powers.

The international security structure, emanating from the geopolitics of energy, clearly shows that India is heavily dependent on the equilibrium of power dominance and projection in which the limits of interdependence between the international system and the countries frequently fluctuates. The sub-regional energy scenario aptly indicates that the access to foreign natural resources will continue to increase, the demand and supply for conventional oil and gas will continue to widen, and the energy logistics in terms of domestic supplies, regional distribution, overseas imports, and storage will dominate the discourse of foreign policy in future. This scenario also presents a low-intensity threat in the maritime security domain. Therefore, India's energy security depends on the maritime cooperation and a stable Indo-Pacific.[57]

Notes

1 Zou, C., Qun Zhao, Guosheng Zhang and Bo Xiong. 'Energy revolution: From a fossil energy era to a new energy era.' *Natural Gas Industry B*, 3, no. 1 (2016), pp. 1–11.
2 Ibid.
3 H.E. Sayed Muazzem Ali, High Commissioner of Bangladesh to India delivered his inaugural Lecture in an International Seminar at School of International Studies, JNU, New Delhi on 19 March 2019.
4 Yergin, D. 'Ensuring energy security.' *Foreign Affairs*, 85, no. 2 (2006), pp. 69–82.
5 Nyman, Jonna. 'Energy and security: Discourse and practices of United Sates and China.' PhD thesis submitted to University of Birmingham, December 2013.
6 Cherp, A. and J. Jewell. 'Measuring energy security: From universal indicators to contextualized frameworks.' In *The Routledge Handbook of Energy Security* edited by B.K. Sovacool, UK and New York: Routledge, 2011, pp. 330–355.
7 Neuwahl, Frederik, Andreas Löschel, Ignazio Mongelli and Luis Delgado. 'Employment impacts of EU biofuels policy: Combining bottom-up technology information and sectoral market simulations in an input–output framework.' *Ecological Economics*, 68, no. 1–2 (2008), pp. 447–460.
8 Checchi, Arianna, Arno Behrens and Christian Egenhofer. *Long-term energy security risks for Europe: A sector-specific approach*. Vol. 309. Brussels: CEPS, 2009.
9 Chester, L. 'Conceptualising energy security and making explicit its polysemic nature'. *Energy Policy*, 38, no. 2 (2010), pp. 887–895; Kruyt, B., D.P. van Vuuren, H.J.M. de Vries, H. Groenenberg. 'Indicators for energy security.' *Energy Policy*, 37, no. 6 (2009), pp. 2166–2181; Mitchell, John V. *Renewing energy security*. London: Royal Institute of International Affairs, 2002.
10 See endnote 4.
11 European Commission, 2000. Energy 2020 A strategy for competitive, sustainable and secure energy. European Commission. 10 November 2010. Accessed 6 March 2021. https://eur-lex.europa.eu/LexUriServ/LexUriServ.do?uri=COM%3A2010%3A0639%3AFIN%3AEN%3AHTML
12 Bohi, Douglas R. and Michael A. Toman. 'Empirical evidence on energy security externalities.' In *The Economics of Energy Security*. Dordrecht: Springer, 1996, pp. 31–58.
13 See endnote 6.
14 Yergin, D. 'Energy security in 1990s'. *Foreign Affairs*, 67, no. 1 (1988), pp. 110–132. Also see endnote 4.
15 Madan, Tanvi. *Energy security of India*. Brookings foreign policy studies, Energy security series. Washington DC: The Brookings Institution, 2006.
16 Ebinger, C.K. *Energy and security in South Asia*. Washington DC: The Brookings Institution, 2011.
17 Dalby, S. *Security and environmental change.* New York: Polity Press, 2009, p. 158. Also see endnote 5.
18 Ibid.
19 Burke, A. 'Security cosmopolitanism.' *Critical Studies on Security*, 1, no. 1 (2013), pp. 13–28.
20 Bhardwaj, Sanjay K. and Pavitra Bhardwaj. 'India-Bangladesh energy cooperation: Policy issues and challenges.' *BEI Journal*, 3, no. 2 (2019), pp. 33–60.
21 Mulligan, S. 'Energy, environment, and security: Critical links in a post-peak world.' *Global Environmental Politics,* 10, no. 4 (2010), p. 89. Also see endnote 5.
22 Cho, J. R. *Prospects for enhancing energy security in Asia and the Pacific through regional trade.* AsiaPacific Research and Training Network on Trade (ARTNeT). 2015.

23 Ciută, F. 'Conceptual notes on energy security: Total or banal security?' *Security Dialogue,* 41, no. 2 (2010), pp. 123–144.
24 Nguyen, A.T. 'Energy use and policy implications for energy security in Asia: A panel data approach'. *Journal of Asian Energy Studies*, (2017), pp. 10–27.
25 Ibid.
26 Lieberthal, K. and M. Herberg. 'China's search for energy security: Implications for U.S. policy.' *NBR Analysis.* 17, no. 1 (2006), pp. 5–42. p. 30.
27 Willrich, M. *Global Politics of Nuclear Energy.* New York: Praeger, 1971.
28 Klare, M. *Rising powers, shrinking planet: How scarce energy is creating a new world order.* Oxford: Oneworld, 2008.
29 Nyman, Jonna (2013).
30 Buzan, B. The South Asian security complex in a decentering world order: Reconsidering regions and powers ten years on. *International Studies*, 48, no. 1 (2011), pp. 1–19.
31 Bhardwaj, Sanjay K. and Pavitra Bhardwaj (2019).
32 Liang-Han Ma, J.-C. H.-H. (2019). Comparing regional difference in global energy performance. *Energy and Environment*, 31, no. 6 (2019), pp. 943–960.
33 See endnote 5.
34 *Insights from the evolving transition scenario – India.* BP Energy Outlook – 2019. Accessed 14 November 2020. www.bp.com/content/dam/bp/business-sites/en/global/corporate/pdfs/energy-economics/energy-outlook/bp-energy-outlook-2019-country-insight-india.pdf
35 See endnote 20.
36 See endnote 34.
37 Bilal Abdi, 'India's crude oil import bill to peak at record $125 bn in current fiscal: Oil ministry', ET Energy World, 22 October 2018, https://energy.economictimes.indiatimes.com/news/oil-and-gas/indias-crude-oil-import-bill-to-peak-at-record-125-billion-in-current-fiscal-oil-ministry/66319124
38 Sampson, Joanna. 'Report finds rise in India's LNG imports, driven by increased consumption.' Gas World, 2 August 2018, www.gasworld.com/report-finds-rise-in-indias-lng-imports/2015192.article
39 'India's coal import rises 35 per cent to 21.1 million tonnes in September.' The Economic Times, 7 October 2018, https://economictimes.indiatimes.com/news/economy/foreign-trade/indias-coal-import-rises-35-to-21-1-million-tonnes-in-september/articleshow/66105510.cms
40 Abdi, Bilal. 'India records lowest crude oil production in nine years'. ET Energy World. 26 March 2019. Accessed 14 November 2020. https://energy.economictimes.indiatimes.com/news/oil-and-gas/india-records-lowest-crude-oil-production-in-nine-years/68580922
41 Abdi, Bilal. 'India's natural gas production at 3-year high.' ET Energy World. 28 March 2019. Accessed 14 November 2020. https://energy.economictimes.indiatimes.com/news/oil-and-gas/indias-natural-gas-production-at-3-year-high/68616034
42 'Existing and proposed LNG terminals in India.' ET Energy World. 15 March 2019. Accessed 14 November 2020. https://energy.economictimes.indiatimes.com/news/oil-and-gas/factbox-existing-and-proposed-lng-terminals-in-india/68420962
43 *Energy Outlook on India.* BP. 2018. Accessed 14 November 2020. www.bp.com/content/dam/bp/en/corporate/pdf/energy-economics/energy-outlook/bp-energy-outlook-2018.pdf
44 Nag, T. 'Barriers to cross-border energy cooperation and implications on energy security: An Indian perspective with reference to energy trade in South Asia.' *Global Business Review*, 2019.

45 Grossman, G.M., Elhanan Helpman. 'The politics of free trade agreements.' *The American Economic Review*, 85, no. 4 (1995), pp. 667–690.
46 Ministry of Power, Government of India. *Guidelines on cross border trade of electricity 2016*. 5 December 2016. Accessed 14 November 2020. https://powermin.nic.in.
47 South Asia Subregional Economic Cooperation. *New CERC regulations to ease cross border electricity trade*. 19 March 2019. Accessed 14 September 2019. www.sasec.asia/index.php?page=news&nid=1008&url=new-cerc-regulations-power-trade
48 South Asian Association for Regional Cooperation. *SAARC framework agreement for energy cooperation (electricity)*. Kathmandu: SAARC Secretariat, 2014.
49 SARI/EI. *Formulation of model set of electricity regulations for implementation of the SAARC Framework Agreement for Energy (Electricity) Cooperation (SFAEC) and for advancing electricity trade in the SAARC countries*. New Delhi: Integrated Research and Action for Development (IRADe), 2018. Accessed 11 March 2019. https://sari-energy.org/wp-content/uploads/2019/04/Report-Formulation-of-Model-set-of-electricity-regulations-for-implementation-of-the-SAARC-Framework-Agreement-for-Energy-Electricity-Cooperation-SFAEC.pdf.
50 North Eastern Electric Power Corporation Limited. *Power potential in the north eastern region*. Shillong: North Eastern Electric Power Corporation Ltd. 2019. Accessed 17 April 2020. https://neepco.co.in/projects/power-potential
51 Ibid.
52 Kaplan, R. D. 'The geopolitics of energy.' *Forbes*. 4 April 2014. Accessed 12 January 2020. www.forbes.com/sites/stratfor/2014/04/04/the-geopolitics-of-energy/#7b0a8cf53b39
53 Milina, V. 'Energy Security and Geopolitics.' *Connections*, 6, no. 4, (2007), pp. 25–44.
54 *OPEC share of world crude oil reserves, 2018*. Vienna: OPEC, 2019. Accessed 12 May 2020, from www.opec.org/opec_web/en/data_graphs/330.htm.
55 'Today in energy.' US Energy Information Administration, 2019. Accessed 2 May 2020. www.eia.gov/todayinenergy/detail.php?id=36952
56 'More than 30% of global maritime crude oil trade moves through the South China Sea'. US Energy Information Administration. 27 August 2018. Retrieved 2 May 2020. www.eia.gov/todayinenergy/detail.php?id=36952
57 Part of this chapter has been developed while guiding Shahab Enam Khan's PhD thesis entitled: *'Comparative Energy Security Discourses in Bangladesh and India'*. Energy Study Programme, SIS, JNU.

2

INDIA'S ENERGY SECURITY IN THE ERA OF GLOBAL ENERGY TRANSITION

Girijesh Pant

Energy today is not limited to hydrocarbons. Energy security is not confined to the security of the hydrocarbon supply only. It is redefined in terms of sustainable and stable energy supply at an affordable price. After the Paris Agreement, discussion on decarbonisation became an indispensable part of the global energy security discourse. Thus, energy security necessitates energy transition for sustainability. India being the leading consumer of hydrocarbon faces the herculean task of changing its energy mix to meet its global commitment. It is well recognised that as a global energy player what it does will have a serious bearing on the global energy market. In fact, India is seen as an agenda setter of the global transition. This precisely is the reason that energy transition has moved to a central position in India's energy security narrative. Indian energy security is equally embedded in its drive to come out of energy poverty. It is thus critically linked to its capacity to mediate and negotiate between competing and conflicting orientation of global and domestic energy regime. It is conflicting because to meet its energy needs India will continue to depend heavily on hydrocarbons including coal, therefore deviating from the global goal to move away from fossil fuel. It is competing because in its drive to change its energy mix by scaling up renewable energy in a targeted way, it relies on importing technology and equipment thus creating new dependency, detrimental to energy security. In addition, it has been adversely impacting on the growth of local renewable industry thereby impeding the possibilities of technological breakthroughs at national level. The present chapter attempts to look at the way India is chartering its roadmap towards a sustainable energy regime to ensure its energy security in the era of the global energy transition.

Global energy transition

With the signing of the Paris Agreement 2016, the process of energy transition has acquired a central position in the global energy affairs. Having committed to nationally determined contributions, the signatory countries have spelled out their respective transition path with differential priorities. Given that thermal power is the major source of electricity, which is the major contributor to emissions, mainstreaming renewables in the global energy mix became central to the global energy discourse. Significantly, the transition to renewables unfolded the possibilities of redefining the very scope of energy security. Renewables are increasingly replacing hydrocarbons and opening the possibilities of countries acquiring a degree of local capacity to meet their demand. Defining the pathways of transition International Renewable Energy Agency (IRENA) suggests that:

> The energy sector needs a total overhaul, with a transformation from fossil-based to zero-carbon energy production by the second half of this century. The transformation to a sustainable energy system with high shares of renewables would meet climate goals and pay for itself. Accelerated deployment of renewable energy and energy efficiency measures form the key elements of the energy transition.[1]

After signing the Paris Agreement, countries declared their INDC with targets and timeline. The targets were committed by countries based on the specificity of their context and priorities, hence their INDCs show a high degree of variation. So, their accomplishments cannot be compared. According to a study by the Energy Transition Commission, five trends emerge from the ongoing transition at global level. These are as follows:[2]

- A massive expansion in renewable electrical energy, especially in developing countries.
- Limited growth in natural gas power generation in developed economies and significant growth in coal-generated power in developing countries.
- Very limited measures to decarbonise energy supply beyond the power sector.
- Average energy productivity to improve by 1.8 per cent a year, but with large variations.
- One fifth of the total emissions reductions depends on international financial support and technology transfer to seven developing countries.

In evaluating the INDCs of different countries, a clear distinction has to be made between countries where energy consumption has reached a point of satiation hence any inclusion of renewables would be displacing fossil fuel but in the case of countries suffering energy poverty the addition of renewables may not lead to cutting down the consumption of fossil fuel. The study thus observes,

> Although current INDCs explicitly define expected expansion in renewable power capacity, they rarely specify whether and to what extent fossil fuel capacity will be phased out. Under current policies, developing countries would in fact still expand fossil fuel power capacity.[3]

The study also observes that despite the rise in net increase in fossil fuel capacity, it share will go down from 67 per cent in 2013 to 54 per cent in 2030. It is expected that the

> developed countries are expecting a net reduction in power capacity generated by fossil fuel of 271 GW, driven by planned declines in coal of 212 GW in coal-fired capacity and 113 GW in oil-fired capacity. – In developing countries, the increase in fossil fuel capacity stems mainly from coal.[4]

Further, in the case of developing countries besides the constraints of resources, path dependency has been the critical factor in restraining the pace and accomplishment of transition,

> industrial economies have been locked into fossil fuel-based energy systems through a process of technological and institutional co-evolution driven by path-dependent increasing returns to scale. It is asserted that this condition, termed carbon lock-in, creates persistent market and policy failures that can inhibit the diffusion of carbon-saving technologies despite their apparent environmental and economic advantages.[5]

Therefore, breaking path dependency, it is argued to be necessary condition for the progress of energy transition.[6] Before looking at the strategies to break this barrier, it will be relevant to summarise the conceptual dynamics of pathways to energy transition.

Energy transitions can be analysed in interdisciplinary frame in co-evolution perspective, i.e.

> (1) techno-economic systems characterised by energy flows like energy production, conversion, and consumption coordinated by the energy markets, (2) socio-technical systems defined by the energy technologies embedded in their socio-technical context, and (3) systems of political actions influencing formulation and implementation of energy policies. These three systems co-evolve and have different boundaries. They are semi-autonomous, but changes are mutually interdependent, which means that the interaction of all three systems must be addressed to fully understand the energy transition processes.[7]

Transition it is argued is 'not determined and linear, but rather involve context-dependent evolutionary processes with emergent properties'.[8] It is defined

> as patterns of changes in sociotechnical systems unfolding over time that lead to new ways of achieving specific societal functions. Transitions pathways involve varying degrees of reconfiguration across technologies, supporting infrastructures, business models and production systems, as well as the preferences and behaviour of consumers.[9]

It is argued that four distinct kind of pathways can be identified namely, (1) Substitution: technological substitution, based on disruptive niche innovations which are sufficiently developed when landscape pressure occurs, (2) transformation, in which landscape pressures stimulate incumbent actors to gradually adjust the regime, when niche-innovations are not sufficiently developed, (3) reconfiguration, based on symbiotic niche-innovations that are incorporated into the regime and trigger further (architectural) adjustments under landscape pressure, (4) de-alignment and re-alignment, in which major landscape pressures destabilize the regime when niche-innovations are insufficiently developed; the prolonged coexistence of 'niche-innovations is followed by re-creation of a new regime around one of them'.[10] The typology is further expanded in terms of enactment by actors and institutions in case of all the four pathways. The substitution pathways assumes struggle not only between incumbents but with outsiders as well. 'New entry may also come from incumbents that diversify from other sectors, e.g. Internet companies moving into renewable energy or driverless cars.'[11] In case of institutions, substitution pathways may have two patterns, first 'fit-and-conform', in which niche-innovations are developed within the existing rules and institutions and 'in second pattern, "stretch-and-transform", where rules and institutions are adjusted to suit the niche-innovation [disruption; displacement]. These institutional changes are likely to involve power struggles, socio-political mobilization and counter-mobilization'.[12]

Unlike the past, the present transition is driven by a larger frame of sustainable energy for all. The terms of reference of transition thus is extended to 'just transition'[13] or fair and equitable transition. It is 'purposive' hence it demands corresponding public policy support.[14] While in the past, transition processes carried with them the elements of disruption in facilitating the progress of the fuel substitution, the present transition is not only driving it at beginning of the end of oil thereby promoting substitute but also encouraging the decoupling energy and growth. According to IEA,

> Global emissions of carbon dioxide stood at 32.1 billion tonnes in 2015, having remained essentially flat since 2013. The IEA preliminary data suggest that electricity generated by renewables played a critical role, having accounted for around 90 percent of new electricity generation in 2015; wind alone produced more than half of new electricity generation. In parallel, the global economy continued to grow by more than 3 percent, offering further evidence that the link between economic growth and emissions growth is weakening.[15]

The peaking of the demand is commented upon by diverse studies. The Mackenzie report observes that the oil demand growth is going to be flattened to 0.4 per cent by 2050. The World Energy Council makes a more alarming prognosis stating that

> Per capita energy demand will peak before 2030, – This is in stark contrast to historic growth levels, which have seen global demand for energy more than double since 1970. Technological innovation, government policies and lower growth expectations will have a significant impact on the sector in the coming decades.[16]

Royal Dutch Shell estimates suggest that, driven by efficiency and substitution, the peak may be possible in the next 5 and 15 years.[17] Michael Liebreich, founder of Bloomberg New Energy Finance, predicts a peak in 2025 and decline in the 2030s.[18] Significantly, OPEC, too, has recognised that oil demand will be peaking in 2040.[19] Clearly, diverse assessments are converging to point out that the global economy is moving to an energy path where oil will remain the vital player but not with the strategic premium that it has been enjoying over the years. Clearly, this changes the very premise of energy geopolitics.

The global energy transition becomes more complex with the energy trilemma emerging as a core dimension of it. According to the World Energy Council

> The energy trilemma recognises the complex interwoven links among the three core dimensions – energy security, energy equity and environmental sustainability – and their importance in ensuring sustainable energy systems. In balance and considered together, these three dimensions are a prerequisite for the prosperity and competitiveness of individual countries.[20]

While the perspective looking at energy security from above made distinct components of the wider energy environment debate, the other from a bottom up perspective looked at the energy security itself in terms of availability, accessibility and affordability as constituents of energy security. In fact, in the context of renewables the issue of acceptability, too, has become integral to the debate.

The dramatic changes in renewable technology has made it possible to counterargue against the high-cost nature of renewables. By making it competitive, the technology opened the possibilities of alternatives to the traditional energy sources. The question of whether renewables can meet all energy needs is largely resolved. What is central to the debate is the pathway, the business model that is competitive and sustainable. It is well recognised that since inclusion is the defining term of the debate, there cannot be one size fits all. The emerging economies facing the challenge of energy poverty do not have the wherewithal to convert their renewable endowment into commercial energy hence have to recognise the inevitability of fossil fuel in their energy mix.

The new energy technology has added a new facet to the debate by contesting the centralised mode of distribution and making the distributive model feasible.

The new paradigm is said to be the closer proximity between producer and consumer. Apart from emerging as an alternative source of energy, the feasibility of its being produced at local level – the off grid system – has extended the debate, i.e. centralised versus decentralised mode of distributive mode. In fact, with the digitalisation of the power system, the new possibility of a consumer producing its own power (prosumer) and, if need be, selling has changed the very organisational principle of the industry. With the relocation of energy security in the sustainable development orbit, the global debate has become germane with derivative issues like energy poverty, energy justice and energy democracy.

The technological breakthrough is not confined to fuel substitution only. It is likely to transform the organising principles of the energy market. The prospects of digitalisation of energy is expected to bring fundamental changes in global energy systems. It is argued that 'the combination of the five S's: software, semiconductors, sensors, solar and storage'[21] is driving the emerging energy revolution, which places people to the centre of the energy system. The World Economic Forum also shares the prognosis,

> The digital transformation of energy systems – smart meters, energy management systems, automated demand response or microgrids – could also help people everywhere access a reliable and affordable source of energy. Two-way communication between energy producers and consumers, as well as the increasing number of prosumers – those who both produce and consume energy – means that distributed energy resources can be dispatched to those areas that need it the most. That could include areas encountering supply shortages and grid stability issues, or those where renewable resources provide only an intermittent energy supply.[22]

The transformational changes are revising producer–consumer relationship–prosumer. Though the twin processes of transition and transformation are technological driven, their trajectory varies contextually. While transition is happening globally, the transformation is more visible in the western economies.

> (Germany), farmers and private individuals own more than 50 percent of the solar output in the country. – Over the course of a full week between the 3rd of May 2016 and the 9th of May 2016, UK's solar panels where generating more electricity from the sun than coal. It is thought to be the first time the UK has been without electricity from coal since the world's first centralised public coal-fired generator opened at Holborn Viaduct in London, in 1882.[23]

In poor countries the population lowest in income ladder are forced to use coal hence have no choice to go to green energy. Yet, given their affirmation of the Paris Agreement, the latter, too, have to calibrate the transition to a low carbon regime by changing their energy mix. This means, in the short to medium time term, the global energy market is going to be segmented between two energy regimes, the transformative regime where oil demand will be peaking and digitalisation is redesigning the energy architecture and the market where due to energy poverty hydrocarbons remain the principal energy supplier but are substituted incrementally by transition processes.

However, the progression of the transition regime is influenced by the pace of developments in transformational regime. Though technological driven, the twin processes of transition and transformation are not linear in nature; the ecosystem plays an equally defining role in their progression or regression. This means crafting an enabling regime to promote human, technical, financial, social, organisational and institutional capacities, compatible for transition and transformation. In the market, where the transition towards low carbon systems has to coexist with the prevailing system, the structural rigidities and preponderance of vested interest demand a huge intervention by the state. Thus, the public policy becomes vital to initiate a road map of transition process where the diverse stake holders perceive the possibilities of gain. The significance of the state intervention in regression is now witnessed in the USA. President Trump's energy policy, America First Energy Plan, not only has restricted the scope of energy transition but has reversed it by plans to bring back hydrocarbons. The premise is that the USA has unexplored hydrocarbon reserves, which need to be harnessed to create 'half a million' jobs. Though the coal does get a reprieve in the US energy basket, the structural shift in the energy sector would not allow the president of the USA to derail or divert the processes set in by transition and transformation.[24] It is argued that

> economics and technological advances are bound to shape the country's energy landscape despite Mr. Trump's very different blueprint. – utilities (not) going back to investing in coal because they have already reduced their infrastructure and they already have commitments geared toward natural gas.[25]

In the context of countries engaged in transition, the state policy has to address the issue of energy poverty, creating the possibilities of access along with those who need to shift their consumption to a more energy efficient mode. The state policy thus has to ensure that the energy transition does not perpetuate the skewed distribution of gains. Hydrocarbon-based energy failed to promote just energy because of its centralised mode of distribution. The economics did not encourage reaching out to markets or habitats located in remote areas or rural settings where the demand has been constrained by poor purchasing power. This means the transition has to address the issues at organisational level. It also raises the issue of ownership and distribution of the energy system. Some leading questions stemming from the transition to be addressed include, what is the proposed organising principle of harnessing energy from the resource? Whether and how can the carbon-based regime address the issue of injustice? How could renewables address the issue of energy justice? The transition trajectory in the countries where transformation is on anvil, shows a strong shift in favour of renewable in decentralised setting. In

> Germany, citizen cooperatives have long been investing in the production of renewable energies and some are now looking at how to buy back the energy grid from the energy companies. – In France, Spain, Croatia and even Greece citizens have started to invest in renewable energy cooperatives.[26]

It is argued that with renewable gaining share in the energy mix particularly in the power sector, distributed generation systems are going to play a vital role in addressing the issue of energy poverty by providing sustainable energy resources. The sustainability lies in its decentralising nature. It is significant that the cost of decentralised energy technologies are falling.

> Energy distribution does not necessarily need to be through major power plants and large grids. It can be more decentralised. That's a major change that might have an even bigger impact on the developing than developed world because it makes investments much lower to build up a functioning energy system.[27]

Thus while in developing economies structural change is reflected more in terms of transition than transformation, in western economies the market is reaching the threshold of transformation. India is an emerging economy with a highly skewed energy market. Its leading position as a global energy consumer makes it imperative to accelerate the twin processes of transition and the transformation simultaneously.

India's energy security in the context of transition

The global shift in energy security discourse beyond securitisation of hydrocarbons to a larger frame of sustainability has its bearing on reconceptualisation of the Indian energy security debate. The Indian debate on renewable energy in the wider context of energy security though influenced by the global debate, has its own issues as well. In fact, prior to the signing of the Paris Agreement, the Indian debate was driven by domestic constraints of supply and towards ensuring it either by domestic production or by imports. It was with the two documents namely Integrated Energy Policy (IEP2006) and National Energy Policy (NEP2017) that renewables gained prominence as a source of energy at commercial level. As the preamble of NEP mentions, 'The NEP builds on the achievements of the earlier omnibus energy policy – the Integrated Energy Policy (IEP), and sets the new agenda consistent with the redefined role of emerging developments in the energy world'.[28] It spells out its objective as 'affordable prices, Improved security and Independence, Greater Sustainability and Economic Growth'.[29] The policy defines energy security in terms of dependence on oil import hence calls upon reducing oil imports by developing resources.

> Energy security may be enhanced through both diversification of the sources of imports and increased domestic production and reduced requirement of

> energy. Given the availability of domestic reserves of oil, coal and gas and the prospects of their exploitation at competitive prices, there is a strong case for reduced dependence on imports.[30]

Significantly, the policy document emphasises that cheap fossil fuel would come in conflict with the goal of energy accessibility at affordable prices and with the goal of sustainability and possibly energy security as well.

> Until such time as the costs of generating, transmitting and distributing renewable energy drop sufficiently to allow its delivery to the customer at lower cost than energy from fossil fuel sources, a conflict is likely to exist among the above three objectives.[31]

The text of India's energy transition is being scripted by the compelling, to some extent, competing imperatives of energy supply security and its environmental ramifications. Its transition to renewables has potentials to secure its vulnerabilities but hydrocarbons remain and will continue to remain the major supplier of energy. The imbalance between growing demand pushed by the proactive rural electrification policy of the government and the supply does promote continuance of reliance on fossil fuel thereby restrict the space of transition for energy security. According to one estimate, 'The country's oil and gas imports are expected to double by 2050 as overall energy demand grows while the dependence on coal reduces'.[32] Moreover, the third largest economy in the world, India, faces acute incidence of energy poverty. Thus, it has to calibrate its roadmap in the context of divergent set of demands having bearing on its energy security policy As observed by IEA, the leading trends having bearing on Indian energy roadmap.[33]

- India is set to contribute more than any other country to the projected rise in global energy demand, around one-quarter of the total: even so, energy demand per capita in 2040 is still 40 per cent below the world average.
- India's urbanisation is a key driver of energy trends: an additional 315 million people – almost the population of the United States today – are expected to live in India's cities by 2040.
- India's need for new infrastructure underlies a strong demand for energy-intensive goods, while the rising level of vehicle ownership keeps transport demand on an even steeper upward curve.
- India's power system needs to almost quadruple in size by 2040 to catch up and keep pace with electricity demand that – boosted by rising incomes and new connections to the grid – increases at almost 5 per cent per year.
- Over 50 per cent of new generation capacity to 2040 comes from renewables and nuclear, while new coal-fired plants in India represent nearly half of the net coal capacity added worldwide.
- A large expansion of coal output makes India the second-largest coal producer in the world, but rising demand also means that India becomes, before 2020,

the world's largest coal importer, overtaking Japan, the European Union and China.

- Production of oil and gas falls well behind the growth in demand: India's reliance on oil imports rises above 90 per cent by 2040, requiring constant vigilance as to the implications for energy security.
- Putting manufacturing at the heart of India's growth model means a large rise in the energy needed to fuel India's development.
- India requires a cumulative $2.8 trillion in investment in energy supply in our main scenario, three-quarters of which goes to the power sector, and a further $0.8 trillion to improve energy efficiency.

The above set of observations point to three leading dimensions of India's energy future. First, given its growth momentum, India has high stakes in the global hydrocarbon market hence it has to position itself to protect and promote its interests. Second, its energy security concerns no longer remain limited to hydrocarbon supply but move to larger resource bases with growing thrust on renewable. Third, the political economy of electoral polity and inclusive growth necessitates revisiting its model of energy governance, and the architecture including institutions and policies.

The policy narrative gained in its content with the state setting ambitious targets and aspires for leadership role for India as a leading energy consumer with critical influence on the pace of global energy transition.[34] Furthermore, the political necessities of electoral politics made it frame it in terms of energy for all. Thus, multiple issues of a competing and conflicting nature make it a complex narrative. At one level of analysis, it appears that sustainable energy for all, i.e. energy security and renewables, are placed in a mutually exclusive premise defined by structural realities where non-renewables are the major provider of energy (electricity to all) and renewables are only to supplement the energy deficit. In other words, renewables are placed along with hydrocarbons to strengthen the prevailing energy order, which has been highly skewed and failed to reach the consumers on the margin. This is despite the fact that renewables, unlike fossil fuel, provides for reaching out to the margins. The point made here is that energy security acquires different connotations when looked at from the perspective of fossil fuel than from renewables. Renewables are not limited to providing light but provide benefits as well.

Re-positioning India in the global energy market

Notwithstanding the adverse impact of Covid-19 on global energy consumption with a larger incidence of hydrocarbons than renewables, it is clear that with the positioning of renewables as an alternative to fossil fuel, the global energy market is passing a phase of transition embedded with a new agenda of inter fuel competition and collaboration. Countries are repositioning as they progress in their respective transition path. India, too, is calibrating its position factoring the composition of its energy mix. India is critically dependent on imports of hydrocarbons and is the emerging player in the global renewable market. It has set an ambitious target to move to renewables and cut down its oil import. Significantly, being the third largest consumer of energy India, enjoys the leverage of its market size in both the hydrocarbon and renewable markets. Indeed, there is a contextual shift, which provides India great opportunity to be energy secured.

India's energy mix is dominated by hydrocarbons and will continue to be so in the near future. The global hydrocarbon market thus remains a critical factor in its global positioning. In the global hydrocarbon market, the oil segment is undergoing structural transformation. The growing profile of USA as a swing player replacing Saudi Arabia has totally altered the oil geopolitics. Further, the peaking of oil demand in industrialised countries has necessitated the oil exporters to look east. The Asian energy market is dominated by China, India, Japan and Korea though ASEAN, too, is looking for oil imports. The third largest importer of oil, India's import demand is expected to be 7.2 mb/d in 2040 next to China. What is changing the balance is the arrival of many new suppliers, giving India, for that matter any oil importing country, to make a choice by factoring economics and security parameter. Significantly, the American decision to lift oil exports and the energy policy of President Trump has added new elements of competition in the market. Reportedly,

> U.S. crude exports to countries other than Canada soared to more than 350,000 bpd in May, less than six months after Washington lifted a four-decade ban on shipments abroad. Including Canada, U.S. exports have doubled in the past two years to almost 700,000 bpd. China and Japan are now regular importers of U.S. crude, with occasional purchases from South Korea, India and Singapore. [35]

President Trump's intent to retrieve space for US oil no doubt adds to strategic shift in favour of oil consumers. The point made here is that with the supply side of the oil market being more diversified and competitive, the Indian position, despite high dependence, is relatively more secured. It is significant that recognising the significance of Iranian oil in Indian imports, America has indicated it will ensure the supply of oil to meet the disruption caused by sanctions on Iran. Even the Gulf countries like Saudi Arabia have promised to contribute to meet the supply coming from Iran.

Transition is having a bearing downstream of the oil industry. The oil and gas industry is transforming to emerge as integrated energy companies. It is observed

> The Energy Transition is disrupting the conventional value chain of the oil and gas industry. This disruption is resulting in overlapping of the energy value chains, e.g., of electricity and oil & gas, and emergence of 'Energy' companies as opposed to 'oil & gas' or 'electricity' companies. Oil & gas companies are diversifying their presence across the energy sources, at the same time a number of new type of players are emerging as well. The oil and gas industry will be transformed and a new energy value chain will emerge.[36]

It is further argued that India has to augment its refining capacities to meet the demands of the market. India is seeking engagement of leading oil exporters to invest its downstream. The UAE and Saudi Arabia are investing in a big way to create refining capacity in India. Indian repositioning in the global hydrocarbon market can be appreciated by the fact that, in building its strategic reserves, India is getting supplies from the UAE and Saudi Arabia and in the USA India is exploring the possibilities of storing oil. The point to be noted is that India is no longer positioning itself as a buyer only but a strategic player in the global hydrocarbon market.

Observations like 'India is now a world leader in renewable energy' by the World Bank or, 'India becoming a global force in wind energy and solar power' in the global forum underline the Indian positioning in the clean energy market. India began its move to renewables as far back as 1982 when the Ministry of Energy Resources was expanded to include Department of Petroleum and Non-Conventional Energy Sources. In 1983, the Advisory Board on Energy was created to formulate an integrated energy policy covering commercial and non-commercial sources of energy. The Department of Non-Conventional Energy Source was upgraded to a ministry in 1992. It was renamed Ministry of New and Renewable Energy in 2006. However, it is the Paris Agreement that could be called the game changer in visualising India's renewable energy policy. India is setting targets, taking initiatives, redefining issues and rewriting the script of its energy policy. NITI Aayog has developed a future energy scenario with reference to 2047 when India completes hundred years of its independence. According to Aayog, a new energy policy is being drafted making departure from earlier policy frame?:

> In this policy we are going to give a lot more emphasis on solar energy as the cost of electricity from solar has come down drastically. Natural gas will also get due importance – the policy will also try to address air quality concerns. However, the concerns addressed will be specific to India and not just air quality concerns being talked about across the world. – Another key feature in the energy policy will be the government's attempt to provide universal electricity and provision of clean cooking fuel. When the erstwhile Planning Commission framed its energy policy, around 37 per cent of the country's population did not have electricity and around 75 per cent of the people used solid fuel for cooking. Therefore, these two areas were not addressed by the energy policy of the Planning Commission.[37]

Seemingly, India is anchoring its transition to renewables to respond its global commitment to climate change and expanding its resource base to meet the challenges of energy poverty.[38] Along with achieving the numbers, equally important in Indian strategy is to meet the objectives of just transition. Synergising just transition in a low carbon economy raises new issues of political economy, namely, what are the organising principles, who sets the terms of transition and for whom. It also poses questions about 'the role of actors, interests and institutions in the energy sector'.[39] This brings into debate the issue of political economy, i.e. who are the players, what are the organisational rules, thus what is the road map. These are central concerns because, India is estimated to be among the top five in the green energy market in the globe and the market seemingly has no concern for being a promoter of a just energy economy. India has targeted 175 GW power generation from renewables by 2022 of which 100 GW would be from solar power, 60 GW from wind, 10 GW from biomass and 5 GW from small hydro power. According to government estimates, it would mean investment of $89.88 billion (Rs 600,000 crore) at the rate of Rs 6 crore per MW at the prevailing rate. Such a huge investment cannot come from the state alone. The Indian government is banking heavily on private financing both from India and abroad. It is pitching for $200 billion investment from India and abroad. According to government sources, about three hundred global and local companies have expressed an intent to be engaged with renewable power investing $310–350 billion in the next ten years.[40] Some of the leading global companies looking for investment in the Indian market include OAO Rosneft (Russia), First Solar (USA) and Trina Solar (China).[41] NITI Aayog, has spelled out the roadmap for renewable by identifying 'RE to be main occupants of the "house" and then work out the rest of the system around RE, essentially, because RE is the future?' Its salient points include the following:[42]

- Treat RE as a resource of national and strategic importance.
- Mandate RE as a significant component of the power sector.
- Take an integrated approach to power sector planning, including generation, transmission, and distribution.
- Make buyers indifferent between conventional and RE resources until grid parity is achieved.
- Give small-scale/distributed RE, close to end users, priority equal to large-scale/centralised.

The report recommends incremental intervention staggered in stages. In the first stage it calls for minimisation of risk perception regarding investor's return expectation. This has to be followed by availability of low-cost finance. In the third stage a central-government entity (e.g. IREDA, PFC) will pool various sources of funds from domestic as well as international sources. The funds could be administered and managed to lend debt (and even part equity, if possible) at lower interest rates. The report also underlines the need to upgrade and integration of the grid system. One of the problems that India faces is of uneven distribution of power, which to a greater extent has been due to the limitation of grids reaching remote areas. The report therefore rightly underlines the importance of an off-grid energy system. It recommends:

- Immediately providing stand-alone off-grid systems in remote rural areas for home lighting and running other basic appliances. Over time, these systems could play the same role as that of rooftop systems in urban areas.
- In parallel, developing district and block-level plans for providing electricity through deployment of micro-grids or mini-grids using RE resources.[43]

The imperatives of reaching targets needs finance. India as observed above is visualising a proactive role of the private players. Consequently, it is responding to their concerns by enabling policy changes. The outreach initiatives to investors are indicative of the policy thrust on promoting a market-based business model. However, from the perspective of accessibility, mere generation of capacities would not address the concern of energy poverty. It is equally critical that renewal transition does not lead to uneven distribution but, in fact, corrects the inequality that a hydrocarbon-based energy system has created in India. This brings into debate the nature of the distribution system, and whether it is premised on a centralised grid model or has space for an off-grid system as well. The point made here is that unlike the hydrocarbon-based system where the distribution logistics require a highly centralised system, renewable energy could be produced at a local level with an off- or mini-grid system. However, the possibilities of mainstreaming a decentralising model may demand change from utilities in their prevailing business model because,

> Some of their most profitable customers will reduce their regular power consumption from the central grid in favor of locally produced power. These customers may still depend on the central grid for their emergency or peak use, so utilities will have to maintain their costly infrastructure and power-generating capabilities even as revenues from consumption decline. In many markets, utilities are working with regulators[44] to adapt to this structural change by promoting a pricing model based more on connectivity and capacity and less on usage.[45]

It is argued that a decentralised energy system could turn out to be cost-effective by discounting the possibility of leakage besides the cost of long-distance transmission. The point is that with renewable energy coming into the mainstream, the carbon energy system too needs to calibrate its business model more so when decentralising model promises more jobs and empowerment of local habitat including the economy as illustrated by episodic experiences from developing and even developed countries like the USA. Apparently, India is visualising the construct of its roadmap largely supported by private players, global financing and technology, and the facilitator's role of the state. Consequently, its solar policy is significantly embedded in promoting a centralised system like the ultra-mega size solar park. This could be further inferred from the limited role visualised for off grid or mini grids in its transition strategy. The leading role of private players can be illustrated by the fact that they have proposed to develop 190 GW of renewable projects, while state-owned entities are expected to be developing 18 GW, foreign investors are expected to develop 58GW.[46]

The government has been floating a number of instruments to raise funds to finance renewables by promoting tax-free green bonds. State companies are expected to raise such funds. 'State-run power giant NTPC is likely to raise around Rs 10,000 crore through green bonds for acquisition of the government's stake in THDC India Ltd (THDCIL) and North Eastern Electric Power Corporation Ltd

(NEEPCO).'[47] So far, most of such financing has come from the government entities and banks including from the private sector but the domestic bond and capital market has yet to show interest. The government has also allowed 100 per cent ownership for foreign companies to attract technological support. It can be argued that India is pitching its energy initiatives to register its presence as the leading nation on the global energy map. This is best illustrated by its initiative to establish the International Solar Alliance as a multilateral platform to promote solar energy across the globe. It is argued that in the backdrop of sustainable energy need, countries located between the Tropic of Cancer and Tropic of Capricorn are so richly endowed with solar radiation that they could move away from dependence on carbon energy provided they could harness it. The Alliance is a joint effort from India and France to bring about 129 countries on a common platform. The platform aims at bringing these countries to be engaged on a cooperative and collaborative mode in developing technology at a cost-effective rate. The idea was given a concrete profile in the side-lines of the Marrakesh meeting in November 2016 where reportedly more than 20 countries signed a framework of agreement, making it an intergovernmental body registered under the UN charter. The objectives of the Alliance are the following: (UNFC) promote solar technologies, new business models and investment in the solar sector to enhance prosperity formulate projects and programmes to promote solar applications, develop innovative financial mechanisms to reduce cost of capita, build a common knowledge e-Portal to facilitate capacity building for promotion and absorption of solar technologies and R&D among member countries. India is pitching its transition beyond the national turf. It is projected in the wider frame of common but differentiated global responsibility. Indian profiling of its renewable objectives has received global endorsement. 'India's plans to virtually triple the share of renewable energy by 2030 will both transform the country's energy supply and have far-reaching global implications in the fight against climate change,' said Kim, the President, World Bank. He further added that 'World Bank Group will do all it can to help India meet its ambitious targets, especially around scaling up solar energy.'[48] The proactive role of the state in pushing energy transition is well evident in its policy initiatives like the fiscal incentives and ease of doing business. The former includes, accelerated depreciation, concessional custom duty, excise duty exemption, income tax holidays for ten tears, etc. Among the critical policy intervention is the provision of Renewable Purchase Obligation, (RPO), 'prescribing purchase of solar energy to promote renewable energy with an aim to reach up to 8 % of total electricity consumption by March, 2022'.[49] With a view to ease the doing business, renewables are reclassified as a 'white category which exempts these projects to exempt from seeking environment clearance'.[50]

While the urban bias of Indian energy transition is visible and possibly explained by the power dynamics, the imperatives of electoral politics has made rural electrification an important deliverable. Thus, the transition regime also talks about decentralising mode of rural electrification. The prevailing view seems to look at DRE as complementary to centralised system It is even argued that,

> there is enough evidence to move beyond the distinction between grid power and off-grid power, and to develop an integrated system where cross cutting, innovative solutions work together and help achieve the ultimate goal of energy access. There is an urgent need for a paradigm shift towards considering DRE solutions as complementary to the grid, and centralised energy providers. not in competition with it. Energy access, being immediate focus, has engaged all stakeholders from the central and state governments, investors, to private developers and consumers. Each stakeholder now needs to understand the importance of an integrated intervention strategy at both the tail-end and the generation side, along with a one track focus on developing and promoting the right solutions for the right applications.[51]

Apparently, the challenge that India faces in defining its energy inclusive transition strategy is to synergise the two distinct trajectories though not conflicting but possibly competing, given the power dynamics, where urban bias is very clearly visible. Further, it is argued that the Indian approach has yet to spell out the institutional frame work to promote an innovative ecosystem that provides a sense of participation among the local stakeholders or communities.[52] The approach appears to be to take a leaf from success stories hoping they might trigger the pace of transition. The experience from other countries suggest that such standalone cases need to be converted into a network to push the processes from the bottom up. In this the role of intermediaries has been found to be vital.[53]

Being the leading energy consumer, India's energy transition has high strategic salience in accomplishing the targets of the Paris Agreement. No wonder that the global stake holders are proactively engaged with Indian story. While such engagement is desirable as far as financing and technology is concerned, the possibilities that it could nudge the leaning of Indian policy towards a centralised path cannot be ignored. Though the Indian state is creating enabling ecosystem, in doing so, the organising principle has not been suitably modified and crafted. It can be argued that its orientation is more of a linear progression. The approach seemingly remains to be tilted in favour of grid extension over decentralised distributed generation. As observed earlier, the findings show that the grid-based centralised system not only faces the constraints of high cost and distributional losses but also fails to address the issue of skewed power distribution especially in rural settings.[54] Further, the studies have also observed that the potential of mini-grids in rural India have been restrained by the absence of private investment. It is also observed 'that mini-grids based on solar PV power and storage are more economical than incumbent energy services available to households without central grid connection'.[55] Moreover, it is also found out that 'the threat of central grid extension is the gateway barrier preventing mini-grid development in India'.[56] Apparently, the imperatives of just sustainable energy services demands reconstruction of the ecosystem not in a piecemeal way but in a wider, integrated perspective. The political economy of sustainable energy transition clearly makes a compelling case of centrality of energy justice in transition trajectory of India.

In conclusion, it is argued that with the onset of a global energy transition, in the backdrop of the UN call for sustainable energy for all, the terms and reference of energy security have been revised fundamentally. For India, heavily dependent on hydrocarbons for its energy needs but with the potential to become energy independent on the strength of its renewable resources, the task of charting a regime for energy security is indeed challenging. It becomes more complex when its energy distribution is highly skewed in favour of urban setting and against the marginal consumer. India thus has to work simultaneously to ensure the supply of hydrocarbons and change its energy mix along with ensuring accessibility. Evidently, the structural changes in the global hydrocarbon market has placed India in a position of advantage compared to the days of scarcity. The world has enough oil thanks to the nonconventional discoveries and renewable energy has emerged as an alternative to fossil fuel. Interestingly, the geopolitical shifts in the hydrocarbon market provides India leverage to redefine its security by becoming part of the supply chain, thus ensuring the supply security of hydrocarbons. Yet it will have to work towards reducing its fossil fuel consumption to minimise its imports. India has set the target to curtail oil import dependence by 10 per cent by 2022. Ironically, the Covid-19 depressed oil market has helped India to fill its strategic reserves to ensure energy security. Global energy transition thus has contributed in creating conditions that, if harnessed, could empower India to negotiate with the challenges of its energy security as defined in wider sense of the term.

Notes

1 IRENA. 'Renewable energy: A key climate solution'. 2017. Accessed 10 November 2020. www.irena.org.
2 Energy Transition Commission. *Pathways from Paris*. London: Energy Transition Commission, 2016, p. 8.
3 Energy Transition Commission. *Road from Paris*. London: Energy Transition Commission, p. 18.
4 Ibid.
5 Unruh, Gregory C. 'Understanding carbon lock-in.' *Energy Policy* 28, no. 12 (2000), pp. 817–830. https://doi.org/10.1016/s0301-4215(00)00070-7.
6 Stein, Amy L. 'Breaking energy path dependencies'. *Brookings Law Review*, 82 no. 559 (2017), pp. 559-604.
7 Bolwig, Simon, Gatis Bazbauers, Antje Klitkou, Peter D. Lund, Andra Blumberga, Armands Gravelsins and Dagnija Blumberga. *Modelling energy transitions pathways*. IST 2018 Conference, 12–14 June 2018 Manchester.
8 Ibid.
9 Geels, F.W. and J. Schot. 'Typology of sociotechnical transition pathways.' *Research Policy*, 36, 3 (2007), pp. 399–417 doi: 10.1016/j.respol.2007.01.003
10 Geels, Frank W., Florian Kern, Gerhard Fuchs, Nele Hinderer, Gregor Kungl, Josephine Mylana, Mario Neukirchc and Sandra Wassermannd. 'The enactment of socio-technical transition pathways: A reformulated typology and a comparative multi-level analysis of the German and UK low-carbon electricity transitions (1990–2014)'. *Research Policy*, 45, 4 (May 2016), pp. 896–916.

11 Ibid.
12 Ibid.
13 Michael, Jakob and Steckel Jan Christoph. 'The just energy transition.' 2016. Accessed 2 November 2020. https://wwfit.awsassets.panda.org/downloads/jakobsteckel_2016_jet.pdf.
14 Graaf, Thijs Van de, Benjamin K., Sovacool Arunabha Ghosh, Florian Kern and Michael T. Klare. *The international political economy of energy*. London: Palgrave Macmillan, 2016, p. 292.
15 IEA. 'Decoupling of global emissions and economic growth confirmed.' 16 March 2016. Accessed 7 March 2021. https://www.iea.org/news/decoupling-of-global-emissions-and-economic-growth-confirmed
16 'World Energy Council: Per capita energy demand to peak before 2030'. Greentechlead. 10 October 2016. Accessed 2 November 2020. https://greentechlead.com/climate/30977-30977
17 Katakey, Rakteem. 'Shell says oil demand could peak in five years.' *Independent*. 4 November 2016. Accessed 2 November 2020. www.independent.co.uk
18 'Liebreich: Peak emissions are closer than you think – and here's why'. Bloomberg NEF. Accessed 2 November 2020. https://about.bnef.com/blog/peak-emissions-are-closer-than-you-think-and-heres why/
19 'OPEC forecasts peak oil demand for first time, but projects quick coronavirus recovery.' S&P Global. Accessed 20 October 2020. www.spglobal.com/.
20 *World energy trilemma*. World Energy Council. 2015. Accessed 2 November 2020. www.cleanenergyministerial.org/sites/default/files/2018-07/CEM6-WEC-2015-World-Energy-Trilemma.pdf
21 Reid, Gerald. 'The five S's that will define the new energy order.' Energypost.eu. 8 November 2016. Accessed 2 November 2020. https://energypost.eu/digitalisation-will-define-new-energy-order-faster-think/
22 Molinaroli, Alex. 'What does digital mean for the future of energy?' World Economic Forum. 2 March 2016. Accessed 7 March 2021. https://www.weforum.org/agenda/2016/03/perspective-distributed-digital-and-demand-side-energy-technology-implications-for-energy-security/
23 Rick, Torben. 'Energy industry on the brink of disruption.' 2016. Accessed 2 November 2020. www.torbenrick.eu
24 'Trump's supply-side energy policy and the low-carbon transition – analysis'. Elcano Royal Institute. 2017 Accessed 2 November 2020. www.eurasiareview.com/20022017
25 Kraus C. and D. Cardwell. 'Policy shift helps coal, but other forces may limit effect'. 2017. Accessed 2 November 2020. www.nytimes.com/2017/03/28
26 *Enabling mini-grid development in rural India*. Working Paper, July, 2016 Stanford Graduate School of Management, EASME. 2015. Spreading the model of renewable energy cooperatives. Accessed 2 November 2020. https://ec.europa.eu/easme/en/news.
27 Carlson, Peter. 'Battery breakthrough 5–8 years away.' Accessed 2 November 2020. https://tbb.innoenergy.com
28 *Draft national energy policy*. NITI Aayog, Government of India, p. 1.
29 Ibid.
30 Ibid.
31 Ibid.
32 'India's oil and gas import to double by 2050: BP Energy Outlook.' *Financial Express*. 15 September 2020. Accessed 20 October 2020. www.financialexpress.com/economy/indias-oil-and-gas-import-to-double-by-2050-bp-energy-outlook/2083387/

33 IEA. *World energy outlook*. Paris: IEA. 2015.

34 In the emerging energy geo-political narrative, India now is the key to global energy decarbonisation plans. The hope is that much of India's yet-to-be installed energy infrastructure could be based on low carbon energy sources. India's energy demand is still projected to account for 30 per cent of the world's incremental energy demand over the next two decades. However, the emphasis has shifted to how this demand can be met from non-fossil fuels. See Joshi, Sunjoy and Lydia Powell. *India: Energy geo-politics.* New Delhi: Observer Research Foundation, 2018.

35 'U.S. crude exports competitive to Asia-Pacific, delivered prices show'. World Oil, 2016. Accessed 20 October 2020. www.worldoil.com/news/2016/9/5/us-crude-exports-competitive-to-asia-pacific-delivered-prices-sho

36 Dua, Vivek. 'Energy transition: Transforming the downstream oil and gas industry.' Kearney-India. AT Kearney. Accessed 7 March 2021. https://www.kearney.in/article/?%2Fa%2Fenergy-transition-transforming-the-downstream-oil-and-gas-industry

37 'NITI Aayog ready with draft national energy policy'. *The Hindu*. 2016. Accessed 2 November 2020. www.thehindubusinessline.com.

38 Pant, Girijesh. 'Global energy transition: Redefining India's energy roadmap'. *Studies in Asian Social Science*, 4, no. 2 (2017), pp. 36–45.

39 Newell, P., Phillips, J., Pueyo, A., Kirumba, E., Ozor, N., and Urama, K. *The political economy of low carbon economy in Kenya.* IDS Working Paper 445. 2014. Accessed 2 November 2020. www.ids.ac.uk/publication20.

40 IBEF. 'Power sector in India'. 2017. Accessed 2 November 2002. www.ibef.org.

41 IBEF. 'Roseneft eyes Indian solar power market'. 2015. Accessed 2 November 2020. www.ibef.org/news/rosneft-eyes-indian-solar-power-market.

42 'NITI Aayog ready with draft national energy policy.' *Business Line*. 5 August 2016. Accessed 2 November 2020. www.thehindubusinessline.com.

43 *Report on India's renewable electricity roadmap 2030: Towards accelerated renewable electricity deployment.'* New Delhi: NITI Aayog, Government of India. 2015.

44 See endnote 38.

45 Brief, Bain. 'Distributed energy: Disrupting the utility business model.' 2014. Accessed 10 November 2018. www.bain.com.

46 'Renewable-energy-transformation'. PWC. 2015. Accessed 2 November 2020. www.pwc.in.

47 'NTPC likely to issue green bonds to raise funds for THDCIL, NEEPCO acquisition.' ET Energy World. 25 November 2019. Accessed 21 October 2020. https://energy.economictimes.indiatimes.com/news/power/ntpc-likely-to-issue-green-bonds-to-raise-funds-for-thdcil-neepco-acquisition/72216052.

48 'Solar energy to power India of the future.' World Bank. 30 June 2016. Accessed 2 November 2020. www.worldbank.org/en/news/feature/2016/06/30/solar-energy-to-power-india-of-the-future.

49 *New and renewable energy sector, achievements report.* New Delhi: Ministry of New Renewable Energy, 2017.

50 Ibid.

51 Gupta, Deepak. 'Leading shift narrative clean energy access India'. New Delhi: Shakti Foundation, 2016.

52 Sarangi, G. K. and A. Mishra. *Mainstreaming off-grid renewable energy systems in India: An integrated approach.* Delhi: TERI University, 2012.

53 Schoffelen, Jorn. 'How to support bottom-up energy transitions? A strategic niche management analysis of intermediary organizations facilitating community energy development in the Netherlands.' Thesis submitted in partial fulfillment of the MSc. Climate studies at Wageningen UR, The Netherlands, 2015.
54 Khandeker, R. S., H. A. Samad, R. Ali and D. F. Barnes. 'Who benefits most from rural electrification? Evidence in India.' *The Energy Journal*, 35, no. 2 (2014), pp. 75–96.
55 Ibid.
56 Ibid.

3

CHALLENGES AND STRATEGY FOR AN ENERGY SECURE INDIA

Shebonti Ray Dadwal

Introduction

From a minor actor in the international energy (mainly oil) oil market less than two decades ago, India is now acknowledged as a major energy player. Positioned as the third largest energy consumer in the world after China and the United States of America (henceforth referred to as the US), India's thirst for energy resources seems almost unquenchable. Although its consumption is not yet anywhere close to the US and China, it has registered one of the fastest growths in energy consumption levels. Moreover, the combination of high population growth, low per capita energy consumption levels and high economic growth, the International Monetary Fund (IMF) projected in its World economic Outlook 2019 that India would grow at a rate of 7.5 per cent per annum in 2019 and 7.7 per cent in 2020.[1] India's status in the energy market is perceived as one that will continue its upward trajectory for decades.[2]

While this fast-paced economic growth and growing energy market status has reaped India substantial dividends with energy producers and suppliers vying for a share of its huge and growing energy market, it has also brought it some unwelcome attention from climate change activists and their advocates, who are demanding that India cut its growing carbon emissions. No doubt, some of this is justified. Recent reports have shown that Indian cities are some of the most polluted in the world; in fact, according to a projection by the Global Carbon Project, India is the fourth highest emitter of carbon dioxide (CO_2) in the world, accounting for 7 per cent of global emissions in 2017, behind China's 27 per cent, the 15 per cent of the US and the European Union's 10 per cent. The cause of the growth in emissions was said to be India's rapid economic growth and the use of large amounts of coal to meet the growing demand for electricity.[3]

The dilemma that policymakers are confronted with, therefore, is to sustain India's economic growth, for which huge amounts of energy resources are required, without increasing its carbon footprint. Moreover, having committed to cut its carbon emissions under the 2015 Paris Agreement by 30–35 per cent by 2030, from a base year of 2005, India has come under increasing international pressure to meet its commitments.

It is in scenario in which India's energy security policy has to be embedded, wherein it needs to devise strategies to ensure that it has access to sufficient resources of energy in order to allow its economy to sustain the high growth levels and to bring down poverty levels, and to do so without further increasing carbon emission levels, which are endangering the ecology and environment.

The Indian energy scenario

According to BP's Energy Outlook 2019, India's share of global demand will rise to 11 per cent in 2040 from 5 per cent in 2016, while its energy demand growth is projected to be around 165 per cent, which is nearly three times the overall non-OECD growth of 61 per cent. Of this, the demand for coal is expected to see the largest growth, expanding by 132 per cent, followed by renewables at 409 per cent, nuclear 412 per cent, hydro 80 per cent, gas 85 per cent and oil 129 per cent. In the transport sector, with the demand for energy growing by 4.4 per cent annually, oil is expected to remain the dominant fuel source with a 96 per cent market share in 2040, despite the recent drive to focus on electric vehicles.[4]

In other words, fossil fuels will continue to meet around 82 per cent of demand in 2040, albeit down from 93 per cent in 2016. Interestingly, India's power consumption is expected to treble – by 241 per cent – with coal remaining the dominant fuel source, although its share of generation is expected to drop from 77 per cent in 2016 to 64 per cent in 2040, while the share of renewables is expected to rise from 5 per cent to 23 per cent.[5]

Given the fact that India's indigenous production of fossil fuels is, and will, continue to be inadequate to meet the country's escalating demand, it will remain dependent on imports of energy resources, mainly fossil fuels and particularly oil and gas. Currently, the import dependency for oil, natural gas and coal are 83 per cent,[6] 45 per cent liquefied natural gas (LNG),[7] and 35 per cent,[8] respectively, as its domestic crude oil production has been declining. In fact, in the 2018–2019 financial year, India had registered the lowest output recorded in the past nine years.[9]

However, the natural gas sector presents a more optimistic picture. According to data sourced from the oil ministry, the output recorded at 30,057 million standard cubic metres (mmscm) in 2018–2019, was the highest in the past three years.[10] Nevertheless, despite the increase in production, any reduction in gas imports is unlikely. In fact, India's gas imports, in the form of liquefied natural gas or LNG, are expected to go up substantially given that the government has stated its intention of moving gradually to a 'gas-based economy'. The fact that some 11 LNG terminals are being planned over the next seven years over and above the existing four, is indicative of two factors: first, that India will be importing a substantial amount of gas in the years to come,[11] and second, that LNG, as opposed to cross-border pipelines, will be the vehicle of gas imports.

In the case of coal, the domestic production has risen by 10 per cent to 433 million tonnes (mt) from April to November 2018, as against 394 mt in the previous fiscal.[12] Nevertheless, and despite being one of the largest producers of coal in the world, India's coal imports have gone up by nearly 8 per cent over the previous year.[13] However, overall, coal imports have been declining and the government has been trying to reform the coal sector and has set a target of one billion tonnes in coal production as part of its policy of self-reliance. Some of the decline has also been attributed to the policy to substitute coal-based power with alternative fuels, including gas-based plants and renewable energy, although whether the trend in reduction can be sustained is yet to be seen. The fact that India witnessed a prolonged winter last year, which resulted in reduced power consumption, and which, in turn, saw the demand for power in general coming down, may not be sustainable. In fact, according to some estimates, the demand for coal imports is projected to rise by 10 per cent.[14]

But it is the oil sector that has faced the most challenging of times. The fall in domestic production of crude oil entails increasing quantities of imports to meet demand. This, in turn, led to a huge outflow of foreign exchange for imports. In fact, oil imports comprise the largest portion of India's overall import bill year after year, leading to Prime Minister Narendra Modi's announcement in 2015 that India would strive to cut its oil imports by 10 per cent by 2022. However, this would require a doubling of India's oil and gas production from 68.4 million tons of oil equivalent (Mtoe) in fiscal 2018 to 129.7 Mtoe in fiscal 2023.

Therefore, India's growing demand for energy, inadequate domestic availability and, consequently, dependence on imports has seen it becoming susceptible to the oil and gas market and to the geopolitics that are an inherent part of the energy market. In fact, the only certainty about global energy markets is that uncertainty will continue to rule due to a combination of factors, from geopolitics to geoeconomics for the foreseeable future. These factors have always impacted on the energy market and given the rapid changes that are taking place in the energy landscape, one can expect a prolonged period of volatility.

Policy initiatives

Domestic oil and gas sector

To deal with this challenge, India has adopted a three-pronged strategy to ensure its energy security. While a large part of the challenge is to manoeuvre in the temperamental international oil and gas markets, many of the challenges are home-grown and require major policy reform and implementation.

First, in keeping with the policy to reduce its dependence on oil imports by 10 per cent by 2022, the focus has been on enhancing domestic production. To that end, periodic rounds of bidding for exploration and production (E&P) are being conducted and oil and gas blocks have been offered under internationally competitive bidding and contractual terms to Indian and foreign oil and gas companies. Second, to ensure the maximisation of the value of discovered reserves through the application of advanced technology; and third, to build up a substantial portfolio of equity oil, gas and even coal reserves in overseas assets.

To encourage production from domestic reserves, a plethora of new reforms with respect to E&P are being undertaken. While NELP or the New Exploration Licensing Policy, which has seen 10 rounds of bidding since it was launched in the late 1990s, is seen as not very successful in attracting the major international oil companies and has also come under criticism for its unattractive contractual terms, which were based on auctioned production sharing contracts, it has now been decided that it will be replaced by HELP or the Hydrocarbon Exploration Licensing Policy, which was launched in 2016. HELP is based on a uniform licensing regime under a revenue sharing model and therefore seen as offering more attractive terms for exploration companies. Another policy, named OALP or Open Acreage Licensing Policy, was launched in 2018, which the government hopes will be a key driver for accelerating E&P activities in India. A second round of OALP along with the National Data Repository (NDR) was launched in early 2019, which the government hopes will attract more investment from domestic as well as foreign companies in the country's upstream hydrocarbon sector, including in shale formations.

With these new bidding rounds under HELP and OALP, the exploration acreage of India was expanded from approximately 90,000 square kilometres in 2017 to 150,000 sq. km after the first round of OALP, and has been enhanced to around 2,20,000 sq. km after four rounds of OALP.[15]

External oil and gas sector

However, given that the domestic reserves, even when fully exploited, are not projected to bear sufficient reserves to meet the growing demand, India will have to continue importing oil and gas. Hence, India has been accelerating its energy diplomacy, which seeks to leverage its growing domestic market to seek energy partnerships as well as tie up long-term contracts with preferential terms for hydrocarbon imports from producers.

An example of its growing energy status is indicated by the willingness of producers to accommodate India in term contracts, which was unheard of earlier. In 2016, India successfully renegotiated its long-term LNG contract with Qatar's RasGas, which was signed in 2003. Following the crash in gas prices in 2015, India sought a downward revision of the price from $12 per mmBtuto less than $5 per mmBtu as well as an additional 1 million tonnes a year of LNG for about 12 years with effect from 1 January 2016.[16] A year later, in 2017, India also got US energy major Exxon Mobil to lower the price of LNG from its Gorgon project in Australia, saving Rs 4,000 crore in import bills, and, in 2018, Russia, too, lowered the price of LNG from its Yamal project. These deals have assisted India in saving millions of dollars in its gas import bill. [17]

Apart from oil and gas purchases, India is also increasing its purchase of energy assets in overseas hydrocarbon blocks, and has succeeded in creating an impressive portfolio of assets. OVL alone has 41 projects across 20 countries and has in its portfolio reserves of 711 million tonnes of oil and oil equivalent natural gas. Domestic energy companies are being encouraged to explore opportunities for joint development of oil fields in various regions, including Russia's Arctic shelf and Pechora and Okhotsk Seas, as well as Africa, Latin America and West Asia.

India is also leveraging its huge and growing energy market to develop stronger bilateral ties with hydrocarbon producers and exporters to gain access to resources on preferential terms. For example, in June 2018, India received LNG from Russia under a long-term deal, at $7 mmBtu, which was $1.5 per mmBtu less than the price that Qatar, India's oldest and largest long-term supplier, offered, as well as shipments procured more recently from Australia and the US.[18] Earlier, India had also successfully re-negotiated the price of the long-term deal with Qatar, which had enabled it to save Rs 8,000 crore.[19]

To further ensure its supply security, India has also built strategic petroleum reserves (SPRs). While three of the SPRs have already been established at Vishakhapatnam, Mangaluru and Padur, two more are being planned at Chandikhol in Odisha and another in Padur, Karnataka, so that a 90-day SPR can be built in the event that a disruption in its oil supplies occurs.[20]

Alternative to hydrocarbons

Biofuels

Another initiative that is being looked at towards achieving its goal of reducing oil imports, is the use of ethanol and biofuels, which will be blended with crude oil. Over the last decade, several initiatives were undertaken to promote biofuels through programmes like Ethanol Blended Petrol Programme, National Biodiesel Mission and Biodiesel Blending Programme. However, due to a number of challenges, these programmes were revamped to make biofuels more acceptable, both for suppliers as well as users. These included issues on pricing, incentives, opening an alternate route for ethanol production, sale of biodiesel to bulk and retail customers, and a focus on research and development (R&D), etc. The goal is to enable the availability of biofuels in the market and increase its blending per centage from the current 2 per cent blend of ethanol in petrol and less than 0.1 per cent of biodiesel blending in diesel. A target of 20 per cent blending of ethanol in petrol and 5 per cent blending of biodiesel in diesel is proposed by 2030. This will be achieved by reinforcing ongoing ethanol/biodiesel supplies through increasing domestic production; setting up second generation bio-refineries; development of new feedstock for biofuels; the development of new technologies for conversion to biofuels and creating a suitable environment for biofuels and its integration with the main fuels. While ethanol will be processed from sugar as well as starch-rich materials such as corn, cassava, rotten potatoes, algae, etc. as well as cellulosic materials such as bagasse, wood waste, agricultural and forestry residues or other renewable resources like industrial waste, the feedstock for biodiesel will be procured processing of lignocellulosic feedstock (agricultural and forestry residues such as rice and wheat straw/corn cobs and stover/bagasse, woody biomass), as well as non-food crops like grasses and algae, or industrial waste and residue streams.[21]

A target to triple the production of ethanol to 450 crore litres by 2022 has been set, which is expected to assist in saving around Rs 12,000 crore in oil import bill, as well as boost farm income. Eleven state oil companies have adopted the modern 'lignocellulosic' or biomass route for establishing 12 2G ethanol plants in 11 states of the country.[22] At the same time, biofuels extracted from jatropha plants is also being attempted. In December 2018, the Indian Air Force (IAF) tested a biofuel-powered Russian-made AN-32 transport aircraft, using 10 per cent biofuel with air turbine fuel (ATF). Once the trials are completed successfully, the same blend will be replicated in other aircraft, including MiG-29s and Su-30 MKIs. According to estimates, the total expenditure on ATF spending will come down by 10–15 per cent. This will amount to huge savings, given that the defence forces are the largest consumers of oil. A few months before the IAF trials, a commercial flight with 25 per cent blended biofuel was also tested successfully.[23]

Green energy

Finally, while fossil fuels will remain the bedrock of the Indian primary energy system, India has been looking increasingly at alternative energy resources, both from an energy security perspective as well as to meet its carbon emission mitigation goals made under the Paris Agreement. But this would entail huge capacity additions, given that the requirement for electricity generation capacity would reach 840 GW by 2030 from 349.2 GW in December 2018, with a substantial amount generated from clean resources. As a result, the government has been devising policies to reduce the share of hydrocarbon imports by diversifying to alternative fuels, both for the power as well as the transport sectors. For the power sector, it has been ramping up its share of alternative fuels, including nuclear and hydro power, as well as renewable energy, particularly solar. In the transport sector, apart from enhancing the quotient of biofuels and ethanol in diesel and petrol (gasoline), the goal is to swiftly increase the number of battery-operated/hybrid electric vehicles, while phasing out internal combustion engineered (ICE) vehicles.

In fact, over the last four years, the drive towards ramping up the share of alternative energy has been impressive. Generation of electricity from renewable energy sources, barring large hydropower, constituted around 34 per cent of total installed capacity. Of this, despite the uncertainties with respect to the solar sector in 2018, the country's solar power installed generation capacity grew to 26,000 MW, and wind-generated power by 35288.10 MW as of 31 January 2019.[24] In fact, of all the renewable energy resources under consideration, solar energy holds pride of place, with a target of generating 100 GW of solar energy by 2022. Although there were some challenges in the form of the imposition of safeguard duty on import of solar modules and equipment, as well as low and falling tariffs and the devaluation of the Indian rupee against the US dollar in 2018, the outlook for the solar sector industry is looking more positive in 2019 on the back of improved capacity addition, favourable policy push and rising demand for clean energy.

Solar power generation capacity grew to 26,000 MW by the end of September 2018 of which grid-based power accounts for 87 per cent (23 GW) and about 13 per cent (3 GW) of rooftop solar projects.

Nuclear energy

But with India planning to generate 49 per cent of its electricity from clean energy resources by 2040,[25] India will require huge capacity additions to not only renewable energy but also other alternative energy resources such as nuclear and hydropower, besides fossil fuel-based energy, given that the projected installed power generation capacity is expected to triple from the current 348 GW.

Although nuclear energy was launched in India as an alternative source of energy to hydrocarbons, and hence critical for the country's energy security, nuclear power in India currently delivers a total capacity of 6.7 GW, contributing just under 2 per cent of the country's electricity supply. However, 21 new nuclear power reactors, with a total installed capacity of 15,700 MW, are expected to be set up by 2031, with nine reactors that are in various stages of construction scheduled to be completed by 2024–2025.

However, as in the case of oil and gas, a major challenge in the nuclear sector is ensuring the availability of uranium. According to the Department of Atomic Energy (DAE) India would require a stockpile of 15,000 tonnes of uranium for achieving supply security of fuel for its nuclear plants that are not under international inspection. India has 22 reactors, 14 of which were placed under international scrutiny. Ten more pressurised heavy water reactors (PHWR) have been sanctioned, although a decision on whether these should be placed under IAEA safeguards has yet to be taken. The government is also planning to build a strategic stockpile to ensure that there is no shortage of uranium for its power reactors.[26]

Although the government is looking at boosting the indigenous production of uranium by tenfold by 2031–2032, it will require substantial quantities of imported uranium – around 30 per cent as per Department of Atomic Energy assessments –to meet its target of around 63,000 MW by 2032, although this target may be amended. To that end, India has signed agreements with a number of countries, namely, the US, Russia, France, the UK, South Korea, the Czech Republic, Canada, Australia, Argentina, Kazakhstan, Mongolia and Namibia, both for nuclear technology as well as uranium supplies. India currently imports uranium from Kazakhstan and Canada and plans to also purchase the fuel from Australia. In January 2019, India signed a deal for long-term supply of uranium from Uzbekistan, during the visit of Uzbek President Shavkat Mirziyoyev.[27]

Hydropower

There is also renewed focus on hydropower, which is accepted as a sustainable and clean alternative to thermal power, and has several other features, such as the ability to ramp up generation swiftly, making it ideal for peak power demand and grid balancing, besides providing water security, irrigation and flood moderation and other socio-economic benefits. Moreover, India is endowed with a potential of 1,45,320 MW of hydropower, although only about 45,400 MW has been utilised so far. Some of the factors that have contributed to the slow-down are social and environmental impact of dams – population displacement and adverse effects on biodiversity, methane emissions from the rotting vegetation in the reservoirs.[28] Another factor that has contributed to the slowdown is the high tariff compared with other energy sources.

However, given the huge potential of enhancing hydropower, ambitious plans were drawn up by the government for setting up hydel plants with the support of the private sector, to stem the slowdown in hydro capacity since 2008. Recently, the government introduced a number of measures, including categorising large hydro projects as renewables, as against the earlier policy to give projects under 25 MW the status of renewable energy. This will allow all hydro projects to get benefits like financial assistance and cheaper credit.[29] The policy decision will also allow the government to reach its target of achieving 225 GW of renewable energy by 2022. With around 45 GW of hydro capacity planned, this will be added to the existing 74 GW of renewables derived from solar, wind and small hydro.

Cross-border power grids

Apart from the focus on developing its domestic hydropower capacity, India is also importing hydro-electric power from neighbouring countries. Moreover, given the strategic geographical position of the northeast region, and its prospects for playing a key role in India's Act East Policy by partnering with ASEAN countries, it was decided to explore the vast potential of region. Not only is the region endowed with abundant untapped natural resources, particularly rare minerals like dolomite, sillimanite, carborundum, etc. it also has substantial oil, gas and uranium reserves and its huge potential for generating hydro-electricity.

A set of plans and guidelines were drawn up to boost infrastructure in the region, which would allow it to perform its envisaged role as a bridge to its eastern neighbourhood. Apart from hydropower, a document – Hydrocarbon Vision 2030 for North East India – was prepared, the aim being to provide a roadmap for the next 15 years to increase the production of hydrocarbons in northeast India and to outline the necessary investment in the sector for enhancing exploration activities, as well as expand the piped natural gas (PNG) network and ensure availability of petroleum products, including LPG, in the remotest corners of the hitherto under-developed region.

Initiatives were also taken to form a sub-regional electricity grid with some of its eastern neighbouring countries. The central power regulatory board announced (amended) regulations in December 2018 which are aimed to facilitate the countries of the region to trade power seamlessly among Bhutan, Bangladesh, India and Nepal (BBIN) without agreements, as against the earlier requirement for bilateral trading using the Indian territories.[30]

Hence, with a clear focus on focusing on clean energy sources, since 2014, India has done well in increasing its renewable energy, assisted by the massive fall in the price of renewable energy. It has now set a goal of achieving 49 per cent of its electricity from renewable energy.

Apart from resources, the government has also set up a number of policy initiatives that will further incentivise the adoption of clean energy, such as the electric vehicle (EV) policy under the Faster Adoption and Manufacturing of Hybrid and Electric Vehicles (FAME-2) –which envisages that by 2030, almost half the vehicles in India, including two and three-wheelers, will be electric –in an attempt to further encourage the move away from fossil fuels. Finally, robust energy efficiency programmes are being evolved that will be evaluated against set targets. Efficiency targets are being set across all energy demand sectors of the economy.

But challenges remain

Despite these initiatives that have been undertaken, will it allow India to become energy self-sufficient? Take the Electric Vehicle (EV) policy, for example. The rationale for adopting electrification of transport was twofold: to reduce petroleum consumption, which would lead to a reduction in oil imports; and second, to bring down emissions and pollution in consonance with commitments taken under the Paris Agreement.

However, as policies to encourage production and use of EVs increase to meet the target of 50 per cent electric mobility by 2030, the demand for power will increase manifold as vehicles are plugged into charging stations at all times of the day.

While the goal is to enhance the share of renewable energy, currently, renewable energy can only be generated to supplement fossil fuel (as well as hydro and nuclear)-based generation as without access to storage technology, renewable energy will be subject to weather conditions – sunlight in the case of solar energy and wind speed in the case of wind energy.

In the case of solar energy, despite the focus of the government in its development, the year 2019 saw a significant dip in generation accretion. Several factors were responsible for the cancellation of projects by solar developers – a combination of low tariffs, and the imposition of safeguard duty on imported solar panels from China and Malaysia of 25 per cent – saw several developers opt out of projects. The rationale for the import duty was to encourage domestic manufacturing of solar panels and to give an advantage to Indian manufacturers since more than 90 per cent of solar panels and modules used in Indian solar projects are imported from China and Malaysia. However, the technology for Indian modules are generally outdated, with an overwhelming dependence on the import of raw materials, as well as limited access to cheap loans and factories, which sees domestic manufacturers often operating below their capacity, resulting in domestic modules costing 10–20 per cent more than imported modules from China, even after the safeguard duty is imposed. Moreover, difficulties in land acquisitions and inconsistencies in policies are also deterring factors in the development of solar energy.

Similarly, in the case of wind energy, although India ranks fifth in the world in terms of the installed capacity for wind energy generation of around 34,043 MW, institutional and technical issues need to be overcome. First, the limitation of existing power grids, including voltage fluctuations and grid frequencies, which make it difficult to efficiently deliver wind generation successfully and leads to wastage, are major challenges. Given the high cost of setting up, operating and repowering, windmills deter private operators. Moreover, unlike solar panels, particularly rooftop panels, wind farms require specific topographic and geological criteria, thereby limiting their diffusion.

Apart from the above challenges, huge amounts of raw materials will have to be made available for the manufacture of renewable energy equipment. Some of the key minerals/raw materials that are required for the manufacture of renewable energy hardware as well as several electronic, as well as defence and aviation sector-related equipment, including smartphones, laptops, pacemakers, automobiles, solar panels and wind turbines, include silicon technology, for which the major raw material is the rock quartzite, while rare earth metals, particularly 'lanthanides' such as neodymium, are required for making the magnets in wind turbine generators, while copper is preferred in making conductors for generator windings, power cables, transformers and invertors in wind power. For storage in both solar power as well as EVs, lithium and cobalt are used. [31]

Of the various minerals, India is mostly concerned with acquiring copper, nickel and cobalt, all of which are required for making clean energy and energy storage equipment, but are not widely available in the country, at least on land. Hence, much of this was required to be imported.

A new kind of import dependence?

With the government now encouraging manufacturing of renewable energy equipment as against importing and assembling the same, it is working towards acquiring the requisite raw materials required for manufacturing solar panels and storage batteries. Recently, the 2019 National Mineral Policy (NMP 2019) was approved, which aims to develop the mining sector in a sustainable manner. NMP 2019 replaces the 2008 National Mineral Policy, which determined mining policies till now. The new policy aims to attract private investment through incentives by granting industry status to mining activities, which in turn will facilitate financing to allow for the buying of mineral assets in other countries by the private sector. Furthermore, a new long-term import-export policy is being formulated.[32]

Furthermore, India is also looking at exploring deep-sea mining, which was earlier seen as too costly and technologically challenging, although the country's deep ocean exploration programme goes back more than two decades, during which the sea floor and testing environmental impacts had been surveyed, according to the National Institute of Oceanography (NIO) in Goa.[33] However, given that the seabed that lies within India's territorial jurisdiction is largely unexplored, the government has initiated plans to explore for sea-bed based minerals.

The world over, sea-beds are scattered with vast amounts of minerals – polymetallic nodules comprising copper, nickel, cobalt, manganese, iron and rare-earth elements. Over the next decade, the Earth Sciences Ministry plans to provide over $1 billion to develop and test deep-sea technologies, including underwater crawling machines and human-piloted submarines, and industrial-scale sea mining, which would be able to reach depths of up to 6 km, where metals can be concentrated more than 15 times than in land deposits. The International Seabed Authority (ISA) – an autonomous international organisation set up to organise and control activities in the maritime space that is beyond the limits of national jurisdiction, with a view to administer the resources of the Area[34] – allows India to explore an area in the Indian Ocean of 75,000 sq. km (about 29,000 square miles), equal to roughly 2 per cent of the country's size. In fact, industrial-scale sea mining could begin as early as 2019.[35]

Most mineral resources that are in demand fall into three categories: polymetallic nodules, which are scattered on the sea-bed at depths of 3.5 to 6 km. They mainly comprise manganese oxides but also contain metals such as nickel, cobalt and copper, and were first identified as potentially economically attractive back in the 1960s.[36]

Second, are Seafloor Massive Sulphides (SMS), which are metal-containing deposits, particularly copper, that are located around mid-ocean ridges where the sea floor is, or was, volcanically active. Third, there are cobalt-rich ferromanganese crusts, found mostly on the flanks of underwater seamounts and extinct volcanoes. They contain iron, manganese, cobalt, nickel and other minor metals. Unlike the other two minerals, mining these may be challenging but are less environmentally damaging.

Given India's huge and growing demand for energy across the board, and the fact that India will not be able to depend on domestic resources for its energy requirements, India will require partnerships for ensuring access to materials and minerals are required, as well as the need for access to the requisite technology for processing minerals like rare earth. Similarly, in the case of storage systems for EVs or solar PV, the lack of metals like lithium and cobalt behove India to depend on imports of the same for the manufacture of batteries, both for renewable energy as well as e-vehicles. A step in this direction has been taken by signing a memorandum of understanding with Bolivia for the development and industrial use of lithium. It was also agreed to extend collaborate to lithium mining areas and other facilities in the Bolivia's Salar de Uyuni, which holds over a quarter of the world's known deposits, to allow India to attain its objective of having 30 per cent electrification in transport.[37]

Conclusion: The road ahead

Expanding and improving energy and associated services including electricity is imperative for India's economic growth and poverty alleviation. Large investments are urgently required to seal energy gaps, initiate and implement reforms to address existing policy and price distortions across the energy sector play a crucial role in energy delivery, avoiding waste, attracting investments, particularly from the private sector and promoting the energy transition toward a cleaner and more sustainable energy mix.

In 2012, India suffered a major blackouts wherein an estimated 600 million people lost power for two days. The blackout was caused by a failure in three of the country's five state-owned electricity grids and plunged the whole of north and eastern India into chaos. Schools, commerce, businesses, hospitals and traffic were all affected for hours, causing immense economic and financial losses, and displaying telling evidence of the critical importance of energy security.

The NDA government has taken several initiatives to address the challenge and reorganise the energy sector. When the current government took office, the installed power generation capacity in the country was 2,485,54.39 MW,[38] but in the last five years, the installed capacity has been increased to around 350 GW, and the power deficit has been brought down sufficiently. Policies like 24×7 Power for All and Saubhagya schemes, among others, whose aim is to provide electricity connections to all households, both urban and rural, including free electricity under the latter by 2019. Although the government is confident of achieving the target, inefficiencies in the electricity supply chain will continue to cause disruptions in energy supply emanating from fuel shortages, both due to access and lack of delivery systems, poorly performing state utilities and wasteful consumption downstream. These are generally attributable to weak governance norms, poor implementation and regulatory distortions resulting from price regulation, subsidies and cross-subsidies.

Moreover, several remote areas of the country are not connected to the grid, sometimes due to challenging terrains. There is an urgent need to enhance and upgrade the national grid capacity in order to absorb capacity additions, both from renewable and non-renewable fuels. Pricing of retail power will also have to be rationalised, particularly if the contradictions in augmenting capacity from cleaner and greener fuel-based generation, as against cheaper but more polluting fuels, are to be addressed. Hence, while grid modernisation and enhancement is a priority, construction of mini-grids to provide decentralised power – preferably renewable –to remote and inaccessible areas is a means to address the problem. A major focus should be developing and supporting research and development in the sector, given the swift changes that are taking place, particularly in the clean energy space as attracting up-to-date technology into the various energy sectors, and the requisite investment, is required in a sector that is hugely capital- and technology-intensive. However, an attractive investment climate, with less bureaucratic red tape, would be necessary to achieve the desired results.

A start has been made and the results have been positive thus far as can be seen from the changes in some of the relevant energy-related ministries. Nevertheless, much is left to be done before India can embark on the path of being energy secure.

Notes

1 Still Sluggish Global Growth, World Economic Outlook Reports, World Economic Outlook, 23 July 2019, https://www.imf.org/en/Publications/WEO/Issues/2019/07/18/WEOupdateJuly2019
2 India Energy Outlook 2021, International Energy Agency, World Energy Outlook Special Report, February 2021, https://www.iea.org/reports/india-energy-outlook-2021
3 'Record carbon emissions seen as energy use grows most in decade.' *Business Line*. 26 March 2019. Accessed 27 March 2019. www.thehindubusinessline.com/news/science/record-carbon-emissions-seen-as-energy-use-grew-most-in-decade/article26641235.ece.
4 'Insights from the evolving transition scenario – India.' BP Energy Outlook, 2019. Accessed 11 February 2019. www.bp.com/content/dam/bp/business-sites/en/global/corporate/pdfs/energy-economics/energy-outlook/bp-energy-outlook-2019-country-insight-india.pdf.
5 Ibid.
6 Bilal Abdi. 'India's crude oil import bill to peak at record $125 bn in current fiscal: Oil ministry.' *ET Energy World*. 22 October 2018. Accessed 11 February 2019. https://energy.economictimes.indiatimes.com/news/oil-and-gas/indias-crude-oil-import-bill-to-peak-at-record-125-billion-in-current-fiscal-oil-ministry/66319124.
7 Joanna Sampson. 'Report finds rise in India's LNG imports, driven by increased consumption.' Gas World. 2 August 2018. Accessed 11 February 2019. www.gasworld.com/report-finds-rise-in-indias-lng-imports/2015192.article
8 'India's coal import rises 35 per cent to 21.1 million tonnes in September.' *The Economic Times*. 7 October 2018. Accessed 19 February 2019.https://economictimes.indiatimes.com/news/economy/foreign-trade/indias-coal-import-rises-35-to-21-1-million-tonnes-in-september/articleshow/66105510.cms.
9 Bilal Abdi. 'India records lowest crude oil production in nine years.' *ET Energy World*. 26 March 2019.Accessed 11 February 2019. https://energy.economictimes.indiatimes.com/news/oil-and-gas/india-records-lowest-crude-oil-production-in-nine-years/68580922.
10 Bilal Abdi. 'India's natural gas production at 3-year high.' *ET Energy World*. 28 March 2019. Accessed 11 February 2019. https://energy.economictimes.indiatimes.com/news/oil-and-gas/indias-natural-gas-production-at-3-year-high/68616034.
11 'Existing and proposed LNG terminals in India.' *ET Energy World*. 15 March 2019. Accessed 11 February 2019. https://energy.economictimes.indiatimes.com/news/oil-and-gas/factbox-existing-and-proposed-lng-terminals-in-india/68420962.
12 'India's coal production has grown 10 per cent to 433 MT in current fiscal so far.' *ET Energy World*. 31 December 2018. Accessed 19 February 2019. https://energy.economictimes.indiatimes.com/news/coal/indias-coal-production-has-grown-10-per-cent-to-433-mt-in-current-fiscal-so-far/67324817.
13 'India's coal import rises 8% to 212 million tonnes in April-February.' Money Control. 7 April 2019. Accessed 19 February 2019. www.moneycontrol.com/news/business/commodities/indias-coal-import-rises-8-to-212-million-tonnes-in-april-february-3778321.html

14 India's thermal coal imports likely to rise 10 pct in 2019 – Adani Power.' *Reuters*. 19 January 2019. Accessed 11 February 2019. https://in.reuters.com/article/india-coal/indias-thermal-coal-imports-likely-to-rise-10-pct-in-2019-adani-power-idINL5N20E27L.
15 National Data Repository, Directorate General of Hydrocarbons (DGH), Ministry of Petroleum and Natural Gas, Government of India, March 7, 2021, https://www.ndrdgh.gov.in/NDR/, accessed on March 7, 2021
16 'LNG import cost falls on revised deal with Qatar: Dharmendra Pradhan.' *Live Mint*. 2 May 2016. Accessed 23 February 2019.www.livemint.com/Industry/ONuOzD5j7S7wiTXzm1Bg9O/LNG-import-cost-falls-on-revised-deal-with-Qatar-Dharmendra.html.
17 'After Qatar and Australia, Russia lowers LNG price for India.' *The Economic Times*. 16 January 2018. Accessed 23 February 2019. https://economictimes.indiatimes.com/industry/energy/oil-gas/after-qatar-and-australia-russia-lowers-lng-price-for-india/articleshow/62525192.cms.
18 'India gets cheapest LNG as Russia's Gazprom begins supplies.' *Times of India*. 4 June 2018. Accessed 23 February 2019. https://timesofindia.indiatimes.com/business/india-business/india-gets-cheapest-lng-as-russias-gazprom-begins-supplies/articleshow/64450442.cms.
19 'After Qatar and Australia, Russia lowers LNG price for India.' *The Economic Times*. 16 January 2018. Accessed 23 February 2019. https://economictimes.indiatimes.com/industry/energy/oil-gas/after-qatar-and-australia-russia-lowers-lng-price-for-india/articleshow/62525192.cms?from=mdr.
20 Strategic Crude Oil Reserves, Ministry of Petroleum & Natural Gas, February 3, 2021, https://pib.gov.in/PressReleasePage.aspx?PRID=1694712
21 *National Policy on Biofuels – 2018*. Ministry of Petroleum and Natural Gas Notification, Govt. of India, 4 June 2018. Accessed 25 February 2019. http://petroleum.nic.in/sites/default/files/biofuelpolicy2018_1.pdf.
22 'PM Modi targets Rs 12,000 crore saving in oil import bill from ethanol use.' *The Economic Times*. 10 August 2018. Accessed 25 February 2019. https://economictimes.indiatimes.com/industry/energy/oil-gas/earlier-govts-not-serious-on-ethanol-output-now-it-will-save-rs-12000-crore-pm/articleshow/65350732.cms?from=mdr.
23 'In a first, India flies military aircraft using blended bio-jet fuel.' *The Economic Times*. 27 December 2018. Accessed 25 February 2019. https://economictimes.indiatimes.com/news/defence/in-a-first-india-flies-military-aircraft-using-blended-bio-jet-fuel/articleshow/67133114.cms?from=mdr.
24 *Programme/scheme wise physical progress in 2018–19 &cumulative upto Jan, 2019*. Ministry of New and Renewable Energy (MNRE), GoI. Accessed 30 March 2019. https://mnre.gov.in/physical-progress-achievements.
25 'Renewable energy will reach 49 per cent in India by 2040: Report.' *ET Energy World*. 17 June 2017. Accessed 30 March 2019. https://energy.economictimes.indiatimes.com/news/renewable/renewable-energy-will-reach-49-per cent-in-india-by-2040-report/59194908.
26 'New reactors under IAEA safeguards: Decision will be based on source of uranium, says official', The Economic Times, 10 February 2019. https://economictimes.indiatimes.com/news/politics-and-nation/new-reactors-under-iaea-safeguards-decision-will-be-based-on-source-of-uranium-says-official/articleshow/67930512.cms. Accessed 6 March 2021. https://economictimes.indiatimes.com/industry/energy/power/15000-tonnes-of-uranium-needed-to-achieve-supply-security-of-fuel-for-nuclear-plants/articleshow/67309739.cms?from=mdr.

27 Chaudhury, Dipanjan Roy. 'India inks deal to get uranium supply from Uzbekistan.' *The Economic Times*. 19 January 2019. Accessed 31 March 2019. https://economictimes.indiatimes.com/news/defence/india-inks-deal-to-get-uranium-supply-from-uzbekistan/articleshow/67596635.cms.

28 Seetharaman, G. 'Hydel power in India is growing at the slowest pace.' *The Economic Times*. 27 January 2019. Accessed 1 April 2019. https://economictimes.indiatimes.com/industry/energy/power/hydel-power-in-india-is-growing-at-the-slowest-pace/articleshow/67704776.cms?from=mdr.

29 Ibid.

30 Hossein, Mollah Amzad. 'India clears BBIN path.' Energy & Power. 7 February 2019. Accessed 1 April 2019. http://ep-bd.com/view/details/article/MzA5NQ%3D%3D/title?q=india+clears+bbin+path.

31 Barron, Andrew. 'Meet the new "renewable superpowers" – nations that boss the materials used for wind and solar.' Phys.org. 19 February 2019. Accessed 1 April 2019. https://phys.org/news/2018-02-renewable-superpowersnations-boss-materials-solar.html

32 'India approves NMP 2019 for sustainable mining sector development.' Mining Technology. 1 March 2019. Accessed 2 April 2019. www.mining-technology.com/news/india-nmp-2019-sustainable-mining/.

33 'Will India's deep dive for minerals boost its economy?' *Business Line*. 5 December 2018. Accessed 2 April 2019. www.thehindubusinessline.com/news/variety/will-indias-deep-dive-for-minerals-boost-its-economy/article25672656.ece

34 The International Seabed Authority was established under the 1982 United Nations Convention on the Law of the Sea and the 1994 Agreement relating to the Implementation of Part XI of the United Nations Convention on the Law of the Sea. The Authority is the organisation through which States Parties to the Convention shall, in accordance with the regime for the seabed and ocean floor and subsoil thereof beyond the limits of national jurisdiction (the Area) established in Part XI and the Agreement, organise and control activities in the Area, particularly with a view to administering the resources of the Area.

35 'India plans deep dive for seabed minerals.' *The Hindu*. 10 December 2018. Accessed 3 April 2019 www.thehindu.com/sci-tech/science/india-plans-deep-dive-for-seabed-minerals/article25711278.ece,

36 Murray, Louise. 'Deep-sea mining: Plundering the sea-floor's minerals.' Engineering & Technology. 18 February 2019. Accessed 5 April 2019. https://eandt.theiet.org/content/articles/2019/02/deep-sea-mining-plundering-the-seafloor-s-minerals/.

37 Gupta, Uma. 'India gets access to Bolivia's lithium for EV batteries.' PV Magazine. 2 April 2019. Accessed 5 April 2019. www.pv-magazine-india.com/2019/04/02/india-gets-access-to-bolivias-lithium-for-ev-batteries/.

38 'All India installed capacity (in MW) of power stations (as on 31.03.2014, CEA).' Accessed 5 April 2019. http://cea.nic.in/reports/monthly/installedcapacity/2014/installed_capacity-03.pdf.

4

ENERGY EFFICIENCY AND CLEAN ENERGY TRANSITIONS IN INDIA

What do these mean for climate change mitigation?

Meeta Keswani Mehra and Deepti Kohli

Introduction and background

Energy plays a crucial role in the development and growth of an economy. It constitutes a critical input for meeting heating, cooling and cooking energy needs in households, processing heat and motive power demands in industries, fuelling of automobiles and other modes of transportation and running of appliances and equipment in the commercial and services sectors. While higher energy use is advantageous for the economy and society, in terms of larger output and improved quality of life, there are negative impacts associated with its use in the form of environmental deterioration. These adverse effects are experienced locally, regionally and globally, in terms of inferior quality of air and water, degradation of soil, depletion of natural resources, noise pollution, ozone depletion and climate change. To mitigate or adapt to environmental change requires both – more efficient use of energy and a switch to cleaner energy forms.

Energy efficiency refers to utilisation of energy in a manner such that energy losses are minimised during energy conversion, transmission and use, leading to lowering of consumption of primary energy for a given level of useful energy delivered for carrying out an economic activity. A switch to cleaner energy, by its very definition, implies change in the energy mix by switching to those fuels that generate lower wastes and, hence, reduced environmental pollution per unit of economic activity. Consequently, energy efficient practices, employment of cleaner technologies and shift to cleaner energy forms not only help utilise less energy for any energy-intensive activity but also help in minimising the associated adverse environmental impacts of energy consumption.

With an expected annual gross domestic product (GDP) growth rate of 7.6 per cent (at constant 2011–2012 prices), India has presently emerged as one of the fastest growing economies in the world. Notwithstanding the ongoing adverse impact of COVID-19, India aims to strive for a higher economic growth path in the medium to long run. Accordingly, from a longer-run perspective, India's energy needs cannot be overlooked. According to India's Energy Outlook, 2015, published by the International Energy Agency, India's total energy demand is slated to more than double by the year 2040.[1] Additionally, IEO/IEA, 2015 forecasts that by 2040, India's aggregate energy consumption will see a phenomenal rise in the off-take of coal, oil and natural gas.[2]

The escalating demand for energy has raised concerns related to environmental sustainability of the growth process. At both local and global levels, greater reliance on conventional sources of energy, like coal, oil and natural gas, constitutes a threat to environmental sustainability. The combustion of fossil fuels releases carbon dioxide (CO_2), sulphur oxides (SO_x), nitrogen oxides (NO_x) and particulate matter (PM), and results in air pollution, subsequently leading to global warming and climate change. In the year 2014, India recorded 2238 million tons of CO_2 emissions, which is much higher than the 2000 level of 1032 million tons. In 2015, the mean annual exposure to particulate matter 2.5 ($PM_{2.5}$) ambient air pollution concentration in India was 74.3 micrograms/cubic metre, way higher than the world average of 44 micrograms/cubic metre, and significantly above the average for high income countries of 16.6 micrograms/cubic metre.[3]

Given this milieu, it is pertinent to address the role of energy efficiency and clean fuel options in mitigating environmental and climate change for India to grow sustainably. In what follows, we place the growth of the energy sector in India within the global order of energy consumption.

India's energy economy in the global order

In terms of the world order of energy consumption, it can be seen in Figure 4.1 that non-OECD (Organization for Economic Cooperation and Development) countries have become the largest global consumers of energy with their share placed at 58.5 per cent, surpassing the OECD's share by 17 per cent. In comparison, Figure 4.2 exhibits the slightly falling trend in OECD countries' energy consumption, contrasting with that of non-OECD countries and energy consumption in the European Union (EU), which has remained fairly constant. The energy consumption in Mtoe

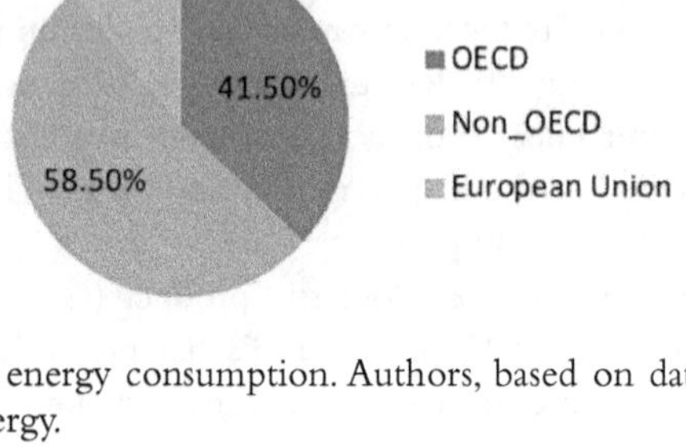

FIGURE 4.1 Share of energy consumption. Authors, based on data from BP Statistical Review of World Energy.

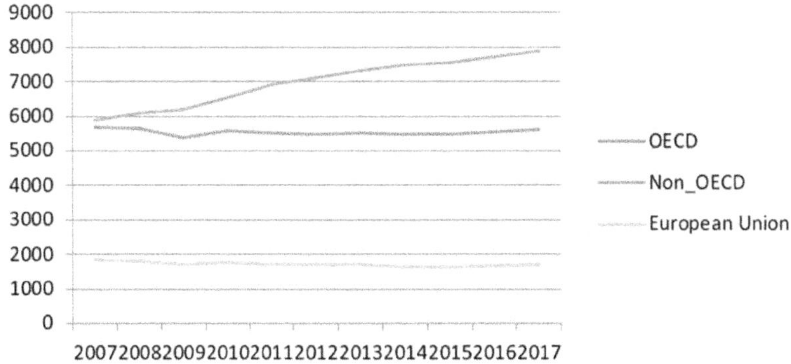

FIGURE 4.2 Primary energy consumption trends. Authors, based on data from BP Statistical Review of World Energy. 2018.

TABLE 4.1 Primary energy consumption across different regions of the world (Mtoe)

Regions	*2007*	*2008*	*2009*	*2010*	*2011*	*2012*	*2013*	*2014*	*2015*	*2016*	*2017*
North America	2809.5	2759.4	2632.5	2720.7	2722.9	2665.1	2738.3	2766.8	2739.7	2761.9	2772.8
South & Central America	587	605.8	596.8	632.5	658.9	676.5	692	697.7	701.1	696.8	700.6
Europe	2041.7	2038.5	1932.1	2001.1	1949.1	1944.3	1934	1871.2	1908.7	1934.6	1969.5
CIS	989.8	998.1	926.8	967.8	1006	1014.1	989.2	987	960.7	972	978
Middle East	618.2	657.1	677.2	714.3	740.9	771.1	795.3	823.1	848.3	869.7	897.2
Africa	346.9	368.7	373.4	386.9	385.6	399.8	410.6	425.1	429.4	438	449.5
Asia Pacific	4195.2	4310.8	4411.1	4696.1	4951.1	5118.2	5269.9	5382.9	5472.4	5585.5	5743.6
World	11588.4	11738.5	11549.9	12119.4	12414.4	12589	12829.3	12953.9	13060.2	13258.5	13511.2

Source: BP Statistics. *BP Statistical Review of World Energy*. 2018.

(million tons of oil equivalent) across different regions of the world over the last decade displays that the major consumers of energy are countries from the Asia-Pacific region, succeeded by North America and Europe (Table 4.1).[4] In contrast, South and Central America, Africa, CIS (Commonwealth of Independent States) and the Middle East fall way behind in primary energy consumption. The general trend indicates a reduction in the share of consumption of energy across European and North American regions.

Furthermore, the shares and growth rates of energy consumption for different regions of the world for the year 2017 are depicted in Figure 4.3. As can be seen in Table 4.1, although Africa and the Middle East are not large consumers of energy (with shares at 3.3 per cent and 6.6 per cent in 2017), their growth rate in 2017 surpassed that of the world (at 2.9 per cent and 3.4 per cent respectively). North and South-Central America had a combined energy consumption growth rate of 1.5 per cent, which is relatively lower than the 2.2 per cent growth rate of the world as

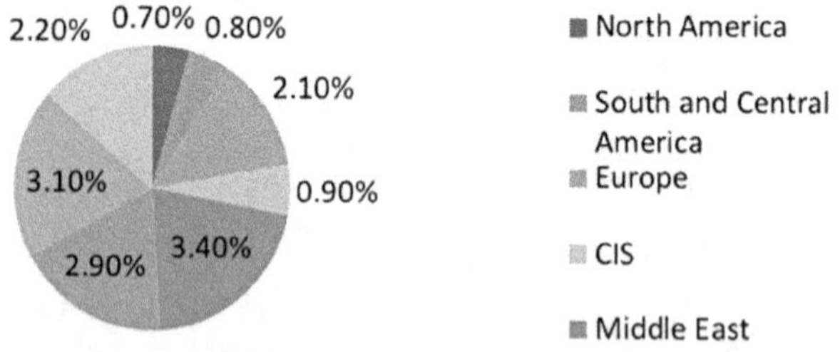

FIGURE 4.3 Growth rate of energy consumption. Authors, based on data from BP Statistical Review of World Energy. 2018.

a whole. Although Europe registered a lower growth rate (2.1 per cent) relative to the world as a whole, it can still be considered substantial relative to the combined growth rate for North, South and Central America (1.5 per cent) given the former's 14.6 per cent share in the world's energy consumption as compared to 25.7 per cent for the latter. The Asia-Pacific region has been the most intriguing: having a 42.5 per cent share in the world's consumption of primary energy, it displayed a very high energy consumption growth rate of 3.1 per cent in 2017, which is second only to the growth rate in the Middle East (3.4 per cent).[5]

Since the Asia-Pacific region comprises a bulk share of world energy consumption, it is imperative to go deeper into the analysis of its energy consumption trends. Table 4.2 contains data on primary energy consumption in South-Asian and South-East Asian countries. As can be seen, within the Asia-Pacific region, China has emerged as the largest consumer of energy, at 3132.2 Mtoe, followed by India's consumption at 753.7 Mtoe. This is not surprising given that China's energy

TABLE 4.2 Primary energy consumption across Asia Pacific countries (Mtoe)

Regions	*2007*	*2008*	*2009*	*2010*	*2011*	*2012*	*2013*	*2014*	*2015*	*2016*	*2017*
Australia	126.7	128.9	128.2	129.2	133.5	132	132.9	135.1	138	139.5	139.4
Bangladesh	17.8	18.8	20.6	21.6	23	25	25.5	26.8	31.1	31.9	33
China	2150.3	2231.2	2329.5	2491.3	2690.1	2799.1	2907	2973.5	3009.8	3047.2	3132.2
India	450.4	476.3	512	538	570.7	600.3	623.6	666.8	686.9	722.3	753.7
Indonesia	134.4	132.7	137.4	150.9	164.6	173.2	177.6	166	165.4	167.4	175.2
Japan	524.4	516.9	472.3	503.8	477.8	475	471.3	456.7	453	451.2	456.4
Malaysia	77.2	80	77.7	81.6	82.9	89.1	93.1	93.9	95.1	97.6	99.6
Pakistan	62	62.4	63.2	63.4	63.5	64.1	64.8	66.7	70.2	76.5	80.9
Philippines	27.1	28	28.3	29.3	29.9	30.9	33.1	34.9	38.3	40.6	43.3
Singapore	55.8	59.3	63.8	68.6	71.3	71.6	73.6	75.8	80.6	83.6	86.5
South Korea	236.7	241.2	242.3	259.7	273	276.3	276.7	279.3	284.9	292.2	295.9
Sri Lanka	5.5	5.1	5.3	5.7	5.9	6	6.1	6.4	7.4	7.4	7.7
Thailand	94.2	95.5	98.8	105	109.1	116.7	118.7	122.1	124.9	126.9	129.7
Vietnam	31.1	38.6	39.4	44.6	51	53.4	57.2	62.7	68.8	73.6	75.3

Source: BP Statistics. *BP Statistical Review of World Energy*. 2018.

consumption share in the world in 2017 was the highest, at around 23.2 per cent, while India's share was only 5.6 per cent. Though the absolute levels of energy consumption of countries like Bangladesh, Indonesia, Philippines, Vietnam and Sri Lanka were relatively lower, their growth rates of energy consumption, respectively at 3.6 per cent, 5 per cent, 6.9 per cent, 2.7 per cent and 4.8 per cent, were quite remarkable.[6]

According to a recent study by the Global Carbon Project, India has emerged as the fourth highest emitter of carbon dioxide (CO_2), accounting for about 7 per cent of world annual emissions of CO_2 in 2017, although it displayed much lower per capita emissions at 1.8 tons in comparison with the 4.2 tons per capita as the global average, 5.3 tons per capita for the US and 3.5 tons for EU in 2016.[7] For the other South Asian and South-East Asian countries, the per capita CO_2 emissions in 2016 were estimated at 0.45 tons per capita for Bangladesh, 2 tons per capita for Indonesia, 1 ton per capita in Philippines, 0.99 tons per capita in the case of Sri Lanka and 2 tons per capita for Vietnam.[8]

In India, policy initiatives like the launch of the National Action Plan on Climate Change (NAPCC) and India's involvement in crucial climate change treaties like the Copenhagen Accord (2009) and the Paris Agreement of Climate Change (2015) have acted as a catalyst in promoting cleaner forms of energy in the country and, consequently, a move towards creation of a low-carbon economy. As a part of the Paris Agreement, India has committed to voluntarily reduce its carbon intensity by 33–35 per cent from the baseline year of 2005 by 2030. By being a major contributor to carbon emissions, India's energy sector is set for an overhaul with setting up 175 Giga Watt (GW) of installed capacity of renewable energy by 2022, 24 × 7 Power for All by 2022, housing for all by 2022, 100 smart cities mission, 10 per cent reduction of oil and gas import dependence by 2022 from 2014 to 2015 levels and provision of clean cooking fuels.[9]

This chapter highlights the importance of energy-efficiency and use of cleaner technologies as an instrument for climate change mitigation with a focus on India, and placing it against other South-Asian and South-East Asian countries. The research finds that in the light of the persisting concerns of climate change, India has developed a wide-ranging policy framework to reduce GHG emissions by emphasising deployment of energy efficient technologies and promoting the share of renewables in the energy mix under the ambit of NAPCC, along with its eight focused missions. In support of these, India has put in place various financial and economic instruments towards energy efficiency, such as the Perform, Achieve, Trade (PAT), a market-based instrument for energy saving and trade, and incentives for dissemination of renewable energy technologies through cuts in subsidy on fossil fuels, taxing carbon, feed-in-tariffs (FiT), renewable purchase obligations (RPOs) and generation-based incentives (GBIs) for renewable energy. To this end, a rapidly growing economy like India has displayed significant efforts to devise ecologically sustainable growth pathways in the face of climate change. These could potentially yield valuable lessons for other growing market economies as well.

Energy sector trends in India

Key energy indicators

According to a report by the Japan Centre for Economic Research, the projected real GDP growth rate of India in 2030 would be around 5.2 per cent, while China, which had the same growth rate as India in 2016 (6.7 per cent) will slow down to 2.8 per cent in 2030. Some of these growth trends might undergo changes in the short run, due to the adverse impacts of COVID-19.[10] The focus of the chapter is on the long-run trajectories. In accordance with the revised population estimates provided by the United Nations, India's population is forecasted to transcend that of China's in the next seven years and rise to around 1.5 billion by 2030 and 1.66 billion by 2050.[11] These high expected economic growth projections, accompanied with structural changes like urbanisation and population growth, will generate persistent and rapid expansion in demand for energy in India.

By 2040, India is expected to constitute 25 per cent of the rise in global energy demand according to International Energy Agency Statistics.[12] According to a report by NITI Aayog, the compound annual growth rate (CAGR) for India's energy demand is estimated to be in the range of 3.7 to 4.5 per cent and India's electricity demand is estimated to grow at a compound rate in the range of 5.4 to 5.7 per cent until 2047.[13] From Table 4.3, it can be noted that the total primary energy supply (TPES) from both conventional and non-conventional sources in India in 2016 was estimated at 862 Mtoe with energy supply from commercial and non-commercial sources at about 643 Mtoe and 191 Mtoe, respectively. Further, per-capita primary energy supply from both conventional and non-conventional sources for India was 0.65 tons of oil equivalent (toe) as compared to 2 toe for the world as a whole. Other Asian countries like Bangladesh, Myanmar and Vietnam fall way behind India in terms of total primary energy supply with their respective estimates being merely 40 Mtoe, 19 Mtoe and 81 Mtoe. As far as per-capita final energy consumption is

TABLE 4.3 Key energy indicators across select countries for 2016

Countries	*TPES* (Mtoe)	*TPES/ Population* (toe)	*TPES/ GDP*	*Electricity/* Population (MWh/capita)	*CO_2 emissions (Mt of CO_2)*
India	862	0.65	0.11	0.92	2077
Bangladesh	40	0.24	0.07	0.35	73
Vietnam	81	0.87	0.15	2	187
Myanmar	19	0.37	0.07	0.29	21
Malaysia	89	3	0.11	5	216
Indonesia	230	0.88	0.08	0.87	455
World	13761	2	0.13	3	32316

Source: IEA. *Data and Statistics.*

concerned, in 2016 India's estimate was 0.43 Mtoe, which was substantially lower than 1.28 Mtoe for the world. The reason for such low per-capita energy consumption levels stems from the fact that with an 18 per cent share of the world population, India consumes a mere 6 per cent of the world's energy.[14]

In so far as aggregate efficiency of energy use is concerned, the data in Table 4.3 suggest that energy intensity measured by the TPES/GDP ratio (where GDP is PPP adjusted and TPES and includes both conventional and non-conventional energy sources) is 0.11 for both India and Malaysia, which is below the world average of 0.13. This means that India uses lower levels of primary energy for producing each thousand dollars of GDP. Moreover, the energy intensity measure for commercial and non-commercial energy sources for India is 0.081 and 0.024, respectively. The corresponding figures for the world are 0.102. However, Vietnam exhibits an energy intensity measure of 0.15, which is greater than the world average, despite having a low level of TPES. Additionally, a comparison for per-capita electricity consumption portrays that the electricity consumption for India was a mere 0.92 MWh per-capita per annum in 2016 as compared to the world average of 3 MWh, while Malaysia and Vietnam's per-capita electricity consumption was quite substantial at 5 MWh and 2 MWh, respectively (see Table 4.3).[15]

The key energy demand and supply patterns in India are outlined in more detail in the following sub-sections.

Energy demand

In India, end-use demand for energy arises in the following sectors: industry, residential, agriculture, transport, commercial and services and non-energy use. The final energy consumption levels rose from 484 Mtoe in 2010 to 572 Mtoe in 2016, registering a CAGR of around 2.85 per cent. The highest annual rates of growth were registered in the transport and agricultural sectors (around 5–7 per cent), with industrial energy growth exhibiting a CAGR of 3.25 per cent from 2010 to 2016. While industry and residential sectors are the largest energy consumers (at 34 per cent and 31 per cent respectively) in 2016, industry overshot the residential sector in terms of shares over the six-year period. Transport notched up its share by registering amongst the highest rates of growth.

The trends for the individual sectors, in terms of the fuel-mix, are also interesting. The total consumption of raw coal by industry rose from 502.82 million tons during 2007–2008 to 841.56 million tons during 2016–2017 with a CAGR of 5.29 per cent according to the Energy Statistics Report by Ministry of Statistics and Programme Implementation.[16] In 2016–2017, the topmost consumer of raw coal was the power generation industry (527.26 million tons of coal), succeeded by steel and washery industries (54.15 million tons), cement industries (6.43 million tons) and sponge iron industries (5.68 million tons).

Natural gas has been utilised for both energy (58.16 per cent) and non-energy (41.84 per cent) purposes. Figure 4.4 depicts the sector-wise natural gas consumption in India during 2016–2017. It can be discerned that the fertiliser industry

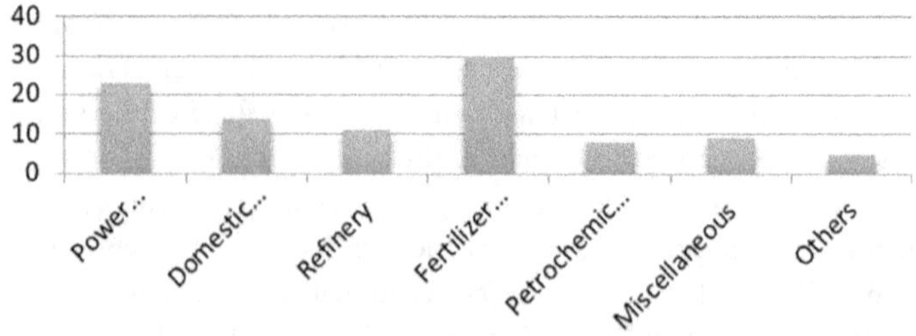

FIGURE 4.4 Sector-wise use of natural gas in India during 2016–2017. Authors, based on data from the Ministry of Statistics and Programme Implementation (MoSPI). Energy Statistics. Central Statistics Office, New Delhi, India: MOSPI, 2018.

(non-energy purpose) has seen a significant utilisation of natural gas (30 per cent) followed by power generation (24 per cent) and domestic fuel (around 14 per cent) for energy purposes. This ties in with the growth in non-energy use.[17]

Besides this, crude oil consumption has shown a stable increase from 156.1 million tons in 2007–2008 to 245.36 million tons in 2016–2017 with a CAGR of 4.63 per cent. Additionally, out of all types of petroleum products, high speed diesel oil accounted for 39.06 per cent of total consumption in 2016–2017. This was followed by petroleum coke (12.31 per cent), petrol/gasoline (12.21 per cent), liquefied petroleum gas (LPG) (11.11 per cent) and naphtha (6.80 per cent). Figure 4.5 shows that reseller/retail sector contributed to 54 per cent in the total consumption petroleum products in India followed by mining and quarrying (16 per cent) and chemicals and petrochemicals (9 per cent) in 2016–2017.[18]

Additionally, the consumption of electricity in India depicted a CAGR of 7.82 per cent from 2007–2008 to 2016–2017.[19–20] Figure 4.6 presents that out of the total electricity consumption in 2016–2017, industry accounted for the largest share (40.01 per cent), followed by domestic (24.32 per cent), agriculture (18.33 per cent) and commercial sectors (9.22 per cent). According to Energy Statistics Report by Ministry of Statistics and Programme Implementation, during 2007–2008 to

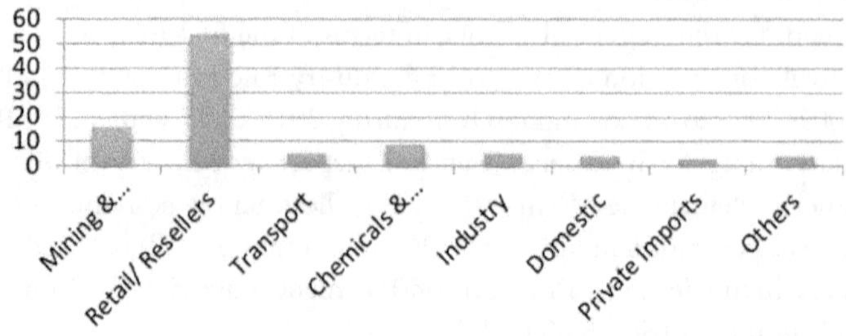

FIGURE 4.5 Sectoral consumption of petroleum products in India during 2016–2017. Authors, based on data from the Ministry of Statistics and Programme Implementation (MoSPI). Energy Statistics. Central Statistics Office, New Delhi, India: MOSPI, 2018.

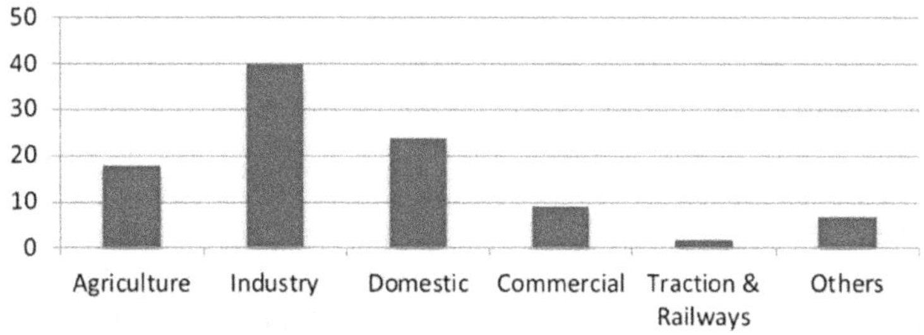

FIGURE 4.6 Sector-wise consumption of electricity in India during 2016–2017. Authors, based on data from the Ministry of Statistics and Programme Implementation (MoSPI). Energy Statistics. Central Statistics Office, New Delhi, India: MOSPI, 2018.

2016–2017, the electricity consumption in industry sector and residential/domestic sector has increased at a much faster pace relative to other sectors with CAGRs of 8.46 per cent and 7.93 per cent, respectively.[21]

Energy supply mix

Aggregate primary energy supply in India rose from 700 Mtoe in 2010 to 862 Mtoe in 2016, registering a CAGR of 3.54 per cent. Given its large domestic endowments, India has had an overwhelming dependence on coal as a source of primary energy supply. Coal contributed 40 per cent (279 Mtoe) of total primary energy supply in 2010, which rose to 44 per cent (380 Mtoe) in 2016, with both domestic production and imports having risen over the analysis period. Coal is followed by oil and oil products in terms of their contribution to total primary energy supply mix, where the latter's levels rose from 162 Mtoe (23 per cent share) in 2010 to 217 Mtoe (25 per cent in terms of share). Importantly, the level of natural gas supplies declined from 54 to 47 Mtoe over the period 2010–2016, and a bulk of this decline was on account of domestic production, while its import levels registered a near doubling (Table 4.4).

TABLE 4.4 Energy demand by end-use sectors

	2010	*2010*	*2016*	*2016*
	Mtoe	*Per cent*	*Mtoe*	*Per cent*
Industry	159	33	193	34
Transport	64	13	90	16
Residential	177	37	178	31
Commercial & public services	17	4	24	4
Agriculture & forestry	19	4	27	5
Non-specified & non-energy use	47	10	61	11
Total	484	100	572	100

Source: IEA Data and Statistics

Nuclear, hydro and imports of electricity rose slightly from 18 to 22 Mtoe, with their share as a group stable at around 3 per cent of total primary energy supply during 2010–2016. Interestingly again, despite the policy push, the share of renewable energy, which includes geothermal, solar, wind, biomass etc. did depict a small increase in the level, from 187 to 197 Mtoe, while in terms of its share, there was a fall from 27 per cent to 23 per cent, to be made up for by fossil energy, mainly coal, oil and oil products in the recent past (Table 4.5).[22] Unless energy efficiency measures are given a stronger thrust, this will have significant implications for the environment.

In physical terms, coal production in India during the year 2007–2008 was 457.08 million tons as compared to 662.79 million tons during 2016–2017, registering a CAGR of 3.79 per cent over 2007–2008 to 2016–2017. Additionally, the production of lignite rose from 33.98 million tons in 2007–2008 to 45.23 million tons in 2016–2017 with a CAGR of about 2.9 per cent. During 2016–2017, crude oil production rose from 34.12 million tons during 2007–2008 to 36.01 million tons, displaying a CAGR of about 0.54 per cent. Furthermore, the CAGRs for natural gas and electricity production were found to be (-) 0.16 per cent and 4.05 per cent respectively for the period 2007–2008 to 2016–2017. More specifically, the net production of natural gas decreased from 32.42 billion cubic metres (BCM) in 2007–2008 to 31.9 billion cubic metres registering a negative CAGR of 0.16 per cent. And as far as electricity production from utilities is concerned, it rose from 722,625 GWh in 2007–2008 to 1,235,358 GWh in 2016–2017, exhibiting a CAGR of around 5.9 per cent over the period in consideration. Furthermore, out of the aggregate electricity generated through utilities in 2016–2017, about 993,516 GWh was generated from thermal, 1, 22,378 GWh from hydro and 37,916 GWh was generated from nuclear sources.[23]

In light of these production trends, it is important to highlight the energy import dependence trends for India.

Energy import dependence

As can be seen from the statistics in Table 4.5, India's energy import dependence, calculated as a ratio of net energy imports to total primary energy supply, increased from 29 per cent in 2010 to 36 per cent in 2016, with the most significant increases found in case of natural gas (21 per cent to 45 per cent) and crude oil and petroleum products (76 per cent to 85 per cent). From 2010 to 2016, coal import dependence was also found to rise from 25 per cent to 29 per cent, respectively.

Table 4.6 below provides trends in international trade in coal, crude oil, petroleum products, natural gas and electricity in India for 2016–2017. Since the average quality of Indian coal is inferior (as it is high in ash content), to meet the requirements of power generation and steel production, it becomes necessary to import high-quality coal. Therefore, imports of coal have consistently risen from 49.79 million tons during 2007–2008 to 190.95 million tons during 2016–2017. However,

TABLE 4.5 Contribution of individual fuel supplies in total primary energy supply

	2010	*2010*	*2010*	*2010*	*2010*	*2010*	*2016*	*2016*	*2016*	*2016*	*2016*	*2016*
	Mtoe	*Mtoe*	*Mtoe*	*Mtoe*	*Mtoe*	*Mtoe*	*Mtoe*	*Mtoe*	*Mtoe*	*Mtoe*	*Mtoe*	*Mtoe*
	Coal	*Crude oil & oil products*	*Natural gas*	*Nuclear, hydro & electricity trade*	*Geothermal, solar, wind, biofuels & waste etc.*	*Total*	*Coal*	*Crude oil & oil products*	*Natural gas*	*Nuclear, hydro & electricity trade*	*Geothermal, solar, wind, biofuel's & waste etc.*	*Total*
Production	213	43	43	18	187	504	271	41	26	22	197	557
Imports	71	185	11	0	0	267	110	253	21	0	0	384
Exports	−1	−61	0	0	0	−62.6	−0.5	−68.7	0.0	-0.6	0.0	−69.8
Stock changes	−3.2	0.0	0.0	0.0	0.0	−3.2	−1.4	−1.6	0.0	0.0	0.0	−3.0
Total Primary Energy Supply (TPES)	279	162	54	18	187	700	380	217	47	22	197	862
% share	40	23	8	3	27	100	44	25	5	3	23	100
Net Imports/ TPES	25	76	21	3	0	29	29	85	45	0	0	36

Source: IEA. *Data and Statistics.*

TABLE 4.6 Trends of foreign trade in India for 2016–2017 (in million tons)

Source of energy	*Gross imports*	*Gross exports*	*Net imports*	*Growth rate of net imports (%)*
Coal (million tons)	190.95	1.77	189.8	−4.03
Crude oil (million tons)	213.93	0.00	213.93	5.46
Petroleum products (million tons)	36.29	65.51	−29.23	−5.97
Natural gas (billion cubic metres)	18.63	0.00	18.63	15.42
Electricity (GWh)	5617	6710	−1093	−1263.76

Source: Ministry of Statistics and Programme Implementation (MoSPI). *Energy Statistics*. Central Statistics Office, New Delhi, India: MOSPI, 2018.

on account of higher domestic production, gross coal imports decreased by 3.84 per cent and net imports by 4.03 per cent in 2016–2017 over 2015–2016. In fact, there was a hike of 27.22 per cent in export of coal during the same period. For crude oil there has been an increase of 5.46 per cent in net imports during 2016–2017 over 2015–2016. Moreover, recording a CAGR of 8.40 per cent, the gross import of natural gas increased from 8.32 billion cubic metres in 2007–2008 to 18.63 billion cubic metres in 2016–2017. Additionally, gross imports of electricity rose from 5230 GWh in 2007–2008 to 5617 GWh in 2016–2017 showing a CAGR 0.72 per cent. Similarly, exports of electricity increased from 290 GWh in 2007–2008 to 6710 GWh in 2016–2017.[24]

This rising import dependence of fossil energy in general and oil imports in particular does not auger well for India's energy security or environmental sustainability. Given all of the above concerns, it would be useful to analyse what the prevailing and past trends in energy demand and supply entail in terms of future energy sector patterns in India.

Future of India's energy economy

The 'India's Energy Outlook' by International Energy Agency (IEA/IEO) makes projections up to the year 2040 for India under two alternative futuristic scenarios: New Policies Scenario and India Vision Case, both linked to the specific policy choices, their implementation and consequent implications for energy demand and supply trends. The New Policy Scenario constitutes the centrepiece of the IEA/IEO analysis and rests on the assumption of both prevailing regulations and policies as also India's proclaimed policy targets, such as those relating to goals for coal usage and renewables as well as the push to provide reliable and ubiquitous electricity access to all. This scenario takes a measured view of the pace of implementation, meaning that some of these ambitious targets may not be attained due to regulatory, financial and administrative constraints. The alternative case, called the India Vision Case, is a more ambitious scenario, and derives from the full realisation of government's policy objectives, especially with regard to universal access to electricity, faster development of environmentally friendly energy sources and energy efficiency. Table 4.7 below provides the projections of total primary energy supply and total final consumption under the two scenarios for the year 2040, while also estimating the rates of change over 2013–2040.[25]

The projections yield that, in the aggregate, primary energy supply will increase from 775 Mtoe in 2013 to around 1908 Mtoe in 2040 in case of the New Policies Scenario and even higher to 1930 Mtoe in the India Vision Case. These would respectively amount to a per-capita consumption level that would be 60–61 per cent of the global average level in 2040, from a current level of 33 per cent. On account of many OECD countries reducing their energy use and China moving into a phase of development marked by lower energy intensity, India is predicted to take over China as the largest single source of demand for both coal and oil by 2040. It is also expected that India will become a significant player in renewable energy markets, from wind and solar to nuclear, hydropower and natural gas.

TABLE 4.7 Projections of total primary energy supply and total final consumption under the two scenarios

	New Policies Scenario				*India Vision Case*		
	2013 (Mtoe)	*2040 (Mtoe)*	*Shares in 2040*	*CAGR (2013-40)*	*2040 (Mtoe)*	*Shares in 2040*	*CAGR (2013-40)*
Total primary energy supply	**775**	**1908**	100	**3.4**	**1930**	100	**3.4**
Coal	341	934	49	3.8	922	48	3.8
Oil	176	458	24	3.6	483	25	3.8
Gas	45	149	8	4.5	151	8	4.6
Nuclear	9	70	4	7.9	70	4	7.9
Hydro	12	29	2	3.3	28	1	3.2
Bioenergy	188	209	11	0.4	203	11	0.3
Other renewables	4	60	3	10.6	73	4	11.4
Total final consumption	**527**	**1275**	100	**3.3**	**1326**	100	**3.5**
Industry	185	572	45	4.3	614	46	4.5
Transport	75	280	22	5.0	292	22	5.2
Buildings	214	299	23	1.2	279	21	1.0
Other	53	123	10	3.2	141	11	3.7

Source: International Energy Agency (IEA). *India Energy Outlook (IEO), World Energy Outlook Special Report*. France: 2015.

And as far as the anticipated primary energy supply by fuels is concerned, the estimates for the period 2013–2040 do not transform into a pronounced shift in the energy mix in India, although some notable changes can be comprehended from the data in Table 4.7. It can be discerned that India's energy mix will evolve gradually with a rise in the share of primary energy supply coming from coal (44 to 49 per cent), natural gas (6 to 8 per cent) and renewable energy (1 to 3–4 per cent) and a fall in the share of bioenergy (24 to 11 per cent). Of these primary fuels, the growth of renewable energy is expected to be the most dramatic, at around 10.6 to 11.4 per cent in the two scenarios, which can be attributed to increasing deployment of modern renewable technologies like wind and solar power.[26]

Additionally, the share of oil, which comprises a significant portion of India's energy mix, will remain steady at around 23–25 per cent over 2013–2040, with the bulk of demand coming from sectors like transport (gasoline and diesel) and residential sector (principally in the form of liquefied petroleum gas). In contrast, the role of natural gas in the Indian energy mix is still peripheral, with the share of natural gas showing only a slight increase from 6 per cent in 2013 to 8 per cent in 2040. The use of natural gas is projected to rise in sectors ranging from power generation to transport, while maintaining a principal role as a feedstock for the fertiliser industry. However, despite its low environmental footprint and protean nature in contrast with coal, its relatively high price does not allow it to supersede other energy forms in an expeditious manner.[27]

In terms of end-use sectors, the share of industry and transport will rise significantly over 2013–2040, while the share of buildings will fall over this period. Industry will clearly emerge as the most significant energy consuming sector.[28]

Energy and climate change in India

India is among the most susceptible countries to adverse impacts of climate change. Thus, it has significant stakes in joining other countries of the world in mitigating or coping with GHG emissions. Despite housing a huge population and having a large economic size, India has accounted for a small share of cumulative global GHG emissions historically, that is, a mere 6–7 per cent of energy-related CO_2 emissions since 1890. However, as per recent data brought out by CAIT Climate Data Explorer, China tops the list of contributors with share at 24.5 per cent of global CO_2 equivalent emissions in 2012, followed by the United States with around 13.9 per cent of the global share. With 6.7 per cent of aggregate emissions, India occupies the third position as an individual country and fourth in case EU is considered as a block. In either case, India has surfaced as one among the five top emitters of the world (Table 4.8).[29]

For India, a bulk of these emissions, nearly 83 per cent in 2013, originated in the energy sector (from fuel combustion and fugitive emissions) (Table 4.9). In fact, according to the GHG Platform India database, the share of energy sector in aggregate GHG emissions (in CO_2 equivalent terms) has increased from 76 per cent in

TABLE 4.8 Share of global emissions and population for major emitters, 2010

Country	*Total GHG emissions excluding land-use and forestry (Mt CO_2 e)*	*Share of world population (per cent)*	*Share of global GHG emissions (per cent)*	*Per capita emissions (t CO_2e)*
China	10975.5	19.2	24.5	8.1
United States	6235.1	4.5	13.9	19.9
EU 28	4399.1	7.1	9.8	8.8
India	3013.8	17.6	6.7	2.4
Russian Federation	2322.2	2	5.2	16.2
Africa	2679.4	15.1	6	2.5
Japan	1344.6	1.8	3	10.5
Germany	887.2	1.1	2	11
South Korea	693.3	0.7	1.5	13.9
Iran	715	1.1	1.6	9.4

Source: CAIT/WRI Climate Data Explorer. 2015.Accessed 9 November 2018. www.wri.org/our-work/project/cait-climate-data-explorer

2005 to 80 per cent in 2010, only to rise further to 83 per cent in 2013.The balance is made up for by agriculture, forestry and land-use (whose contribution has fallen from 13 per cent to 7 per cent during 2005 to 2013), and industry and waste heat, whose combined share has been stable at around 10 per cent.[30]

As can be seen from Figure 4.7, India's CO_2 emissions have been increasing continuously over the years from 529.06 million tons in 1990 and reaching a level of around 2026.11 million tons in 2015, indicating a nearly four-fold increase.[31]

The picture in per capita terms is somewhat different. Figure 4.8 depicts that for the period 1990–2015 the per-capita CO_2 emissions of India translate to a rather low level as compared to the world. This can be attributed to India's significantly large population base as compared to other important CO_2 polluters. However, this average has been increasing over the years from 0.61 tCO_2 in 1990 to 1.55 tCO_2

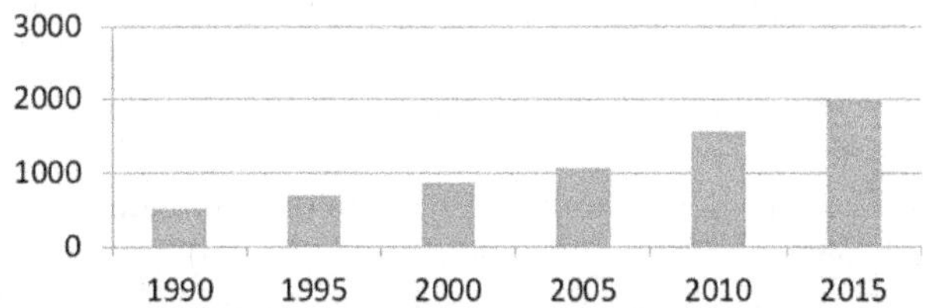

FIGURE 4.7 CO_2 emissions in India during 1990–2015 (million tons). Authors, based on data from the International Energy Agency (IEA). India Energy Outlook (IEO), World Energy Outlook Special Report. France: 2015.

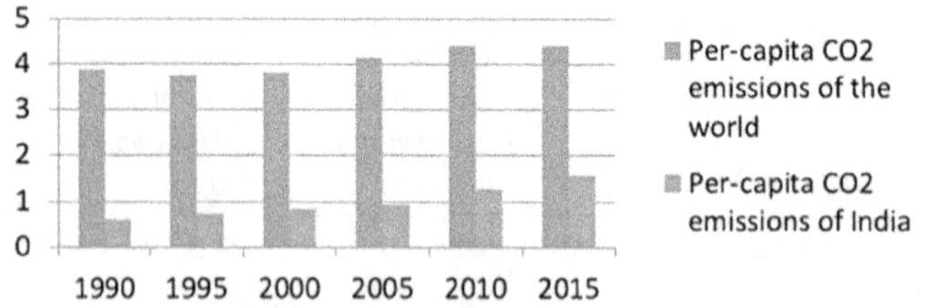

FIGURE 4.8 Per-capita CO_2 emissions in India and the world for 1990–2015. Authors, based on data from the International Energy Agency (IEA). India Energy Outlook (IEO), World Energy Outlook Special Report. France: 2015.

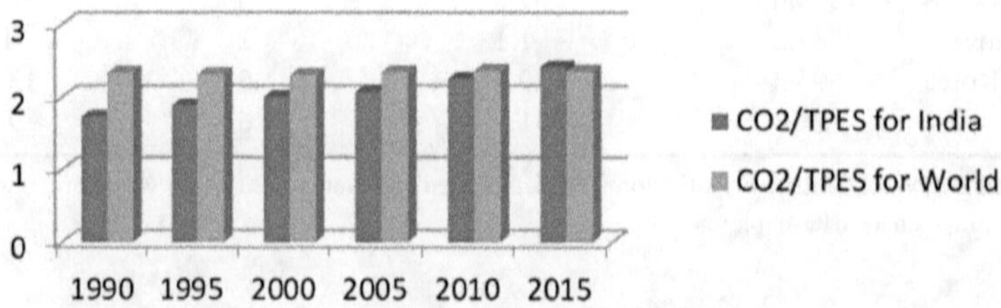

FIGURE 4.9 CO_2/total primary energy supply (TPES) for India and the world. Authors, based on data from the International Energy Agency (IEA). India Energy Outlook (IEO), World Energy Outlook Special Report. France: 2015.

in 2015, with rising commercial energy consumption. The corresponding values of the world are 3.89 tCO_2 in 1990 and 4.4 tCO_2 in 2015; thus, India falls short of the world average values in per capita terms.[32]

Furthermore, Figure 4.9 depicts the CO_2 emissions per unit of total primary energy supply for India and the world. It can be perceived that for the period 1990 to 2010, India has remained below the world level but in 2015 it exceeded the world level of 2.36 tCO_2/toe by reaching a value of 2.42 tCO_2/toe. This indicates that India's CO_2 emissions relative to its primary energy supply have risen while the overall world's CO_2 emissions relative to the overall primary energy supply have reduced a little, a trend corroborated by India's fuel combustion share in total GHG emissions in CO_2 equivalent terms (see Table 4.9).[33]

As a part of international cooperative efforts, the challenge that India faces is to curtail the rate at which its future emissions would grow, while still providing ample headway for economic growth. In the aggregate, as part of its Intended Nationally Determined Contribution (INDC) submitted in October 2015, India has committed to keep its future per-capita emissions beneath those of industrialised countries. As discussed earlier, it also envisages a reduction in the intensity of emission of the economy by 33–35 per cent by 2030, in comparison with the level in 2005.

IEA/IEO predicts that India would account for about 25 per cent of the rise in global energy use by 2040 and will display the largest absolute growth in both the consumption of coal and oil. A greater reliance on fossil fuels is likely to result in

TABLE 4.9 GHG emissions inventory (in CO_2 equiv terms) and key contributing sectors

	Aggregate GHG emissions (CO_2equiv) in million tons (Mt)			*Shares in per cent*		
	2005	*2010*	*2013*	*2005*	*2010*	*2013*
Agriculture, forestry and other land use	**202**	**215**	**172**	13	10	7
Energy, of which						
• Fuel combustion emissions	1146	1616	1961			
• Fugitive emissions	36	47	39			
Energy total	**1181**	**1663**	**2000**	76	80	83
Industrial product and process Use	**98**	**136**	**156**	6	6	6
Waste	**66**	**73**	**89**	4	4	4
Grand total	**1547**	**2086**	**2417**	**100**	**100**	**100**

Source: GHG Platform India. Accessed 9 December 2018. www.ghgplatform-india.org/

TABLE 4.10 Aggregate CO_2 emissions in India under the Alternative IEA Scenarios

	New Policies Scenario				*India Vision Case*		
	2013 (Mt)	*2040 (Mt)*	*Shares in 2040*	*CAGR (2013–40)*	*2040 (Mtoe)*	*Shares in 2040*	*CAGR (2013–40)*
Total CO_2	**1880**	**5147**		**3.8**	**5157**		**3.8**
Coal	1348	3623	72	3.7	3581	70	3.7
Oil	447	1213	24	3.8	1261	24	3.9
Gas	85	311	5	4.9	315	6	5.0

Source: International Energy Agency (IEA). *India Energy Outlook (IEO), World Energy Outlook Special Report.* France: 2015.

a surge in India's aggregate energy-related CO_2 emissions (Table 4.10). The aggregate emissions of CO_2 from the energy sector are anticipated to rise at a CAGR of around 3.8 per cent between 2013 and 2040, with emissions in 2040 at 5147 Mt under the New Policies Scenario and slightly higher at 5157 Mt in the India Vision Case.[34]

However, even as India's share of global CO_2 emissions is expected to rise from 6 per cent in 2013 to 14 per cent in 2040 in the New Policies Scenario, in per capita terms the emissions will be 3.2 tons in 2040, 79–80 per cent of the global average of 4.1 tons of CO_2 per capita. Associated with improvements in energy efficiency and transition to more efficient fuels, IEA/IEO projects that the energy intensity of GDP will reduce from a base of 100 in 2013 to 45 in 2040 while the carbon intensity of power generation will fall from a base level of 100 in 2013 to 71 in

2040. Thus, the future of the energy sector allows for the possibility of decoupling of growth from energy use and de-carbonised energy sector mix.[35]

The specific policies and measures that underlie trends in energy efficiency and shifts to cleaner energy mix are now discussed.

Transition in India's energy economy: Role of energy efficiency and clean energy

Energy efficiency improvement trends indicate a temporal decline in the intensity of energy use in generating economic output or GDP. In comparison, the shift to cleaner energy is defined as the change in the composition or mix of energy in producing the aggregate output. In general, for an economy seeking improvement in energy use pattern and cleaner energy mix, the twin channels of energy efficiency improvement and cleaner energy transitions will have to work complementarily. For India, in particular, as a part of its commitments under the Paris Agreement, the government envisages significant reduction in energy and carbon intensity of the economy by the year 2030. To this end, both energy efficiency gains and move to cleaner energy will have important contributions to make.

Energy efficiency in India

A typical pattern of energy intensity trend for across a large spectrum of countries displays a bell-shaped curve. This implies that initially the countries use more energy per unit of GDP until it peaks, and eventually declines at higher levels of GDP. This pattern corroborates a customary pattern of economic development that relates to the structure of output of an economy. That is, commercial energy intensity first increases sharply as production operation switch from agriculture to industry, that is, from low energy intensive activities to high energy intensive activities. It then wanes gently as economic activity is transferred in favour of less energy-intensive services sectors.[36]

Table 4.11 shows that the energy intensity of India has been declining continually and remains steadily below the global energy intensity level right up to 2030. Evidence in this regard can be found in the transition from industrial to services-driven economy. This is because, on account of globalisation, most fuels can now be traded internationally, and technologies are becoming increasingly shared across international borders. Moreover, the consumption baskets (end-use of energy) are also becoming more standardised and similar across countries and cultures, which were formerly very different from each other.

Sectoral energy efficiency patterns

Both the scale and intensity of energy consumption are used as indicators to identify target or priority sectors and specific industries therein. Bearing in mind the total amount of energy consumed across sectors as well as the potential for cost effective

TABLE 4.11 Overall energy intensity of India and world from 1990 to 2030

Year	*India*		*World*	
	Energy consumption (Mtoe)	*Energy intensity (toe/ million $2010 PPP)*	*Energy consumption (Mtoe)*	*Energy intensity (toe/ million $2010 PPP)*
1990	181	142	8109	197
1995	236	151	8578	187
2000	296	147	9382	174
2005	364	119	10801	165
2010	524	117	12002	155
2015	676	107	13360	142
2020	871	102	14627	129
2025	1048	94	15635	115
2030	1262	88	16632	103

Source: Rühl, C., P. Appleby, J. Fennema, A. Naumov and M. Schaffer. 'Economic Development and Demand for Energy: A Historical Perspective on the Next 20 years', *Energy Policy*, 50 (2012), 109–116.

improvements, the role of sectoral energy efficient activities is expected to become exceedingly important. For India, we explore possible energy efficiency scenarios for the three most important energy demand sectors, namely, industry, agriculture and transport. It can be seen from the data in Table 4.12 that out of these three sectors, transport has the highest energy intensity value of 0.02 in 2015–2016. This means that targeting the transport sector for energy efficiency would generally lead to attainment of higher energy efficiency gains as compared to the other two sectors. In 2016–2017, however, industrial sector emerges as the most important from the point of view of attaining energy efficiency with a higher energy intensity value of 0.0094. It can also be seen that for both transport and industry, the energy intensity has fallen over in 2015–16 to 2016–2017, while that of agriculture has remained fairly constant.[37]

TABLE 4.12 Sectoral energy intensity for India (thousand Indian rupees (INR))

	2015-16	*2016-17*
Industry	0.013	0.0094
Agriculture	0.001	0.00102
Transport	0.02	0.00831

Source: Ministry of Statistics and Programme Implementation (MoSPI). *Energy Statistics*. Central Statistics Office, New Delhi, India: MOSPI, 2017 and 2018.

According to IEA/IEO, industrial energy demand in India is expected to rise fast, by 4.4 per cent per year right up to 2040, so as to absorb more than 50 per cent of final consumption by 2040, relative to the current consumption of 40 per cent. Coal currently accounts for almost 50 per cent of industrial energy use thus emerging as the predominant source of energy for this sector. In addition, the share of coal is projected to rise further to 56 per cent in 2040 under the New Policies scenario on account of the perpetual growth in demand from different industries like steel, bricks and cement, and is strengthened further by the lower cost of coal relative to alternative fuels. The structure of energy consumption in different industrial sub-sectors in India is very different: some energy-intensive industries, including chemicals, cement, aluminium and, to some extent, steel, are dominated by large enterprises; others, particularly brick-making, food etc. consist of thousands of small and medium enterprises (SMEs). The latter, in particular, usually exhibit a mediocre energy performance.[38]

A joint report by Bureau of Energy Efficiency (BEE), The Energy Resource Institute (TERI) and Indo-German Energy Forum considers two scenarios of energy use: Reference Scenario and Efficiency Scenario and shows that by years 2021, 2031 and 2041, the industrial sector can provide energy savings to the tune of 3.85, 40.15 and 73.7 Mtoe respectively, which account for about 1 per cent to 8 per cent energy savings over the entire time period. The energy savings for the individual sectors under industry can be inferred from the data in Table 4.13, according to which, energy efficiency has the largest scope in the iron and steel sub-sector, followed by paper and pulp sector and finally bricks sector.[39]

In India, to achieve energy efficiency across industries such as thermal power, steel, aluminium, cement, chlor-alkali, fertiliser, paper and textiles industries, the Perform, Achieve and Trade (PAT) scheme was introduced in 2012 under the Energy Conservation Act. This is a market-based trading program for efficiency

TABLE 4.13 Energy saving by end-use based on efficiency scenario (in per cent)

	2021	*2031*	*2041*
Iron & steel	1	18	19
Brick	3	7	10
Cement	0	2	3
Aluminium	2	7	12
Fertiliser	1	6	14
Paper and pulp	14	18	22
SME & other industries	1	2	3

Source: Bureau of Energy Efficiency (BEE), The Energy Resource Institute (TERI) and Indo-Germen Energy Forum (IGEF). *Energy Efficiency Potential in India*. India: BEE, Ministry of Power, Government of India, 2018.

certificates and describes energy saving targets for 478 units with an energy consumption exceeding 30 thousand tons of oil equivalent (ktoe).[40] The first phase of the PAT scheme (from 31 March 2012 to 31 March 2015) aimed for a reduction of about 4 per cent from the baseline level for these plants. In this three-year cycle, except for thermal power generation, all sectors among the assessed plants have not only met their set target but have also surpassed the target by about 30 per cent.[41]

Currently, the largest industrial energy consumer in India is the steel sub-sector, and is expected to retain this position right up to 2040, rising from the current 46 Mtoe to up to nearly 200 Mtoe. As it stands, 20 per cent of inputs to the steel industry are constituted of coal-based sponge iron (or direct reduced iron (DRI)), with the remaining comprising of traditional pig iron from blast furnaces. For large-scale DRI production, Indian integrated steel plants primarily utilise coal in place of natural gas, even as the energy consumption of coal-based DRI can be double that of gas-based DRI.[42] Although India has three major gas-based DRI producers, these exhibited a utilisation rate of less than 30 per cent in 2013, owing primarily to the scarce availability of domestic natural gas.[43] In 2013, almost a third of India's steel was manufactured in electric arc furnaces and a similar per centage in small-scale induction furnaces, both of which utilise electricity as an energy input, and have a narrowed scope for enhancements in energy efficiency. In the years ahead, it is expected that the Indian steel sector will become less dependent on the DRI route, switching instead towards the blast furnace method for steel-making as was used traditionally, with reduced dependence on electricity use. This technology transition, combined with growing energy efficiency gains, especially in blast furnaces, finished steel making and utilisation of waste heat from the DRI processes, and a moderately increased share of metal scrap-based production, is expected to contribute to lowered energy intensity in the Indian iron and steel sector.[44]

India's brick industry is the second-largest energy demand sector, after iron and steel. Due to its reliance on traditional production technologies, brick making has a huge potential for improved energy efficiency. Employment of latest production techniques in brick manufacturing, like the zig-zag firing, can bring down the specific energy consumption from nearly 1.4 megajoules per kilogram (MJ/kg) to around 0.8 to 1.1 MJ/kg, resulting in more than 20 per cent energy saving. While the energy intensity in the Indian brick industry is anticipated to fall by around 30 per cent by the year 2040, through a combination of energy efficiency and a shift towards production of hollow and perforated bricks, realising these goals of efficiency gains will be challenging in the face of lack of awareness, as well as high payback periods associated with energy efficiency measures and financing constraints.

In the fertiliser sector, the intensity of energy use in urea production has declined markedly from 0.84 toe/ton urea in 1990 to around 0.64 toe/ton urea in 2013. IEA/IEO has projected that energy intensity of urea production will decline further to 0.55 toe/ton urea by 2040. The cement industry in India is one of the world's most energy-efficient, with relatively large-scale production units and reliance on latest technologies. In the future, the clinker-to-cement ratio is likely to reduce from the prevailing 0.74 to 0.62 in 2040, thus saving on energy intensity of cement production by around 13 per cent.[45]

Agriculture is another prominent energy consumer, and is responsible for 15 per cent and 18 per cent of the total final consumption of diesel and of electricity respectively, for land preparation (tractors and power tillers) and water-pumping (diesel and electric pumps) end-uses. According to IEA (2015) predictions, energy consumption in agriculture will increase by 27 Mtoe to 50 Mtoe by 2040, with electricity and diesel constituting about 68 and 30 per cent of the 2040 share. There are also considerable energy efficiency gains within India's irrigation system. The system relies heavily on electric pumps that are generally of very poor efficiency (20–35 per cent). To add to it, flood irrigation, again with a water-use efficiency which is very low, about 35–40 per cent, is still the most widely used irrigation method. If these two issues could be overcome, it can help reduce the over-use of electricity in the sector as well as bring down the water consumption, but this requires a carefully integrated approach; as was evident in the mixed results of efforts at reform in Andhra Pradesh, Gujarat and West Bengal, among others. According to BEE/TERI/IGEF, agriculture will save up to 4 per cent energy in 2021, 12 per cent in 2031 and 19 per cent in 2041. Within agriculture, irrigation end-use sector emerges as the major source of potential energy savings, with approximately 1 Mtoe (6 per cent), 4 Mtoe (16 per cent) and 6 Mtoe (25 per cent) being saved by 2021, 2031 and 2041 respectively due to efficiency improvements in the Efficiency Scenario.[46]

With an average growth rate of 6.8 per cent per year since 2000, transport is now the most rapidly growing of all energy end-use sectors, with around 90 per cent of the increase due to oil use in road transport. In the New Policies Scenario of IEA/IEO, transport fuel demand is expected to reach 280 Mtoe in 2040. A lot will depend on India's capability to stem the tendency towards individual vehicle ownership, mainly in cities, by improving the public transport systems. To make Indian cities smarter in areas related to transport and mobility, policies in India would have to include fuel-efficiency standards for passenger vehicles, increasing growth and construction of metro train systems and also the Smart Cities Mission. According to IEA/IEO, energy use in other transport sectors remains low in the New Policies Scenario. Domestic aviation, rail and navigation combined together contribute only 4 per cent to total energy demand growth in transport, even when they continue to grow swiftly. The global targets for reducing aviation fuel consumption, adopted through the International Civil Aviation Organization, could curtail any future demand growth in India. Indian railways still predominantly rely on diesel as a fuel, but there is a drive towards electrification and the advent of high-speed trains between major Indian cities has begun.[47] The huge increase in transport energy demand, and the anticipation that the growth will continue has led to a demand of policies to promote the use of alternative fuels, like natural gas, biofuels, or even electricity, which are the thrust of new policies emerging in this regard.

The buildings sector consumes about 30 per cent of annual electricity consumption of India and is the second highest emitter of GHGs. The energy demand from India's buildings is estimated to increase by more than 800 per cent by 2047 as

TABLE 4.14 Energy saving in building sector based on the Efficiency Scenario

	2021	*2021*	*2031*	*2031*	*2041*	*2041*
	Mtoe	*per cent*	*Mtoe*	*per cent*	*Mtoe*	*per cent*
Educational buildings	0.02	3	0.2	12	0.6	17
Hospitals	0.53	34	1.7	39	4.1	40
Hotels	0.48	15	2.6	33	6.6	41
Shops and malls	1.18	18	5.5	34	15.0	40
Offices	0.46	15	2.8	37	7.8	47

Source: Bureau of Energy Efficiency (BEE), The Energy Resource Institute (TERI) and Indo-Germen Energy Forum (IGEF). *Energy Efficiency Potential in India.* India: BEE, Ministry of Power, Government of India, 2018.

compared to 2012.[48] With the Indian government's plan to build 100 smart cities in India, the buildings sector has an immense potential to achieve enhanced efficiency. According to BEE/TERI/IGEF, under the Efficiency Scenario, the building sector will contribute potential energy savings to the tune of 7 per cent, 15 per cent and 18 per cent by 2021, 2031 and 2041, respectively. Table 4.14 projects the energy saving potential of different types of buildings in India for the years 2021, 2031 and 2041. It can be perceived that the potential for energy efficiency in buildings is the largest in the category of hospitals, followed by shops and malls, offices and hotel buildings.[49]

An important regulatory measure for introducing energy efficiency in the building sector is energy codes. The commercial sector among buildings has been addressed by the Energy Conservation Building Code (ECBC) for commercial buildings launched by BEE, Government of India in 2007. It has specified minimum energy standards for new commercial buildings that have a connected load of 100 kW and above. ECBC requires adoption by states as well. An updated version of ECBC for commercial buildings was launched in June 2017. It is estimated that energy demand in the buildings sector will rise from around 350 billion units (terawatt hour) in 2018 to approximately 1000 billion units by year 2030. In a case study of Ahmedabad, it was found that the application of ECBC 2017 could lead to savings of more than 8 per cent by 2047 relative to 2017 (Rawal et al., 2018). Further, the energy savings potential at the city level with respect to BAU by application of ECBC 2017 ranges from 0.5 per cent to 10.5 per cent. Energy savings not only reduce the cost of production, they also help reduce the amount of GHG generation, of which CO_2 is a major component. In this context, Rawal et al. (2018) estimate that about 0.3 million tons of CO_2 savings in the year 2022 can be expected, which could increase to 3.5 million tons by the year 2047.

The residential sector consumes about 39 per cent of final energy consumption in India, though it accounts for only 19 per cent of final commercial energy consumption, since biomass and other traditional forms constitute a large share of household energy use in rural areas. A high energy demand from the residential sector is a result of speedy dissemination of electrical appliances, coupled with the heightened success of rural electrification programs and dissemination of LPG for domestic cooking.

In residential and commercial sectors, Standard and Labelling (S&L) (introduced by BEE in May 2006) have been dexterous measures for attaining energy efficiency as these focus on appliances that consume large amounts of electricity. This program currently includes 21 appliances, of which 5 have been under mandatory labelling. During 2016–2017, three more appliances (direct cool refrigerator, colour television and storage type electric water heater) have been brought into the mandatory regime raising the total mandatory appliances to 8, while 13 are under the voluntary domain.[50] This scheme has been able to generate awareness among consumers about energy efficient appliances and has been successful in reducing electricity bills nationwide. According to BEE/TERI/IGEF, the residential sector is expected to save energy up to 0.15 per cent in 2021, 2 per cent in 2031 and 8 per cent in 2041. Table 4.15 contains shows that in the residential sector, the energy saving potential in space/air conditioning and lighting ranges respectively from 2 per cent to 28 per cent and 6 per cent to 30 per cent.[51]

According to a primary survey on 5000 consumers, 642 retailers and 45 manufacturers to understand consumer behaviour, perception and awareness towards the S&L program, along with consequences on sales of energy efficient products, energy savings and mitigation of GHGs. The study found that the awareness level for energy efficiency has risen from 33 per cent in 2010 to 63 per cent in 2014. Table 4.16 presents the energy savings, avoided generation capacity and GHG reduction for different appliances for the year 2012. It can be seen that the maximum energy savings are yielded by direct cool refrigerators and room air conditioners, followed by frost-free refrigerators and tubular fluorescent lamps. Accordingly, for direct cool refrigerators and room air conditioners, GHG reduction was estimated to be 2.46 million tons of CO_2 and 1.19 million tons of CO_2, respectively. This was followed by frost-free refrigerators (0.91 million tons), tubular fluorescent lamps (0.56 million tons) and geysers (0.17 million tons).[52]

The S&L program is now being readied to take another leap through BEE's Super-Efficient Equipment Program (SEAP) so that appliances with efficiency

TABLE 4.15 Energy saving in residential sector based on Efficiency Scenario

	2021	*2021*	*2031*	*2031*	*2041*	*2041*
	Mtoe	*per cent*	*Mtoe*	*per cent*	*Mtoe*	*per cent*
Space conditioning	0.2	2	4.6	13	17.9	28
Lighting	1.11	6	5.1	17	10.7	30
Refrigeration	0.03	1	0.4	2	1.9	5

Source: Bureau of Energy Efficiency (BEE), The Energy Resource Institute (TERI) and Indo-Germen Energy Forum (IGEF). *Energy Efficiency Potential in India.* India: BEE, Ministry of Power, Government of India, 2018.

TABLE 4.16 Cumulative energy saving, avoided generation capacity and GHG reduction

Appliance	*Energy savings (MWh)*	*Avoided capacity (MW)*	*GHG reduction (million tons of CO_2)*
Direct cool refrigerators	2,641,604	529	2.46
Frost-free refrigerators	973,314	195	0.91
Room air conditioners	1,281,183	1,872	1.19
Tubular fluorescent lamps (36 watts)	602,381	880	0.56
Colour television sets	16,532	4	0.02
Ceiling fans	903,815	20	0.04
Geysers	185,264	1,300	0.17
Distribution transformers	210,996	32	0.20
Pumps	803	15	0.00
Total	5,954,072	4,847	5.55

Source: Dhingra, N., A. Walia and P.K. Mukherjee. *Measuring the Impact of India's Standard and Labelling Programme*. Washington: CLASP, 2016.

surpassing even the five-star label can be identified and promoted. The aggressive S&L scenario (which considers further tightening of the standards every two years as suggested by BEE) is projected to result in 16.7 million tons of avoided CO_2 emissions in 2020 while the scenario with the SEAP is anticipated to avoid 47.9 million tons of CO_2 emissions.[53] Other policies like Housing 2020 and Deendayal Upadhyaya Gram Jyoti Yojana for rural electrification, both of which are crucial in promoting national and social infrastructure, will unambiguously increase energy demand. To offset this, schemes like UJALA (LED replacement program) with focus on installing LED lights in public buildings and spaces, have been implemented. This scheme has helped to save more than 35 million kWh of energy per day and 2667 MW of avoided power generation capacity. Additionally, this scheme has been incessantly working towards fuel savings equalling nearly 23 million tons of coal per year.[54] The Pradhan Mantri Ujjwala Yojana has aimed to upgrade cooking techniques used by the rural households. The basic idea adopted by the latter policy to create a shift from the use of traditional biomass fuels to efficient LPG and solar cookers. According to many recent reports, this policy has a huge potential in reducing solid fuel use to minimum levels and has managed to attain a significant result as almost half of the targeted recipients have been provided with LPG connections; besides, lakhs of solar cookers have also been distributed.

In a most recent step in attaining energy efficiency in the residential sector, the Energy Conservation Building Code for Residential Buildings (ECBC-R) has also been promulgated to set minimum building envelope performance standards. The ECBC-R was established by the government of India in December 2018 to promote design and construction of residences including apartments and complete townships to provide benefits of energy efficiency to the occupants. The Part-I of the code has the capacity for energy savings of nearly 125 billion units of electricity by the year 2030, which amounts to around 100 million tons of CO_2 emissions saved.

Some barriers in implementation of energy efficiency measures

Despite endeavours towards energy efficiency being rational, both in terms of cost effectiveness and avoided environmental damages, it is generally difficult to incentivise managers of companies (and individuals) to act upon these. All stakeholders tend to stick to the status quo, which is often a less efficient situation, and only mobilise towards improvements in energy efficiency once a stringent policy or a crisis induces them to act. This inherent inertia may be reinforced by a number of institutional, financial and technical barriers to energy efficiency programs.

India needs to do a lot for significant attainment of energy efficiency goals due to the presence of certain barriers in different sectors of the economy. For instance, in the iron and steel sector, there are barriers in the form of apprehensions associated with high investment costs and production losses as well as exaggerated claims of high benefits from energy efficient technologies under Indian conditions. This concern becomes more pronounced in new emerging technologies that are yet to be adopted commercially.

The government of India is directing large industries to reduce their current energy consumption levels through the PAT mechanism. However, there are many sub-sectors including SMEs, which are energy intensive but presently outside the ambit of PAT mechanism. Hence, efforts need to be directed towards developing programs for this sector, which is a very important contributor to the Indian economy and has a large energy saving potential.

As far as the S&L program for appliances is concerned, certain studies through conduct of surveys have found that although this has increased the consumer awareness levels, it is yet to reach a significant portion of the population. Moreover, studies find that for a significant majority of population, energy efficiency still ranks below other factors such as price and brand of the appliance.[55] India also faces other significant barriers in the achievement of energy efficiency, such as policy challenges due to diversity in sectors, market failure in that the investment towards end user energy efficiency improvements remain low, behavioural aspects where end users prefer the least cost option of energy-efficient technology and price sensitivity of market where users don't prefer energy efficient technologies as they look for immediate benefits rather than long term gains.

Clean energy in India

Renewable or environmentally cleaner energy technologies are known as 'cutting-edge' technologies despite being highly cost-intensive in the initial stages as compared to the energy efficiency measures. A shift towards renewables supports sustainable energy production and leads to a lowered dependency on imported energy. For large-scale setups, commonly available renewable technologies are electricity generation based on biomass, grid connected solar photovoltaic (PV), on-shore and off-shore wind energy, geothermal energy and large-scale hydropower. For small-scale operations, technologies that can replace electricity or gas supplies include solar water heaters for heating water, small-scale wind generators and mini-hydro systems and rooftop solar photovoltaic cells for electricity generation, and small-scale biomass setups for heat and electricity.

In 2018, at 69 GW, renewable capacity accounted for around 20 per cent of the total installed energy capacity in India. Wind energy comprises a major portion of India's renewable energy industry at 34 MW (49 per cent) of its installed capacity. Additionally, solar power, biomass and small hydro contribute 22 GW (31 per cent), 9 GW (13 per cent) and 4 GW (6 per cent), respectively, to this capacity. There has been a significant recent thrust by the government on greater dissemination of renewable energy towards low-carbon energy development in India, with a target of a 40 per cent non-fossil fuel-based power capacity by 2030. India has huge untapped potential for renewable energy resources with the highest levels of solar irradiation in the world as well as an expansive coastline and areas with high wind velocities. In addition, India has a number of rivers and waterways indicating significant opportunities for hydropower generation. Moreover, with plenty of agricultural and forest residues, India has a huge capacity for biomass-based energy sources as well.

According to the 2016 annual report of the Ministry of New and Renewable Energy (MNRE), out of the total estimated renewable energy potential of 896.6 GW in India, the potential of wind power is estimated to be about 102.77 GW as in 2016. This sector was provided an impetus through preferential tariffs, accelerated depreciation and generation-based incentives (GBI) along with renewable purchase obligations (RPOs). It is evident that wind energy will be pivotal in raising India's renewable energy share in future. Currently, India's goal is to reach 60 GW of wind power installed capacity by 2022. Looking at the tremendous energy saving potential that the wind energy sector offers, the Indian government has undertaken new initiatives for the growth of the wind energy sector, such as the formulation and issuing of extensive directions for evolution of on-shore wind power projects, issue of guidelines for enactment of 'Scheme for Setting up of 1000 MW Inter-State Transmission System (ISTS) – connected Wind Power Projects', the release of Policy for Repowering of the Wind Power Projects to foster optimal use of wind energy resources by providing a smooth structure for repowering.[56]

In India, hydro projects having a capacity of up to 25 MW are categorised as small hydro power projects. Small hydro is a well-known technology that proffers lucrative projects to investors that have low risk and high potential yields. Currently, small hydro has, on an average, the lowest generation costs among all renewable energy technologies in India. Until 2013, about 5415 potential sites with an aggregate capacity of 14.3 GW for small hydro projects had been identified by the MNRE. It is anticipated that these projects will play a key role not only because of their suitability for implementation in outlying and inaccessible regions, but also because of the vast untapped potential of the resource.

The promulgation of the National Solar Mission (NSM) under the NAPCC has given a boost to India's solar energy market by focusing on attaining grid parity for solar energy and raising grid-connected solar power projects. The NSM aims for a manufacturing capacity of 4–5 GW by 2020, which includes capacities for polysilicon, a resource for which India currently depends heavily on imports. Over 2005–2018, India has shown a remarkable advancement in its solar power capacity by raising it from 3.7 MW in 2005 to 21651 MW in 2018 representing a CAGR exceeding 94 per cent over the past 13 years. A major hindrance in the path of increased uptake of solar energy is its cost since it is believed that energy procured from conventional sources is cheaper than that obtained from solar power. Nonetheless, the module costs of solar energy have declined considerably over the years by virtue of new developments in technology and increased deployment of solar energy projects. To boost the solar energy sector, the government offers numerous incentives, which include a ten-year tax holiday for solar power projects, an assured market access for states through solar power purchase obligation, a 30 per cent subsidy of project costs for off-grid PV and solar thermal projects, provision of loans at discounted rates for off-grid applications and many more.

As on 2016, the energy potential for biomass is 25.1 GW for India.[57] To promote ecologically sustainable development using bioenergy, the MNRE has taken an initiative in the form of Integrated National Bio-energy Mission to be implemented in consortium with state governments, the public and private sectors and other principal stakeholders. This mission aims to achieve GHG emissions reduction targets that would be in consonance with NDCs. This is expected to be achieved through a commingling or a complete replacement of fossil fuels like coal, petrol, diesel, natural gas and LPG with biomass pellets, bioethanol, biodiesel, biomethane and other green fuels for both electrical and non-electrical uses. In a bid to encourage biomass-based power in India, MNRE is also contemplating the feasibility of creation of a fund for renewable energy generation, including generation of bioenergy.

Since 2014, the government of India has actively facilitated and worked for the promotion of non-conventional energy as a viable energy source. The India government has set a 175 GW goal for renewable power capacity comprising 100 GW from solar, 60 GW from wind, 10 GW from bio-power and 5 GW from small hydro power to be attained by 2022. In 2015–2016, the addition to wind power capacity and solar power capacity was around 3423 MW and 3019 MW, respectively. For both wind and solar energy, the added capacity surpassed the target by 43 per cent and 116 per cent, respectively. Moreover, to develop and promote solar energy, an International Solar Alliance (ISA) was initiated to act as a platform for mutual cooperation among 121 solar resource rich countries at COP21 in Paris in 2015, with headquarters in India. On 15 November, 2016, after conduction of an intense dialogue with various stakeholders, the Framework Agreement of ISA was finalised and signed by 20 member countries including India, France, Brazil and others at Marrakech, Morocco.[58]

Several state governments, apart from the central government have also attempted to boost renewable energy in India. Some of the initiatives include investor-friendly policies to induce investment, financing of Research and Development (R&D) and implementation of the Electricity Act in 2003, which provided the outline for renewable power generation in India by focusing on optimum resource utilisation, furtherance of electricity from renewables and fitting measures for grid connectivity. Furthermore, the National Electricity Policy mandates State Electricity Regulatory Commissions (SERCs) to set RPOs that allow for differential tariffs for non-conventional energy. Finally, the Integrated Energy Policy's longstanding vision for non-conventional energy encompasses a special support for renewables for a well-marked period in addition to providing stimulus to generation rather than capacity addition.[59]

Barriers to renewable energy installation

One possible disadvantage associated with renewable energy use is the intermittency of supply due to the fluctuating nature of these resources. For instance, solar energy production is fully reliant on distinct seasons; with production peaking to a maximum in summer and minimum in winter. On the other hand, for a wind energy system, energy produced depends on the wind speed power curve and the prevailing wind speed frequency distribution at the installation site.[60] This may result in irregular supply of power thus causing problems. This can be avoided by utilising a hybrid system that consists of, one, a renewable energy source, two, a diesel genset or a secondary energy source and three, a shortage system to guarantee a stable output during time of shortages. In addition, recently apprehensions have been expressed with regard to meeting the targets of renewable energy capacity installation, given the constraints such as the policy structure shifting from feed-in-tariffs to reverse auctions-based purchases, lack of grid infrastructure and evacuation restrictions.[61]

Implications for the environment and climate change indicators

Commensurate with the gains in energy efficiency and clean energy initiatives, studies project changes in key indicators of low carbon pathways for India. In particular, IEA/IEO predicts that, along the New Policies Scenario, the energy intensity of GDP and carbon intensity of power generation is expected to fall by around 65 per cent and 29 per cent between 2013 and 2040. The energy efficiency gains accrue even as India's energy consumption grows, and so do the CO_2 emissions in proportion to the global emissions.[62] Another estimate puts the decline in India's aggregate energy intensity by 40 per cent between 1995 and 2015, with likely gains between 2015 and 2040 hovering around 30–40 per cent thus, supporting the government's NDC targets.[63]

Conclusion

India, being one of the fastest growing economies in the world, is trying to variegate its energy portfolio such that it results in a reduction of carbon emissions without compromising on the rising demand for energy. For this, India is following a two-pronged approach – adoption of various energy efficiency measures and a push towards cleaner forms of energy as a replacement of the conventional forms of energy. This chapter highlights the importance of energy-efficiency and use of cleaner technologies as an instrument for climate change mitigation focusing on India, and places it against other South-Asian and South-East Asian countries.

Numerous initiatives to achieve energy efficiency have been launched in the domain of household lighting, commercial buildings, standards and labelling of appliances, besides focusing on demand side management in agriculture, SMEs and large industries. Additionally, under NAPCC, a National Mission for Enhanced Energy Efficiency (NMEEE) has been initiated, which seeks to explore the market for energy efficiency estimated to be worth Rs. 74,000 crores.[64] Specifically, the target of this mission at its full implementation stage is to attain a total avoided capacity addition of 19,598 MW, 23 million tons per year of fuel savings and reduction in GHG emissions to the tune of 98.55 million tons per year.

Furthermore, India has developed a comprehensive policy structure under the NAPCC umbrella to reduce its emissions by promoting the use of renewable energy and increasing the deployment of greener technologies. In addition to subsidy cuts on fossil fuels, carbon taxes and subsidising various renewable energy projects, India's energy sector is set for an overhaul, starting with attaining a renewable energy installed capacity of 175 gigawatt (GW) by 2022, 24 × 7 Power for All by 2022, housing for all by 2022, 100 smart cities mission, 10 per cent reduction of oil and gas import dependence by 2022 from 2014 to 2015 levels. All these measures indicate that a country like India, that is significantly dependent on its natural resource base and predominantly climate-sensitive sectors; has shown kinetic efforts to chart out an ecologically sustainable growth model in the light of climate change, which could furnish gainful experience for other developing nations.

Notes

1 International Energy Agency (IEA). *India Energy Outlook (IEO), World Energy Outlook Special Report*. France: IEA, 2015.

2 Ibid.

3 World Bank. *World Development Indicators Data Bank*.Accessed 2 November 2020. https://databank.worldbank.org/source/world-development-indicators.

4 BP Statistics. *BP Statistical Review of World Energy*. 2018. Accessed 4 October 2018. Available on www.bp.com/content/dam/bp/en/corporate/pdf/energy-economics/statistical-review/bp-stats-review-2018-full-report.pdf .

5 Ibid.

6 Ibid.

7 Global Carbon Project. 2018. Accessed 2 November 2020. www.globalcarbonproject.org/

8 IEA. *World Energy Balances*. 2018. Accessed 2 November 2020. www.iea.org/statistics/?country=WORLD&year=2016&category=Energy%20supply&indicator=TPESbySource&mode=table&dataTable=INDICATORS

9 1 GW=10^9 watts. National Institution of Transforming India (NITI) Aayog. *Energizing India: A Joint Project Report of NITI Aayog and Institute of Energy Economics*. Japan, New Delhi: Government of India, 2017.

10 Japan Center for Economic Research. *Digit Asia 5.0 – Innovation Changes Economic Power Relationships, Third Medium-Term Forecast on Asian Economies: 2017–2030*. Japan: Japan Center for Economic Research, 2017.

11 United Nations. *World Population Prospects: The 2017 Revision, Department of Economic and Social Affairs*. New York, USA: United Nations, 2017.

12 See endnote 1.

13 National Institution of Transforming India (NITI) Aayog. *Energizing India: A Joint Project Report of NITI Aayog and Institute of Energy Economics*. Japan, New Delhi: Government of India, 2017.

14 International Energy Agency. *Data and Statistics*. Accessed 2 November 2020. www.iea.org/data-and-statistics?country=WORLD&fuel=Energy%20supply&indicator=TPESbySource

15 IEA. *Data and Statistics*. 1 MWh = 10^6 Watt hours.

16 Ministry of Statistics and Programme Implementation (MoSPI). *Energy Statistics*. Central Statistics Office, New Delhi, India: MOSPI, 2018.

17 Ibid.

18 Ibid.

19 1 GWh=10^9 watt hour = 10^6 kilowatt hour

20 Ibid.

21 Ibid.

22 See endnote 15.

23 See endnote 16.

24 Ibid.

25 See endnote 1.

26 Ibid.

27 Ibid.

28 Ibid.

29 CAIT/ WRI Climate Data Explorer. 2015. Accessed 9 November 2018. www.wri.org/our-work/project/cait-climate-data-explorer

30 GHG Platform India. Accessed 9 December 2018. www.ghgplatform-india.org/

31 See endnote 1.

32 Ibid.

33 Ibid.

34 Ibid.

35 Ibid.

36 Rühl, C., P. Appleby, J. Fennema, A. Naumov and M. Schaffer. 'Economic Development and Demand for Energy: A Historical Perspective on the Next 20 years', *Energy Policy*, 50 (2012), 109–116.

37 Ministry of Statistics and Programme Implementation (MoSPI). *Energy Statistics*, Central Statistics Office, New Delhi, India: MOSPI, 2017.

38 See endnote 1.

39 Bureau of Energy Efficiency (BEE), The Energy Resource Institute (TERI) and Indo-Germen Energy Forum (IGEF). *Energy Efficiency Potential in India*. India: BEE, Ministry of Power, Government of India, 2018.

40 See endnote 1.

41 WRI / Mitra, A., P. Chitkara, K. Ross, M. Singh, S. Sawhney, S. Keswani, J. C. Altamirano, T. Fransen, S. Majumdar, and P. Batra. 'Pathways for Meeting India's Climate Goals'. WRI Working Paper, 2017.

42 IEA. 2017.

43 Joint Plant Committee (JPC). *Annual Statistics 2013–14*. Kolkata, India, 2014.

44 Ibid.

45 See endnote 1.

46 See endnote 38.

47 See endnote 1.

48 See endnote 13.

49 See endnote 38.

50 Bureau of Energy Efficiency (BEE). *Annual Report*. New Delhi India: Ministry of Power, Government of India, 2016.

51 See endnote 38.

52 Dhingra, N., A. Walia and P.K. Mukherjee. *Measuring the Impact of India's Standard and Labelling Programme*. Washington: CLASP, 2016.

53 Chunekar, A., K. Kadav, D. Singh and G. Sant. *Potential Savings from Selected Super-Efficient Electric Appliances in India*. Pune, India: Prayas Energy Group, 2017.

54 Ebinger, C.K. *India's Energy and Climate Policy, The Energy Security and Climate Initiative*. Washington, DC: The Brookings Institution, 2016.

55 Chatterjee, B. and S. P. Singh. *Energy Efficient Products and Indian Consumers*. Jaipur, India: CUTS International, 2012.

56 Ministry of New and Renewable Energy (MNRE). *Annual Report*. New Delhi, India: Government of India, 2016.

57 Ibid.

58 Ibid.

59 Ministry of New and Renewable Energy (MNRE). *Annual Report*. New Delhi: Government of India, 2013.

60 Lanjewar, R. and S. Dutt. 'Assessment of Sustainability Indicators for Off Grid Energy System'. *International Journal of Engineering and Computer Science*. 3, 2014, 7253–7256.

61 Sree Ram R. 'Renewable energy future hinges on policy execution'. *Live Mint*. 28 December 2017. Accessed 26 May 2020. www.livemint.com/Money/vd9N429itd0KU-jcFb7NxoM/Renewable-energy-future-hinges-on-policy-execution.html.

62 See endnote 1.

63 Chaturvedi, V, P. N. Koti, and A. R. Chordia. *Sustainable Development, Uncertainties, and India's Climate Policy: Pathways towards Nationally Determined Contribution and Mid-Century Strategy*. New Delhi: Council on Energy, Environment and Water (CEEW), 2018.

64 1 crore = 10 million.

5

LOW-CARBON ENERGY SECURITY FOR INDIA

Exploring Asia-Pacific cooperation*

Sacchidananda Mukherjee

Introduction

International Energy Agency (IEA) defines energy security as the 'uninterrupted availability of energy sources at an affordable price'. There are many aspects of energy security; long-term energy security mainly deals with timely investments to supply energy in line with economic developments and environmental needs. On the other hand, short-term energy security focuses on the ability of the energy system to react promptly to sudden changes in the supply–demand balance.[1] *Sustainable Development Goal (SDG)-7: Affordable and Clean Energy* stresses universal access to affordable, reliable and modern energy services by 2030.[2] Availability and affordability are the two major dimensions that drive any country's energy security. Providing access to reliable and clean energy at a affordable price is a challenge that many developing countries like India are facing today.

Achieving India's energy security is important to sustain economic growth and socio-economic well-being of the vast population of India. According to *Energy Balance of India for 2016–17*,[3] India's total consumption of energy is 871.83 million tonnes of oil equivalent (Mtoe), of which 484.06 Mtoe (55.5%) is sourced from domestic origin and 325.92 Mtoe (37.4%) is net import. India's high dependence on imports to achieve energy security is a cause of concern for the current account deficit. In 2016–2017, India's trade deficit in 'mineral fuels, mineral oils and products or their distillation; bituminous substances; mineral waxes' is Rs. 474.44 thousand crore, which is 65 per cent of total trade deficit (i.e. Rs. 728.24 thousand crore) of the

* An earlier version of this chapter was presented at the International Conference on *India's Energy Security: Inter-regional Cooperation to Energy Secure Society* at the School of International Studies (SIS), Jawaharlal Nehru University (JNU), New Delhi. Suggestions and comments received from participants of the conference, Prof. U. Sankar and Dr. Paul Burke are gratefully acknowledged. The usual disclaimer, nevertheless, applies.

year. India's net import of coal is 122.36 Mtoe, crude oil is 218.62 Mtoe, and natural gas is 17.14 Mtoe. India's power sector consumes 292.44 Mtoe of primary energy, which is 33.5 per cent of total consumption, and produces 192.73 thousand GWh of power. The Indian power sector is the predominant end user of coal, consumes 63 per cent of the total available coal, and the rest by the Indian industry. Total available petroleum products for final consumption is 209.64 Mtoe, of which 62.37 Mtoe (30%) is consumed by Indian industry, 37.4 Mtoe (18%) by transport sector and the rest by other uses like residential, agriculture, etc. The high dependence of Indian industry on coal and petroleum products is partly attributable to irregular electricity supply, which compels industries to install captive power generation plants. The installed capacity of such non-utilities has gone up from 24,986 Megawatt (MW) in 2007–2008 to 50,289 MW in 2016–2017, showing a compound average annual growth rate (CAAGR) of 8.42 per cent.[4] In the utility sector, the installed capacity has gone up from 143,061 MW in 2007–2008 to 326,833 MW in 2016–2017 with a CAAGR of 8.61 per cent. In total installed capacity of non-utilities, 59.4 per cent is steam, 25.6 per cent is diesel and 12 per cent is gas based.[5]

With a rising demand for energy, India's contribution to the world's energy-related total CO_2 emission is expected to go up from 6.7 per cent in 2017 to 10.6 per cent in 2030.[6] Though India's per capita CO_2 emission is one-third of the world's average, the rising contribution in CO_2 emission is mostly attributable to the high emission intensity of India's GDP. It is expected that India will be the single largest driver of global growth in total energy-related CO_2 emission in 2017–2030.[7] Achieving energy security along with reducing the emission intensity of Gross Domestic Product (GDP) would be important for India to sustain high economic growth and achieve socio-economic-environmental well-being of the Indian populace. The objective of this chapter is to explore possible pathways to achieve low carbon energy security in India through regional energy cooperation in the Asia-Pacific region.

Structure of India's demand for primary energy

In the World Energy Outlook 2018,[8] the International Energy Agency has expected that India's total primary energy demand (TPED) will reach 1465 Mtoe in 2030 and 1880 Mtoe in 2040 from 862 Mtoe in 2016 (Table 5.1). It is also expected that the growth rate of India's TPED will be the single largest driver of global growth in TPED. India's share in the world's TPED will go up from 6.3 per cent in 2016 to 9.1 per cent in 2030 and 10.6 per cent in 2040. India was experiencing a CAAGR of 4.3 per cent in TPED during 2000 to 2016, and it is expected to grow at 3.9 per cent during 2016 to 2030 and thereafter it will fall to 2.5 per cent during 2030 to 2040. Demand for coal constitutes nearly two-fifth of total demand for primary energy in India during 2000–2016. It is expected that CAAGR in demand for coal will fall from 6.2 per cent during 2000–2016 to 4.1 per cent during 2016–2030 and further to 2.7 per cent during 2030–2040. However, the share of coal in TPED is expected to increase and reach nearly half of TPED by 2040. Demand for oil

TABLE 5.1 Source-wise projection of India's total primary energy demand (TPED) (IEA's New Policies Scenario)

Energy source	*Energy demand (Mtoe)*							*CAAGR (%)*		
	2000	*2016*	*2017e*	*2025*	*2030*	*2035*	*2040*	*2000–2016*	*2016–2030*	*2030–2040*
TPED	**441**	**862**	**898**	**1238**	**1465**	**1683**	**1880**	4.3	3.9	2.5
Coal	146	380	400	561	668	773	868	6.2	4.1	2.7
Oil	112	217	223	300	350	392	421	4.2	3.5	1.9
Gas	23	47	49	81	104	126	147	4.6	5.8	3.5
Nuclear	4	10	11	28	43	58	71	5.9	11.0	5.1
Hydro	6	12	12	17	22	26	30	4.4	4.4	3.2
Bioenergy	149	192	195	220	222	224	224	1.6	1.0	0.1
Other renewables	0	6	7	32	55	85	119	n.a.	17.1	8.0
Energy source	As per centage share in TPED							Average share 2000–2016	Change in share 2000–16 to 2030	Change in share 2000–16 to 2040
Coal	33.1	44.1	44.5	45.3	45.6	45.9	46.2	38.6	7.0	7.6
Oil	25.4	25.2	24.8	24.2	23.9	23.3	22.4	25.3	−1.4	−2.9
Gas	5.2	5.5	5.5	6.5	7.1	7.5	7.8	5.3	1.8	2.5
Nuclear	0.9	1.2	1.2	2.3	2.9	3.4	3.8	1.0	1.9	2.7
Hydro	1.4	1.4	1.3	1.4	1.5	1.5	1.6	1.4	0.1	0.2
Bioenergy	33.8	22.3	21.7	17.8	15.2	13.3	11.9	28.0	−12.9	−16.1
Other renewables	0.0	0.7	0.8	2.6	3.8	5.1	6.3	0.3	3.4	6.0

Note: * CAAGR: Compound average annual growth rate, 2017e implies estimated.Source: International Energy Agency (IEA). *World Energy Outlook 2018*. Paris, France: International Energy Agency. 2018.

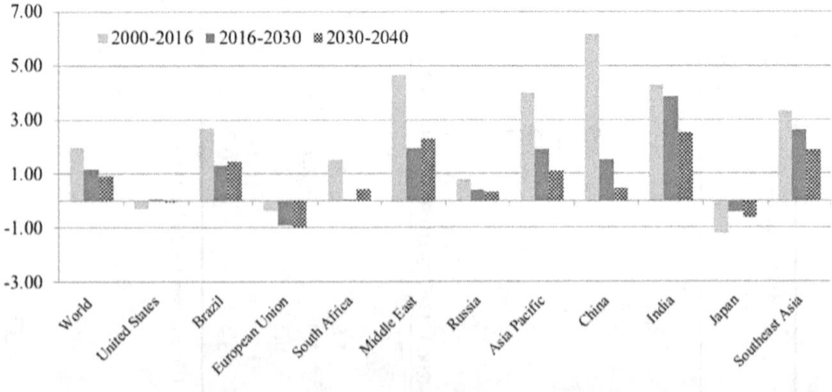

FIGURE 5.1 Compound average annual growth rate of TPED (%) (IEA's New Policies Scenario). Authors, based on data from the International Energy Agency (IEA). *World Energy Outlook 2018*. Paris, France: International Energy Agency, 2018.

constitutes the second largest source of India's TPED, it contributes nearly one-fourth, and it is expected that CAAGR in oil demand will fall in the future. The structural composition of India's TPED is expected to move away from bioenergy and oil to coal, non-hydro renewables, gas and nuclear energy (Table 5.1).

Figure 5.1 shows that expected India's growth in TPED during 2016–2030 and 2030–2040 will be the single largest driver of global growth in TPED. Like many regions/countries, India's growth rate in TPED is also expected to fall in the future. To sustain economic growth in India, energy will play an important role. However, it will be important for India to decouple economic growth from energy consumption.

Coal and oil are the two major primary energy sources of India and contribute 44 and 25 per cent of TPED in 2016 respectively. Therefore, discussing coal and oil balances of India is important to achieve low carbon energy security. High dependence on imports to meet these primary energy sources make the Indian economy vulnerable to shocks associated with volatilities of global energy prices and the exchange rate of the Indian rupee. To achieve macro-economic stabilisation, India may consider gradual reduction of imports of such primary energy sources where these energy sources are predominantly used for power generation. Given the large potential that exists in renewable power generation in India, mainly from solar (649.3 GW in 2017) and wind (302.3 GW),[9] mobilising finance to invest in such renewable power generation and transmission infrastructures may help in reducing India's dependence on imported primary energy sources for electricity generation. Since electricity demands in neighbouring countries are growing, any surplus electricity in India will find immediate markets in the neighbourhood. India also needs to invest in improving domestic interconnections to facilitate development of domestic markets for electricity. Access to grid connectivity could play an important role in increasing efficiency of production and distribution of electricity across sources. In the long run, India may also explore available options to generate hydrogen from solar and wind power generation plants to reduce dependence on imports of combustible fuels (like oil and natural gas) used in transport sector. India also needs to reorganise energy baskets by giving more importance to those primary energy sources where international market prices are comparatively less volatile as compared to traditional energy sources like coal and oil.

India's demand for coal

According to *Energy Balance of India* for 2016–2017, the total coal available in 2016–2017 is 576.6 Mtoe, of which 63 per cent is used in the Indian power sector and the rest is by Indian industry as final consumption (Table 5.2). India is the second largest producer of coal in the world and produced 730 million tonnes (Mt) in 2017 and contributes 9.7 per cent in the world's total coal production.[10] China holds the top position in production of coal with 3376 Mt, which is 44.7 per cent of the world's total coal production. China also holds the first position in importing coal (263 Mt in 2017) and India is in the second position (207 Mt). In the Asia-Pacific region, Indonesia (first position with 387 Mt) and Mongolia (7th position with 33 Mt) are two prominent net exporters of coal. Australia (379 Mt) and Russian federation (161 Mt) also hold significant shares in the world's total exports of coal (1263 Mt). CAAGR of net import of coal in India is 16.4 per cent during 2007–2008 to 2016–2017. To reduce India's dependence on imported coal, the Indian power sector needs to give larger importance to invest in renewable sources of energy. Since wholesale electricity prices have been steadily declining in most mature power markets,[11] initially India may also consider importing electricity through CBET not only from neighbouring countries in Asia but also from the Asia-Pacific region to reduce dependence on imports of coal and oil for power generation.

TABLE 5.2 Coal balance of India for 2016–2017 (provisional)

Supply side (Ktoe)		*Demand side (Ktoe)*		
Production	*394,724.94*	*Main activity producer electricity plants*	*363,982.83*	*(63.1)*
Imports	123,552.77	Energy industry own use	167.62	(0.03)
Exports	-1195.34	Final consumption	212,491.29	(36.8)
Stock changes	7388.67	of which Industry	212,491.29	(36.8)
Total primary energy supply	524,471.04	*Iron & steel*	*40,310.83*	*(7.0)*
Statistical differences	52,170.70	*Chemical and petrochemical*	*2286.49*	*(0.4)*
		Paper, pulp and print	*917.41*	*(0.2)*
		Construction	*4552.37*	*(0.8)*
		Textile and leather	*497.24*	*(0.1)*
		Non-specified (industry)	*163,926.96*	*(28.4)*
Total	576,641.74	Total	576,641.74	

Note: Figures in the parenthesis show the per centage share in total demand.Source: Central Statistics Office (CSO). *Energy Statistics 2018 (Twenty Fifth Issue)*. New Delhi: Ministry of Statistics and Programme Implementation, Government of India. 2018.

India's demand for petroleum products

More than 80 per cent of India's demand for crude oil is met through imports. The high dependence of India on imported crude oil is one of the major causes of India's high trade deficit. Volatility in international crude oil prices and foreign exchange rate are the causes of volatility in domestic prices of refined petroleum products. India is a net exporter of refined petroleum products with an installed refinery capacity of 233.97 million metric tonnes per annum (MMTPA). During 2016–2017, 245.36 million tonnes of crude oil is refined in India. In total, 30 per cent of refined petroleum products are used in Indian industry, 18 per cent in transport and 48 per cent in other uses (including agriculture and other non-specified uses) (Table 5.3). Improving the quality of electricity supply could reduce industrial uses of refined petroleum products (e.g. diesel) where it is mostly used to generate power in captive power generation plants. Among the distillates, light distillates constitute 27.3 per cent (LPG 10%, Petrol 11%), middle distillates 41.4 per cent (SKO 2.5%, HSDO 35.4%) and heavy ends 19 per cent. In total, 12.6 per cent of refined petroleum products is used as cooking fuel (LPG and SKO) where the government provides considerable subsidies.[12] Many studies have shown that anaerobic digestion of bio-wastes (including cattle manure and faecal sludge) in India has the potential to

TABLE 5.3 Crude oil and petroleum products balances of India for 2016–2017 (provisional)

Crude Oil			
Supply side (Ktoe)		*Demand side (Ktoe)*	
Production	36,801.12	Oil refineries	250,759.40
Imports	218,618.60	Losses	20,511.49
Exports			
Stock changes			
Total primary energy supply	255,419.71		
Statistical differences	15,851.18		
Total	**271,270.89**		**271,270.89**
Petroleum products			
Supply side (Ktoe)		*Demand side (Ktoe)*	
Production	248,741.88	Main activity producer electricity plants	823.79
Imports	36,327.16	Final Consumption	209,638.14
Exports	-68,429.32	Of which	
Stock changes		*Industry*	*62,368.47*
Total primary energy supply	216,639.72	*Transport*	*37,396.77*
Statistical differences	-6,177.78	*Other*	*101,068.12*
		Non-energy use industry/ transformation/ energy	8,804.77
Total	**210,461.94**	**Total**	**210,461.92**

Source: Central Statistics Office (CSO). *Energy Statistics 2018 (Twenty Fifth Issue)*. New Delhi: Ministry of Statistics and Programme Implementation, Government of India. 2018.

meet the demand for cooking fuel and therefore could save substantial government resources as well as foreign exchange.[13]

India's total consumption of natural gas is 49.1 Mtoe in 2016–2017, of which 17.1 Mtoe (35%) is imported and the rest is domestic production. Natural gas is mostly used in generation of electricity, oil refineries, energy industries and fertiliser industry. India needs to explore options to reduce import of natural gas for electricity generation and other uses where other energy substitutes are available at lower prices.

India also needs to reduce dependence on imports of high value primary energy sources, especially oil and natural gas initially and coal in the long run, for generation of electricity – both in the utility and non-utility sector (captive power generation plants) – to achieve macro-economic stability and contain current account deficit.

Energy consumption and emission intensity of Indian GDP

India's per capita total primary energy supply (TPES) is only 0.65 tonnes of oil equivalent (toe) in 2016 and it is nearly one-third of the global average (i.e. 1.85 toe).[14] India's per capita TPES is lower than many neighbours in Asia (Table 5.4). Per capita electricity consumption in India was only 918 KWh in 2016 and it is 3.4 times lower than the global average (i.e., 3110 kWh). There is an increasing relationship between per capita electricity consumption and per capita income, and therefore it is expected that providing access to quality electricity could play an important role in human capital formation (education and health achievements), generation of employment and value addition. However access to quality electricity supply is still lacking in many rural habitations in India. According to the Census of India 2011, nearly 400 million populations are outside the grid connection.[15] India's CO_2 emission intensity of TPES is higher than the world's average whereas the emission intensity of GDP was marginally lower than the world's average in 2016. Though India's per capita CO_2 emission is one-third of the world's average, India needs continuous efforts in greening up GDP growth.

In 2000, except for China and an average of North America and upper middle income countries, India's energy intensity of GDP was higher than other regions (Figure 5.2). As compared to 2000, Indian energy intensity has gone down in 2014 and it is lower than an average of East Asia and Pacific and Middle East and North Africa regions. This shows that India needs continuous efforts to improve energy efficiency.

In 2000, except China, average of East Asia and Pacific and upper middle income countries, India's CO_2 emission intensity of GDP was higher than other regions (Figure 5.3). As compared to 2000, Indian emission intensity decreased in 2014 and it was lower than the world's average. This shows that India needs to put continuous efforts to decouple economic growth from CO_2 emission.

Drivers for low carbon energy security in India

With rising demand for primary energy, it is also expected in the World Energy Outlook 2018 that the growth rate of India's energy-related CO_2 emission will be

TABLE 5.4 Selected indicators for 2016

Country	*TPES/ pop (toe/capita)*	*Elec. cons./pop (kWh/capita)*	*CO_2/pop. (tCO_2/ capita)*	*TPES/ GDP(PPP) (toe/000 2010 USD)*	*CO2/TPES (tCO_2/ toe)*	*CO2/ GDP (PPP) ($kgCO_2$/ 2010 USD)*
Australia	5.29	9918	16.02	0.12	3.02	0.35
Bangladesh	0.24	353	0.45	0.07	1.85	0.14
Brazil	1.37	2504	2.01	0.10	1.46	0.15
China	2.15	4279	6.57	0.15	3.06	0.47
India	**0.65**	**918**	**1.57**	**0.11**	**2.41**	**0.26**
Indonesia	0.88	865	1.74	0.08	1.98	0.17
Japan	3.35	7971	9.03	0.09	2.7	0.24
Malaysia	2.85	4654	6.93	0.11	2.43	0.28
Myanmar	0.37	293	0.40	0.07	1.09	0.08
Nepal	0.44	172	0.29	0.20	0.66	0.13
Philippines	0.53	799	1.11	0.07	2.09	0.16
Russian Federation	5.07	6717	9.97	0.23	1.96	0.45
Sri Lanka	0.55	627	0.99	0.05	1.79	0.09
South Korea	5.51	10627	11.51	0.16	2.09	0.33
South Africa	2.51	4032	7.41	0.21	2.95	0.62
Thailand	2.01	2866	3.55	0.13	1.77	0.23
United Kingdom	2.73	5037	5.66	0.07	2.07	0.15
United States	6.7	12825	14.94	0.13	2.23	0.29
Viet Nam	0.87	1616	2.02	0.15	2.31	0.35
OECD	4.11	8051	9.03	0.11	2.2	0.24
World	**1.85**	**3110**	**4.35**	**0.13**	**2.35**	**0.30**

Source: International Energy Agency. *Key world energy statistics 2018*. Paris, France: International Energy Agency. 2018.

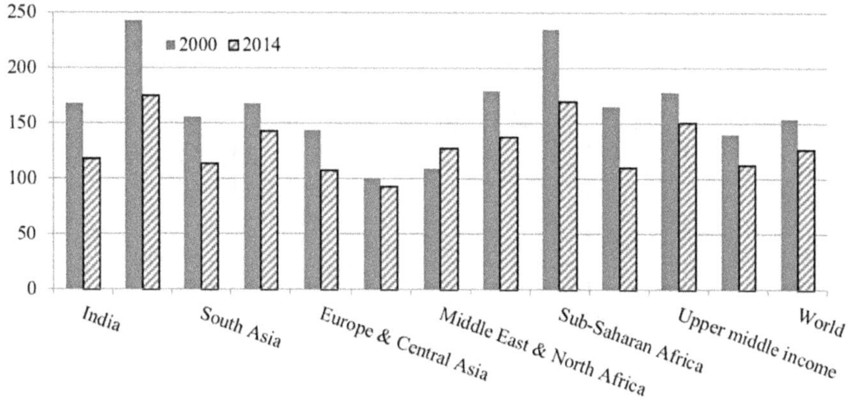

FIGURE 5.2 Energy intensity of GDP (kg of oil equivalent per $1000 GDP at constant 2011 PPP). World Bank. *World Development Indicator Database.*

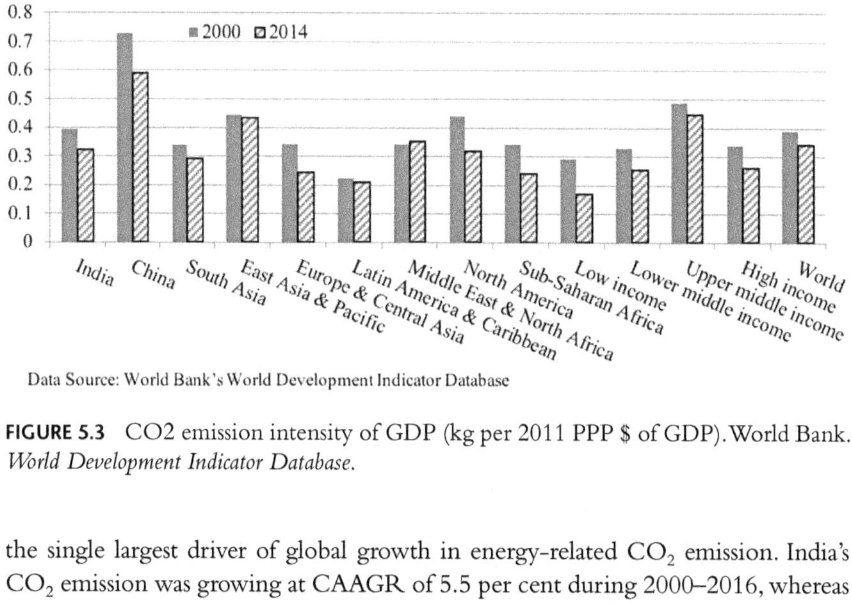

FIGURE 5.3 CO2 emission intensity of GDP (kg per 2011 PPP $ of GDP). World Bank. *World Development Indicator Database.*

the single largest driver of global growth in energy-related CO_2 emission. India's CO_2 emission was growing at CAAGR of 5.5 per cent during 2000–2016, whereas it was 6.9 per cent in China. It is expected that India's CO_2 emission will grow at CAAGR of 4.2 per cent during 2016–2030, as compared to 0.4 per cent in China. The fall in growth rate in CO_2 emission is expected in India during 2030 to 2040, at CAAGR of 2.6 per cent (Table 5.5). Since many countries are reducing their energy-related CO_2 emission, there will be considerable expectation from India to cut CO_2 emission (Figure 5.4). Therefore, it will be important for India to follow the 'low-carbon energy security' path to sustain economic growth as well as socio-economic-environmental well-being of the Indian populace.

Coal is the single largest source of India's energy-related CO_2 emission, contributed 71 per cent in 2016 (Table 5.5). It is expected that the contribution of

TABLE 5.5 India's energy-related CO_2 emission (IEA's New Policies Scenario)

	CO2 emission (Mt)							*CAAGR (%)*		
	2000	*2016*	*2017e*	*2025*	*2030*	*2035*	*2040*	*2000–2016*	*2016–2030*	*2030–2040*
Total CO_2	*885*	*2075*	*2195*	*3076*	*3673*	*4242*	*4738*	*5.5*	*4.2*	*2.6*
Coal	572 (64.6)	1468 (70.7)	1568 (71.4)	2182 (70.9)	2593 (70.6)	2993 (70.6)	3360 (70.9)	6.1	4.1	2.6
Oil	277 (31.3)	534 (25.7)	527 (24)	726 (23.6)	860 (23.4)	982 (23.1)	1066 (22.5)	4.2	3.5	2.2
Gas	36 (4.1)	73 (3.5)	100 (4.6)	169 (5.5)	221 (6)	267 (6.3)	312 (6.6)	4.5	8.2	3.5
Power sector	459 (51.9)	1071 (51.6)	1160 (52.8)	1471 (47.8)	1685 (45.9)	1887 (44.5)	2062 (43.5)	5.4	3.3	2.0
Total final consumption	393 (44.4)	965 (46.5)	995 (45.3)	1560 (50.7)	1937 (52.7)	2299 (54.2)	2614 (55.2)	5.8	5.1	3.0

Note: Figures in the parenthesis shows the per centage share in India's total energy-related CO_2 emission. Source: International Energy Agency (IEA). *World Energy Outlook 2018*. Paris, France: International Energy Agency. 2018.

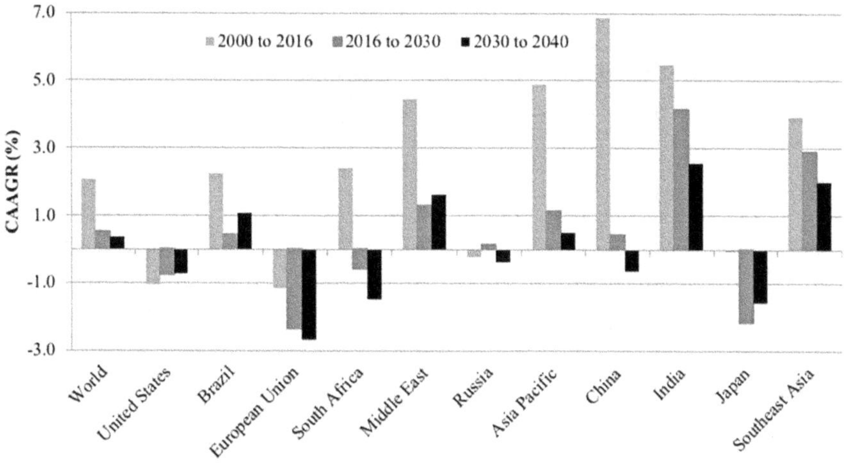

FIGURE 5.4 Compound average annual growth rate of energy-related CO_2 emission (IEA's New Policies Scenario). Authors, based on data from the International Energy Agency (IEA). *World Energy Outlook 2018.* Paris, France: International Energy Agency, 2018.

coal in India's energy-related CO_2 emission will remain at 71 per cent until 2040. CAAGR of CO_2 emission from coal was 6.1 per cent during 2000–2016, and it is expected to fall to 4.1 per cent during 2016–2030 and further to 2.6 per cent during 2030–2040. The Indian power sector is the single largest user of coal and therefore reducing dependence on coal in the power sector would be the foremost priority to achieve low carbon energy security in India. The share of oil is the second largest source India's CO_2 emission, contributed 26 per cent in 2016. However, it is expected that the contribution of oil will go down to 23.4 per cent in 2030 and 22.5 per cent in 2040. Oil used in the transport sector contributes the largest share in total CO_2 emission from oil.

The power sector is the single largest source of energy-related CO_2 emission in India and contributes 52 per cent in 2016. However, the share is expected to go down to 46 per cent in 2030 and 44 per cent in 2040. It is expected that with a larger share of renewables in the Indian power sector, CO_2 emission will reduce (Figure 5.5). India needs to accelerate investment in renewable source power generation infrastructures to reduce dependence on energy imports as well as greening the power sector. However, sustaining investment in India's renewable energy sector requires mobilisation of finances as well as technology transfers.

India's energy demand and CO_2 emission scenarios

In World Energy Outlook 2018, IEA has presented India's demand for TPED and corresponding energy-related CO_2 emissions in three alternative scenarios – New Policies Scenario (NPS), Current Policies Scenario (CPS) and Sustainable

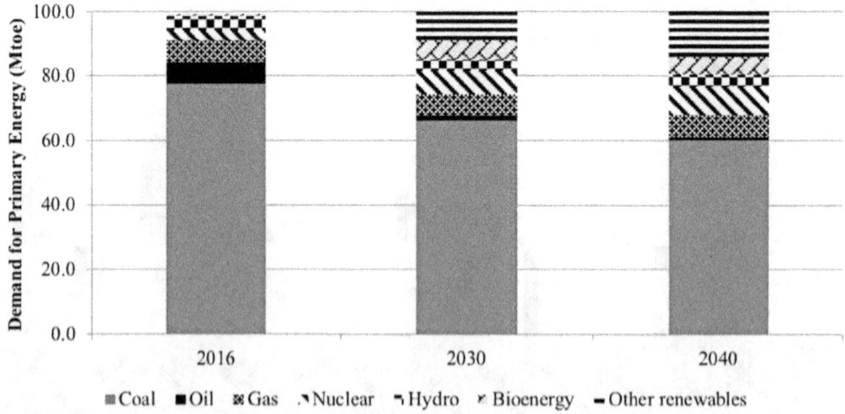

FIGURE 5.5 Present and future energy demand by fuel in Indian the power sector. Authors, based on data from the International Energy Agency (IEA). *World Energy Outlook 2018*. Paris, France: International Energy Agency, 2018.

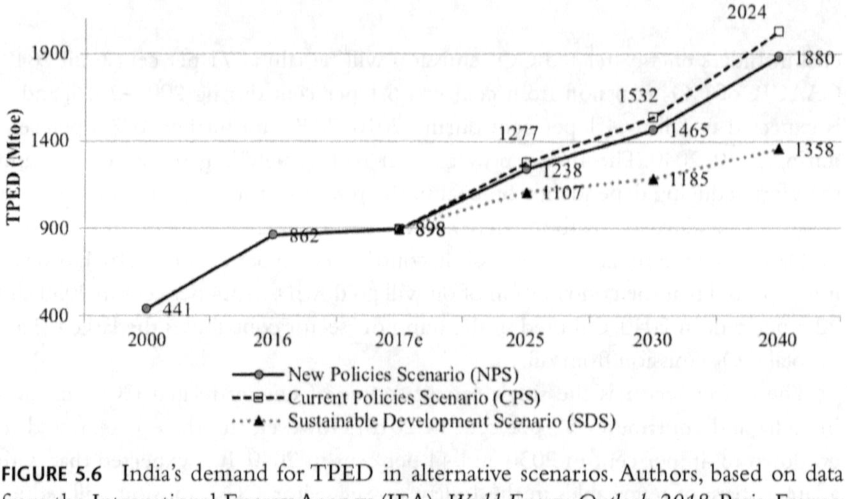

FIGURE 5.6 India's demand for TPED in alternative scenarios. Authors, based on data from the International Energy Agency (IEA). *World Energy Outlook 2018*. Paris, France: International Energy Agency, 2018.

Development Scenario (SDS) – where CPS serves as the baseline scenario. The detail descriptions of these scenarios are presented in Table A.5.1 in the Appendix. Figure 5.6 shows that in NPS, India's TPED will be moderately lower than CPS. However, India's TPED will fall if India follows the SDS. It is desirable for India to follow policies associated with SDS to save energy as well as reduce dependence on energy imports.

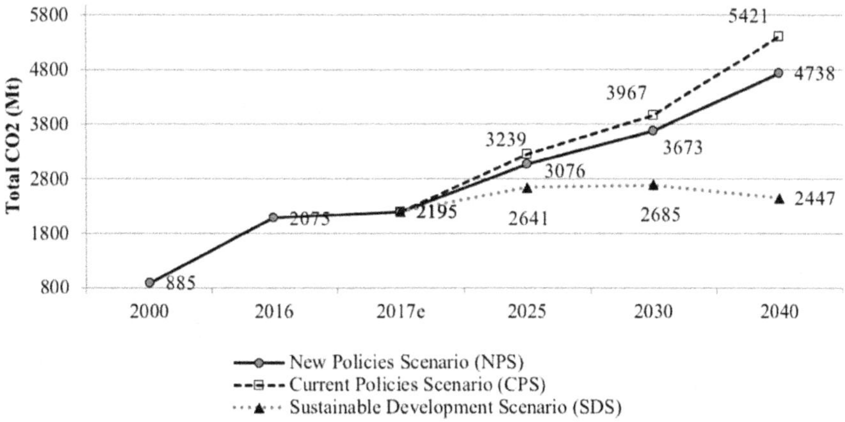

FIGURE 5.7 India's energy-related CO_2 emissions in alternative scenarios. Authors, based on data from the International Energy Agency (IEA). *World Energy Outlook 2018*. Paris, France: International Energy Agency, 2018.

Corresponding to three alternative scenarios, India's energy-related CO_2 emissions are presented in Figure 5.7. It shows that by following SDS, India will not only save in energy but also global environmental space for CO_2 emission. India's objectives to achieve energy security and environmental sustainability needs to be integrated and following a 'low carbon energy security' path could help India to achieve this objective.

India's cross border electricity trade and role of Asia-Pacific energy cooperation

To achieve energy security, India may consider exploring possible regional energy cooperation with energy surplus countries in Eastern South Asia and South East Asia. Table 5.6 shows that Indonesia, Malaysia, Myanmar and Vietnam are net energy exporters whereas Bangladesh and India are net energy importers. Any regional energy cooperation among countries presented in Table 5.6 (excluding Australia and Thailand) may result in additional energy available for cross border trade. However, the available energy may not be sufficient to sustain for long, given the rising demands from origin countries. Moreover, it is to be noted that China is the largest Asian county with a mammoth trade deficit in energy and therefore India may face competition from China to access any surplus energy available in the Asian region. Except for a few countries in Asia and due to historical and geo-political reasons, China's investment in the Asia-Pacific region is much higher than India. Therefore, it would be beneficial for India to expand the scope and coverage of energy cooperation beyond the Asian region and look for opportunities of energy trade (including electricity) in the Asia-Pacific region. To reduce energy-related CO_2 emission and the vulnerability of the Indian economy due to volatility of international prices

TABLE 5.6 Net energy imports of selected countries in Asia Pacific region (Mtoe)*

Country	*2010*	*2011*	*2012*	*2013*	*Remarks***
Australia	−196.05	−184.49	−194.22	−218.09	ESC
Bangladesh	4.43	5.36	5.91	5.08	EDC
India	196.52	212.33	238.87	251.99	EDC
Indonesia	−167.66	−218.03	−227.27	−244.23	ESC
Malaysia	−15.93	−11.28	−9.24	−5.06	ESC
Myanmar	−8.54	−8.34	−7.25	−6.61	ESC
Thailand	47.26	49.03	50.75	57.64	EDC
Vietnam	−7.48	−9.40	−9.43	−9.05	ESC
Total	**−147.44**	**−164.81**	**−151.88**	**−168.34**	**Energy surplus**
Total excluding Australia	***48.61***	***19.67***	***42.34***	***49.75***	***Energy deficit***
Total excluding Australia & Thailand	***1.35***	***−29.35***	***−8.41***	***−7.89***	***Energy surplus***
China	**299.31**	**332.62**	**418.01**	**443.42**	**EDC**

Note: * Energy imports, net (Mtoe) = [Energy imports, net (% of energy use)* Energy use (kg of oil equivalent) per $1,000 GDP (constant 2011 PPP)* (GDP, PPP (constant 2011 international $)/1000)]/10⁹

** ESC – Energy surplus country, EDC – Energy deficit country

Source: Computed based on: World Bank. *WDI Database.*

of primary energy sources, India needs to consider expanding the horizon of energy trade beyond primary energy sources to electricity through cross border electricity trade (CBET). However, expanding the scope of energy cooperation in the Asia-Pacific region also require inclusion of all countries to reduce cost of transmission of electricity and improve connectivity of grids. Any energy cooperation among selected countries in Table 5.6 (including Australia and Thailand) may assure energy availability for relatively longer time horizon. Given the vast potential exist in India for renewable source power generation, in such energy cooperation India may not necessarily be a net importer of electricity. Modernisation and connectivity of grids in the Asia-Pacific region would be the foremost priority to operationalise CBET in the region.

India's demand for electricity is ever increasing with rising per capita income, urbanisation and coverage of rural habitations under electricity network. According to *Energy Balance of India* for 2016–2017, India exports 577.06 Ktoe (6710 GWh) of electricity and imports 483.06 Ktoe (5617 GWh). India is a net exporter of electricity and India's CBET is limited to neighbouring countries like Bangladesh, Bhutan, Nepal and Myanmar (only 3 MW from Manipur) (Table 5.7). India imports 5427 GWh electricity from Bhutan and exports 3764 GWh to Bangladesh, 100 GWh to Bhutan and 1778 GWh to Nepal. India's CBET is mostly driven by availability of hydro-electricity in the neighbouring countries located in the Himalayan region. However, Himalayan region is identified as one of the most vulnerable regions for geological and hydro-climatic hazards and therefore construction of hydro-electric power projects may result in environmental hazards as well as financial risks associated with natural calamities.[16]

Table 5.7 Export and import of electricity, 2016

From/To (GWh)	*Bangladesh*	*Bhutan*	**India**	*Myanmar*	*Nepal*	*Sri Lanka*	*Thailand*	*Others*	**Total Export**
Bangladesh		–	**–**	–	–	–	–	–	**–**
Bhutan	–		**5,427**	–	–	–	–	–	**5427**
India	**3764**	**110**		**N.A.**	**1778**	**–**	**–**	**–**	**5652**
Myanmar	–	–	**–**		–	–	–	–	**–**
Nepal	–	–	**–**	–		–	–	–	**–**
Sri Lanka	–	–	**–**	–	–		–	–	**–**
Thailand	–	–	**–**	–	–	–		1,385	**1385**
Others	–	–	**–**	–	–	–	19,825		**19,825**
Total import	**3764**	**110**	**5427**	**–**	**1778**	**–**	**19,825**	**1,385**	**32,289**

Source: South Asia Regional Initiative for Energy Integration (SARI/EI). *BIMSTEC Energy Outlook 2030*. 2017. Accessed 16 March 2019. https://irade.org/SARI-EI-Report-on-BIMSTEC-Energy-Outlook-2030.pdf.

Given India's energy-related CO_2 emission projections, any plan to decarbonise the Indian energy basket in general and the power sector in particular may induce India to explore the horizon of CBET beyond Asia. India envisages increasing import of electricity between 4 to 35 GWh by 2032 and between 10 to 60 GWh by 2047. India also plans to export electricity between 1.5 to 3.5 GWh by 2032 and 2 to 10 GWh by 2047 (Figures 5.8 and 5.9).

To achieve the desired label of CBET, India needs to explore energy cooperation beyond Asia. It is reported in World Energy Outlook 2018 that the Asia-Pacific region is adding considerable capacity in generation of both traditional as well as

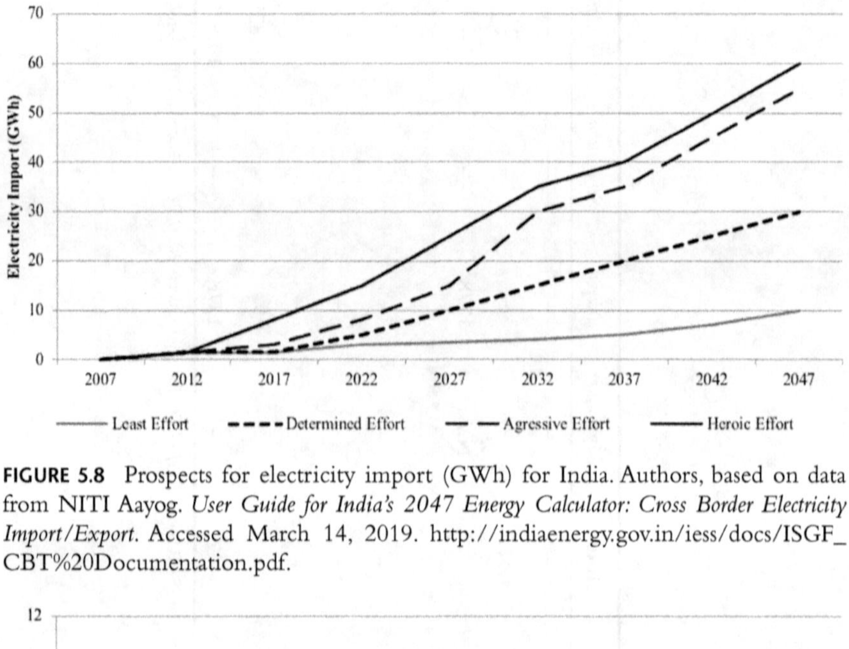

FIGURE 5.8 Prospects for electricity import (GWh) for India. Authors, based on data from NITI Aayog. *User Guide for India's 2047 Energy Calculator: Cross Border Electricity Import/Export*. Accessed March 14, 2019. http://indiaenergy.gov.in/iess/docs/ISGF_CBT%20Documentation.pdf.

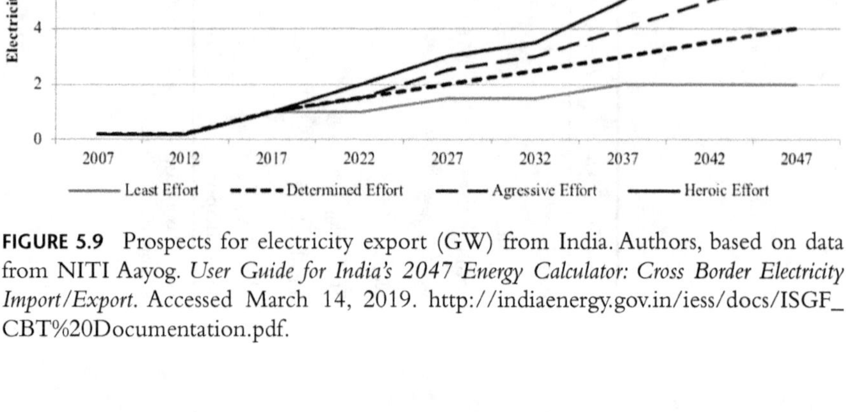

FIGURE 5.9 Prospects for electricity export (GW) from India. Authors, based on data from NITI Aayog. *User Guide for India's 2047 Energy Calculator: Cross Border Electricity Import/Export*. Accessed March 14, 2019. http://indiaenergy.gov.in/iess/docs/ISGF_CBT%20Documentation.pdf.

non-hydro renewable source power generation. The Asia-Pacific region is leading in investment to generate electricity from non-hydro renewable sources – nearly 150 GW in solar PV and 80 GW of wind – which will be operational by 2020.[17] In future, the energy cooperation in the Asia-Pacific region will not be restricted to trade in primary energy sources and electricity only but also hydrogen produced using renewable power.[18]

Recent studies show that Australia has an abundance of non-hydro, renewable energy electricity generation potential, especially in Western Australia.[19] The Asian Renewable Energy Hub (AREH) is one such example where Australia–Indonesia cooperation has proposed to set up a 11 GW capacity renewable electricity plant in the Western Australia. The proposed project will provide electricity to Indonesia and Singapore (Box 5.1).

Major factors that will drive the CBET are mobilising finance to invest in power generation and transmission infrastructures, volatility of electricity prices in international markets and geo-political security/stability (including environmental sustainability) for sustaining energy cooperation in the region.

With reference to average wholesale electricity prices in selected competitive markets, IEA in World Energy Outlook 2018 has observed that 'Since 2010, some electricity markets have experienced a decline in wholesale energy prices brought about by stagnant demand, low natural gas prices and higher output of generation with low marginal costs'.[20] International Renewable Energy Agency has also observed that the cost of electricity from renewables has declined for the majority of renewable sources during 2010 to 2017 (Table 5.8).[21] The highest fall in prices is observed for solar photovoltaic (72 per cent) followed by concentrating solar power (32 per cent), onshore wind (25 per cent) and offshore wind (18 per cent).

BOX 5.1 ASIAN RENEWABLE ENERGY HUB (AREH)

The Asian Renewable Energy Hub (AREH) is one of the most exciting energy projects in the world, with the potential to solve several key energy and sustainable development challenges facing Indonesia. The project will harness Western Australia's abundant wind and solar resources, to export renewable energy to Indonesia via subsea power cables. The proposed project includes, 7.5+ GW of wind generation and 3.5+ GW of solar generation, 8GW+ of generation for green hydrogen production, transmission power lines to major electrical loads, two subsea power cables from Australia to Jakarta and Singapore, over 40 TWh of total annual generation, of which 20 TWh would be exported overseas for new export revenues and regional economic interconnectedness and a design life of 50+ years.

Source: 'Asian Renewable Energy Hub.' Asian Renewable. Accessed 16 March 2019. https://asianrehub.com/.

TABLE 5.8 Cost of electricity from renewable sources

Renewable energy source	*Global levelised cost of electricity from utility-scale power generation technologies, 2010–2017 (2016 USD/kWh)*		*Global weighted average total installed costs, 2010–2017 (2016 USD/kW)*	
	2010	*2017*	*2010*	*2017*
Solar photovoltaic (PV)	0.36	0.10	4394	1388
Concentrating solar power (CSP)	0.33	0.22	7583	5564
Offshore wind	0.17	0.14	4331	4239
Onshore wind	0.08	0.06	1843	1477

Source: International Renewable Energy Agency (IRENA). *Renewable Power Generation Costs in 2017.* Abu Dhabi: International Renewable Energy Agency. 2018.

Since both costs of production and market prices are falling, it may be beneficial for importing countries to import electricity rather than primary energy sources for power generation. Table 5.8 also shows that the cost of installation of solar PV has gone down by 68 per cent during 2010 to 2017. Similarly, installation cost of concentrating solar power (CSP) has gone down by 27 per cent, onshore wind by 20 per cent and offshore wind by 2 per cent. The falling costs of installation and generation of electricity may be good signs for countries having renewable source power generation potential to invest in such plants, but any decision of investment needs to be based on detailed benefit–cost analysis backed by future prospective market price of electricity. Countries having considerable domestic demand of electricity may find it beneficial to invest in generation of power from renewable sources at this time, given the present and future prospects of prices of electricity.

In addition to the cost of installation, for CBET there will be the additional cost of infrastructure for transmission of electricity, operation and maintenance costs of those infrastructure and any un-anticipated costs associated with risks of natural calamities/ hazards etc. The estimated costs of transmission electricity through high-voltage DC link lines in the ASEAN region is presented in Table 5.9. Setting up an HVDC line submarine would be 1.6 times costlier than a HVDC line on the ground, therefore active participation and cooperation of all countries in the Asia-Pacific region in CBET could help in minimising the cost of transmission.

Existing agreements/ forums on regional energy cooperation in Asia could play an important role in operationalising Asia-Pacific electricity transmission corridor. One of the key initiatives under the ASEAN (Association of Southeast Asian Nations) Plan of Action for Energy Cooperation (APAEC) is multilateral electricity trading to accelerate the realisation of the ASEAN Power Grid (APG).[22] It could be beneficial for India to join the ASEAN Power Grid initiative to connect and transmit non-hydro renewable power available in Australia and other countries in the Asia-Pacific region.

TABLE 5.9 Cost assumptions for high-voltage DC (HVDC) cables in AUD

Description	*Capex*	*Opex fix annual ($/kW$_{NTC}$/ km/a)*	*Opex var ($/kWh$_{NTC}$)*	*Lifetime years (a)*
HVDC line on the ground	\$0.955 /kW$_{NTC}$/km	0.0117	0	50
HVDC line submarine	\$1.548 /kW$_{NTC}$/km	0.00156	0	50
HVDC converter pair	\$281 /kW$_{NTC}$	2.808	0	50

Source: Wang, Changlong, Roger Dargaville and Matthew Jeppesen. 'Power system decarbonisation with Global Energy Interconnection – a case study on the economic viability of international transmission network in Australasia.' *Global Energy Interconnection* 1, 4 (2018): 507–519.

In 2014, member states of SAARC (South Asian Association for Regional Cooperation) signed 'SAARC Framework Agreement for Energy Cooperation (Electricity)' with the following objectives:[23]

a. to facilitate integrated operation of regional grid across SAARC region and cross border trade.
b. to enable cross-border trade of electricity amongst the Member States on a voluntary basis subject to the laws, rules and regulation of the respective Member States. CBET could facilitate transmission of surplus power of one number state to other state(s) in a short to long-term time frame.

It is evident that CBET is one of the thrust areas of regional energy cooperation in Asia. However, it would be beneficial to extend the scope and coverage of the energy cooperation in the Asia-Pacific region. Mobilising finance to invest in the Asia-Pacific electricity trade/transmission corridor could be an issue where multilateral development banks (e.g. Asian Development Bank, World Bank) and dedicated infrastructure banks (e.g. Asian Infrastructure Investment Bank) could play important roles.[24]

Conclusions

In World Energy Outlook 2018, International Energy Agency projects that India's TPED will grow at CAAGR of 3.9 per cent during 2016 to 2030, whereas the world's TPED will grow at 1.2 per cent. India's growth in TPED would be the single largest driver of the world's growth in TPED. With rising growth, India's share in the world's TPED is expected to rise from 6.3 per cent in 2016 to 9.1 per cent in 2030. Source-wise composition of India's TPED reveals that coal holds the largest share (44% in 2016) and it will increase to 46 per cent by 2030. CAAGR of demand for coal will remain higher than the TPED growth rate. The share of oil in TPED was 25 per cent in 2016 and it is expected to fall in future. With rising demand for energy, India's energy-related CO_2 emission is also expected to grow at CAAGR of 4.1 per cent during 2016 to 2030 and India's share in world's total energy-related CO_2 emission is expected to increase from 6.5 per cent in 2016 to 10.6 per cent in 2030. Coal and oil are the major contributors of India's total CO_2 emission and contributed 71 per cent and 26 per cent respectively in 2016. Though India's per capita CO_2 emission is one-third of the world's average, both energy and emission intensity of Indian GDP is higher than global average. Therefore, India's energy security needs to be integrated with environmental sustainability to sustain high economic growth and achieve socio-economic-environmental wellbeing of Indian population.

India's energy security is significantly dependent on imports of primary energy sources. A large part of India's imported energy sources are used – either directly and/or after refinement – for generation of electricity. Therefore to achieve energy security as well as reduce the current account deficit, it will be important for India to gradually reduce imports of high value primary energy sources like crude petroleum and natural gas which are used for power generation. In the long run India also needs to reduce dependence on imported coal for power generation. Given the vast potential exist in India in renewable source power generation (mainly solar and wind power), accelerating investment in domestic electricity generation, modernisation and interconnections of power grids may help to reduce dependence on imported primary sources for electricity generation. In future, it would be important for India to explore the Asia-Pacific region in mobilising finance to invest in an inter-regional electricity transmission infrastructure to facilitate cross border electricity trade (CBET). The high dependence of Indian industry on coal and petroleum products is partly attributable to an irregular electricity supply, which compels industries to install captive power generation plants. India needs an additional 15 per cent in the existing installed capacity under utility sector to ensure an uninterrupted power supply to industries/ establishments. There may be some specific advantages of distributed production of electricity but efficiencies of the captive power generation plants vary across units and there is a need for intensive monitoring to control emissions from these plants. Moreover, these plants are mostly located in the vicinity of habitations and cause maximum health hazards to urban population. Therefore, it would be important for India to improve the quality of the electricity supply to industries and establishments so that dependence on captive power generation will go down gradually over the years. Petroleum products provides mobile sources of energy security for transport sector and to reduce the dependence on petroleum products from the transport sector, the adoption of electrical vehicles (EVs) needs to be encouraged, at least in metros and class I cities, along with improvement in mass rapid transport infrastructure. However, given the dependence on transport fuels (mainly diesel and petrol) for revenue generation, it would be against the revenue interests of the governments to promote EVs unless the government deregulates the electricity price as well as puts tax on electricity at per with other transport fuels. In future, hydrogen produced using renewable power may reduce India's dependence on imports of oils for the production of combustible fuels for the transport sector.

Appendix

TABLE A.5.1 India's policy scenarios with reference to TPED and CO_2 emission

Scenarios	*Cross-cutting policy assumptions*	*Power sector policies and measures*	*Transport sector policies and measures*
Current Policies Scenario (CPS)	**Assumptions** • National Mission on Enhanced Energy Efficiency • National Clean Energy Fund (NCEF) to promote clean energy technologies based on a levy of INR 400 ($6) per tonne of coal. • 'Make in India' campaign to increase the share of manufacturing in the national economy.	**Assumptions** • Renewable purchase obligation and other fiscal measures to promote renewables. • Increased use of supercritical coal technology. • Restructured Accelerated Power Development and Reform Programme to finance the modernisation of transmission and distribution networks. • Pollution control rules limiting emissions from coal power plants.	**Assumptions** • Increasing blending mandate for ethanol and support for alternative-fuel vehicles. • LDVs: Bharat IV emissions standards and Euro 4 equivalent fuel sulphur standards. • HDVs: Bharat IV emissions standards and Euro IV equivalent fuel sulphur standards.

(*Continued*)

TABLE A.5.1 (CONTINUED)

Scenarios	*Cross-cutting policy assumptions*	*Power sector policies and measures*	*Transport sector policies and measures*
New Policies Scenario (NPS)	• Nationally Determined Contributions (NDC) Greenhouse Gas (GHS) Target: reduce emissions intensity of GDP 33–35% below 2005 levels by 2030. • NDC energy target: achieve about 40% cumulative installed capacity from non-fossil fuel sources by 2030 with the help of technology transfer and low-cost international finance. • Efforts to expedite environmental clearances and land acquisition for energy projects. • Opening of coal, gas and oil sectors to private and foreign investors.	• Environmental (Protection) Amendment Rules. • Universal electricity access achieved by 2023. • Strengthened measures such as competitive bidding to increase the use of renewables towards the national target of 175 GW of non-hydro renewables capacity by 2022 (100 GW solar, 75 GW non-solar). • Expanded efforts to strengthen the national grid, upgrade the transmission and distribution network, and reduce aggregate technical and commercial losses to 15%. • Increased efforts to establish the financial viability of all power market participants, especially network and distribution companies.	• Declared intent to move to 30% electric share in vehicle sales by 2030. • Extended support for alternative-fuel two/three-wheelers, cars and public buses. • National Biofuel Policy with indicative blending share targets for bioethanol and biodiesel. • LDVs: Bharat VI emissions standards by 2020; fuel-economy standards at 130 g CO_2/km in 2017 and 113 g CO_2/km in 2022. • HDVs: Bharat VI emissions standards by 2020; fuel-economy targets for 2018 and 2021. • Dedicated rail corridors to encourage shift away from road freight.
Sustainable Development Scenario (SDS)	• Provides an integrated strategy to achieve the key energy-related elements of the United Nations Sustainable Development agenda, including energy access, air quality and climate objectives. The emissions trajectory of the SDS is fully in line with achieving the long-term objectives of the Paris Agreement. • To deliver the outcomes of this scenario, the power sector proceeds further and faster with the deployment of low-emissions generation. Renewable energy technologies provide the main pathway to the provision of universal energy access. All economically viable avenues to improve efficiency are pursued, keeping overall demand in 2040 at today's level.		

Scenarios	*Industry sector policies and measures*	*Buildings sector policies and measures*
	Assumptions	**Assumptions**

Current Policies Scenario (CPS)	• Energy Conservation Act:
	  • Mandatory energy audits.
	  • Appointment of an energy manager in seven energy-intensive industries.
	• National Mission on Enhanced Energy Efficiency (NMEEE):
	• Cycle II and III of Perform, Achieve and Trade (PAT) scheme, which benchmarks facilities' performance against best practice and enables trading of energy savings certificates.
	• Income and corporate tax incentives for energy service companies, including the Energy Efficiency Financing Platform.
	• Framework for Energy-Efficient Economic Development offering a risk guarantee for performance contracts and a venture capital fund for energy efficiency.
	• Energy efficiency intervention in selected SME clusters including capacity building.
		• Universal electricity access achieved by 2023.
		• Rural electrification under Deen Dayal Upadhyaya Gram Jyoti Yojana scheme.
		• Promotion of clean cooking access with LPG, including free connections to poor rural households through *Pradhan Mantri Ujjwala Yojana*.
		• Measures under the National Solar Mission.
		• Energy Conservation Building Code 2007 with voluntary standards for commercial buildings.
		• 'Green Rating for Integrated Habitat Assessment' rating system for green buildings.
		• Promotion and distribution of LEDs through the Efficient Lighting Programme.

(*Continued*)

TABLE A.5.1 (CONTINUED)

Scenarios	*Industry sector policies and measures*	*Buildings sector policies and measures*
New Policies Scenario (NPS)	• Further implementation of the NMEEE's recommendations including: • Tightening of the PAT mechanism under Cycle III. • Further strengthening of fiscal instruments to promote energy efficiency. • Strengthen existing policies to realise the energy efficiency potential in SMEs.	• Standards and Labelling Programme, mandatory for air conditioners, lights, televisions and refrigerators, voluntary for seven other products and LEDs. • Phase out incandescent light bulbs by 2020. • Voluntary Star Ratings for the services sector. • Measures under the National Mission on Enhanced Energy Efficiency. • Energy Conservation in Building Codes made mandatory in eight states that regulate building envelope, lighting and hot water. • Efforts to plan and rationalise urbanisation in line with the '100 smart cities' concept. • Enhanced efforts to increase electricity access for households.

Source: World Energy Outlook 2018. Paris, France: International Energy Agency. 2018.

Notes

1 'Energy Security – Topics.' International Energy Agency. 1 July 2020. Accessed 22 March 2019. www.iea.org/topics/energy-security.
2 'Goal 7 | Department of Economic and Social Affairs.' United Nations. Accessed 22 March 2019. https://sdgs.un.org/goals/goal7.
3 Central Statistics Office (CSO). *Energy Statistics 2018 (Twenty Fifth Issue)*. New Delhi: Ministry of Statistics and Programme Implementation, Government of India. 2018.
4 Ibid.
5 Ibid.
6 International Energy Agency (IEA). *World Energy Outlook 2018*. Paris, France: International Energy Agency. 2018.
7 Ibid.
8 Ibid.
9 See endnote 4.
10 International Energy Agency. *Key world energy statistics 2018*. Paris, France: International Energy Agency. 2018.
11 See endnote 7.
12 Total subsidy/ under-recovery on petroleum products is Rs. 28,684 crore for 2017–2018. See: Petroleum Policy and Analysis Cell (PPAC). *Subsidy/Under-recovery on Petroleum Products*. Accessed March 26, 2019. www.ppac.gov.in/WriteReadData/userfiles/file/PS_2_b_UR_on_SensitiveProducts(H).xls.
13 Breitenmoser, L., T. Gross, R. Huesch, J. Rau, H. Dhar, S. Kumar, C. Hugi and T. Wintgens. 'Anaerobic digestion of biowastes in India: Opportunities, challenges and research needs.' *Journal of Environmental Management* 236 (2019): 396–412. Also see: Chaurasiya, Pawan Kumar. 'A detailed study of cattle dung based biogas plant for cooking fuel and organic fertilizer.' 2020. Accessed 16 October 2020. DOI: 10.13140/RG.2.2.18496.97282. Mukherjee, S. and D. Chakraborty. 'Turning human waste into renewable energy: Opportunities and policy options for India.' *Turkish Economic Review*, 3, 4 (2016): 610–628.
14 International Energy Agency. *Key world energy statistics 2018*. Paris, France: International Energy Agency. 2018
15 Registrar General & Census Commissioner (RG&CC). *Indian Census, 2011: Houses, Household Amenities & Assets*. Ministry of Home Affairs, Government of India, Houses, Household Amenities & Assets. 2011.
16 Huber, Amelie, 'Hydropower in the Himalayan Hazardscape: Strategic Ignorance and the Production of Unequal Risk.' *Water*, 11, 3, 414 (2019). Accessed March 22, 2019. www.mdpi.com/2073-4441/11/3/414.
17 See endnote 6, p. 294.
18 International Renewable Energy Agency (IRENA). *Hydrogen from Renewable Power: Technology Outlook for the Energy Transition*. Abu Dhabi: International Renewable Energy Agency. 2018.
19 ANU Energy Change Institute, Australian National University. *Zero-Carbon Energy for the Asia-Pacific*. Accessed 16 March 2019. http://energy.anu.edu.au/files/ECI%20Grand%20Challenge%20Public%20Pitch.pdf.
20 See endnote 6, p. 315.
21 International Renewable Energy Agency (IRENA). *Renewable Power Generation Costs in 2017*. Abu Dhabi: International Renewable Energy Agency. 2018.
22 Zamora, Christopher G. *ASEAN Plan of Action for Energy Cooperation (APAEC) 2016–2025*. Jakarta, Indonesia: ASEAN Centre for Energy. 2015.

23 'SAARC Framework Agreement for Energy Cooperation (Electricity).' Ministry of Power. Accessed 22 March 2019. https://powermin.nic.in/en/content/saarc-framework-agreement-energy-cooperation-electricity.

24 Sengupta, Ramprasad, Sacchidananda Mukherjee and Manish Gupta. *Financing for Infrastructure Investment in G-20 Countries*, Working Paper No. 2015-144. New Delhi: National Institute of Public Finance and Policy (NIPFP). 2015.

PART II

India's Act East policy and energy cooperation

6

INDIA'S ENERGY COOPERATION WITH SOUTHEAST ASIA UNDER ACT EAST POLICY

S.D. Muni

Introduction

India's Act East policy, launched in 2014, is a carryover of the Look East policy initiated during the early 1990s. India has, however, been looking towards and engaging its extended neighbours for the centuries, even before the beginning of the Christian era. The link and continuity between the two policies is acknowledged officially. Foreign Minister Dr S. Jaishankar, in a Conference key Note address on Indo-Pacific in Maldives on 3 September 2019 said, 'to begin with, Indo-Pacific must be perceived as the further extrapolation of the Act East-Look East policy'.[1]

The Look East policy had both strategic and economic orientation, though it is popularly known to have had a sharper focus on economic engagement. Energy has been an important component of this engagement. It may, however, be borne in mind that India has been having energy cooperation with some of the Southeast Asian countries even before the launching of the Look East policy. These countries included Myanmar, Vietnam and Indonesia.[2] Subsequently, energy cooperation was explored also with Bangladesh, which has gradually grown in dimensions. We shall come back to this aspect of bilateral cooperation later. A robust push to India's energy cooperation was provided by Mr Mani Shankar Aiyar, during 2005–2006, when he held the portfolio of Petroleum and Natural Gas Ministry of Government of India under Dr Manmohan Singh's prime ministership. He initiated a policy to set up a firm and cooperative network of oil and gas pipelines with all the neighbouring countries including Pakistan and China. Regarding cooperation with China in third countries he said:

> While China has indeed had a head-start on us in looking for opportunities in third countries, in recent years India has established a presence in E&P projects in 14 countries, including Sakhalin-I in the Russian Federation, and

> is in discussion or negotiation for hydrocarbon cooperation in some 50 countries around the globe. Almost everywhere we go, we meet our Chinese friends. Thus far we have usually met as friends but commercial competitors. We are now entering the era of meeting as friends and partners. Cooperation between India and China in third countries is not only eminently desirable, it is also entirely feasible.[3]

This approach included laying down oil and gas pipe lines with the Southeast Asian countries via India's Northeastern region. The significance of this region in India's Look East policy had only begun to be realised in economic and energy areas. One can argue that Mr Aiyar's energy cooperation policy was not conceived strictly within the framework of the Look East policy, but it was bound to have a significant impact there. He was conscious of the energy needs of the fast-growing economies like Japan, South Korea, India and China, the four largest energy importers, as well as of energy suppliers like Myanmar, Malaysia, Indonesia and Papua New Guinea, among India's eastern neighbours. He made a strong plea for energy cooperation among all to build Asian century.[4] However, Aiyar's approach came in conflict with the priorities of the Ministry of External Affairs and India's security establishments. Accordingly, this approach could not be pursued after his exit from the Petroleum Ministry. The US pressures have also been referred to as a factor in thwarting Aiyar's approach for energy partnership with China.[5]

The idea of a broader cooperation with China in the energy sector has remerged. The present Petroleum Minister in the Modi regime, Dharmendra Pradhan, has proposed that India and China should join hands in coping with the challenge of 'crude volatility', i.e. fluctuating prices of crude oil in the global market. He has gone to the extent of proposing a block of Asia's four highest oil consumers and importers to form a 'buyers' block' to negotiate with the oil exporters.[6] Since transporting Russian oil to India is uneconomical, India has also proposed to swap this oil with China in return for oil and gas that China is extracting from other third countries like Myanmar.[7] These are innovative proposals and will transform the nature of India's energy relations with its eastern neighbours. However, there is a big strategic hurdle in turning these proposals into reality. Strategic relations between India and China are anything but smooth despite informal summits between Prime Minister Modi and Chinese President Xi in Wuhan (April 2018) and Chennai (September 2019). It may be kept in mind that it was the strategic factor that had blocked Aiyar's ideas from being pursued.

India's Northeast region has a critical role in energy linkages with India's eastern neighbours. The Look East policy had initially ignored the development of this region as it was focussed on advancing trade and investment cooperation with the Association of Southeast Asian Nations (ASEAN). However, with the constitution of the DoNER (Development of North-East Region) as a separate department in 2001 and then upgrading it to a full-fledged Ministry in 2004, this gap was filled. With the initiation of India's Act East policy, emphasis on the development of the Northeast region has been stepped up. This region is critical for establishing connectivity – both physical and energy related – with the ASEAN neighbours. Energy cooperation under the Act East policy is being pursued at two levels: through regional organisations and also bilaterally. At the regional level, ASEAN, Bay of Bengal Initiative for Multi-Sectoral Technical and Economic Cooperation (BIMSTEC) and Mekong- Ganga Cooperation (MGC) are relevant organisations. Bilateral cooperation has to be strengthened and explored with the energy producers of the region like Myanmar, Vietnam, Indonesia, Malaysia and Brunei. Let us look at the regional and bilateral areas of energy cooperation in some details.

Energy at regional level

ASEAN

ASEAN was a critical component of India's Look East policy and it continues to remain so for the Act East policy as well. India's cooperation with BIMSTEC and MGC is also carefully coordinated with the overall objectives and priorities of ASEAN. There is considerable attention in ASEAN on ensuring its energy security and ASEAN is working systematically for this. In January 1999, ASEAN set up an ASEAN Centre for Energy as an inter-governmental organisation to develop innovative approaches for energy security and also to coordinate and synergise approaches of the ASEAN member states towards their developmental needs for energy. This Centre has been revamped and upgraded to become a knowledge hub on energy for ASEAN and help 'unify and strengthen ASEAN energy cooperation and integration'.[8]

Regional energy security is integral to the ASEAN vision 2020 and would remain so subsequently also. It is working on an ASEAN regional power grid. Since 2002, ASEAN has been working on the Trans-ASEAN Gas Pipeline, which also includes constructing regasification terminals. This is to enhance energy connectivity and accessibility for all the member countries. ASEAN is also working on coal and clean coal technology. Under a comprehensive ASEAN energy management system, attention is also paid to energy efficiency and conservation. Yet another area of energy focus for ASEAN is renewable energy involving biofuels and solar systems. ASEAN is closely engaged in this area with its +3 partners (i.e. China, Japan and South Korea), India, as well as countries like Germany and Canada.

Energy has appeared in the India-ASEAN cooperation from the beginning, but ideas about the nature of cooperation in this sector have evolved gradually. In the first ASEAN-India Plan of Action to implement their partnership for 'Peace, Progress and Shared Prosperity', drawn in 2004, emphasis was on trade and investment in gas and electricity projects, as also on energy efficiency and renewable energy.[9] Not much of significance was added in the next Plan of Action 2010–2015. It only endorsed the ASEAN Plan of Action for Energy Cooperation, underlined the importance of institutional linkages in the area of energy cooperation and committed India to support the rural household electrification of ASEAN Member States, particularly, in the CLMV (Cambodia, Laos, Myanmar and Vietnam) countries.

Under the next Plan of Action for 2016–2020, the past commitments were reiterated with the promise to 'promote ASEAN-India New and Renewable Energy initiative'. A meeting of the senior officials of the two sides was constituted for this purpose and the private sector's engagement in the 'development and utilisation of renewable and alternative energy resources.'[10]

Despite these declarations, nothing substantial has taken place between ASEAN and India in the field of energy cooperation. In April 2019, after a meeting of the senior officials of India and ASEAN in New Delhi, the 'need to impart urgency to cooperation in renewable energy' was underlined. The target of this urgency was the holding of a conference on this subject in 2019. It is really frustrating that even after four years of preparing the Plan of Action, holding a conference is becoming a problem. Why is it that cooperation between India and ASEAN has not proceeded along desired lines? To begin with, not enough resources have been allocated to the projects of exploring renewable and alternate energy resources. India's ASEAN Fund for Science and Technology supported these programmes but that is not enough. India has invested more than US$10 billion in improving its renewable energy sources like solar, wind and biogas. ASEAN is collaborating with more resourceful countries like Germany, Japan and Canada and perhaps India does not fit into its priorities in this sector. This could be one of the reasons for encouraging the private sector to come and contribute as was underlined in the 2016–2020 Plan of Action.

There are other difficulties also confronting cooperation in energy sector. ASEAN countries are at different levels of development and their energy needs vary significantly from each other. Many of them are rich in hydrocarbons and hydropower and may not have huge interest in devoting their attention to renewable energy sources. Besides the intensity of interest, there are also 'structural and systemic' constraints in terms of infrastructure for renewable energy and a culture of political decision-making. The medium- and long-term renewable targets of renewable energy set by countries like 'Cambodia, Malaysia, the Philippines, Thailand and Vietnam … differ greatly in quantitative objectives, time, and specificity due in part to their varying levels of economic development'.[11] An ASEAN analyst rightly observed:

> The real test of ASEAN – India renewable energy cooperation will be its contribution to fulfilling the energy needs of local communities in a sustainable and efficient way. The documents and pledges for energy collaboration should not be an end in itself … initial efforts must translate to actions. It is crucial, now more than ever, to demonstrate the willingness and determination of both ASEAN and India to develop this collaborative venture given the concrete gains it can offer to the people and the environment.[12]

India on its part is more than prepared and willing to train ASEAN people and share its technical expertise with them, which willing Member States of the organisation, like the Philippines, can take advantage of. Overall substantial energy cooperation between ASEAN and India will, it seems, move at a slow speed.

BIMSTEC and MGC

BIMSTEC was established in 1997, reflecting the convergence of India's Look East policy and Thailand's Look West approach. Initially, it was a five-member grouping of Bangladesh, India, Myanmar, Sri Lanka and Thailand and was named by taking the first alphabet of all the member countries for economic cooperation. By 2004, Nepal and Bhutan became its full-fledged members and with the same acronym; its name was changed to Bay of Bengal Initiative for Multi-Sectoral Technical and Economic Cooperation. The group started to focus on six areas of cooperation, namely, trade, technology, energy, transport, tourism and fisheries. By 2008, eight more areas were added, i.e. agriculture, public health, poverty alleviation, counter-terrorism, environment, culture, people to people contacts and climate change. Lately, since 2017, security issues, including maritime security, have also been brought on the board.

Energy cooperation has been one of the priority areas for this grouping as they are endowed with significant energy resources: Nepal, Bhutan and India's Northeast region with hydropower, India with coal and Bangladesh and Myanmar with natural gas. According to one estimate, the energy potential of the BIMSTEC region has 65 billion tonnes of coal, 6.4 billion barrels of crude oil, 87 trillion cubic feet of natural gas, 243 million tonnes of biomass and 390 gigawatts of hydropower.[13] All these countries are developing economies in need of growing energy consumption. Unfortunately, some of the member countries like Nepal have only just begun to pay attention to harnessing their energy potential (hydropower) adequately. All forms of energy sources including conventional, such as hydrocarbons and hydropower, as also unconventional and renewable like solar, wind and wave energies were broadly identified for cooperation. Emphasis has, however, been mainly on natural gas and electricity. It is possible that hydropower and other energy sources may also be harnessed in future. The first BIMSTEC summit held in Myanmar in 2004 agreed 'to promote sustainable and optimal energy utilization through development of new hydrocarbon and hydro-power projects, inter connection of electricity and natural gas grids and energy technologies'.

The enthusiasm for trans-BIMSTEC natural gas grids had been triggered by the estimates of rich potential in this respect in Myanmar and Bangladesh, and also by discoveries of natural gas in Indian river basins. But soon Bangladesh dampened this enthusiasm by putting on hold its export of natural gas until it had met all its own needs.[14] Now the emphasis is on trans-national power grids and transmission lines. BIMSTEC Plan of Action for Energy Cooperation was finalised in 2005, but very little achievements are visible on the ground. The BIMSTEC Kathmandu Summit in August 2018 concluded and signed the Memorandum of Understanding on BIMSTEC Grid Interconnection. The summit also instructed 'the relevant agencies to take concrete measures to initiate harmonization of technical, planning and operational standards for removing barriers to grid interconnections and also ensure early establishment of a BIMSTEC Grid'.[15] This can be cited as the only concrete outcome of a number of conferences, workshops, task force reports and meetings of the energy ministers of BIMSTEC for the past more than two decades. One can possibly also refer to the establishment of the BIMSTEC Energy Centre in Bangalore, India, in 2008. The mandate of the Centre is to help BIMSTEC coordinate its energy cooperation and explore new and effective ways of energy cooperation in the region. But more than ten years have gone without making this Centre get operationalised formally. The 2018 Kathmandu Summit had given a call for its early operationalisation to strengthen energy cooperation.

Obviously, the achievements of BIMSTEC in energy cooperation have fallen far short of its promise and expectations. Indian foreign minister Dr S. Jaishankar told the visiting BIMSTEC secretary general on 24 July 2019 in New Delhi that there was 'need to invest more energy in BIMSTEC'. Earlier at the Kathmandu ministerial meeting of the grouping, the host, Foreign Minister of Nepal, had lamented the overall poor progress in concrete terms. With regard to the energy sector, Thailand presented a paper on reprioritising BIMSTEC. The paper asked to reduce the current 14 areas, to seriously advance cooperation. The new areas suggested were, namely, connectivity; trade and investment; people to people contacts; counter-terrorism; trans-national crime and security, and science and technology. Energy was *not* in there. Though this is not the collective view of all the members, it underlines the extent of the frustration among its members.

Several factors have contributed to the lack of energy cooperation in BIMSTEC despite a strong desire to the contrary. One may be hopeful and optimistic that this negative situation will change in future as there is potential and there is need for cooperation. Among many factors that have come in the way of advancing energy cooperation, lack of financing resources for energy projects has been an important one. In a number of ministerial meetings, this aspect has been underlined and efforts for mobilising finances from within and outside the region have been called upon. The private sector has also been invited to play a major role in energy cooperation projects. But lack of incentives and support from the governments has kept the situation unchanged. Lidia Powell, a dedicated analyst at the Observer Research Foundation New Delhi, rightly observed in this respect that:

> Viewed through the lens of regional cooperation the absence of trans-national energy infrastructure like pipelines and transmission lines in the BIMSTEC region is the result of market failure. Markets have always been unable to provide public goods such as energy security. The benefits of energy security accrue to the nation and not to market participants as also there is little incentive, if at all, for market participants to invest in cross border energy infrastructure. Market participants also have a tendency to depend on states to secure their interests, primarily by reducing risk and uncertainty. In trans-border projects the costs for market participants to manage risk and uncertainty is higher than the benefits that may accrue from techno economic efficiencies. In the absence of state participation that would reduce risk and uncertainty, trans-border infra-structure is unlikely to materialise.[16]

The state participation has been hesitant because of a lack of political will. Regional cooperation at its core is a strategic exercise. Unless the strategic interests of the participating countries converge, substantial cooperation would not occur despite sincere intent and attractive rhetoric. The problem of lack of political will and commitment has also been sounded clearly in BIMSTEC meetings, both at the ministerial and summit levels. Five of the seven BIMSTEC members are also SAARC members and if their cooperation in SAARC was not satisfactory, how could it be otherwise in BIMSTEC only because of the absence of Pakistan? It may be recalled that four of these countries, Bhutan, Bangladesh, India and Nepal (BBIN), have also not succeeded in advancing their sub-regional cooperation since 2014 in a desirable way. China also heavily impinges on other BIMSTEC members and has a competitive relationship with India.

The MGC was established in November 2000 for cooperation between India and the Mekong countries, namely, Myanmar, Laos, Thailand, Cambodia and Vietnam. Four areas of cooperation earmarked for this grouping were identified as tourism, culture, education and transportation. Energy did not figure among them in any significant way. India has extended considerable support to the MGC countries, specially Myanmar, Cambodia, Laos and Vietnam, in the areas of connectivity, capacity building, creation of border economic zones and overall development activities. A specially dedicated unit in the Ministry of External Affairs looks after these countries. Of the Mekong countries, Myanmar and Vietnam are rich producers of hydrocarbons and India has been cooperating with them for energy imports on bilateral level. Laos, Myanmar, Cambodia and Vietnam have capacities in hydropower. Laos depends on Thailand for buying its surplus power. India has extended lines of credit to support construction of hydropower projects, electrical transmission lines, creation of power sub-stations and projects of rural electrification in Laos, Myanmar, Cambodia and Vietnam.[17]

Cooperation at bilateral level

Notwithstanding hurdles in the regional cooperation arrangements, India has continued to seek cooperation with its eastern neighbour in the energy sector bilaterally. This has, however, not been in conflict with the priorities set in regional cooperation arrangements. In some cases, like Vietnam, bilateral cooperation began even before the launching of the Look East policy. India had started extracting oil in Vietnam from the continental shelf and extended economic zone in 1980s. Initially, the aim was to access energy sources from the neighbouring countries but gradually the area of cooperation has been expanded and diversified. Impetus has been given to this cooperation under the Act East policy. There are clearly two dimensions of this cooperation: one in relation to the immediate sub-regional neighbours that include Nepal, Bhutan, Myanmar and Bangladesh and another in relation to the extended eastern neighbours like Malaysia, Indonesia, Brunei and Vietnam.

In accessing energy from the eastern neighbours, India has been working with international oil and gas conglomerates. In Vietnam, India's Oil and Natural Gas Corporation

(ONGC-*Videsh*) had been working with a joint venture of Vietnam and then Soviet Union, Vietsov, even before 1988 when it started exploring energy blocks independently. Subsequently, ONGC also partnered with British Petroleum (BP), Amoco and Norwegian Statoil. In Myanmar, Korea's Daewoo Oil Corporation sold off 30 per cent of its shares of oil extraction contracts to Indian companies – 20 per cent to ONGC-*Videsh* and 10 per cent to Gas Authority of India Ltd. (GAIL) in 2001.[18] Subsequently, India has gained experience and developed relevant technologies to undertake oil and gas exploration independently also in these countries. Both Vietnam and Myanmar are also keen to encourage Indian participation in order to maintain balance among the foreign participants involved in their energy-harnessing activities.

India's approach for strengthening connectivity with the neighbours has also covered connectivity in energy sector. This has been pursued through laying down of cross-boundary gas and oil pipelines and establishing power grid for pooling and distributing electricity in the immediate neighbouring region. Expressions like energy diplomacy and pipeline diplomacy are used by India's petroleum minister and his associates in the context of energy cooperation with various countries, including the eastern neighbours. There were three identifiable routes for gas and oil pipelines with Myanmar; across Myanmar's Kaladan river, between Sittwe port and west Bengal and through Bangladesh. Of these the last one is closest and most preferred and was seriously pursued both by India and Myanmar for the past more than a decade. However, Bangladesh did not agree to join, despite the potential of earning rich transmission revenues. The reasons were largely political, related to bilateral differences with Myanmar on border and other issues, and the fear of sovereignty breach with India. India is now determinedly pursuing the proposal and hopes to expand its domestic gas pipeline project to Myanmar through Bangladesh.[19] More pipeline routes between India and Myanmar have also been identified. There is a bilateral oil pipeline project between India and Bangladesh to transport diesel through a 137 km long pipeline linking Siliguri in the West Bengal province of India to Parbatipur in the Dinajpur district of North Bangladesh. This project is expected to cost INR360 crores and will be completed in 27 months.[20] After delaying it for years, India has also completed, in record time, an oil pipeline with Nepal, which will ensure interrupted supplies and benefit consumers in Nepal by reducing transportation cost.[21] India is expanding the pipeline infrastructure both within the country and with neighbours as it has reformed its policy parameters and huge investments to the extent of $60 billion are expected in this sector.

BIMSTEC has been working on a sub-regional electricity transmission grid since 2003. An MoU for such a grid was signed by the BIMSTEC Member States on 31 August 2018 at its Kathmandu Summit as noted earlier. Once the grid is established and operationalised, it would be easy for the countries to have electricity trade amongst them. The grid will facilitate:

- the optimization of using the energy resources in the region for mutual benefits on non-discriminatory basis subject to laws, rules and regulations of the respective Parties;

- the promotion of efficient, economic, and secure operation of power system needed through the development of regional electricity networks;
- the necessity of optimization of capital investment for generation capacity addition across the region; and
- power exchange through cross border interconnections.[22]

India has been supplying electricity to all its neighbours, Nepal, Bhutan, Bangladesh and Myanmar, through its own national grid. There was hesitation in pushing for a regional grid earlier as that would have deprived India of its discretion and influence. But in view of the growing demand from the neighbours and for putting dynamism in its Act East policy, the regional grid has been accepted and, hopefully, will come into operation soon. This will facilitate regional trade in electricity and enhance mutual cooperation, development and trust.[23]

Besides oil and gas pipelines and the regional electricity grid, India has also been pursuing cooperation with its eastern neighbours in other forms of energy sources, especially renewable energy. We have noted that in ASEAN and BIMSTEC, India has laid emphasis on renewable energy and actively pursued its initiative on solar alliance. India has established a separate Ministry for Renewable Energy in pursuit of reducing its dependence on fossil fuels and is keen to cooperate with its neighbours in this sector. In all its bilateral engagements, renewable energy has emerged as an important aspect of development cooperation. India has offered training and technology support to its neighbours in harnessing solar, wind and biomass energy based on its own experience and investments in this sector. In Vietnam, India has invested US$814 million in 176 solar and wind power projects.[24] India helped Myanmar set up a biomass gasifier plant since Myanmar has large forest areas.[25] In Vietnam and Bangladesh, India has also been supporting the use of nuclear energy for peaceful purposes. For instance, during Vietnamese President Tran Dai Quang's visit to India in March 2018, it was noted:

> President Tran Dai Quang welcomed Indian companies to invest in renewable energy and energy conservation projects in Viet Nam and thanked India for extending support to Viet Nam in building a research reactor for the purpose of peaceful uses of atomic energy.
>
> The Vietnamese side took note of the request by the Indian side on actively considering signing the Framework Agreement of the International Solar Alliance with a view to strengthening the cooperation in the renewable energy space.[26]

Under its Act East policy, India has sought to institutionalise its cooperation with the eastern neighbours in the energy sector. This has been done by creating mechanisms like Joint Working Groups and Joint Steering Committees at the appropriate level for continuous consultations and cooperation. Where desirable, separate Joint Working Groups for oil and gas, coal and renewable energy have been designated.

With Indonesia, an 'Energy Forum' for Government to Government (G2G) and Business to Business (B2B) interaction has been in place since 2011.[27]

Summing up

India has been pursuing energy cooperation with its eastern neighbours before and during its Look East policy launched during the early 1990s. The Act East policy pronounced in 2014 added dynamism to this cooperation both at the level of regional organisations such as ASEAN, BIMSTEC, MGC, etc. as well as bilateral levels. The outcome of this cooperation has remained much below expectations and known potential. There are several reasons behind this that include lack of adequate funding of the energy cooperation projects, lack of political will, differing needs of energy and capacities to harness the potential, levels of relevant infrastructure and so on. But efforts of India and its neighbouring countries will continue to address these issues as they are all convinced of the benefits of cooperation in the energy sector. India, in particular, may emerge as the largest energy consumer by 2030–2035. It would not be able to meet its energy requirements affordably without cooperation, not only with its eastern neighbours but all over the world.

In the context of the eastern neighbours, there are two other challenges to India's Act East policy for energy cooperation. One is that India's Northeastern region, which is so critical to energy cooperation with the neighbouring countries, is still at a work-in-progress level in internal connectivity as well as harnessing of its energy potential. Assam and Tripura are very rich in petroleum, Arunachal Pradesh in hydropower, Meghalaya has substantial deposits of coal and uranium and a good part of the region can be invested with solar energy. Developing this potential will give a huge boost to energy trading with the neighbouring countries. Connectivity within the Northeast region is being enhanced, but it will take time to attain satisfactory outcomes.

The second challenge is of competition and rivalry with China in the field of energy.[28] China has raised serious objections to India's energy exploration in Vietnam's territorial waters. But even in the face of China's objections, Vietnam has offered oil and gas blocks to India for exploration.[29] In Myanmar, the energy scene is dominated by China and, on occasion, China has successfully defeated Indian bids for exploration contacts.[30] The answer to this challenge lies in mutual cooperation as is now being initiated by both the sides. Indian Petroleum Minister Dharmendra Pradhan's call for a buyer's club may be recalled in this respect. Mutual cooperation and coordination between these two Asian giants look like a formidable task but it is hoped that the compulsions of their needs will nudge them together for understanding in this field.

Notes

1 On transition from the Look East to Act East policy, see Muni, S.D., and Rahul Mishra. *India's Eastward Engagement: From Antiquity to Act East Policy*. New Delhi: Sage, 2019.

2 Aspects of this cooperation have been discussed in Muni, S.D. and Girijesh Pant. *India's Energy Security: Prospects for Cooperation with Extended Neighbourhood*. Delhi: Rupa & Co., 2005.
3 Mr Aiyar's speech in China on 12 January 2006 while having delegation level talks with China's National Development and Reforms Commission. Text of the speech in Press Information Bureau, Government of India, 13 January 2006.
4 See Aiyar's speech in Beijing as reproduced in, Aiyar, Mani Shankar. 'Asia's quest for energy security.' Frontline. 24 February 2006. Accessed 21 October 2020. https://frontline.thehindu.com/the-nation/article30208451.ece.
5 See, for instance, Jayaswal, Rajeev. 'Chapter 1.' In the *The Lobbysts: Untold Story of Oil, Gas and Energy Sector*. New Delhi: Bloomsbury Publishing, 2017, Footnote 19, under the Subtitle 'The Chinese Checker' (page not mentioned).
6 *Economic Times*. New Delhi, 1 May 2019.
7 Ibid.
8 'Introduction.' ASEAN Centre for Energy. Accessed 28 October 2018. www.aseanenergy.org/about-ace/introduction/ .
9 Text of the plan of action in ASEAN Documents Series 2004. *Plan of Action to Implement the ASEAN-India Partnership for Peace, Progress and Prosperity*. Vientiane, Laos, 30 November 2004, p. 85. Accessed 23 October 2019. https://www3.nd.edu/~ggoertz/rei/reidevon.dtBase2/Files.noindex/pdf/d/ASEAN-treaties-2004.pdf .
10 *ASEAN-India Plan of Action to Implement the ASEAN-India Partnership For Peace, Progress and Prosperity* Para 2.3 Energy. Accessed 23 October 2019. https://asean.org/wp-content/uploads/images/2015/August/POA_India/ASEAN-India%20POA%20-%20FINAL.pdf .
11 Villaruel, Jimimah Joanne C. 'ASEAN-India renewable energy cooperation: Opportunities and challenges'. FSI Insights, 4, no.1. Foreign Service Institute, Government of Philippines, June 2017. Accessed 11 November 2019. www.fsi.gov.ph/wp-content/uploads/2014/08/2014-08-FSI-Insights.jpg.
12 Ibid.
13 South Asian Regional Initiative for Energy Integration. *BIMSTEC Energy Outlook 2030*. New Delhi: SARI, December 2017, p. 106. Accessed 17 October 2019. https://irade.org/SARI-EI-Report-on-BIMSTEC-Energy-Outlook-2030.pdf.
14 See endnote 2, the chapter on Bangladesh.
15 '4th BIMSTEC Summit Declaration' Kathmandu, 30–31 August 2018, annex to the declaration, para 16. Accessed 5 November 2019. www.narendramodi.in/fourth-bimstec-summit-declaration-kathmandu-nepal-august-30-31-2018--541302 .
16 Powell, Lydia. *Energy Cooperation Under BIMSTEC: Are Techno-Economic Rationales Sufficient?* ORF Issue Brief, no. 206, p. 3. New Delhi: Observer Research Foundation, 2017. (The author here may be rationalising the behaviour of the private sector but the argument makes sense on the hard ground of reality as it exists in the region.).
17 For some details see RIS, ASEAN-India Centre. *Mekong-Ganga Cooperation: Breaking Barriers and Scaling New Heights*. New Delhi: RIS, 2017, Appendix 2, pp. 13–15.
18 For more details, see endnote 2, pp. 150 and 200.
19 'India to expand gas pipeline to Myanmar through Bangladesh', 9 December 2018. Accessed 10 November 2019. http://energyinfrapost.com/india-expand-gas-pipeline-myanmar-bangladesh/.
20 Bose, Pratim Ranjan. 'Construction of India-Bangladesh pipeline to begin this month', *The Hindu Business Line,* 31 August 2018, Accessed November 2, 2019. www.thehindubusinessline.com/news/construction-of-india-bangladesh-oil-pipeline-to-begin-this-month/article24835076.ece.

21 'India-Nepal PMs launch cross-border oil pipeline; linking Motihari with Amlekhganj', *The Economic Times*, 11 September 2019. Accessed 15 October 2019. https://economictimes.indiatimes.com/industry/energy/oil-gas/narendra-modi-k-p-sharma-oli-jointly-inaugurate-motihari-amlekhganj-petroleum-product-pipeline/articleshow/71061712.cms.

22 Government of India, Ministry of Power, 'Memorandum of Understanding for Establishment of the BIMSTEC Grid Interconnection'. Accessed 30 October 2019. https://powermin.nic.in/en/content/memorandum-understanding-establishment-bimstec-grid-interconnection .

23 Ahmad, Omair. 'India eyes regional ambition through energy trade.' 10 June 2019. Accessed 28 October 2019. www.thethirdpole.net/2019/06/10/india-eyes-regional-ambitions-through-energy-trade/. Also see, Anbumozi, Venkatachalam, Ichiro Kutani, Mahendra Lama. *Energy Connectivity between Northeast India and its Neighbours*. Economic Research Institute for ASEAN and East Asia (ERIA), and Confederation of Indian Industry (CII), 2019. Accessed October 28, 2019. www.eria.org/publications/energising-connectivity-between-northeast-india-and-its-neighbours/.

24 'Indian Investors keen on Energy projects in Vietnam', *Vietnam Investment Review*, 17 April 2018. Accessed 3 November 2019. www.vir.com.vn/indian-investors-keen-on-energy-projects-in-vietnam-58147.html.

25 For details on multi-dimensional energy cooperation between India and Myanmar, see Chatterji, Rakahari, Anusuya Bose and Pratnashree Bose. *India-Myanmar Connectivity: Possibilities and Challenges*. Kolkata: Observer Research Foundation, 2015, pp. 47–62.

26 Text of the Joint Statement issued on the occasion which had three paras on energy cooperation. See: 'India-Vietnam Joint Statement during State Visit of President of Vietnam to India (3 March 2018).' MEA: Statements: Bilateral/Multilateral Documents. Ministry of External Affairs, Government of India. Accessed 25 October 2019. www.mea.gov.in/bilateral-documents.htm?dtl%2F29535%2FIndiaVietnam+Joint+Statement+during+State+visit+of+President+of+Vietnam+to+India+March+03+2018.

27 'India-Indonesia economic and commercial relations'. Embassy of India, Jakarta. 30 May 2019.Accessed on 14 October 2020. www.indianembassyjakarta.gov.in/users/assets/pdf/menu/jakarta_june14.pdf.

28 Chauhan, Priyanshi. 'Cooperation against competition: India and China in energy sector'. South Asian Voices. 16 July 2019. Accessed on 5 November 2019. https://southasianvoices.org/cooperation-against-competition-india-china-energy-sector/.

29 See the Joint Statement issued at the end of the visit of India's President to Vietnam in November 2018, 'India-Vietnam joint statement during state visit of president to Vietnam.' MEA: Visits: Outgoing Visit: Visit Detail. Ministry of External Affairs, Government of India, 21 November 2018. https://mea.gov.in/outoging-visit-detail.htm?30615%2FIndiaVietnam+Joint+Statement+during+State+Visit+of+President+to+Vietnam. Also, Joint Statement on the visit of Indian Vice-President on 9–12 May 2019, to Vietnam, 'Official visit of Vice President of India to Vietnam (9–12 May, 2019).' MEA: Statements: Press Releases. Ministry of External Affairs, Government of India, 12 May 2019. https://mea.gov.in/press-releases.htm?dtl%2F31246%2FOfficial+Visit+of+Vice+President+of+India+to+Vietnam+912+May+2019.

30 Sethi, Nitin. 'Pipped to post: India loses Myanmar's gas to China, well almost'. *Down to Earth*. 4 July 2015. Accessed on 27 October 2019. www.downtoearth.org.in/news/pipped-to-the-post-7808. Also see, Hong, Zhao. 'China-Myanmar energy cooperation and its regional implications.' *Journal of Current Southeast Asian Affairs*, 30, no. 4 (2011): 89–109.

7

INDIA'S ACT EAST POLICY

The energy dimension

G.V.C. Naidu

If there is one foreign policy issue that has been very successful as far as India is concerned is the Look East policy that was launched in the aftermath of the cold war. It has since been upgraded as the Act East policy after Narendra Modi ascended to power in 2014 to underscore the ever-growing salience of the region towards India's east. Indeed, East Asia's significance is not limited just to India but virtually to the entire world. As it rises economically, the global centre of gravity is inexorably shifting to this region and it is not an exaggeration to contend that what happens here will have significant implications for the rest of the world. In every possible parameter one can think of, East Asia is likely to be far ahead of any other region in the coming years. It is the fastest growing region, has the largest and fastest growing markets, is economically the most dynamic in every sense of the term, three out of four largest economies are located here and will undoubtedly be the driver of the global economy in the coming years. Importantly, the intra-regional economic cooperation is growing rapidly and that is aiding greater economic integration. A number of free trade agreements – both bilateral and multilateral – have been finalised including the mega Regional Comprehensive Economic Partnership (RCEP) and the Comprehensive and Progressive Trans-Pacific Partnership (CPTPP), which, in turn, will result eventually in the emergence of the world's largest common market. All these developments are also helping to develop a robust regional value chain. Against this backdrop, it is little wonder that India has been trying to step up its engagement as its economic future lies in this region and hence does not have many options other than constantly finding ways to hitch its economic wagon to this region. To understand to what extent it has been successful in this effort, one needs to keep in mind the fact that it is a two-way process but what matters the most are the proactive and innovative initiatives that New Delhi is taking.

From an Indian perspective, while East Asia in general constitutes the main focal point, the Southeast Asian subregion holds greater significance not merely because of strong historical and cultural connections and geographical proximity and but for strategic and economic reasons as well. The repeated enunciation that regional organisation ASEAN is at the heart of India's policy is a testimony to this. Both from geostrategic and geoeconomic perspectives, Southeast Asia is critical to Indian interests and that has warranted India to evolve a multi-faceted policy over the years. A particular dimension of this engagement is energy cooperation, which for some reason or other has neither generated much interest nor has witnessed notable progress in actual terms despite the fact that there are five countries in the region that have fairly large proven hydrocarbon reserves. In the following, the chapter endeavours to map out the distinctive contours of the Act East policy and the prospects for energy cooperation in terms of India's engagement of Southeast Asia.

Act East Policy

The backdrop to the relaunch of India's engagement of Southeast Asia in 2014 in what is purported to be a more invigorated policy is, in fact, a continuation of its previous incarnation, the Look East policy with an expanded agenda. Initiated in the early 1990s in the wake of the economic crisis that the country was faced with resulting in ushering in market reforms, which sought to emulate the development philosophies of East Asia, the Look East policy's principal aims were to attract investments from this region and also align its economy increasingly to the world's economically the most vibrant region. Of course, there were also other factors that prompted New Delhi to embark on this policy such as a rapidly growing Chinese role and influence in the region in the aftermath of the end of the Cold War and also to revive and strengthen political contacts that had witnessed a steady decline during much of the Cold War. This policy resulted in India gradually becoming a factor in ASEAN-led multilateralism such as becoming a Dialogue and Summit Partner and securing membership in most other region-wide mechanisms that ASEAN led such as the ASEAN Regional Forum, East Asia Summit, ASEAN Defence Ministers Meeting-Plus, etc. Simultaneously, India also sought stronger economic relations by forging comprehensive economic cooperation/partnership agreements with ASEAN collectively and many other countries individually such as Singapore, Malaysia, Japan and South Korea. India was also involved in the creation of RCEP but withdrew at the last minute due to concerns about the Chinese goods inundating the Indian market in the absence of certain measures in RCEP.

The Look East policy began to take root mainly in three areas – political, strategic and economic. While politically developing institutional linkages with ASEAN and participation in regional multilateralism constitutes the key aspects, strategically fashioning a variety of defence and security links and understandings comprise the main focus. The third dimension, that is, economic relations, have certainly come a long way when seen in the backdrop of India being almost irrelevant to the regional dynamics in the 1990s, yet it remains the weakest leg.

In order to expand the footprint of the Act East policy, to further deepen relations by including several other dimensions, and to enhance its overall involvement in regional affairs, it became imperative for New Delhi to intensify its engagement with newer initiatives. The Act East policy, thus, is a reflection of proactive measures that the Indian government purported to be taking. It has become vital for India to evolve a robust strategy to engage East Asia even while the region undergoes fundamental shifts in its economic and security composition. In any case, India's stakes and interests in this region have been growing rapidly and that warrants greater attention.

Thus, the Act East policy is nothing but an indication of India's stepped up engagement with East Asia. It may be remembered that the government, as in the case of the Look East policy, has not published any policy paper or indicated what new things will be included in this. To be sure, this policy is not a replacement of the Look East policy but an extension of it. The idea appears to be to expand the purview of the new policy by bringing in new elements and facets that can further deepen India's relations with East Asia, on one hand, and strengthen those links that are weak, on the other. Quite obviously, it has been necessitated by India's rapidly growing economic and strategic interests in the region. Now let us look at the new aspects that are being emphasised.

As noted, East Asia is witnessing profound shifts and a notable aspect is its rapidly rising economic significance in the world. There is no question that this region will soon emerge as the major driver of global economic development. It is not simply the rise of China or India but the entire East Asian region comprising nearly 50 per cent of the world's population is on the rise – a phenomenon unprecedented in history. The regional economic cooperation is growing leading to greater integration. It is these aspects that matter the most for India. If, for instance, one takes the example of trade, India's trade with its immediate neighbours in South Asia (the SAARC countries) was less than 7 per cent in 2016–17, whereas it was about 13 per cent with the European Union and nearly 30 per cent with East Asia. India's trade has been growing the fastest with this region than any other. Similarly, some of the major investors in India are from East Asia.

There is no question that India's economic future is in East Asia; however, economic links are weak when compared to the other big powers. While all other major powers were expanding and consolidating their economic relations, India remained on the margins. There was a realisation that India would have to find new avenues of cooperation, which could contribute to the overall deepening of relations with Southeast Asia. 'Make in India' has become the leitmotif of India's foreign policy under Modi. In the Act East policy that Prime Minister Modi has announced, economic relations are taking pride of place since they happen to be the weakest link.

The second aspect in many ways connected to the above is poor connectivity between India and the countries of East Asia, which is a major impediment for relatively weak bonds. Connectivity is not simply physical such as road, rail, air and sea, but also includes institutional and people-to-people connectivity. Whereas India has fared better in forging institutional connectivity, it has a long way to go on other fronts. Currently, an all-weather Tri-Nation Highway is being built involving India, Myanmar and Thailand through the Northeast. Once that is completed, theoretically goods can travel all the way to Singapore covering all the countries in the mainland Southeast Asia. It can also link up to southwestern China such as Yunnan. Second, many sea ports are being modernised and expanded, and new ones are being built along India's east coast. In terms of air connectivity, there are a large number of flights from almost all of major airports from India that fly but, unfortunately, most of them are limited to cities such as Bangkok, Kuala Lumpur and Singapore. For instance, there is no direct flight to Jakarta, capital of Indonesia, the largest country in Southeast Asia. Air connectivity is very important because it is the only way people-to-people contacts can be increased. As India's economic links improve, it is expected that air connectivity too will get better.

The third aspect is to enhance and capitalise on its 'soft power' potential in East Asia. The consciousness that India is an ancient civilisation and that it had hugely influenced virtually the entire Asian region from Central Asia to East Asia has always been quite high. It is particularly more pronounced in the case of the region towards its east with which it had established links more than two millennia back. Strong historical, cultural and other connections associated with these are often said to be a pivotal source of soft power. India is one of those very few countries that can boast of age-old connections with Southeast Asia. The enormous cultural and influences that India exercised through these ancient links are far more enduring and robust and hence could potentially become repositories of soft power influence if nurtured and channelled appropriately. There is belated recognition in India that the ancient cultural and spiritual bonds could be made use of more gainfully. Thus, the strengthening of cultural and other links has become a part and parcel of the new revamped Act East policy.

India's economic relations

As far as East Asia is concerned, it should be reasonably clear that economics is security. Much of the security discourse in many ways is dependent on the nature of economic relations. Not many realise that this region has been peaceful and stable for more than four decades except for a few skirmishes and occasional tensions over territorial disputes. It is a far cry from the times when this region witnessed communal riots, armed insurgencies and economic backwardness during the previous four decades of highly destructive wars, and as a corollary this was politically the most instable region in the world. In almost all major wars that the region witnessed, such as the Korean War, India–China War, Indochina wars, China–Soviet War and the China–Vietnam War, the one common factor was China's involvement in all of them. Post-1979 reforms in China, not a single major armed conflict has taken place. By any stretch of the imagination, a major war is unlikely to occur for the foreseeable future. The region has successfully used this rare historic opportunity of peace and stability to focus on economic development. It has been so successful in doing this that the global centre of gravity has already shifted to the East from the Trans-Atlantic West that dominated global economic activity for nearly three centuries. The single most important factor, among others, that has contributed to the present state of affairs is unprecedented economic cooperation that the countries have forged.

It is, thus, pivotal that major developments in the regional economy need to be factored in any assessment of India's relations with East Asia generally and Southeast Asia specially, especially in the context of the Act East policy. India remains relatively not a major player in East Asian affairs compared either to its GDP (US$2.7 trillion in nominal and US$10.3 trillion in PPP terms in 2018) or its market size – 1.3 billion people. It is the third largest economy in Asia in nominal exchange terms and the second largest in PPP and its economy is much larger than all ten ASEAN countries put together measured in PPP. Yet, it remains a marginal player in the East Asian economic equilibrium and punches far below its weight. Its performance either in attracting investments or in trade dwarfs in front of much smaller countries such as Vietnam and Thailand. That is because of its relatively weak economic links with East Asia. For instance, the country that is closest to India is Japan but its share of direct investments is less than 1 per cent of its total overseas investments. The same is true for trade. Japanese investments in and trade with Vietnam, a country about 1/14th the size of India in terms of population, are much more than India. There is no question that India's trade at around 27 per cent with East Asia is the largest compared to any other region and is growing the fastest; nonetheless, from an East Asian perspective India remains economically a marginal player. India's participation in the rapidly growing East Asian regional value chain is still very low at around 15 per cent compared to China's more than 85 per cent. Hence, it is important that India spares no effort to align itself with East Asia in order reap the benefits of the region's unprecedented dynamism. This was one of the major objectives of the Act East policy when it was announced.

India–ASEAN economic relations

The following table gives an idea about India's trade with the ASEAN countries (Figure 7.1 and Table 7.1).

India's real standing in Southeast Asian economic relations can only be understood if seen relative to other major economies. China's trade with ASEAN has gone up from US$213 billion in 2010 to $514 billion in 2017 and is likely to be more than 570 billion in 2018. The Japan–ASEAN trade stood at US$218 billion in 2017; however, Japan's biggest strength is its huge investible capital. It has invested more than $400 billion in Southeast Asia, which makes it the largest investor in

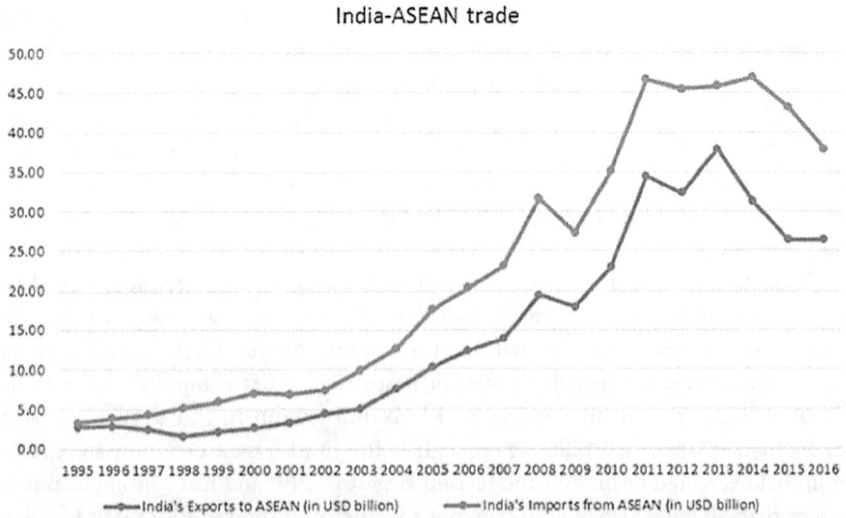

FIGURE 7.1 India–ASEAN trade. Authors, based on data from the Ministry of Trade and Industry, Government of India

TABLE 7.1 India's trade balance with ASEAN members (USD million)

Country	*2008*	*2009*	*2010*	*2001*	*2012*	*2013*	*2014*	*2015*	*2016*	*2017*
Brunei	−300	−462	−186	176	−725	−696	−900	−577	−424	−471
Cambodia	50	38	53	80	100	109	137	103	66	76
Indonesia	−3533	−4991	−5147	−7135	−8205	−10035	−10808	−10930	−9161	−12150
Lao	4	20	−12	−52	−113	−66	4	−91	−148	−205
Malaysia	−4416	−1459	−2446	−5205	−6370	−4008	−6372	−4622	−4453	−3088
Myanmar	−677	−985	−848	−791	−817	−699	−532	−160	70	329
Philippines	523	383	407	561	624	960	1035	790	1016	901
Singapore	365	674	1824	7917	7089	6482	2574	295	852	3855
Thailand	−590	−1092	−1804	−1843	−2008	−1548	−2202	−2505	−2355	−2769
Vietnam	1612	1296	1488	1864	1677	2465	3729	2654	2849	3969
ASEAN	−6963	−6579	−6669	−4428	−8747	−7036	−13335	−15044	−11686	−9553

Source: *Direction of Trade Statistics*. IMF. 2018

Southeast Asia. Whereas, in the case of India it went up from $56 billion in 2010 to was about $72 billion in 2017. The above in many ways indicates where India stands vis-à-vis other Asian major economies. Bilateral investment has also witnessed a progressive development, from US$10.7 billion in 2010 to US$15.8 billion in 2015 (Figure 7.2 and Tables 7.2 to 7.5).[1]

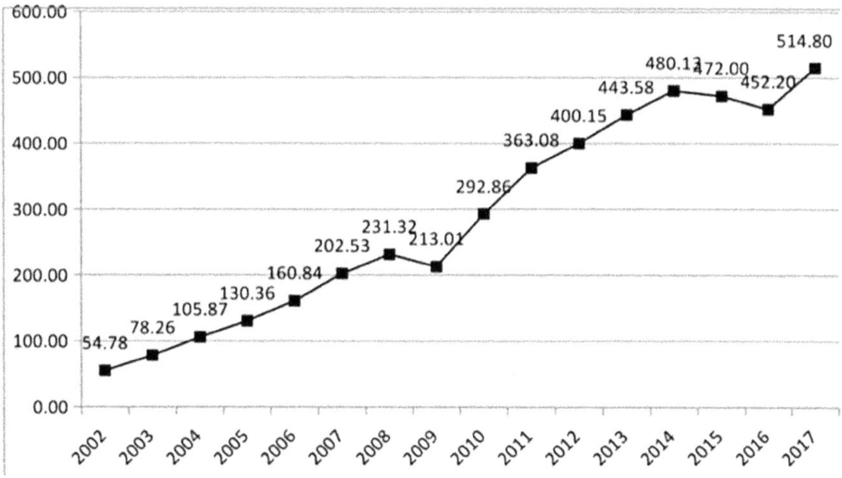

FIGURE 7.2 China–ASEAN trade. Authors, based on data from the Direction of Trade Statistics. IMF.

TABLE 7.2 India's imports from select ASEAN countries ($mn)

Country	*2013*	*2014*	*2015*	*2016*	*2017*
Indonesia	15232.09	15260.84	13883.31	12303.98	16229.43
Malaysia	9061.16	10976.59	9563.19	8650.69	8898.34
Myanmar	1372.73	1401.03	1023.70	1086.54	739.60
Vietnam	2838.08	2779.38	2683.83	3107.45	4147.51

Source: Direction of Trade Statistics. IMF.

TABLE 7.3 India's exports to select ASEAN countries ($mn)

Country	*2013*	*2014*	*2015*	*2016*	*2017*
Indonesia	5197.41	4453.09	2953.34	3143.36	3763.72
Malaysia	5053.54	4604.96	4940.74	4198.04	5548.70
Myanmar	673.70	869.04	864.18	1156.35	1058.68
Vietnam	5302.62	6508.22	5337.68	5956.33	8121.12

Source: Direction of Trade Statistics. IMF.

TABLE 7.4 FDI in ASEAN

	Cumulative	*Share*
Japan	101.4	12.9
United States	100.6	12.8
Netherlands	51.6	6.6
China	**47.0**	**6.0**
Hong Kong (China)	40.6	5.2
Luxembourg	32.6	4.2
S. Korea	27.9	3.6
United Kingdom	25.6	3.3
Australia	21.7	2.8
Taiwan Province of China	14.7	1.9
India	**14.4**	**1.8**
Ireland	11.0	1.4
France	9.9	1.3
Canada	9.7	1.2
Seychelles	7.5	1.0
Top 15 non-ASEAN investors	516.2	66.0

TABLE 7.5 Indian energy investments in Southeast Asia

Indian company	*Name of JV or WOS*	*Host country*	*Industry*	*Investment value ($ mn)*
Oil India	Oil India International Pte Ltd	Singapore	Mining	824
Bharat Petroresources	BPRL International Singapore Pte Ltd	Singapore	Mining	772
Indian Oil Corporation	IOCL Singapore Pte Ltd	Singapore	Mining	662
Indian Oil Corporation	IOCL Singapore Pte Ltd	Singapore	Mining	303
Dee Development Engineers	Dee Piping Systems (Thailand) Co Ltd	Thailand	Manufacturing	1
ONGC Videsh	Petroleum Production Sharing Contract	Myanmar	Mining	0.8
SMS	SMS Mines Indonesia	Indonesia	Mining	0.6
ONGC Videsh	Petroleum Production Sharing Contract	Myanmar	Manufacturing	0.48

Compiled from various sources.

A few Indian MNEs and SOEs have invested in extractive industries in ASEAN, primarily in oil and gas exploration and production, as well as in coal mining. These companies include Essar, Century Ply, Jubilant Oil and Gas, ONGC Videsh, Reliance Industries and Oil India, which have operations in Myanmar. Punj Lloyd is involved in a gas and oil pipeline in Myanmar. Tata Power is involved in coal mining and power generation activities in Indonesia and Myanmar, while Essar Global and Monnet Ispat are involved with coal mining in Indonesia (Tables 7.6 and 7.7).

TABLE 7.6 Natural resources exploration

Access to natural resources	Ispat and energy investment in coal mining in Indonesia
Oil and gas exploration and production	ONGC Videsh in Vietnam and Myanmar for extraction of crude petroleum and natural gas
Mining of coals	Adani Welspun in Thailand for oil and exploration and production

TABLE 7.7 Indian FDI in ASEAN (000s US$)

Industry	*2012*	*2013*	*2014*	*2015*	*2016*	*2012–2016*
Agriculture, forestry and fishing	8.7	4.6	4.7	3.5	4.4	25.8
Mining and quarrying	(0.7)	0.4	(0.1)	0.2	2.9	2.7
Manufacturing	109.4	66.2	34.2	(131.4)	20.2	98.6
Services	7,193.7	2,036.9	1,177.4	1,089.3	1,021.1	12,518.4
Of which: Wholesale and retail trade; repair of motor vehicles and motorcycles	633.9	192.1	25.1	131.5	199.0	1,181.6
Transportation and storage	(451.5)	(17.0)	36.6	0.4	41.0	(390.5)
Finance and insurance	5,619.6	1,067.6	771.5	525.7	(578.4)	7,405.9
Real estate	9.1	1.3	428.7	296.0	276.2	1,011.4
Total	7,311.1	2,108.1	1,216.2	961.6	1,048.6	12,645.5

Energy connectivity

India's national interest, and even national security, is premised on achieving high economic growth. The challenges posed by stubbornly high inflation, poor industrial growth, and a sluggish and debt-ridden global economy can be met only by a resurgent and economically strong India. Energy is a key component of such economic growth. India's 'Energy Elasticity of GDP' ratio stands at 0.8; a 10 per cent growth in GDP would require 8 per cent growth in energy supply. This ratio is adversely affected by increased expenditure on imports of fossil fuels, especially if their prices rise as well. Some writers have proposed, in response, that India achieve 'energy independence' (self-sufficiency in energy supply). Such proposals, while correctly emphasising the role of oil and natural gas imports in energy security, remain more visionary than practical.[2]

Connectivity has been one of the major areas of thrust under the Act East policy. Connectivity has several dimensions such as physical connectivity, digital connectivity, people-to-people connectivity and institutional connectivity. While physical connectivity includes road, rail, air and sea connections, institutional connectivity comprises establishing solid links with various institutional mechanisms both at the bilateral as well as regional level. Now India is trying to establish energy connectivity with its neighbours such as Nepal and Bhutan, which have immense hydro potential, and Bangladesh and Myanmar, which have vast hydrocarbon reserves, especially gas. The energy connectivity denotes not merely importing petroleum and natural gas that India badly needs for its rapidly expanding economy but also connecting electricity and gas grid where possible. Entering into multilateral complex swap arrangements is another facet of energy connectivity. For instance, India is trying for a swap arrangement on natural gas along with Russia, China and Myanmar. There is obviously a strong geopolitical dimension to the energy connectivity as it would help establish mutually beneficial relations with neighbouring countries. Thus, the energy connectivity has several facets and hence has been attached considerable significance under the Modi government. It is particularly pertinent with respect to Myanmar and Bangladesh and hence ONGC Videsh Ltd has been actively involved in prospecting for hydrocarbons.

India–Southeast Asia energy cooperation

In terms of cooperation with Southeast Asia, energy has always figured as one of the top areas; however, it has for some reason failed to make much progress except for involvement in oil and gas exploration in the South China Sea in collaboration with Vietnam. It is indeed surprising that, given Southeast Asia's close geographical proximity and India's relentless efforts for energy security, very little movement has taken place in this direction. Even by way of investments, India's involvement in the region is limited. True, the oil reserves in Southeast Asia have been limited compared to the Middle East, Africa or the Russian Far East, but there are huge proven gas reserves in most countries such as Indonesia, Malaysia, Brunei, Vietnam and Myanmar. Insofar as India's concrete cooperation is concerned, although efforts began in the mid-1990s, actual cooperation is still limited and that too basically limited to Vietnam and Myanmar. Perhaps it may be about time to revisit several aspects of energy cooperation with some of these countries as that would not merely enhance energy security but would also contribute to further strengthening of economic relations, which, as noted, have not made the anticipated growth in India's quest to engage Southeast Asia robustly.

Energy includes numerous aspects from the production of electricity from renewable and non-renewable sources, its transmission, and its efficient use. The other dimensions of energy are fossil fuels and a range of issues related to them from evolving a suitable strategy to ensure their uninterrupted supplies, the security of their transportation without disruption and their efficient use for various purposes. Thus, it is important to delineate the focus of the study. In the following, the chapter tries to assess three dimensions of India's energy cooperation with select Southeast Asian countries such as Indonesia, Malaysia, Vietnam and Myanmar. First, the chapter will discuss Indian involvement in the exploration of hydrocarbons in one or more of these countries. Second, the chapter will explore energy cooperation in general including in the non-renewable fields. Finally, the chapter analyses exports of finished petroleum products to these countries.

India–Vietnam energy cooperation

Among all the countries, Vietnam was the first country India entered into an agreement on energy cooperation, which can be traced to 1988 when the Indian public sector oil major, Oil and Natural Gas Corporation Videsh Limited (OVL), ventured to invest in the South China Sea in the waters claimed by Vietnam. The OVL held 45 per cent, British Petroleum 35 per cent and PetroVietnam 20 per cent. After a few hiccups and controversies, the OVL continued with drilling and claimed that it had begun commercial production of gas in January 2003 and achieved a significant milestone when its gas sales revenue from Block 6.1 crossed US$100 million by December 2004.[3] Subsequently, the company acquired two exploration blocks – Block 127 and Block 128 – in 2006. While Block 127 was relinquished due to poor prospects, the other block was retained. The first extension followed China putting the area under Block 128 for global bidding. These two blocks especially have acquired considerable geopolitical salience as China has claimed sovereignty over much of the South China Sea and thus raised objections to joint exploration activity between India and Vietnam. Despite continued efforts, the OVL has not been successful even in Block 128 and media reports suggested that it would withdraw from this block as well due to commercial unviability. Although it was denied, it was apparent from the fact that the OVL wanted to swap this block with another because 'OVL doesn't want to drill there given the risks involved.' It has 'requested to swap the block with some other block,' said one person aware of the development, requesting anonymity.'[4] From a company's point of view, Block 128 is not economically viable but from a geopolitical perspective, it is very important for

India, for abandoning the site would amount to acquiescing to China's sovereignty contention, which means weakening Vietnam's stand. However, the fact that India continues to operate here indicates that geopolitical factors and strategic partnership with Vietnam have outweighed the economic considerations.

Interestingly, there seem to be efforts to expand the energy cooperation between India and Vietnam beyond hydrocarbons as references have been made to enhance cooperation on 'peaceful uses of atomic energy' between the two countries. They have entered into the Framework Agreement on Cooperation in the Peaceful Uses of Atomic Energy in December 2016 and have signed an MOU between the Institute of Atomic Energy of Viet Nam and India's Global Center for Nuclear Energy Partnership in March 2018.

During President Tran Dai Quang's visit to India in March 2018 both sides decided to expand energy cooperation. The Joint Statement said,

> President Tran Dai Quang welcomed Indian companies to invest in renewable energy and energy conservation projects in Viet Nam and thanked India for extending support to Viet Nam in building a research reactor for the purpose of peaceful uses of atomic energy … The two sides agreed to step up the implementation of agreements signed, and to hold the first meeting of the Joint Committee at the earliest.[5]

It explicitly mentions India's assistance in the building of a 'research' nuclear reactor in Vietnam without giving details whether it is a prelude to building full-fledged reactors that can produce power. Vietnam has been toying with the idea of constructing several civilian nuclear power plants since the mid-1990s. Several countries from Russia, the U.S., Japan to South Korea have shown enormous interest in participating in this mammoth programme[6] but nothing much has come to fruition so far probably because of huge costs involved and, of course, safety concerns especially after the 2011 Fukushima accident.

More recently, during the visit of Indian President Ram Nath Kovind to Vietnam in November 2018, the joint statement stated:

> The two Leaders agreed to continue promoting bilateral investment, including cooperation projects between PVN and ONGC in oil and gas exploration on land, continental shelf and Exclusive Economic Zone (EEZ) of Viet Nam, and encouraged the two sides to be more active in identifying models for cooperation, including those involving third country. The Vietnamese side welcomed and agreed to create facilitating conditions for Indian companies to invest into new thermal energy and renewable energy projects in Viet Nam.[7]

Thus, if India was indeed involved in building an atomic reactor, that would be a major breakthrough in which case Vietnam will be the first country that it would have ventured into.

Myanmar

One of the reasons why New Delhi decided to re-engage Myanmar in the early 1990s even though the military was in power (because of which India maintained minimal interactions) was the vast deposits of oil and natural gas that were found both offshore and onshore. Myanmar is estimated to have about 600 million barrels of oil and around 90 trillion cubic feet of gas, which is almost as much as Indonesia has. The discovery of vast gas reserves in the Gulf of Bengal attracted a lot of attention and intense bidding, most prominently by India and China.

India joined a consortium led by Daewoo of South Korea (60 per cent) with Korea Gas Corporation (10 per cent) and the OVL (20 per cent) and Oil and the Gas Authority of India Ltd. (10 per cent) for exploration in blocks off the Arakan coast. According to the OVL, in October 2013, ONGC Videsh was awarded two onshore blocks, namely B-2 and EP-3, in the Myanmar Onshore Bidding Round 2013. Block B2 is located in the Zebyutaung–Nandaw area and geologically in the Northern part of the Chindwin Basin of Myanmar and Block EP-3 is located in the Central Burma Basin (BagoYoma Sub Basin). PSCs for these blocks were signed on 8 August 2014.[8]

In 2007, consequent to the award of 100 per cent participating interests in the AD-2, AD-3 and Ad-9 Blocks, the OVL committed to invest US$150 million spread over several years.[9] The OVL merely mentions on its homepage that it is involved in six projects in Myanmar, although no details are provided.

The Indian Minister of Petroleum and Natural Gas, Dharmendra Pradhan, stated that the Numaligarh refinery in Assam was exploring options to build diesel storage and distribution sector in Myanmar. The Indian Oil Corporation Ltd is also working with Myanmar companies in setting up LPG storage facilities, and Petro LNG Ltd is working on setting up an LNG terminal. The Hydrocarbon Vision 2030 for North East India envisages a natural gas pipeline from Numaligarh towards Sittwe (in Myanmar) in different phases. The gas pipeline will open future possibilities of gas exchange and grid connectivity.[10]

In a significant development, India sent the first consignment of 30 MT high-speed diesel from NRL refinery in Assam located some 420 kilometres from the border to Myanmar in September 2017 through the National Highway 37 across the Moreh Custom Checkpoint on the Indian side and Tamu Custom Checkpoint on the Myanmar side. These supplies, especially to the northern regions of Myanmar, have acquired enormous significance because of poor connectivity, especially during the rainy season. NRL had already exported 1700 MT of paraffin wax to Myanmar. It was a special privilege for India to contribute hand-made wax candles to the 2500-year-old Shwedagon Pagoda.[11] The OVL already maintains an office in Yangon and more Indian oil and gas companies are planning to set up offices in Myanmar.[12]

A major issue that India has to grapple with is the intense competition that China poses. Given its deep pockets and politically close links with the ruling elite in Myanmar and sharing[which shares] a border with one of the vibrant and rapidly growing provinces of China, that is Yunnan, which in turn is well connected to the rest of the country, Beijing is far better placed than India in establishing strong energy links with Myanmar. Moreover, China is not only the largest trading partner and largest investor but also the biggest aid provider to Myanmar. Myanmar is also one of the key target countries in China's Belt and Road Initiative. Just as with the massive China–Pakistan Economic Corridor, Beijing is also building the China–Myanmar Economic Corridor involving investments worth several billion US dollars.

The other problem is transporting the gas from Myanmar to India. The most cost-effective way to bring Myanmar gas to India is by pipelines provided Bangladesh allows India to lay the pipelines through its territory. Reportedly, Dhaka is making too many demands such as reducing the bilateral trade deficit, duty-free movement of goods and transit rights to transport energy from Nepal and Bhutan to Bangladesh. The other way is to bring gas by building pipelines through Northeast India but this will cost almost three times as much besides many other logistical problems. The best way is a tripartite agreement between India, Myanmar and Bangladesh so that refined petroleum products can be exported to Bangladesh and Myanmar by India and gas can be imported from Myanmar and possibly from Bangladesh as well.

Indonesia

India also took the initiative for energy cooperation with Indonesia in the early 2000s. Indeed, these two created several mechanisms to promote energy cooperation in an expansive and comprehensive way covering a variety of areas such as oil and gas, renewable energy, coal, research and development on energy, technology transfer, etc. Eager to supply crude oil, it was reported that Indonesia was willing to send two cargos of oil to evaluate if Indian companies could refine it[13] but it did not materialise.

Three different Joint Working Groups on Oil and Gas, Coal, and on New and Renewable Energy have been created. To further strengthen bilateral energy cooperation, an India–Indonesia Energy Forum to be led by cabinet ministers was launched and its first meeting was held in 2017 to which the above mentioned three Working Groups presented their reports.

> A Memorandum of Understanding between the Ministry of Petroleum and Natural Gas, Government of India and the Ministry of Energy and Mineral Resources of the Republic of Indonesia on cooperation in the field of Oil and Gas was signed on the occasion. The MOU seeks to establish a cooperative institutional framework to facilitate and to enhance bilateral cooperation in the field of oil and gas sectors on the basis of equality and mutual benefit.[14]

India and Indonesia have also agreed to create a policy framework on oil and gas infrastructure development, opportunities in capacity building and business opportunities in oil and gas sector in both countries. The main issues of discussion were coal resources development, capacity building, research and development and issues and concerns of the private sector. The Working Group on New and Renewable Energy discussed

> policy framework and investment opportunities in India and Indonesia. Both sides agreed to focus on Capacity building, Exchange of Scientific and Technological information and data,Transfer ofTechnology on Non-commercial basis in bio fuel and geothermal area, Development on Joint Research or Technical Projects on subject of Mutual interest, Encouragement and promotion of investment and Encouragement of policy Dialogue in solar park.[15]

While there are continued efforts to forge broad-based energy cooperation between the two countries, the importing of coal from Indonesia has emerged as the most significant energy item for India. For instance, thermal coal imports jumped 19 per cent to 172 million tons in 2018, the highest since 2014. And the value of all coal imports for the year ending 31 December 2018 was 28.7 per cent higher at $24.25 billion than in 2017. Importantly, Indonesia provided more than 61 per cent of India's thermal coal imports, while South Africa accounted for 22 per cent and the United States more than 7 per cent. Indonesia is likely to remain a preferred option because its coal is cheaper and due to lower freight costs.[16] Although India does not import much hydrocarbons, the prospects to forge a strong energy partnership with Indonesia encompassing a large canvass of issues from investments in prospecting for oil and gas, technology transfers, R&D sharing, especially in renewable sources, efficient transmission and use of electricity, etc.

Malaysia

The other Southeast Asian country that has fairly large hydrocarbon reserves is Malaysia. However, India does not seem to have any hydrocarbon-related investments. Except for a mention about cooperation in new and non-renewable energy, there is no concrete cooperation agreement on energy. The Joint Statement issued during Prime Minister Narendra Modi's visit to Malaysia in November 2015 stated:

> Sustainable Energy development has been a key component towards achieving energy security in the future with both Malaysia and India having actively pursued to increase renewable energy sources so as to strengthen their energy security while increasing energy access. Noting that, both sides agreed to set up a Joint Working Group on New and Renewable Energy at the earliest that would serve as a good platform for both countries to exchange ideas and forge mutually beneficial collaboration. [17]

Conclusion

It is a well-established fact that energy is a critical aspect of a country's economic development and hence ensuring energy security continues to be one of the top priorities of India. The issue of ensuring reliable oil and gas supplies began in the mid-1970s in the wake of conflicts in the Middle East and the subsequent use of oil as a strategic weapon. As the Indian economy started to expand rapidly, it became imperative to evolve an elaborate strategy to not only guarantee an uninterrupted supply of hydrocarbons but also to look at energy in a comprehensive fashion encompassing its various dimensions, including harnessing new and renewable energy and efficient use energy sources. As part of this exercise, the ONGC Videsh Ltd has been tasked with finding sources of hydrocarbons both within India as well as overseas. Thus, OVL has invested nearly US$35 billion in many countries from Africa to the Soviet Far East and from Venezuela to Southeast Asia. As far as Southeast Asia is concerned, until recently much of the focus has been on Vietnam and Myanmar and that, too, limited to investments in prospecting for oil and gas but it has yielded only limited success. With the launch of the Act East policy by the Modi government in 2004 with an attempt to reinvigorate its engagement with East Asia, several new dimensions have been identified that could deepen and strengthen India's relations especially with Southeast Asia. Having realised that India has remained on the margins when it came to economic relations and since economics constitutes the core of both East Asian geopolitics as well as geoeconomics, it became crucial for New Delhi to craft a new economic policy that would help both in qualitatively enhancing India's economic links and make itself a key player in the evolving East Asian economic equilibrium. One of them is the energy dimension. India somehow was not enthused by the Southeast Asian hydrocarbons except in Vietnam where it became involved in prospecting for oil and gas in the late 1980s. The OVL managed to produce gas commercially only much later after becoming embroiled in some controversy. The blocks that it acquired later on turned out to be economically unviable. While Block 127 was returned, it is still involved in Block 128 mainly for geopolitical reasons. A crucial energy dimension is India's involvement in building a research nuclear reactor in Vietnam, which potentially can pave the way for constructing larger civilian commercial nuclear reactors.

In Myanmar, India has been facing intense competition from China, which has been aggressively seeking to secure exploration rights. India has managed to get a few good blocks where gas is being produced commercially. Importantly, India is exporting refined petroleum products such as high-speed diesel to Myanmar. New Delhi is also trying to expand energy links by building LNG storage facilities. A major impediment has been transporting natural gas to India. The cheaper way is to use gas pipelines through Bangladesh but that approach has not materialised. With Indonesia, India has begun an Energy Forum encompassing not merely natural gas (which Indonesia has proven large reserves) but by including other aspects such as renewable energy, technology transfer, research and development in energy, etc. Although not very successful in importing gas, India has emerged as one of the largest markets for Indonesian coal.

India's energy engagement with Southeast Asia, especially the three key countries – Vietnam, Myanmar and Indonesia – has multiple benefits. Besides strengthening economic bonds and serving geopolitical interests, it would also contribute to India's energy security efforts. For that, it is important to build energy connectivity with this region.

Notes

1 CEIC. 2016. Accessed 2 November 2020. www.ceicdata.com/en; Ministry of Commerce, People's Republic of China 2016.
2 'India setting up energy cooperation network with neighbours: Dharmendra Pradhan.' *The Financial Express*. 7 August 2017. Accessed 18 September 2018. www.financialexpress.com/industry/india-setting-up-energy-cooperation-network-with-neighbours-dharmendra-pradhan/797722/.
3 'ONGC Videsh Realizes US$ 100 Million from Vietnam Project.' *Rigzone*. 10 January 2005. Accessed 16 March 2005. www.rigzone.com/news/oil_gas/a/19303/ongc_videsh_realizes_us_100_million_from_vietnam_project/.
4 'ONGC Videsh wants to swap South China Sea block with another in Vietnam.' *Mint*. 4 March 2019. Accessed 5 March 2019. www.livemint.com/industry/energy/ongc-videsh-wants-to-swap-south-china-sea-block-with-another-in-vietnam-1551650387112.html.
5 Ministry of External Affairs, Government of India. *India-Vietnam Joint Statement during State visit of President of Vietnam to India*. New Delhi, 2018. Accessed 4 March 2018. www.mea.gov.in/bilateral-documents.htm?dtl/29535/IndiaVietnam+Joint+Statement+during+State+visit+of+President+of+Vietnam+to+India+March+03+2018.
6 For details, see: 'Nuclear Power in Vietnam.' World Nuclear Association. Accessed 2 April 2019. www.world-nuclear.org/information-library/country-profiles/countries-t-z/vietnam.aspx.
7 Ministry of External Affairs, Government of India. *India-Vietnam Joint Statement during State Visit of President to Vietnam*. 21 November 2018. Accessed 21 October 2020. www.mea.gov.in/bilateral-documents.htm?dtl/30615/IndiaVietnam_Joint_Statement_during_State_Visit_of_President_to_Vietnam.
8 Oil and Natural Gas Corporation Limited. 'ONGC Videsh Limited (OVL).' Accessed 20 October 2020. www.ongcindia.com/wps/wcm/connect/en/about-ongc/subsidiaries/ongc-videsh-limited/.
9 'ONGC to invest $150 million in 3 new offshore blocks in Myanmar.' 24 September 2007. Accessed 20 October 2020. www.domain-b.com/companies/companies_o/ongc/20070924_invest.htm.
10 *Assessing India's Connectivity with Its Neighbourhood*. New Delhi: Confederation of Indian Industries, 2018. Accessed 25 February 2018. www.vifindia.org/sites/default/files/Assessing-India-s-Connectivity-With-its-Neighborhood.pdf.
11 Government of India. 4 September 2017. Accessed 4 March 2018. http://pib.nic.in/newsite/mbErel.aspx?relid=170509.
12 'India plans to set up LNG terminal in Myanmar.' *Press Trust of India*. 3 August 2018. Accessed 26 October 2018. www.asianage.com/business/in-other-news/030818/india-plans-to-set-up-lng-terminal-in-myanmar.html.
13 'ONGC May Explore Oil in Indonesia.' *Press Trust of India*. 27 January 2013. Accessed 22 November 2018. www.business-standard.com/article/specials/ongc-may-explore-oil-in-indonesia-100092501004_1.html.
14 'First India Indonesia Energy Forum held in Jakarta.' *Press Information Bureau*. Government of India. 22 April 2017. Accessed 22 October 2018. http://pib.nic.in/newsite/PrintRelease.aspx?relid=161220.

15 Ibid.
16 'India's 2018 thermal coal imports grew at fastest pace in 4 years.' *Press Trust of India*. 28 January 2019. Accessed 20 October 2020. https://economictimes.indiatimes.com/industry/indl-goods/svs/metals-mining/indias-2018-thermal-coal-imports-grew-at-fastest-pace-in-4-yrs/articleshow/67718101.cms.
17 Ministry of External Affairs, Government of India. *Joint Statement on enhanced Malaysia-India Strategic Partnership*. 23 November 2015. Accessed 5 January 2019. https://mea.gov.in/bilateral-documents.htm?dtl/26057/Joint+Statement+on+enhanced+MalaysiaIndia+Strategic+Partnership+November+23+2015.

8

INDIA'S ENERGY TRADE WITH SOUTHEAST ASIA

Opportunities and challenges

Amita Batra and Priyanshi Chauhan

Introduction

Over the last decade and a half India has been among the fastest growing emerging market economies in the world.[1] India's economic dynamism has been accompanied by urbanisation and consequent consumption and lifestyle changes that have been increasingly energy intensive. Simultaneously though, a little less than one-fourth of its 1.34 billion population lives below the poverty line[2] and ensuring access to reliable energy supply to all is likely to further accentuate the demand for energy.[3] For example, the launch of various schemes like *Saubhagya* and *Deen Dayal Upadhyay Gram Jyoti Yojna* (DDUGJY) by the Government of India in making power accessible and affordable for all may add to the growing energy demand in the coming years by more than 28 GW.[4] The International Energy Agency (IEA) has predicted that 'India alone will account for nearly 30 percent of the entire global increase in energy demand through 2040'.[5] Increasing pressure on demand for energy as a key input to sustain and accelerate economic growth and development is amply reflected in India's increased import dependence, with imported energy that accounted for 8.79% of total energy used in 1991 having increased to 34.6% in 2014. Notwithstanding, in 2017–18, India experienced a power deficit where peak demand was 164,066 MW compared to the peak demand met at 160,752 MW. India, today, therefore faces the challenge of developing innovative ways to secure access to affordable, continuous and sustainable energy supplies to all its people.[6]

One possible way to effectively address the issue of supply–demand mismatch of energy is through regional cooperation. Towards this end, regional initiatives like the SAARC Energy Ring, establishing the South Asian Energy Centre (SEC) through the 2005 Dhaka Declaration and the 2014 SAARC Framework Agreement for Energy Cooperation (Electricity) have been undertaken. Such initiatives recognise the significance of energy cooperation for development in South Asia but the progress in developing interconnected energy markets and its enabling infrastructure has been limited. While the existence of tariff and non-tariff barriers to trade including the lack of adequate infrastructure for trade facilitation, geo-political and security concerns in the region, hostile India–Pakistan relations, and lack of mutual trust have prevented expansion of intra-regional trade in general in South Asia, domestic factors like inadequate economic reforms including state ownership of the energy sector and high subsidies, lack of enabling infrastructure, low tariffs, and poor financial health of electricity utilities also contribute to limited energy trade in the region. However, at the bilateral level, energy trade exists, particularly in electricity, between India–Nepal, India–Bhutan and more recently between India and Bangladesh. As options on the western front are limited due to hostile relations with Pakistan, India should focus on the existing energy trade partners such as Nepal and Bangladesh and continue to expand energy corridors in the Southeast Asia through Myanmar to Thailand, Vietnam, Malaysia and Indonesia, which can be further extended to connect the adjoining sub-regions as part of a broader Asia-Pacific energy integration.[7]

In this context, this chapter attempts to explore the opportunities for India's energy trade with Bangladesh, Myanmar, Thailand, Vietnam, Malaysia and Indonesia in the larger framework of enhancing India's cooperation with Southeast Asia. For this, key trends in the energy sector of the countries will be examined to identify the rationale for trade. Further, challenges to the proposed energy trade will also be studied, with a focus on economic, geopolitical and security, and environmental concerns both at the domestic and the regional level.

BOX 8.1 TRENDS AND FORECASTS

- 2000–2014: India's energy consumption doubled.
- 2017: At 753.7 million tonnes of oil equivalent, India had the world's third largest energy demand, which is a quarter of the Chinese level, and a third of the US, but it is growing much faster than either of the two.
- India is expected to outpace Chinese growth before 2030 owing to a more energy-intensive development pathway.
- India will overtake China as the largest growing energy market beyond 2020.
- India alone will account for nearly 30% of the entire global increase in energy demand through 2040.
- India's imports of all forms of energy are expected to rise from 36% of primary consumption to as high as 55% by 2040.

Source: BP Statistical Review of World Energy 2017. BP, 2018.

Rationale for energy trade: A study of key trends

This section identifies key trends in the energy sector of each country to understand the driving forces of energy cooperation amongst them.

Resource endowments, rising demand and single-source dependence

The overall trend in demand for energy is increasing but there are variations in the production of fuels in the Southeast Asian countries and consequent supplies to meet the demand. The International Energy Agency report titled *Southeast Asia Energy Outlook 2017* highlights the gap between supply and demand that the Southeast Asian countries are likely to face and presents a fuel-wise production scenario until 2040.[8] The report suggests that, by 2040, there will be a decline in oil production in Southeast Asia owing to the decreasing production in Indonesia, Malaysia and Thailand while the 'demand for oil will continue to grow robustly propelled by increase in demand for mobility'. It further states that the coal production in Indonesia will fall due to the government's plans to 'cap coal production at 400 million tonnes (around 300 Mtce) from 2019 onwards'. On the other hand, 'Vietnam sees its coal production rise modestly' till 2040. The report also states that Indonesia will 'remain the largest producer of gas in the region with output growing from 77 bcm in 2016 to 90 bcm by 2040'; however, Malaysian gas production will drop to approximately '20 percent below 2016 levels'. The mismatch between demand and supply of energy is further accentuated by the dependence on single source of energy as shown by the energy mix of selected countries in Figure 8.1.

For instance as is evident from Figure 8.1, 60% of India's energy mix is dependent on coal whereas in Indonesia it is 44%. In Myanmar, biomass forms 55% of its

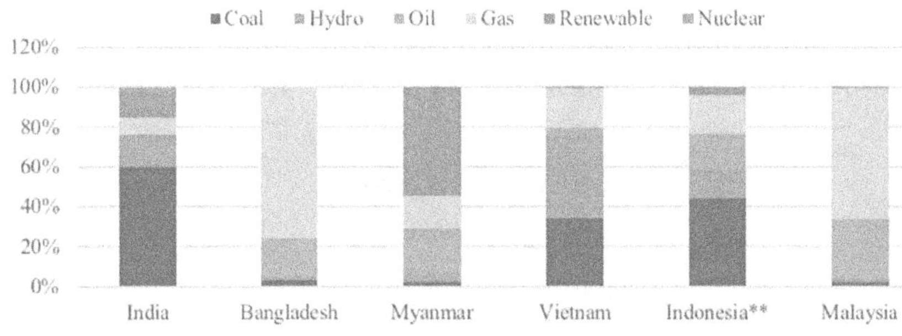

FIGURE 8.1 Energy mix (MW). ** Biomass is used as proxy for renewable energy. Source: Authors, based on data from, 'Draft Central Electricity Regulatory Commission (Cross Border Trade of Electricity) Regulations, 2017 – Explanatory Memorandum'. Central Electricity Regulatory Commission. Ministry of Power, Government of India, 2017. Accessed 15 March 2019. www.cercind.gov.in/2017/draft_reg/Expl7.pdf. Also see: *Southeast Asia Energy Outlook 2017*. OECD/IEA. Accessed October 17 November 2019. www.iea.org/publications/freepublications/publication/WEO2017SpecialReport_SoutheastAsiaEnergyOutlook.pdf

energy mix, whereas in Vietnam hydrogen forms 42% of the energy mix. Natural gas is a major source of energy in Bangladesh and Malaysia with a 75% and 66% share in the energy mix, respectively.

Interestingly, even though these countries are primarily dependent on a single source to meet their domestic energy requirements, complementarities in the resource endowments of these countries are evident when considered in a cooperative context, allowing thereby for pooling and allocation of energy resources in a way that optimises energy. This will also lead to reduction in the costs of production since the participating economies will be able to buy from the least cost energy source.[9] For instance, the importing of thermal power from India by Bangladesh and Myanmar will reduce the costs of electricity production by current expensive means of all natural gas production.[10] The diversity and complementarities of energy resources in the countries therefore offers opportunities for trade and cooperation in energy in a regional arrangement.

Import of energy resources

Since the demand of energy is increasing at a faster pace than the available supply from the domestic resources, countries are importing/exporting less energy sources to augment the domestic resource endowment. Figure 8.2 shows the status of the net energy imports as a percentage of energy use for these selected countries for 2014. It is observed that while India and Bangladesh are the net importers of energy resources with imports amounting to 34% and 17% of their energy use, Myanmar, Vietnam, Malaysia and Indonesia are net exporters of energy.

An examination of trends in the net energy imports as a percentage of energy use for the period 2000–2014, as shown in Figure 8.3, shows that India's dependence on the imports has continuously increased in the given period. In the case of Bangladesh, the imports show a declining trend until 2009 and then again show an increasing trend. This may be attributed to the introduction of Independent Power Producers (IPPs) and privatisation of power in 1996.[11] The opening up of

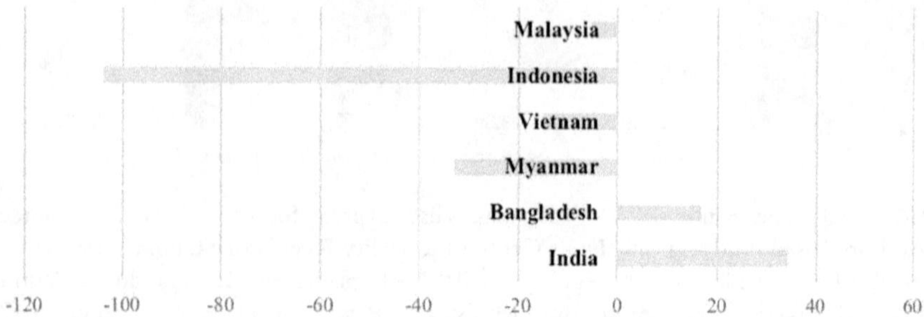

FIGURE 8.2 Net energy imports as a percentage of energy use (2014). 'Energy Imports, Net (% of Energy Use).' Data. World Bank. Accessed 21 October 2020. https://data.worldbank.org/indicator/EG.IMP.CONS.ZS.

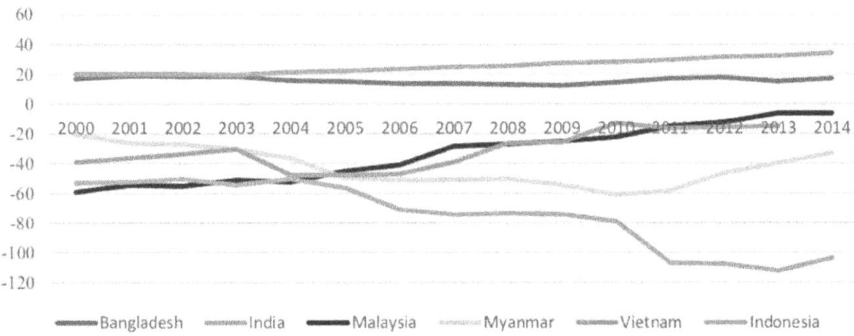

FIGURE 8.3 Net energy imports as a percentage of energy use 2000–2014. 'Energy Imports, Net (% of Energy Use).' Data.World Bank. Accessed 21 October 2020. https://data.worldbank.org/indicator/EG.IMP.CONS.ZS.

the power sector to the private utilities increased the power generation capacity of Bangladesh and thus reduced its dependence on imports to meet energy requirements. However, this decreasing dependence on imports could not continue after 2009 because domestically produced power could not keep pace with the increasing demand as shown in Figure 8.3. As a result, the net energy imports as a percentage of energy use again started to show an increasing trend for Bangladesh as well.

In Myanmar, Vietnam and Malaysia there has been a decline in the amount of exports as a percentage of energy use as shown in Figure 8.3. Indonesia is the only country that has shown a continuous increase in the net energy exports until 2013. However, post 2013, Indonesia's exports also have shown a declining trend as shown in Figure 8.3.

Modern energy use and accessibility

Trends in the levels of access to modern energy uses in the countries reveal differences across countries. An examination of per capita electric power consumption in KWh in 2014, as shown in Figure 8.4, highlights that India, Bangladesh, Myanmar, Vietnam and Indonesia have a consumption much below the average world level consumption of 3127 KWh. Per capita electric power consumption in Thailand is 2540 KWh, which is lower than the world level but the difference is not much. The case of Malaysia is different with per capita consumption of electricity at 4596 KWh being much higher than that of the world average.

In terms of access to electricity as a percentage of population in 2016, as shown in Figure 8.5, while Vietnam, Thailand and Malaysia have achieved universal access to electricity, and Indonesia is closing the gap with 97.6% of population having access to electricity, there is a significant population in India, Bangladesh and Myanmar that lacks access to electricity despite increasing imports of energy fuels. Myanmar has the lowest access to electricity, with only 57% of the population having access to electricity. India and Bangladesh perform relatively well with 85% and 76% of the

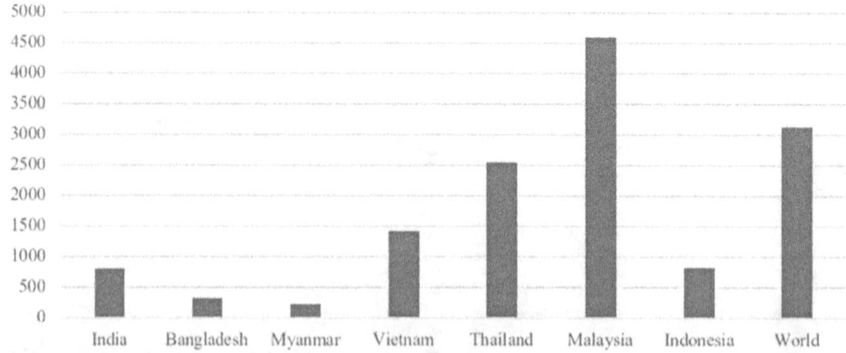

FIGURE 8.4 Per capita electric power consumption (KWh) 2014. 'Electric Power Consumption (KWh per Capita).' Data. World Bank. Accessed 21 October 2020. https://data.worldbank.org/indicator/EG.USE.ELEC.KH.PC.

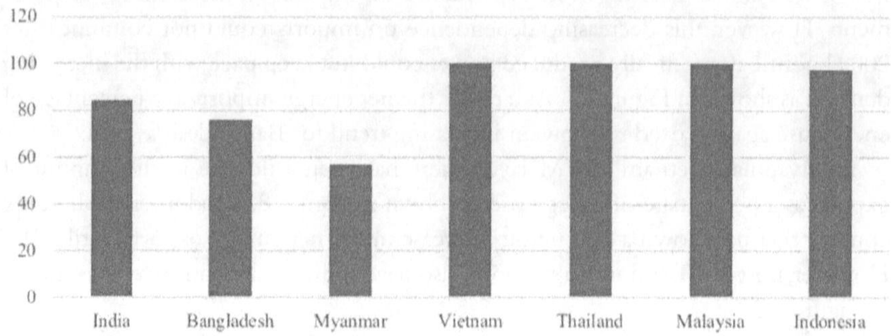

FIGURE 8.5 Access to electricity (percentage of population) 2016. 'Access to Electricity (% of Population).' Data. World Bank. Accessed 21 October 2020. https://data.worldbank.org/indicator/EG.ELC.ACCS.ZS.

population having access to electricity. In the case of India and Bangladesh, the situation in terms of access to electricity does not seem dismal when seen in percentage terms. But owing to their high population, the absolute number of people without access to electricity is large, which in the case of India is approximately 240 million people and more than 30 million households.[12]

Analysing the trends in accessibility of electricity together with the trends in imports of energy sources highlights the rationale for trade in electricity among these countries. Vietnam, Thailand, Malaysia and Indonesia, which have achieved universal electrification in their countries, are all energy-exporting countries that can find a huge market for their exports in India and Bangladesh, which will increase the foreign exchange earnings and contribute to their export-led growth. The improved cash flow will also lead to postponement of large domestic capital investment needs and avoid crowding out other important investment needs. Further, an integrated energy market could increase output and FDI, particularly through tariff cuts, subsidy reductions and more infrastructure investments.[13] Energy cooperation will also have positive environmental and climate change implications. This is especially relevant for the countries because of their excessive reliance on oil and coal, which is expected to increase further despite being signatories to the Paris Agreement and commitments on Nationally Determined Contributions (NDC). Imported natural gas and hydropower would help in moderating this increase to some extent.[14] The management of regional sources of energy and the use of other primary energy sources enabled by trade thus will be optimised for the benefit of all, and address the issues of the supply–demand mismatch, along with concerns around energy security and environment.

Status of existing energy cooperation

The energy trade of India with its eastern neighbours can be seen as part of the larger interest in regional trade and cross border market integration. Prior to the economic reforms of 1991, the energy trade was strictly limited to the importing of oil and oil products only, despite serious problems faced by the domestic power companies due to poor quality coal to produce electricity.[15] With liberalisation, there was a change in the political mindset and economic policy, which called for ensuring energy security by diversification of energy sources supplemented by LNG imports, coal imports and acquisition of oil and gas fields abroad.

India is engaged in bilateral trade in fuels as shown in Table 8.1, with Thailand, Indonesia and Malaysia being significant source countries for India's fuel imports, while major exporting destinations for India include Bangladesh, Myanmar, Vietnam and Malaysia. Further, India also exports electricity to Bangladesh.[16]

Evaluation of trends in India's fuel trade (Figures 8.6–8.11) also suggest that Bangladesh, Myanmar and Vietnam are destinations of India's energy exports while Indonesia, Thailand and Malaysia are important sources for India's energy imports. With Bangladesh, India's exports of fuels have been consistently more than India's imports between 2006 and 2018 as shown in Figure 8.6. Since 2013, India has also been exporting electricity to Bangladesh. In the case of Myanmar, India's exports of fuels have increased significantly post 2016 as shown in Figure 8.7. However,

TABLE 8.1 Exports and imports of fuel by India (US thousand $)

Countries	*Fuel export of India 2018*	*Fuel import of India 2018*
Bangladesh	876,545.62	81.48
Myanmar	215,819.69	1.52
Thailand	94,205.87	121,743.14
Vietnam	10,004.33	0.77
Indonesia	276,841.80	8,437,460.88
Malaysia	2,405,535.83	3,375,393.85

Source: 'Trade Statistics by Country / Region.' World Integrated Trade Solution. Accessed 21 October 2020. https://wits.worldbank.org/countrystats.aspx?lang=en.

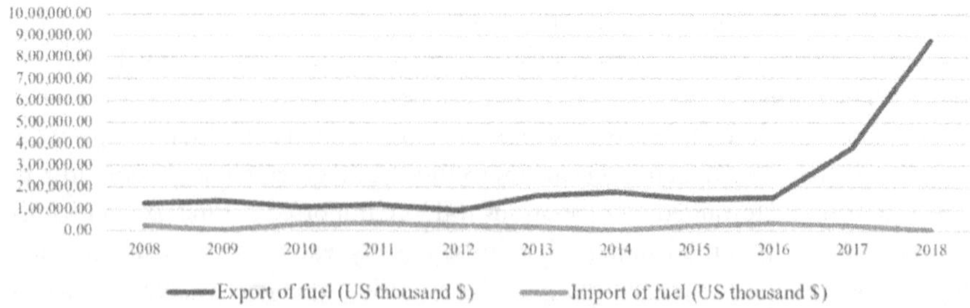

FIGURE 8.6 India's export and import of fuel with Bangladesh 2006–18. 'Trade Statistics by Country/Region.' World Integrated Trade Solution. Accessed 21 October 2020. https://wits.worldbank.org/countrystats.aspx?lang=en.

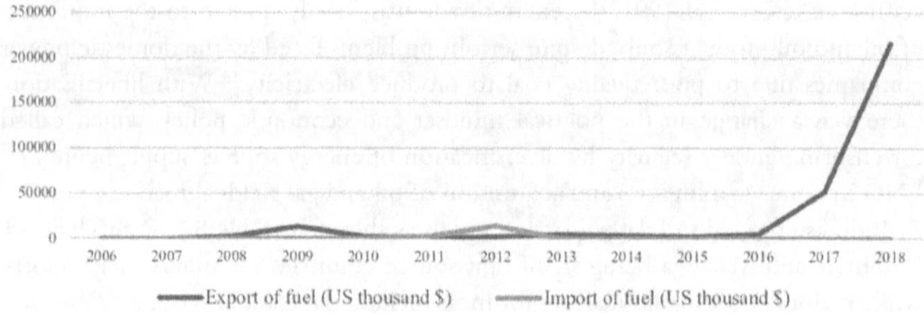

FIGURE 8.7 India's export and import of fuel with Myanmar 2006–18. 'Trade Statistics by Country/Region.' World Integrated Trade Solution. Accessed 21 October 2020. https://wits.worldbank.org/countrystats.aspx?lang=en.

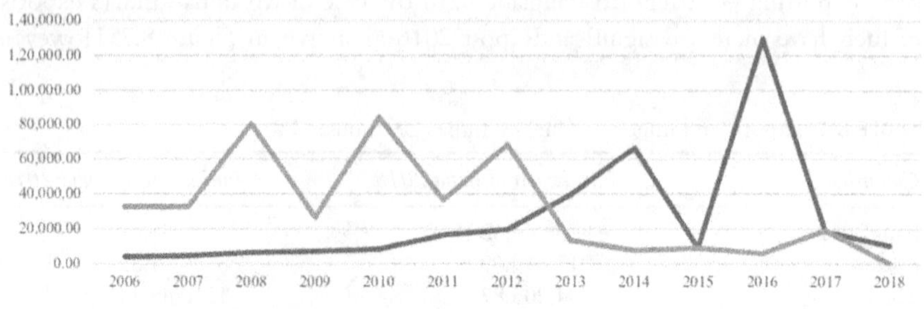

FIGURE 8.8 India's export and import of fuels with Vietnam 2006–18. 'Trade Statistics by Country/Region.' World Integrated Trade Solution. Accessed 21 October 2020. https://wits.worldbank.org/countrystats.aspx?lang=en.

with the discovery of new fields in Bangladesh[17] and Myanmar,[18] the prospects of importing energy resources from these countries to India have considerably increased and India, being a huge market, will help increase their foreign exchange earnings. Further, this will help enhance efficiency in electricity production through diversification of sources following import of cheap thermal resources from India.[19] In the case of Bangladesh, it will, in addition, help address the problem of its burgeoning trade deficit with India.[20] In the case of energy trade with Vietnam, India's fuel imports have declined dramatically and are less than India's exports of energy fuels to Vietnam post 2013 as shown in Figure 8.8. After 2016, there was a dramatic decline in India's fuel exports to Vietnam, with imports and exports being at almost the same level in 2017 after which a gap emerged with India's exports exceeding its imports again. Despite Indonesia, Malaysia and Thailand being significant sources of fuels for India, India's total imports from these countries saw a declining trend until 2016 (2017 in case of Thailand) after which there was a reversal of trend with India's fuel imports increasing again as shown in Figure 8.9, 8.10 and 8.11 respectively.

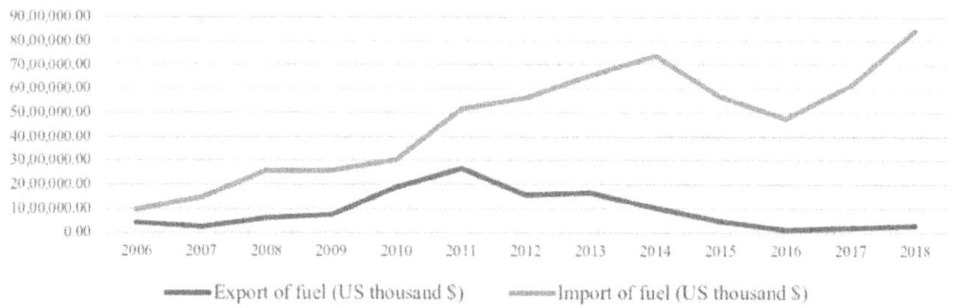

FIGURE 8.9 India's trade in fuels with Indonesia 2006–2018. 'Trade Statistics by Country/Region.' World Integrated Trade Solution. Accessed 21 October 2020. https://wits.worldbank.org/countrystats.aspx?lang=en.

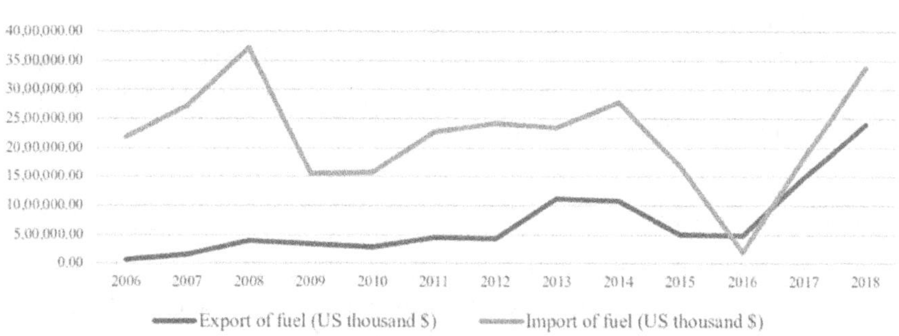

FIGURE 8.10 India's trade in fuels with Malaysia 2006–2018. 'Trade Statistics by Country/Region.' World Integrated Trade Solution. Accessed 21 October 2020. https://wits.worldbank.org/countrystats.aspx?lang=en.

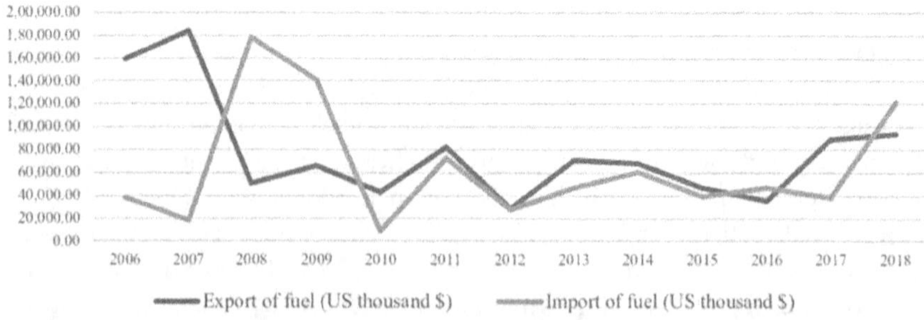

FIGURE 8.11 India's trade in fuels with Thailand 2006–2018. 'Trade Statistics by Country/Region.' World Integrated Trade Solution. Accessed 21 October 2020. https://wits.worldbank.org/countrystats.aspx?lang=en.

BOX 8.2 STATUS OF INDIA'S EXISTING ENERGY COOPERATION

India–Bangladesh

- Bangladesh imported 3822 GWh of electricity from India in 2015 through interconnections in Bheramara and Tripura.
- Commissioning of second cross border interconnection between Surjyamaninagar (Tripura) in India and South Comilla in Bangladesh.
- The 1320 MW coal fired Maitree thermal power plant, a 50:50 JV between NTPC and BPDB is being developed at Rampal.
- In 2017, agreements for generation/supply/financing of more than 3600 MW electricity were signed between Indian public/private companies and Bangladesh.
- India has agreed to fund the construction of India–Bangladesh Friendship Pipeline from Siliguri to Parbatipur for supply of diesel to Bangladesh from Numaligarh Refinery Limited.

India–Myanmar

- In 2001, India started negotiations about buying gas from Myanmar.
- A MOU was signed on Renewable Energy on Myanmar President U Htin Kyaw state visit to India in 2016 with the objective to encourage and promote bilateral technical cooperation on new and renewable energy, namely solar energy, bio energy and wind energy.

India–Vietnam

- During the state visit of Vietnamese Prime Minister Nguyen Tan Dung to India in October 2014, seven agreements including one on energy were signed.
- In 2016, when Prime Minister Modi paid an official visit to Vietnam, both the prime ministers agreed to further enhance cooperation in the oil and gas sector and urged both sides to actively implement the Agreement signed in 2014 between PVN and OVL on cooperation in new blocks in Vietnam.
- The Vietnamese side welcomed the long-standing investment and presence of ONGC Videsh Limited (OVL) and its partnership with PetroVietnam (PVN) for exploration of oil and gas in Vietnam and also welcomed Indian oil and gas companies to avail themselves of opportunities in participating in mid-stream and down-stream sectors in Vietnam.

India–Indonesia

- In 2017, the first India Indonesia Energy Forum was held in Jakarta, where a MoU was signed between the Union Ministry of Petroleum and Natural Gas and the Indonesia's Ministry of Energy and Mineral Resources on cooperation in the field of oil and gas which sought to set up an institutional framework for bilateral cooperation in the sector.
- India and Indonesia have agreed to explore cooperation in the following areas: (a) Upgrading of refineries in Indonesia, (b) sharing the expertise of Indonesia in gasification of fuel oil, (c) relocation of gas-based plants from India to Indonesia, (d) exploration of oil, gas and coal fields, (e) sharing of experience in use of LEDs and renewable energy in India.

India–Malaysia

- In the Malaysian energy sector, Indian Oil Corporation (IOC) is involved in a joint venture with Petronas of Malaysia.

Source: 'Ministry of External Affairs, Government of India.' Ministry of External Affairs, Government of India. Accessed 21 October 2020. www.mea.gov.in/.

Opportunities for energy trade: Interconnected power transmission grid and natural gas pipeline

Given the existing status of energy trade and resource endowments in the region, the main opportunities for energy trade are in the electricity sector and the natural gas sector.[21]

India's electricity trade exists with Bhutan, Nepal and Bangladesh at bilateral level only. The new 'Guidelines for the Import/Export of Cross Border Electricity' by India facilitate this arrangement by allowing Bangladesh, Nepal and Bhutan to sign a tripartite agreement for electricity trade and providing for a transmission corridor on the Indian territory.[22] This is an improvement over the 2016 guidelines, which excluded private companies in these countries and gave India disproportionate control over the electricity trade through Indian territory.[23] The new guidelines provide an enabling policy framework to support regional trade in electricity, which may evolve into regional electricity trading arrangements within the BBIN. This can be further integrated with the ASEAN Power Grid (APG) through the northern sub-region via Bangladesh and Myanmar.[24]

In line with the existing power trading arrangements, Myanmar will play an important role and act as a bridge between South Asia and Southeast Asia. India is currently developing the Tamanti multipurpose project close to the India–Myanmar border, with an installed hydropower capacity of 1200 MW in the first stage, 400 MW in the second stage, and 700 MW in the third stage.[25] Myanmar can also be linked with the proposed transmission grid between Nepal, Bhutan and Bangladesh via India.

ASEAN is also developing the Trans-ASEAN Gas Pipeline (TAPG), a physical energy infrastructure project to support new market opportunities, and ensure energy security amongst the ASEAN states through an interconnected gas pipeline infrastructure for ASEAN members and connectivity through LNG regasification terminals to enable gas to be transported across the borders of the member states. According to the IEA (2017) report, the prospects for the natural gas production and exports are high in the years to come. With its increased production, Myanmar will find markets for its natural gas both in India and Bangladesh. The re-election of Ms Hasina as the prime minister of Bangladesh is a good signal to resume talks on the 2009 MIB pipeline.

Challenges to energy trade

The energy trade in the region is limited due to challenges that are present both at the regional and the domestic level. This section attempts to identify the challenges with a focus on geopolitical, economic and environmental concerns.

The China factor[26]

As the world's most populous country with a high GDP growth rate,[27] there has been an increase in energy demand of China over the years. In 2017, China witnessed the fastest primary energy consumption growth of 2.2% since 2013.[28] Moreover, 'energy consumption rose by 3.1 percent in 2017 and China was the largest growth market for energy in the 17th consecutive year'.[29] The rising energy demand has, however, not been met with sufficient domestic energy supply. Consequently, China is increasingly relying on energy imports as is evident in Figure 8.12, and is further

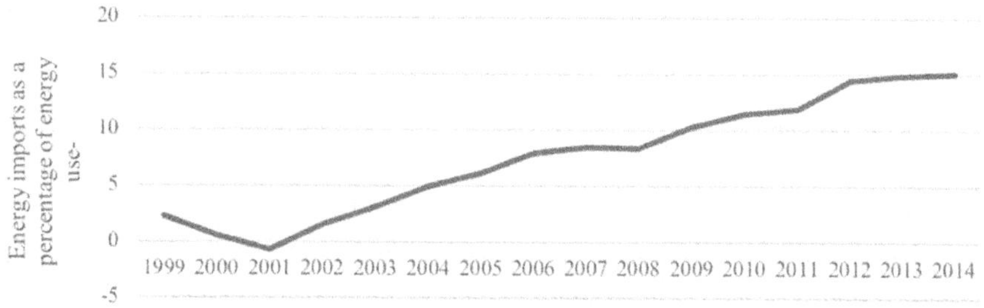

FIGURE 8.12 China's net energy imports (as a percentage of energy use): 1999–2014. 'Energy Imports, Net (% of Energy Use).' Data.World Bank. Accessed 21 October 2020. https://data.worldbank.org/indicator/EG.IMP.CONS.ZS.

expected to rise with IEA's projections suggesting that China is set to become the world's largest consumer and importer of oil by 2040.[30]

Not only this, China's over dependence on the Middle Eastern oil is a cause for concern and therefore it has prioritised diversification of sources of energy.[31] One of the major challenges facing China to ensure its energy security is to secure its vital energy routes. In total, 72% of China's oil imports transit through the Straits of Malacca, a narrow strait connecting South China with the Indian Ocean and the Pacific Ocean. Further, 42% of the total oil transit through the South China Sea is for China as compared to 20% for Japan and only 3% for the US (Figure 8.13). With 80% of its oil imports passing through the Malacca Straits, the risk of a possible maritime disruption and blocking China's supply of oil by choking the Straits is very significant. This is referred to as the 'Malacca Dilemma'.[32] What amplifies the

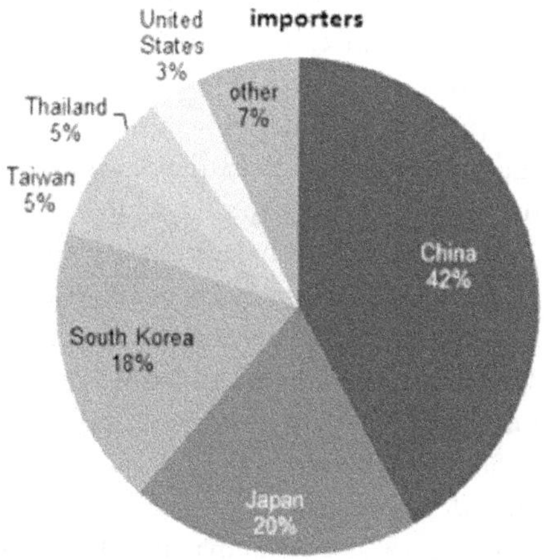

FIGURE 8.13 Import of crude oil through the South China Sea. 'More than 30% of global maritime crude oil trade moves through the South China Sea'. US Energy Information Administration, 2018. Accessed 20 January 2020 from www.eia.gov/todayinenergy/detail.php?id=36952.

problem is the lack of alternate viable routes connecting the South China Sea with the Indian Ocean. The two prominent transit routes that exist are the Sunda Strait and the Lombok Strait but transit through the Malacca Strait is preferred due to its short distance, which makes it more economical. In addition, the difficulty in navigating the Sunda Straits as they are shallow and the Lombok Strait is far too much of a detour from the trans-Malacca route to be economically viable.[33]

China has responded to its energy needs and has prioritised not only ensuring energy supply, but to diversify its sources and look for new routes for energy trade. Accordingly, the Belt-and-Road Initiative launched in 2013, has energy security as one of its main agendas with a focus on promoting energy cooperation through infrastructure, oil and gas pipelines, cross-border electricity interconnections, and development and exploitation of natural energy resources. In addition, a study of the routes and corridors in the BRI suggests that there exists an overlapping of the maritime route and land based corridors in the BRI with the existing energy transit routes for China covering all the major importers. The Maritime Silk Road connects China with the Southeast Asian countries, Gulf of Oman in West Asia followed by Africa and Europe. This corresponds with the China's maritime oil transit route, passing through the Straits of Malacca. Such similarities are also observed in the land-based corridors, thereby connecting it with Central Asia and Southeast Asia.[34] For instance, BRI through the China-Central-West Asia Economic Corridor (CCWAEC) has connected north-western China with the resource-rich Central Asia and West Asia. The Chinese companies are investing in energy and transportation projects including the China–Kazakhstan oil pipeline, China–Kazakhstan gas pipeline and the Central Asia–China gas pipeline that runs through Uzbekistan, Tajikistan and Kazakhstan to Xinjian in China. The CCWAEC has further provided a land-based route to the oil imports from West Asia, which are currently transited through the shipping routes. Similarly, the China–Mongolia–Russia Economic Corridor (CMREC) gives China access to the Mongolian renewable energy sources, particularly solar and wind energy resources.[35] In the Southeast Asia, negotiations concern the Kra Canal Project, 150 km across the Kra Isthmus in Thailand linking the South China Sea to the Andaman Sea, thereby connecting the Pacific and the Indian Ocean respectively and reduce its reliance on the Malacca Straits. Similar trends are also observed in the China–Pakistan Economic Corridor (CPEC) which has 16 energy projects of 10,400 MW as priority projects to address Pakistan's energy security concerns.[36] Furthermore, the CPEC connects the Gwadar Port of Pakistan with Kashgar Port in Western China, thus allows for rerouting of oil imports from West Asia instead of passing through the Malacca Straits and the South China Sea. Likewise, the Bangladesh–China–India–Myanmar Economic Corridor (BCIMEC) has also covered two of the significant gas producing countries of Bangladesh and Myanmar in China's neighbourhood. A gas pipeline project was initiated in 2009 between China and Myanmar, which was set to provide 6.5 Tcf of gas from Shwe field and Shwe Phyu field (Block A1) and Mya field (Block A3) to China over the next 30 years to China's Yunnan province.[37] In March 2018, Myanmar, Bangladesh and China also agreed on a Power Integration

Project, which seeks to build a 600 kV MTDC system with a total power transmission capacity of around 3,000 MW. While China will transmit power to Myanmar and Bangladesh in the short run, in the long run it is expected that Myanmar may transmit power to Bangladesh and China owing to its abundant energy resources.[38]

There are similarities in the trends in the region-wise dependence for India and China as shown in Figure 8.14, with highest dependence on the MENA region followed by East Asia and Pacific. Owing to its energy demand, China is importing greater amounts of fuels from all the regions with the exception of the MENA region and North America, where the difference is not very large. With reference to fuel trade in the selected Southeast Asian countries as well, China's are imports of fuel are much more than that of India as shown in Figure 8.15. This means that both India and China are looking forward to the similar source countries to meet their domestic energy requirements, thereby generating competition for scarce regional resources.

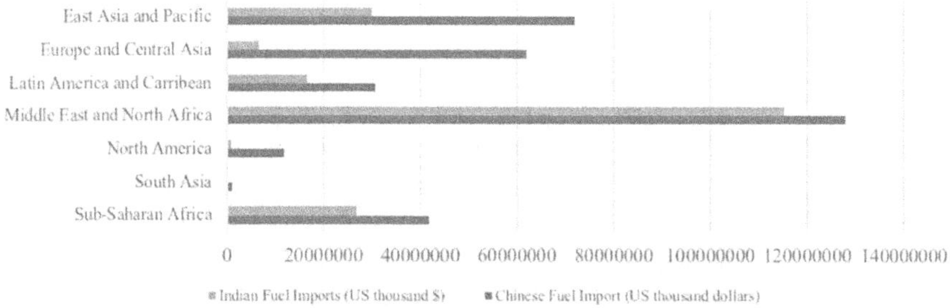

FIGURE 8.14 Comparison of region-wise fuel imports: 2018. 'Trade Statistics by Country / Region.' World Integrated Trade Solution. Accessed 21 October 2020. https://wits.worldbank.org/countrystats.aspx?lang=en.

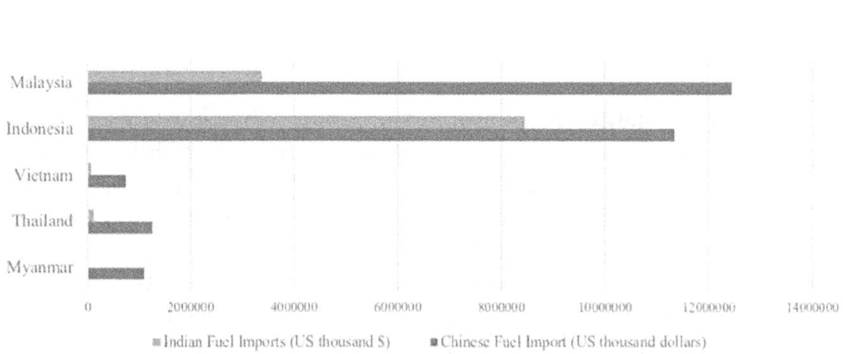

FIGURE 8.15 Comparison of fuel imports of India and China from selected Southeast Asian countries: 2018. 'Trade Statistics by Country/Region.' World Integrated Trade Solution. Accessed 21 October 2020. https://wits.worldbank.org/countrystats.aspx?lang=en.

Competition among the energy importing countries gives an undue advantage to the exporting countries and allows them to hike the prices and adopt discriminatory pricing to their benefit. This has been evident in the function of the Organisation of Petroleum Exporting Countries (OPEC), which increased oil prices from $30 a barrel to $80 in 2018[39] and imposes an 'Asian Premium'[40] on oil exports to Asian countries. This has put energy-importing countries like India and China at a disadvantageous position by adversely affecting their balance of payments and reducing their energy security. As a result, both India and China have initiated cooperation and are working on reducing the cartel's influence on the oil market and increasing their own bargaining powers. Towards this end, India had discussed with China the possibility of forming an 'Oil Buyer's Club' at the International Energy Forum (IEF) meeting in April 2018, to be extended to Japan and South Korea to negotiate better terms with sellers and do away with the discriminatory pricing, and also to reduce the dominance of the cartel.[41] Therefore, owing to the existing competition for similar regional energy resources between India and China, they should not isolate each other but should cooperate on mutually beneficial terms.

Investment

Regional cooperation in energy requires huge investments for creating infrastructure, particularly transmission lines and distribution networks for an interconnected power grid, and pipelines for natural gas, and for LNG regasification terminals, respectively. The electricity sector in particular has the highest demand for investment approximately ranging from $3 billion per year in Southeast Asia to $3.6 billion per year in 2010–2020.[42] If energy cooperation between South Asia and Southeast Asia increases, Southeast Asia will witness an increase in investment costs of about $4 billion by 2030, mostly in natural gas sector and the oil sector, with a simultaneous increase in revenues owing to its exports to South Asia.[43] South Asia will, however, not witness any increase in investment due to its enhanced energy cooperation with Southeast Asia.[44]

According to IEA,[45]

> the total cumulative investment in energy supply infrastructure amounts to $2.1 trillion, of which the power sector accounts for over half. The annual average investment requirement of around $90 billion corresponds to around 3% of the region's total GDP in 2016. Investment in fossil-fuel production and related infrastructure makes up around 40% of total supply-side investment to 2040 in the New Policies Scenario, totalling around $800 billion. Of this, more than half is for natural gas, with around $100 billion required for pipelines and $30 billion for LNG facilities including for small floating regasification terminals to supply gas to island networks in Indonesia. Investment in oil infrastructure totals around $350 billion, a third of which is for refining, a significantly higher proportion than the global average of 10%.

> The relatively higher share for refineries reflects the need to expand capacity to meet increasing demand for oil products in the region.

The report further estimates that

> the cumulative investment needed in the power sector to 2040 is $1.2 trillion, an annual average of around $50 billion. This corresponds to around 10% of total government revenue in Southeast Asia, or around 40% of total foreign direct investment in the region in 2015, illustrating the potentially large burden on government budgets if there is not meaningful private sector participation. Investment for transmission and distribution (T&D) accounts for over half of total power sector investment, reflecting the substantial need to strengthen the current network, as well as to extend grids for access and to meet rising demand in urban areas and to refurbish existing T&D lines. About $570 billion of investment is needed for new power plants, of which about 40% is for fossil-fuel plants and 60% for renewables-based generation. Cumulative investment for renewables-based power generation amounts to over $300 billion to 2040, of which around 45% is for hydropower and 40% for solar PV and wind.

Market structures and sector reforms, and lack of harmonisation of standards

The market structures of countries is such that there is a significant state presence in the energy sector, with the private sector being limited to the exploration of energy resources and production of electricity in the form of IPPs. In addition, the prices of both energy sources and electricity are regulated by the government and are not determined by the market forces of demand and supply. The monopoly market structures do not generate enough finances to invest in the infrastructure for trade and in the expansion of generation capacities required to the new markets. Also, state ownership does not offer enough incentives to adopt cost-reduction techniques. The burden of financing the energy sector and its new projects thus lies on the state funds. In contrast, the private power utilities are ready to adopt cost-effective techniques, invest in new projects and increase their business. Therefore, a greater degree of competition, privatisation and liberalisation of the energy sector is more likely to improve the prospects of energy trade in the selected countries. While this holds true for all the countries under study, there have been some cases of a move towards market forces. For instance, Thailand has made a move towards market-determined pricing of electricity by dividing the tariff structure into a base tariff and fuel adjustment charge.[46] Similarly, Malaysia has introduced deregulation to its gas and power sector and has paved the way for the introduction of IPPs to the supply function of the sector, helping the government to reduce the costs and administration involved in the exploration of new natural gas fields.

Further, there are differences in standards across the selected countries across technical, regulatory, and policy frameworks. For instance, India's electricity laws are governed by the Electricity Act 2003 while Bangladesh electricity laws are governed by the Electricity Act 1910 with some amendments and other policy framework including Policy Guidelines for the Enhancement of Private Participation in the Power Sector (2008), Power Pricing Framework and Vision Statement of the Government of Bangladesh to Provide Access to Affordable and Reliable Electricity to All by the Year 2020, among others. In addition, differences also exist in terms of the structure and mandate of the regulators. Their roles range from multisector regulation and overall energy sector regulation. As a first step, these regulators need to work together to develop a roadmap for harmonising the relevant regulations.[47] Subsequently, institutional and governance framework at the regional level will have to be established to evolve legal rules of governance for trade in energy including the disputing settling mechanism.

Environmental and humanitarian concerns

Myanmar and Bangladesh are countries with a flat and low-lying landscape, so the coastal areas of these countries are highly vulnerable to floods. Sundarbans on the Indian side are similarly ecologically sensitive. Thus, energy cooperation in the region will have to be ecologically sustainable owing to the sensitive climatic conditions. Apart from natural gas, Bangladesh has high-quality coal reserves in abundance. Despite the availability and desperate need to diversify sources of energy, coal mining has not proceeded satisfactorily due to the lack of a comprehensive coal mining policy and inability to address the social and environmental concerns associated with coal mining. The coal reserve region of Bangladesh is densely populated. Coal mining would create concerns related to food security and the livelihood of farmers. This would also create problem of internally displaced persons (IDPs). Hydrological management is another area of concern. On the one hand, pumping out large amounts of water from the ground for open-pit mining will create environmental problems and, on the other hand, closed-pit mining increased the likelihood of floods and high water flow in coal layers, which makes mining difficult and also contaminates adjacent aquifers.[48] This highlights the fact that a consensus among people has not been established, halting cooperation with India.

In the case of Myanmar, there has been a proposal for the construction of six dams in the mainstream river, Kunlong dam (1400 MW), Nong Pha dam (1000 MW), Mong Ton dam (7110 MW) and Manntaung (Tasang) on a tributary of the Salween (200 MW) in Shan state, Ywa Thit dam in Kayah state (4000MW) and Hatgyi dam in Karen state (1360 MW). And without consulting with Myanmar's people, it has been agreed that 90% electricity from these six schemes will be exported to the neighbouring countries of China and Thailand. Opposition has been raised to these proposed projects around issues concerning human rights and environment, as well as ongoing armed conflict between Burmese security forces and ethnic groups along the river. The proposed site for dams are active civil war zones; increased militarisation at the sites has escalated abuse of local population and forcible relocation.[49] Among the major environmental cost of the cascade, Tasang dam will flood the pristine teak forest and Hatgyi dam will flood two wildlife sanctuaries in Karen state.

Conclusion

Against the background of the fast-paced economic growth of India, the need for social development and the consequent increase in demand for energy calls for an increasing energy cooperation with the neighbouring countries. The western neighbours including Central Asian countries and Russia are rich in hydrocarbons, the hostile Indo-Pakistan relations have denied India the benefit of such trade by not allowing it to access these regions via the land route. In such a scenario, South East Asian countries via Bangladesh and Myanmar are an alternative with prospects in energy trade, particularly in electricity and natural gas. Such regional cooperation gains more significance in the light of the Chinese ambitious BRI and the economic, geopolitical and security concerns associated with it. While there exist various challenges to cooperation both at the regional level and domestic level, India should make concerted effort to develop a model for regional cooperation under multilateral framework. Further, there is a need for a model that offers an alternative to the BRI and does away with its limitations of infringing the territorial sovereignty, interference with domestic matters and debt trap diplomacy. Further, India should also look for possibilities of cooperation with China to increase their bargaining power with the oil exporting countries, and address the concerns around energy security of the two largest consumers of energy in the world.

Notes

1 Acknowledgement: Presented at the International Conference on 'India's Energy Security: Inter-regional Cooperation to Energy Security Society', 19 March 2019.

2 'India.' Data. World Bank. Accessed 21 October 2020. https://data.worldbank.org/country/india.

3 There is a close link between demand for energy and the socio-economic development of a country. Energy is a crucial input for socio-economic development and is essential commodity for most human activities. Poor access to reliable and modern energy services therefore acts as a barrier to socio-economic development. See: Bargasse, Emanuel, Wojciech Paczynski, Marek Dabrowski, and Luc Dewulf. *The Relationship between Energy and Socio-Economic Development in the Southern and Eastern Mediterranean*. Energy and Climate Change Mitigation, MEDPRO, 2013.

4 'No Free Power for Poor under Saubhagya; Demand to Rise by 28GW.' *The Economic Times*, 27 September 2017. Accessed 21 October 2020. https://economictimes.indiatimes.com/industry/energy/power/no-free-power-for-poor-under-saubhagya-demand-to-rise-by-28gw/articleshow/60857027.cms?from=mdr.

5 *World Energy Outlook 2017* . International Energy Agency, 2018.

6 'Power Sector at a Glance ALL INDIA.' Ministry of Power. Ministry of Power, Government of India. 2018. Accessed 21 October 2020. https://powermin.nic.in/en/content/power-sector-glance-all-india.
7 *Strengthening Transport Connectivity From/To Port of Selected Countries.* UNESCAP, 2018. Accessed 21 October 2020. www.unescap.org/sites/default/files/PORT%20TRANSPORT%20CONNECTIVITY.pdf.
8 *Southeast Asia Energy Outlook 2017.* OECD/IEA. October 2017. Accessed 17 November 2019. www.iea.org/publications/freepublications/publication/WEO2017SpecialReport_SoutheastAsiaEnergyOutlook.pdf
9 *Connecting South Asia and Southeast Asia.* Tokyo: Asian Development Bank Institute, 2015.
10 *Potential and Prospects for Regional Energy Trade In the South Asia Region.* World Bank, 2007. Accessed 20 November 2018. http://siteresources.worldbank.org/SOUTHASIAEXT/Resources/223546-1192413140459/4281804-1192413178157/4281806-1194474073434/SAR_Energy_Trade_Nov_07.pdf.
11 Ali, Fahd, and Fatima Beg. Working paper Series 106. *The History of Private Power in Pakistan.* Islamabad: Sustainable Development Policy Institute, 2007.
12 Singh, Rajesh Kumar, and Saket Sundria. 'Living in the Dark: 240 Million Indians Have No Electricity.' Bloomberg, 24 January 2017. Accessed 21 October 2020. www.bloomberg.com/news/features/2017-01-24/living-in-the-dark-240-million-indians-have-no-electricity. Also see: Singh, Rajesh Kumar, and Saket Sundria. 'India Nears Power Success, But Millions Still in the Dark.' Bloomberg.com. Bloomberg, 26 April 2018. Accessed 21 October 2020. www.bloomberg.com/news/articles/2018-04-26/india-nears-power-success-but-millions-are-still-in-the-dark; and D'Cunha, Suparna Dutt. 'Modi Announces '100% Village Electrification', But 31 Million Indian Homes Are Still In The Dark.' *Forbes Magazine*, 7 May 2018. Accessed 21 October 2020. www.forbes.com/sites/suparnadutt/2018/05/07/modi-announces-100-village-electrification-but-31-million-homes-are-still-in-the-dark/.
13 See endnote 9.
14 See endnote 10.
15 The import substitution strategy of the pre-reform era was considered to be reducing the energy security of the country by increasing the dependency on imports, exposing itself to the greater risk of disruption and putting pressure on the already limited foreign currency. Reference: Ibid.
16 It began in 2010 when Bangladesh and India signed a memorandum of understanding (MOU) to exchange electricity through a cross-border interconnection from Bheramara (Bangladesh) to Baharampur (India). In 2012, an electricity purchase pact was inked between NTPC Vidyut Vyapar Nigam in India and Bangladesh Power Development Board (BPDB) in Bangladesh for the import of electricity to Bangladesh. This is a 25-year government-to-government electricity purchase agreement, which involves providing 250 MW of coal-fired electricity from India to Bangladesh. The commissioning of this first cross-border interconnection in 2013 has given a major boost to export of power from India to Bangladesh. It was further augmented by commissioning of a second cross-border interconnection between Surjyamaninagar (Tripura) in India and South Comilla in Bangladesh. In 2017, around 600 MW of power was being exported to Bangladesh. See: 'India Becomes Net Exporter of Electricity for the First Time.' Press Release. Press Information Bureau, 29 March 2017. Accessed 14 July 2019. https://pib.gov.in/ErrorPage.html?aspxerrorpath=/newsite/PrintRelease.aspx.
17 Bangladesh Petroleum Exploration and Production Company Limited (Bapex) has discovered the presence of natural gas at an exploratory well in Bhola's Bheduria upazila with approximately 600 Bcf of gas. See: Rasel, Aminur Rahman. 'Bapex Discovers New Gas

Field in Bhola.' *Dhaka Tribune*, 15 January 2018. Accessed 21 October 2020. www.dhakatribune.com/bangladesh/power-energy/2018/01/15/bapex-discovers-gas-bhola-2.

18 The Schwe Yee Htun-2, an appraisal well I offshore block a-6, was tested to be able to produce natural gas, according to an official announcement from the Ministry of Electricity and Energy (MOEE) on 22 September 2018. See Htwe, Chan Mye. 'Myanmar Defence Forum.' Pakistan Defence, 24 September 2018. Accessed 15 March 2019. https://defence.pk/pdf/threads/myanmar-defence-forum.347379/page-136.

19 See endnote 9.

20 For the year 2017, India's total exports to Bangladesh were US $ thousand 7,210,099.52 and India's imports from Bangladesh were US $ 591,575.73. See: 'Trade Statistics by Country / Region.' WITS. World Integrated Trade Solution. Accessed 21 October 2020. https://wits.worldbank.org/countrystats.aspx?lang=en.

21 See endnote 9.

22 'Guidelines for Import/Export (Cross Border) of Electricity-2018-.' Ministry of Power, Government of India, 18 December 2018. Accessed 21 October 2020. https://powermin.nic.in/sites/default/files/uploads/Guidelines_for_ImportExport_Cross%20Border_of_Electricity_2018.pdf.

23 The 2016 guidelines prevented anyone other than Indian generators in the neighbouring countries, or generators owned by that country's government from selling power to India, thereby excluding many privately held companies in these countries and restricting their access to the vast Indian market. See: 'Guidelines on Cross Border Trade of Electricity.' International Cooperation in Electricity. Ministry of Power, 5 December 2016. Accessed 20 March 2018. https://powermin.nic.in/en/content/international-cooperation-electricity.

24 APG is proposed under ASEAN Plan of Action for Energy Cooperation (APEC), which is a collection of interconnected national grids offering bilateral exchanges of electricity, and will subsequently evolve into a sub-regional and regional grid. Three sub-regions have been identified within APG, namely, the northern, eastern and southern sub-regions. The northern sub-region encompasses Vietnam, Lao PDR, Myanmar and Thailand; the southern sub-region covers Peninsular Malaysia and Sumatra (Indonesia); and the eastern sub-region includes Philippines, Borneo Island (including Brunei) and Sulawesi (Indonesia). See: *ASEAN Plan of Action for Energy Cooperation (APAEC) 2016–2025*. ASEAN Centre for Energy, 2015. Accessed 15 March 2019. https://aseanenergy.org/resources/publications/asean-plan-of-action-for-energy-cooperation-apaec-2016-2025/.

25 *SAARC Regional Energy Trade Study*. Kathmandu, Nepal: SAARC Secretariat, 2010. Accessed 21 October 2020. www.sasec.asia/uploads/publications/srets_a.pdf.

26 The section partly uses contents of the article: Chauhan, Priyanshi. 'Energy Dimension of the Belt and Road Initiative: Implications for India's Energy Security.' *Indian Journal of Asian Affairs* 32, no. 1–2 (2019): 119–52.

27 The GDP growth rate for China in 2017 was 6.9%. See: 'China.' Data. World Bank. Accessed 21 October 2020. https://data.worldbank.org/country/china.

28 *BP Statistical Review of World Energy 2017*. BP, 2018. Accessed 21 October 2020. www.bp.com/content/dam/bp/business-sites/en/global/corporate/pdfs/energy-economics/statistical-review/bp-stats-review-2018-full-report.pdf.

29 Ibid.

30 China is a major force in oil markets, and the gap between rising demand of 11.5 million barrels per day (mb/d) in 2016 and falling production of 4 mb/d has made China the largest oil importer in the world. By 2030, continued increases in demand for transport fuels means that China becomes the world's largest oil consumer, taking over from the United States. See: 'World Energy Outlook 2017: China – Analysis.' IEA, November 2017. Accessed 21 October 2020. www.iea.org/reports/world-energy-outlook-2017-china.

31 Jian, Zhang. Rep. *China's Energy Security: Prospects, Challenges and Opportunities*. Washington DC: The Brookings Institution, 2011. Accessed 21 October 2020. www.brookings.edu/wp-content/uploads/2016/06/07_china_energy_zhang_paper.pdf.

32 In 2003, Hu Jinatao, the former President of People's Republic of China, in a speech to senior party members at an economic work conference highlighted concerns regarding encroachments and possible restrictions to free navigation through the Malacca strait what he called Malacca Dilemma. See: Storey, Ian. 'China's 'Malacca Dilemma." The Jamestown Foundation, 20 September 2016. Accessed 21 October 2020. https://jamestown.org/program/chinas-malacca-dilemma/.

33 Rusli, Mohd Hazmi bin Mohd. 'CO12024: Maritime Highways of Southeast Asia: Alternative Straits?' S. Rajaratnam School of International Studies, 10 February 2012. Accessed 21 October 2020. www.rsis.edu.sg/rsis-publication/rsis/1686-maritime-highways-of-southeast/.

34 The BRI initiative includes six international corridors spanning Asia, Europe and Africa, namely, (i) the new Eurasia land bridge, (ii) the China–Mongolia–Russia economic corridor, (iii) China–Central–West Asia economic corridor (CCWAEC), (iv) China–Indochina Peninsular Economic Corridor, (v) China–Pakistan Economic Corridor, and (vi) Bangladesh–China–India–Myanmar Economic Corridor. These corridors will be made up of networks of rail routes, roads, waterways, pipelines and information highways that link industrial and energy clusters and will contain both an overland and a maritime component. See: Lu, Hui, Charlene Rohr, Marco Hafner, and Anna Knack. Rep. *China Belt and Road Initiative Measuring the Impact of Improving Transportation Connectivity on Trade in the Region*. RAND Corporation, 2018. Accessed 21 October 2020. www.rand.org/pubs/research_reports/RR2625.html.

35 The National Renewable Energy Centre (NREC) estimates that Mongolia's total renewable energy potential is 2.6 terawatts (TQ), a potentially huge resource base for electricity production and export. See: 'Mongolia's Vast Renewable Energy Resources Can Power Sustainable Development.' Press Release. International Renewable Energy Agency, 21 March 2016. Accessed 21 October 2020. www.irena.org/newsroom/pressreleases/2016/Mar/Mongolias-Vast-Renewable-Energy-Resources-Can-Power-Sustainable-Development.

36 Ministry of Planning, Development & Reform 'P' block Pak-Secretariat. 'CPEC-Energy Priority Projects.' Energy | China-Pakistan Economic Corridor (CPEC) Official Website. Ministry of Planning and Development. Government of Pakistan. Accessed 15 March 2019. http://cpec.gov.pk/energy.

37 Thandi, D. 'The Myanmar Pipedream: Myanmar-Bangladesh-India Pipeline'. Centre for Land Warfare Studies, 25 December 2013. Accessed 19 March 2021. https://archive.claws.in/1128/the-myanmar-pipedream-myanmar-bangladesh-india-pipeline-daaman-thandi.html.

38 *ASEAN Power Cooperation Report 2017*. ASEAN Energy Centre, 2017. Accessed 15 March 2019. www.aseanenergy.org/resources/reports/asean-power-cooperation-report/.

39 'India's Plans to Float 'Oil Buyers Club' with China to Cut OPEC's Dominance.' *Business Standard*, 2 July 2018. Accessed 21 October 2020. www.business-standard.com/article/economy-policy/india-s-plans-to-float-oil-buyers-club-with-china-to-cut-opec-s-dominance-118070201063_1.html.

40 Asian Premium is the discriminatory pricing practiced by the OPEC for oil importing countries in Asia. It has its origins in the late 1980s when Saudi Arabia, the de-facto OPEC leader, adopted a marker-based price system for its oil exports. The Asia marker was costlier than the American and European ones, and did not reflect market dynamics due to lack of substantial production centres and oil derivatives market in Asia. Also,

Asian countries dependent heavily on oil imports, were essentially price takers. Therefore, oil exporters used their superior bargaining power to squeeze Asian oil importers while charging less to their American and European customers. See: Kalyanaraman, Anand. 'Scrap 'Asian Premium' on Oil.' *Business Line*, 19 June 2018. Accessed 21 October 2020. www.thehindubusinessline.com/opinion/columns/from-the-viewsroom/scrap-asian-premium-on-oil/article24202983.ece.

41 PTI. 'India Discusses 'Oil Buyers Club' with China; Seeks US Crude.' *The Times of India*, 13 June 2018. Accessed 21 October 2020. https://timesofindia.indiatimes.com/business/india-business/india-discusses-oil-buyers-club-with-china-seeks-us-crude-to-counter-opec/articleshow/64575528.cms.

42 See endnote 9.

43 Ibid.

44 Ibid.

45 *Southeast Asia Energy Outlook 2017*. Paris, France: OECD/IEA, 2017.

46 While the base tariff is set by the government, the fuel adjustment charge is an automatic mechanism that reflects the changes in base-case assumptions that are beyond the control of power utilities, e.g. a higher-than-forecast fuel price increase.

47 Rahman, Mustafizur. *Sustainable Exploitation of Bangladesh's Coal Resources: An Intractable (?) Policy Dilemma*. Dhaka: Centre for Policy Dialogue, 2011.

48 Ibid.

49 At the Tasang dam site area and floodplain alone, over 60,000 people have been forcibly relocated. Also, ethnic minority groups are not only being systematically and forcibly moved from their homes but also robbed, tortured, raped and executed. See: 'Salween.' International Rivers, 2016. Accessed 15 March 2019. www.internationalrivers.org/where-we-work/asia/salween/.

9

ASEAN–INDIA ENERGY COOPERATION

Current status and future scope of cooperation*

Prabir De and Durairaj Kumarasamy

Introduction

In January 2018, the leaders of ASEAN countries and India issued the *Delhi Declaration* to mark the 25th Anniversary of the ASEAN–India Partnership. They recommended:

> Continue to enhance cooperation for ensuring long term food and energy security in our region through strengthening cooperation in agriculture and energy sectors; work together to promote the development of renewable energy technology through international platforms including the International Solar Alliance (ISA) where applicable.[1]

The renewable energy has become the key focus of ASEAN–India energy cooperation.[2] Since renewal energy sources produce very negligible or zero global warming emissions, deeper cooperation in renewal energy may help countries moving towards a low-carbon growth path. ASEAN has set a target of securing 23 per cent of its primary energy from renewable sources by 2025, whereas India aims to achieve 40 per cent of power capacity to be based on non-fossil fuels and reduction in emission intensity by 33–35 per cent by 2030.[3] The leaders of ASEAN and India have,

* An earlier version of the paper was presented at the International Conference on India and Its Neighbours, Organised by the Centre for South Asian Studies, Jawaharlal Nehru University (JNU) on 24–25 March 2019, and at the Indian Oil Institute of Petroleum Management (IIPM), Gurgaon on 2 August 2019 by the first author. The authors are grateful to seminar participants for their comments. The authors are also grateful to Dr Anbhumozhi Venkatachalam, Senior Economist, ERIA, Jakarta, and the ASEAN Centre for Energy (ACE) for sharing their perspectives on ASEAN energy cooperation. Authors also had detailed discussions with the Ministry of Power and Ministry of New and Renewable Energy on India's activities on energy cooperation with South and Southeast Asian countries. Views expressed by the authors are their own. Usual disclaimers apply.

TABLE 9.1 Targets for SDG 7

1. By 2030, ensure universal access to affordable, reliable and modern energy services.
2. By 2030, increase substantially the share of renewable energy in the global energy mix.
3. By 2030, double the global rate of improvement in energy efficiency.
4. By 2030, enhance international co-operation to facilitate access to clean energy research and technology, including renewable energy, energy efficiency and advanced and cleaner fossil-fuel technology, and promote investment in energy infrastructure and clean energy technology.
5. By 2030, expand infrastructure and upgrade technology for supplying modern and sustainable energy services for all in developing countries, in particular the least developed countries, small island developing states and land-locked developing countries, in accordance with their respective programmes of support.

Source: 'SDG 7: Affordable and Clean Energy.' United Nations. United Nations, 2020. https://in.one.un.org/page/sustainable-development-goals/sdg-7/.

therefore, called for a stronger collaboration to achieve energy security and to meet the Sustainable Development Goals (SDG) for ensuring access to affordable, reliable, sustainable and modern energy for all.

The energy cooperation between ASEAN and India appears to be more promising if we consider the countries' commitments under the Sustainable Development Goals (SDG). ASEAN countries and India are committed to achieve SDG 7, which aims to ensure access to affordable, reliable, sustainable and modern energy for all by 2030 (Table 9.1). Therefore, to expand energy access, it is crucial to enhance energy efficiency and to invest in renewable energy.[4] These targets may seem ambitious, but with better cooperation between ASEAN and India, it can become a possibility. Therefore, strengthening the discourse on renewable energy cooperation will help meet the twin targets – SDG as well as climate change.

ASEAN–India energy cooperation has huge potential to accelerate the engagements in renewable energy. India shares both land and maritime borders with ASEAN. Both have wide access to ocean, wind, solar and other forms of renewable energy sources. While India's power grid is connected with Myanmar on a small scale, several ASEAN countries are now members of India's International Solar Alliance (ISA). When the countries in ASEAN and India face common SDG targets and challenges in renewable energy, regional cooperation makes sense to generate wider benefits, particularly through exchange of know-how, conduct of training and capacity building while dealing the common challenges together.

India's energy trade with South and Southeast Asian countries

South Asian countries are endowed with energy resources, which are unevenly distributed and underutilised. India's energy trade with South Asian countries is below the optimal capacity. The imbalance in supply and demand in energy resources in the region can be minimised through energy trading among the South Asian countries. For instance, India, Pakistan and Bangladesh have large reserves of gas and coal, while Nepal and Bhutan have a high potential for hydro-electric power. Among South Asian countries, India holds more than 95 per cent of coal resources, oil and natural resources.[5] India also holds a major share of biomass and hydro resources, followed by Nepal and Bhutan. In the case of renewable energy like solar energy, South Asian countries have been producing at the same capacity. India has huge potential and capacity in wind energy, compared to other South Asian countries (see Tables 9.2 and 9.3).

India's power trade with its neighbours is largely one-sided. India annually imports around 1,200 MW power from Bhutan, and exports 1,200 MW to Bangladesh, 450 MW to Nepal and 3 MW to Myanmar.[6] In the case of high-speed diesel (HSD), India's exports to South Asian countries are mostly directed to Bangladesh, Bhutan, Nepal and Sri Lanka (Table 9.4). India's export of HSD to Bangladesh has witnessed a massive rise of 195.4 per cent in the last two years. India has started exporting HSD to Myanmar via land border since 2017–18. The cross-border electricity trade in the South Asian region has the potential to grow to 60,000 MW through 2045 with the likely strengthening of regional power cooperation among countries including India, Bhutan, Bangladesh, Nepal, Pakistan, Sri Lanka and Myanmar.[7] Currently, about 3,000 MW of electricity is being traded in the region among the seven countries, which is likely to be doubled by 2020.[8]

TABLE 9.2 Energy resource potential in South Asia

	Coal (million tonnes)	*Oil (million barrels)*	*Natural gas (trillion cubic feet)*	*Biomass (million tonnes)*	*Hydropower (gigawatts)*
Afghanistan	440	–	15	18–27	25
Bangladesh	884	12	8	0.08	0.33
Bhutan	2	–	–	26.60	30
India	90085	5700	39	139	150
Nepal	–	–	–	27.04	83
Pakistan	17550	324	33	–	59
Sri Lanka	–	150	–	12	2
Regional Total	108961	5906	95	223	349.33

Source: Asian Development Bank (2012).

TABLE 9.3 Renewable energy potential in South Asia

	Bangladesh	*India*	*Nepal*	*Bhutan*	*Pakistan*	*Sri Lanka*
Solar power (Kmh/ sq.m. per day)	3.8–6.5	4–7	3.6–6.2	2.5–5	5.3	NA
Wind (MW)	Limited potential	151918	3000	4825	24000	25000

Source: Asian Development Bank (2012).

TABLE 9.4 India's export of HSD to South Asian countries (US$ million)

	2016–2017	2017–2018	Growth (%)
Bangladesh	91.94	271.61	195.4
Bhutan	65.43	107.91	64.9
Nepal	513.59	931.22	81.3
Sri Lanka	314.49	358.48	13.9
Myanmar	0.00	0.02	
Total	985.45	1669.24	69.4

Source: Calculated based on EXIM Databank, Ministry of Commerce and Industry, India.

Bhutan has an installed generation capacity of 1,606 MW currently and exports around 70 per cent of its annual electricity production to India.[9] For Nepal, its overall electricity supply is inadequate to meet the rising power demand and therefore the country relies on imported diesel from India. The current installed power generation capacity of Nepal is around 792 MW, out of which 734 MW (93 per cent) is generated from hydro resources and 53 MW (7 per cent) is generated from thermal resources.[10] Nepal imports about 450 MW power from India through 11 cross-border interconnection lines. Apart from the huge potential of hydro and coal reserves, South Asia is also rich in natural gas. For example, natural gas contributes about 78 per cent of Bangladesh's total power generation.[11]

The Motihari–Amlekhgunj petroleum product pipeline between India and Nepal was inaugurated in September 2019. The 69 km-long pipeline from Motihari in Bihar to Amlekhgunj in Nepal is the first-ever cross-border petroleum product pipeline in the South Asia region. Built by Indian Oil Corporation (IOC) and Nepal Oil Corporation (NOC), the pipeline has the capacity to carry two million metric tonnes of clean petroleum products to Nepal. This oil pipeline has several advantages for Nepal such as it reduces the retail pump price in Nepal, prevents pilferage and adulteration and ensures an uninterrupted supply during blockades or unrest.[12]

IOC is also planning to set up a LPG storage and liquefied petroleum gas (LPG) import terminal in Myanmar. The terminal to import natural gas will be in addition to the similar facilities planned by Indian firms in Bangladesh and Sri Lanka as part of larger plan of energy connectivity in the South Asian neighbourhood. Numaligarh Refinery Ltd (NRL) in Assam has started supplying diesel to Myanmar and is looking at options to build fuel storage and distribution sector in that country. The Hydrocarbon Vision 2030 for North East India envisages a natural gas pipeline from Numaligarh towards Sittwe (in Myanmar) in different phases.

NRL exports diesel through a rail rake from Siliguri in West Bengal to Parbatipur in Bangladesh and are in the process of constructing a 130 km long product pipeline for uninterrupted supply. In addition, Indian companies are working on connecting India's gas grid with that of Bangladesh and supply gas for power generation at Khulna Power Plant. In Sri Lanka, India is jointly developing Trincomalee oil storage tank farm and is also working on setting up an LNG terminal and a 500 MW

LNG-fired power plant near Colombo. Also, there is a proposal to develop city gas distribution (CGD) and CNG market and infrastructure in Sri Lanka. India is working with Sri Lanka on a proposal to set up a solar power plant at Sampur, which would be of 50 MW to begin with.

The energy cooperation between India and Bangladesh was signed in October 2013 through the initiation of two collaborative power projects. The first project involves a transmission line to supply 500 MW of power from West Bengal to Bangladesh. This 125 km grid is a cross-border link between the Bheramara of the western electrical grid of Bangladesh and the Baharampur of the eastern electrical grid of India. The system was started with an initial power flow of 500 MW into Bangladesh from the Indian grid, with a provision to boost the power flow to 1,000 MW.[13] The second project includes a 1,320 MW thermal power undertaking in Bangladesh named 'Maitri'. The Bangladesh–India Friendship Power Company is a joint venture between the National Thermal Power Corporation (NTPC) of India and the Bangladesh Power Development Board.[14]

In South Asia, only India and Bhutan trade electricity. In addition, India supplies some power to Bangladesh. Demand for electricity in South Asia and particularly in Bangladesh, Bhutan, India and Nepal has been growing rapidly, which can be addressed through regional cooperation on energy trade.[15] For example, India is assisting Bhutan to build a 10,000 MW hydropower project with concessional finance, with a total investment of about US$10 billion. Hydro electricity from the river power plant built on the Mangdechhu River in Bhutan will be taken towards the Eastern and Northeastern region of India. PTC India Ltd (PTC) signed a Power Purchase Agreement (PPA) with Druk Green Power Corporation Ltd (DGPC) to purchase surplus power from 720 MW Mangdechhu Hydro Electric Project in Bhutan for 35 years. In addition, India has an extensive engagement in Bhutan's hydro power sector. Since 1961, India has helped Bhutan to develop several hydro power plants such as Tala, Chuka, Jaldhaka, among others.

For a long time, ASEAN countries such as Malaysia, Indonesia, Thailand and Brunei have been important sources of India's crude oil. In recent years, however, India's trade in energy products has undergone some major changes. While India has become a major importer of coal, India has also become a major exporter of refined petroleum products. As of now, petroleum products constitute the largest export item of India. India's petroleum products like HSD are exported to Southeast Asian countries such as Singapore, Thailand and Myanmar. However, India's exports of petroleum products are moving more towards some other regions/countries such as EU, UAE, South Africa and some ASEAN countries like Singapore and Thailand (Table 9.5).

Myanmar has an estimated hydropower potential of 39,720 MW, of which only about 2 per cent has been developed. India and Myanmar have collaborative agreements for the development of the Sedawyagi and Yeywa hydropower projects. India is also participating in the Tamanti multipurpose project with a hydropower component of 1,200 MW in the first stage. Inadequate investments in transmission and distribution grids meant to export power from Nepal to the Northeast region of

TABLE 9.5 India's export of high-speed diesel, top ten destinations

Country	*2010–11*	*Country*	*2015–16*	*Country*	*2017–2018*	*Country*	*2019–20*
Netherland	1,989.22	Saudi Arab	1,021.90	Singapore	4,054.27	Singapore	2,493.19
Brazil	1,821.21	Singapore	921.36	Israel	1,044.23	Netherland	1,603.27
Singapore	1,443.66	Turkey	828.91	Turkey	912.72	Mozambique	1,579.16
France	1,212.30	Israel	801.56	Malaysia	901.53	Israel	1,284.77
Israel	1,163.46	Kenya	724.43	Netherland	886.38	Nepal	931.22
UAE	691.11	Mozambique	713.89	Australia	795.09	Turkey	841.93
Tanzania	598.23	Gibraltar	651.4	Nepal	722.05	Malaysia	781.46
Belgium	558.82	Netherland	632.42	South Africa	629.75	Tanzania	681.9
Kenya	506.23	Australia	629.45	Tanzania	597.82	South Africa	543.53
South Africa	465.55	Tanzania	582.23	Mozambique	531.74	Belgium	497.43

Source: Calculated based on EXIM Databank, Ministry of Commerce and Industry, India.

India (although already synchronised with the eastern and northern regions) hampers the power trade between these two countries.[16]

India is already active in the ASEAN region through investment in energy sector as well as development of energy infrastructure. While the focus of Indian companies investing in the region are Myanmar, Vietnam, Indonesia and Malaysia, its involvement in energy infrastructure development is by and large limited to CLMV countries through development cooperation and construction of facilities. The major investments made by Indian firms in Myanmar are in oil and gas sector (98 per cent of India's total investment in Myanmar), of which, almost 90 per cent of India's investment in Myanmar has been made by ONGC Videsh Ltd (Table 9.6). The company has invested via JV and WOS with various India-based and foreign-based firms in Myanmar. ONGC Videsh Ltd (OVL) has also invested in the oil and gas sector in Vietnam. The other major Indian firms in the oil and gas sector are Gas Authority of India Limited (GAIL), Jubilant Oil and Gas Private Limited, Oil India Limited, Petro Engineering and Construction Pvt Ltd, etc.[17]

Similarly, OVL has also invested heavily in the Vietnam. OVL aims to support India's oil and gas security through overseas participation in oil and gas exploration and production activities. OVL has won two on-land oil blocks in Myanmar in 2013, which have strengthened its presence in the Southeast Asian nations. OVL has stakes in the A-1 and A-3 gas discovery blocks and three other offshore acreages in Myanmar. The Ministry of Energy, Myanmar, has awarded 13 blocks onshore blocks, out of which OVL received Blocks B-2 (Zebyutaung-Nandaw) and EP-3 (Thegon-Shwegu) for exploration. In order to attract FDI in its production sharing contract (PSCs), Myanmar has reduced the income tax rate from 30 per cent to 25 per cent and extended an existing three-year tax holiday to five-year.

The other major Indian firms of both public and private enterprises in oil and gas and power sector are Gas Authority of India Ltd (GAIL), Jubilant Oil and Gas Private Ltd, Oil India Ltd, Petro Engineering and Construction Pvt Ltd, The Tata

TABLE 9.6 Major Indian firms invested in energy sector in ASEAN: 2008–19 (US$ million)

Country	*Indian firm*	*Foreign firm*	*JV/WOS*	*Major activity*	*Value*
Indonesia	Welspun Steel Limited	Pt. Batubara Energy Indonesia	JV	Wholesale, retail, restaurants and hotels	892.8
Indonesia	Confidence Petroleum India Ltd	Surya Gio Gas Indonesia	JV	Manufacturing	416.9
Indonesia	Tridem Port and Power Company Private Limited	Pt ISMT Resources	WOS	Agriculture and mining	257.8
Indonesia	Gulf Oil Corpn Ltd	Pt Gulf Oil Lubricants Indonesia,	WOS	Manufacturing	164.3
Indonesia	Sea 6 Energy Pvt Ltd	Pt Sea Six Energy Indonesia	WOS	Finance, insurance and Business Services	135.1
Malaysia	Jaybee Energy Pvt Ltd	Umw Sher (L) Ltd	JV	Agriculture and mining	250.4
Myanmar	ONGC Videsh Ltd.	Shwe Offshore Pipeline	JV	Agriculture and mining	272.5
Myanmar	Gail (India) Ltd.	Shwe Offshore Pipeline	JV	Agriculture and mining	253.1
Myanmar	Oil India Limited	Block Yeb	JV	Agriculture and mining	228.7
Myanmar	Gail (India) Ltd	Petroleum Production Sharing Contract in Myanmar, Block A-1	JV	Manufacturing	227.2
Myanmar	Gail (India) Ltd	Petroleum Production Sharing Contract in Myanmar, Block A-3	JV	Manufacturing	227.2
Singapore	The Tata Power Company Limited	Trust Energy Resources Pte Ltd	WOS	Electricity, gas and water	48535.2
Singapore	Bhuruka Gases Ltd	Bhoruka Overseas Pte Ltd	WOS	Manufacturing	44357.7
Singapore	GVK Power & Infrastructure Limited	GVK Coal Developers (Singapore) Pte Ltd	JV	Transport, storage and communication services	40745.1

Singapore	Gupta Coal India Limited	Transasia Pacific GNR Pvt Ltd	WOS	Wholesale, retail, restaurants and hotels	39367.7
Singapore	Ankur Scientific Energy Technologies Pvt Ltd	Helios Renewables Pte Ltd	WOS	Manufacturing	37847.2
Vietnam	ONGC Videsh Ltd.	Petroleum Production Sharing Contract in Vietnam	JV	Manufacturing	282.8
Vietnam	ONGC Videsh Ltd.	Block 128 Oil and Gas Exploration Project Vietnam	WOS	Manufacturing	210.2
Vietnam	ONGC Videsh Ltd.	Block 127 Oil and Gas Exploration Project Vietnam.	WOS	Manufacturing	68.4
Vietnam	Adani Green Energy Limited	Adani Phuoc Minh Solar Power Company Limited	JV	Electricity, gas and water	41.8

Source: Authors' calculation based on RBI data.

Power Company Ltd, Adani Green Energy Ltd, Jaybee Energy Pvt Ltd, GVK Power & Infrastructure Ltd, etc. (see Table 9.6)

To conclude, India highly depends on crude oil imports for its energy demand mainly. India imports nearly 80 per cent of its domestic crude oil requirements mainly from West Asia. It also gets more than 10 per cent of its domestic coal requirements mainly from Indonesia, Australia, and South Africa.[18] Cross-border linkages include the importing of power from Bhutan and exporting of power to Nepal. While India is a net importer of energy, the increase in refining capacity has helped turn India into a net exporter of refined petroleum products.

ASEAN approach to energy cooperation

Region-wide energy cooperation in ASEAN started in 1976 when the ASEAN Council for Petroleum (ASCOPE) was established. In the initial phase, the focus was on oil and power grid cooperation. The objective of ASCOPE was to promote active collaboration and mutual assistance in the development of petroleum resources. The ASEAN level cooperation started in this regard in 1981 as it established a task force involving the Heads of ASEAN Public Utilities Authorities (HAPUA) with the objective of promoting cooperation on power grid connections. The main focus was on establishing mechanisms to avoid supply disruptions.

In another important development, the ASEAN Energy Cooperation Agreement (AECA) was signed in 1986 through which the member countries agreed to cooperate on a wide range of issues to foster efficient development and use of all forms of energy. Cooperation activities included planning, development of resources, conservation, security of supply, capacity building and exchange of information. In addition, an important milestone was achieved in the form of ASEAN Petroleum Security Agreement (APSA) in 1986, which was a binding agreement that put obligations on member countries. It established the ASEAN Emergency Petroleum Sharing Scheme (AEPSS) to ensure mutual supply of oil by six countries in sudden shortfalls in supplies.

ASEAN Plan of Action of Energy Cooperation (APAEC) (2016–2025)

In terms of energy consumption, the ASEAN region is projected to double its energy usage between 2010 and 2035. Fossil fuels will remain the dominant source of energy, with oil consumption projected to double; while the use of natural gas expected to triple.[19] Coal consumption is also projected to rise to over 80 per cent during the same period. Studies indicate that continued reliance on fossil fuels to meet energy demands will have serious environmental consequences, affecting air and water quality, water availability, land use and even the global climate. Hence, there is a crucial need to ensure that energy sources will not only be affordable but also environmentally sustainable in the long run. Recognising the urgency of the ASEAN region's energy predicament, the ASEAN Plan of Action for Energy Cooperation 2010–2015 (APAEC) was prepared to serve as a blueprint on ASEAN cooperation on energy. APAEC is a series of policy documents to support the implementation of multilateral energy cooperation to advance regional integration and connectivity goals in ASEAN.[20] ASEAN recognises the critical role of an efficient, reliable and sustainable energy in stimulating regional economic growth and development.

The fourth APAEC (2016–2025)[21] was launched at the 32nd ASEAN Ministers on Energy Meeting (AMEM) held on September 2014 in Vientiane, Laos PDR endorsed the theme as 'Enhancing Energy Connectivity and Market Integration in ASEAN to Achieve Energy Security, Accessibility, Affordability and Sustainability for All'. The APAEC 2016–2025 is being implemented in two phases. Phase I covers the period 2016–2020 for the implementation of short to medium-term measures to enhance energy security cooperation and to take further steps towards connectivity and integration.

ASEAN welcomes collaborative partnerships with development partners and international organisations to achieve the aspirations of the ASEAN Community Vision 2025. Engagement with development partners and international organisations will play a key role in meeting ASEAN's energy objectives and targets under the APAEC 2016–2025. The APAEC strategies are broad and flexible enough to meet the ever-changing global and regional energy environments and to support the goals of the ASEAN Economic Community Blueprint 2025. ASEAN has had strong support from development partners (Australia, China, EU, India, Korea, Japan, the US, Russia) and international organisations (International Energy Agency (IEA), IRENA and International Atomic Energy Agency/IAEA), over a broad range of activities like joint research studies, capacity building workshops, and publications.

The key strategies of the seven programme areas of the APEC 2016–2025 phase 1 are summarised as follows:

(i) ASEAN power grid to initiate multilateral electricity trade in at least one sub-region by 2018. To meet the electricity demand in ASEAN, HAPUA implemented strategies to expand the cross-border ASEAN power grid system at sub-regional level and then finally integrated the whole ASEAN region. Through the interconnection project (Figure 9.1), the power exchange and purchase would almost triple from 3,489 MW in 2014 to 10,800 MW in 2020 and further increase to 16,000 MW post-2020.[22]

(ii) Trans-ASEAN Gas Pipeline (TAGP) to enhance connectivity for energy security and accessibility via pipelines and regasification terminals. The ASCOPE is responsible for the effective implementation of the TAGP Project through multiple physical pipeline interconnections and regasifiation terminals (RGT).[23] As of 2015, a total of 13 bilateral gas pipeline interconnection projects connecting six (6) countries bilaterally and with a total length of approximately 3,673 km have been successfully commissioned. Driven by economic growth, natural gas demand in the region is expected to grow from 14.5 billion standard cubic feet per day (BSCFD) in 2013 to 23 BSCFD by 2035. Considering the challenges in global gas developments, including the east Natuna Gas Field, the strategic focus of TAGP will expand from piped gas to LNG as the option for gas supply in

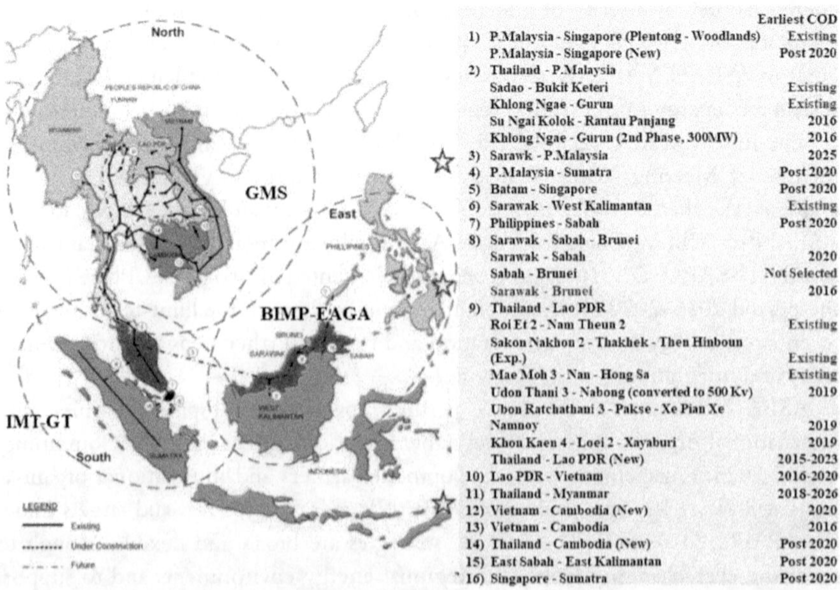

FIGURE 9.1 Interconnection Projects of ASEAN Power Grid. ASEAN Centre for Energy (ACE).

the region. In this regard, further to the four (4) RGTs, it is expected that there will be at least one additional RGT in operation by 2020.[24]

Coal and clean coal technology to enhance the image of coal through promotion of clean coal technologies (CCT), ASEAN Forum on Coal (AFOC) is responsible for promoting the development and utilisation of clean coal technologies and facilitating intra-ASEAN coal trade towards enhancing regional energy security and sustainable development. Coal is expected to continue to be a major fuel for power generation in the future. Consequently, CCT is important in helping to ensure that coal is used in a sustainable manner that will contribute to significant improvements in coal utilisation efficiency and environmental performance compared to existing coal plants. ASEAN will continue its effort to adopt the most appropriate, efficient and clean coal technologies in the region.

(iii) Energy efficiency and conservation to reduce energy intensity by 20 per cent in 2020 based on 2005 level.[25] To address the limited global reserve of fossil fuels and volatile energy prices, the ASEAN Member States (AMS) have been following a deliberate policy of diversifying and using energy sources efficiently. The Energy Efficiency and Conservation Sub-sector Network (EE&C-SSN) is responsible for the coordination of ASEAN's collective efforts on energy efficiency towards its target of reduction in energy intensity. A large number of programmes were implemented, jointly with DPs like the EU, Japan, Korea, the USA and international organisations like the United Nations Environment Programme (UNEP) to improve energy efficiency in all major energy consumption areas including the residential, commercial buildings, industry and transport sectors.

(iv) Renewable energy: Target to increase the component of renewable energy to 23 per cent by 2025 in ASEAN Energy Mix.[26] The AMS deployment of renewable energy technologies was initially based on policies to reduce oil consumption but later included policies to mitigate environmental impacts of fossil fuel use, including the potential effects of climate change. The Renewable Energy Sub-sector Network (RE-SSN) is responsible for carrying out the implementation of renewable energy programmes to increase the diversity of energy supply and to reduce the environmental impact of energy use in the region. In 2013, the amount of ASEAN's electricity produced from renewable energy sources was 169.34 terawatt hours (TWh), accounting for about 21 per cent of total electricity generation. In the same year, ASEAN marked an unprecedented success, achieving 25 per cent share of renewable energy in total installed capacity or about 45.7 GW. This exceeded the 2015 collective target set out in APAEC 2010–2015 of 15 per cent for regional renewable energy of total installed power capacity.[27] The development of renewable energy in the AMS covers hydro, geothermal, solar photovoltaic, solar thermal, wind, bioenergy (bio-ethanol, bio-diesel, biogas, bio-oil) and waste. Others, such as ocean energy (thermal, wave, and tidal), fuel cell, hydrogen and coal liquefaction/gasification are in the research, development and demonstration stages. Solar and wind energy are still considered capital intensive and not as affordable as conventional energy. ASEAN needs more technology transfer and meaningful partnerships to make these energy sources viable, to meet its increasing requirements. The AMS also recognise that renewable energies are crucial for increasing the diversity of energy supply and reducing the environmental impact of energy use in the region.

(v) Regional Energy Policy and Planning (REPP) to better profile the energy sector internationally. With the aim of enhancing ASEAN's engagement with development partners and international organisations, REPP-SSN's key achievement was the successful signing of the ASEAN-IEA MoU in 2011 on the sidelines of the 29th ASEAN Ministers of Energy Meeting (AMEM) in Brunei Darussalam. The MoU has enabled ASEAN to collaborate and benefit from IEA through Ministerial Dialogues and expertise in key areas of ASEAN's interest, including energy data collection/analysis, gas market industry dialogue, emergency preparedness, etc.

(vi) Civilian nuclear energy to build capabilities in policy, technology and regulatory aspects of nuclear energy. Civilian nuclear energy, as a clean source of energy can help ASEAN meet its growing energy demand in the region. To enhance cooperation in areas such as public information/awareness, capacity building, including human resource development, education and training, nuclear safety, emergency preparedness and regulatory framework of civilian nuclear power plants (NPPs) in ASEAN, the Nuclear Energy Cooperation-SSN (NEC-SSN) collaborating with international organisations made several international agreements.

ASEAN renewable energy targets

According to the ACE study, regional renewable energy can also enhance energy security as it reduces import dependencies. Energy security refers to the availability of energy at affordable prices. Figure 9.2 illustrates ASEAN country-wise renewable energy targets. As countries invest more in renewable energy, they would be less dependent on energy imports to fuel their nation's energy consumption needs. For example, ASEAN members with similar energy security challenges can coordinate the development of renewable energy in the region. Overall, this would improve the energy mix and grow their energy security.

Regional cooperation is imperative if ASEAN wants to achieve their renewable energy target for 2025. One of the benefits of cooperation among ASEAN states with regards to renewable energy is that it would create space for dialogue and better coordination. India and ASEAN may consider setting up ASEAN–India Energy Forum to exchange knowledge and to put into practice examples of the implementation of renewable energy policies.

FIGURE 9.2 ASEAN Renewable Energy Targets. Authors' own based on ASEAN Centre for Energy (ACE).

ASEAN have already made positive moves towards more cooperation within the region for renewable energy. ASEAN and IRENA signed an MoU in September 2018 for long-term cooperation between the two bodies and to harness ASEAN's renewable energy potential.

ASEAN is also implementing the ASEAN Power Grid, which aims to enhance electricity trade across regional borders – complementing the rise in demand for electricity. The ASEAN Power Grid looks to integrate infrastructure that is both clean and sustainable. One of the projects under the ASEAN Power Grid is the Laos–Thailand–Malaysia–Singapore Power Integration Project. This project involves Malaysia purchasing up to 100 megawatts (MW) of hydro power from Lao PDR through Thailand's transmission grid. This is beneficial for Malaysia because it would also improve the share of sustainable energy in their total energy mix.

The study by ACE also shows that while there can be huge benefits from regional cooperation,[28] there are also strong obstacles that could impede them. One of the biggest challenges is financial constraints. The study shows that the deployment and transfer of renewable energy technologies requires large funding. It was reported in the media last year that half of Southeast Asia's renewable energy projects are not financially viable.

This poses a serious problem if ASEAN wants to meet its target by 2025. Especially with IRENA reporting that the region's energy demand has grown by 60 per cent over the past 15 years, and is only expected to keep on growing. Clearly, ASEAN governments need to seriously consider renewable energies when planning their energy mix.

ASEAN's energy cooperation programme with neighbouring countries

ASEAN has been engaging in a number of bilateral and multilateral initiatives with the neighbouring countries on energy cooperation. Energy cooperation related issues are the focused areas in the meetings among the ASEAN+3 energy ministers (AMEM),[29] to promote wider use of energy efficiency and conservation measures, diversification of types and sources of energy and development of indigenous petroleum. ASEAN+3 cooperation on energy security also encourages effective dialogue and cooperation between ASEAN+3 and major energy producing countries both within and outside of the region. ASEAN has also organised the Energy Security Forum in cooperation with China, Japan and Korea to work in formalising a mechanism for regional consultation and coordination strategies in case of emergency energy shortages within the region.

ASEAN and China have energy cooperation in the areas of planning nuclear energy programmes and promotion of clean energy and also support at capacity building on civilian nuclear energy.[30] Japan initiated the Hiranuma Initiative at the 8th International Energy Forum in 2002 at Osaka to promote cooperative dialogue between energy producing and consuming countries. The initiative has listed five priority areas for Asian energy cooperation, such as (i) energy security network; (ii) oil stockpiling; (iii) studies on the oil market; (iv) promotion of natural gas usage and (v) renewable energy.[31]

In the event of East Asia Economic (EAS) Summit in 2007 (including India, Australia and New Zealand in addition to ASEAN+3 countries) has initiated the Cebu Declaration on East Asian Energy Security for the promotion of energy efficiency and conservation, voluntarily formulate energy efficiency goals and action plans. In support of Cebu Declaration, Japan has proposed Abe Initiative to help promote energy conservation, the use of biomass energy, the development of clean coal technology and the use of energy for poverty eradication.

Prospects for India–ASEAN energy cooperation

From the above section, it is evident that ASEAN has introduced a comprehensive regional energy cooperation programme; whereas India's regional cooperation within South Asia is mostly at the bilateral level particularly in the electricity sector. Given the huge potentials in the Southeast Asia, India is yet to explore the potential energy resources to access natural gas and hydro power with the region. India has already engaged in energy infrastructure development in the ASEAN region, particularly in the CLMV countries such as building hydropower projects, power transmission lines and substations and oil and gas pipelines etc.

Energy sector machineries, equipment and other goods can also open up possibilities for substantial trade. ASEAN is developing a region-wide grid of natural gas pipelines and electricity transmission lines. India can possibly get connected through these two ASEAN-wide grids by developing transmission line and gas pipeline connections with Myanmar. The Indian electricity grid is already connected with the Bangladesh electricity grid. The proposed pipeline would extend from Block A-1, through Bangladesh, to India and various design options are being considered, including a land route via the eastern Indian states of Tripura and Mizoram, an offshore route through the coastal areas of Bangladesh and a deep-sea route.

India is the fourth largest energy consumer in the world behind China, the US, and Russia, importing 80 per cent of its crude oil and 25 per cent of its natural gas requirements. India is the sixth top investing country among the top ten investing countries in renewable energy with an increase of 22 per cent amounting to US$10.2 billion. For solar energy, India represents as a low-cost destination for grid-connected solar power. Further development of solar power in India would reduce emissions per unit of GDP by 20 to 25 per cent in 2020 and produce clean energy for the country.[32] The Ministry of New and Renewable Energy (MNRE) has also set up a Solar Energy Centre to test solar thermal and solar photovoltaic materials, devices, and systems in addition to its applied research and training on solar power development. In addition, wind power dominates the renewable energy industry of India, representing 70 per cent of its total renewable energy capacity. This can be attributed to the considerable support from government by providing significant tax incentives that have induced substantial investments in wind energy projects.

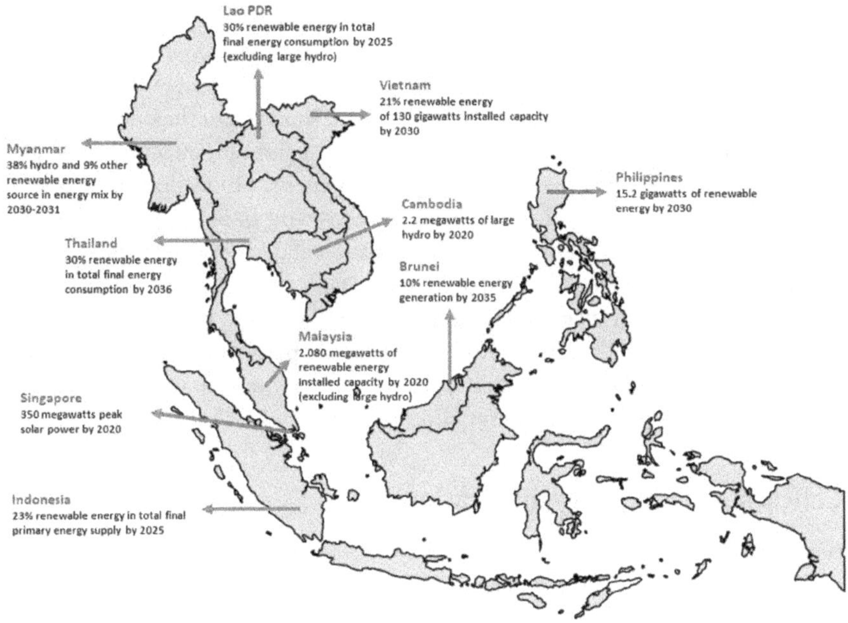

FIGURE 9.3 SDG 7 and India SDG 7 and India United Nations, 2020 https://in.one.un.org/page/sustainable-development-goals/sdg-7/

India is projected to be a significant contributor to the rise in global energy demand, around one-quarter of the total. However, as of 2016, more than 207 million people in India do not have access to electricity. Figure 9.3 illustrates India's commitments under the SDG 7. The government's National Solar Mission is playing an important role in the work towards renewable energy, and interventions in rural electrification and new ultra-mega power projects are moving India towards achieving universal energy access.

In exploration of renewable energy, particularly naturally abundant solar and wind energy, India has initiated the International Solar Alliance (ISA), which now has more than 121[33] prospective member countries. Most of the ASEAN countries are prospective members of ISA, among which Cambodia has signed and Myanmar has signed and ratified the ISA Framework Agreement. The aim of the ISA is bringing together a group of nations to endorse clean energy, sustainable environment, public transport and climate through solar power utilisation and moving towards low-carbon growth path. India has aims to achieve 100 GW solar energy, 175 GW renewable energy by 2022, and reduction in emission intensity by 33–35 percent by 2030. The ISA has also been committed to invest US$ 1 trillion in the exploration of solar energy.

The official discussion on energy cooperation between India and ASEAN has focused widely on renewable energy. The first meeting on ASEAN–India renewable energy cooperating in 2012, both parties emphasised on ways to complement each other on respective renewable energy policies to mutually address the energy needs. India has developed significant capability in electricity generation through wind energy. Similarly, Indonesia and the Philippines have developed geothermal energy and Singapore is generating significant electricity from waste. India and Thailand have some explore in solar power as well. India is also the only country to generate nuclear power and use biofuel to generate significant quantity of electricity. These countries can help others in developing energy production capabilities in the respective sub-sectors. Therefore, both ASEAN and India have huge scope in renewable energy cooperation through information and knowledge sharing to help to develop national policies. ASEAN member states stand to benefit from India's expertise on wind and solar energy. In this case, ASEAN and India should establish a coordinating mechanism through which energy experts from ASEAN and India will be able to share knowledge and expertise necessary in formulating sound, feasible, and practical policies on energy collaboration.

Conclusions and policy implications

Both ASEAN and India are committed to SDGs to ensure access to affordable, reliable, sustainable and modern energy for all by 2030 and targets to reduce global warming emissions through promoting different means of renewable energy source, which shows the need of deeper energy cooperation between ASEAN and India (see Figure 9.4). The energy cooperation between ASEAN and India appears to be more promising if we consider the countries commitments under ASEAN–India should engage in joint research and development in the energy sector. Particularly, with regards grid stability, cleaner deeper management and green management are the potential areas for cooperation. The private sector should engage in both conventional and renewable energy in ASEAN power projects.

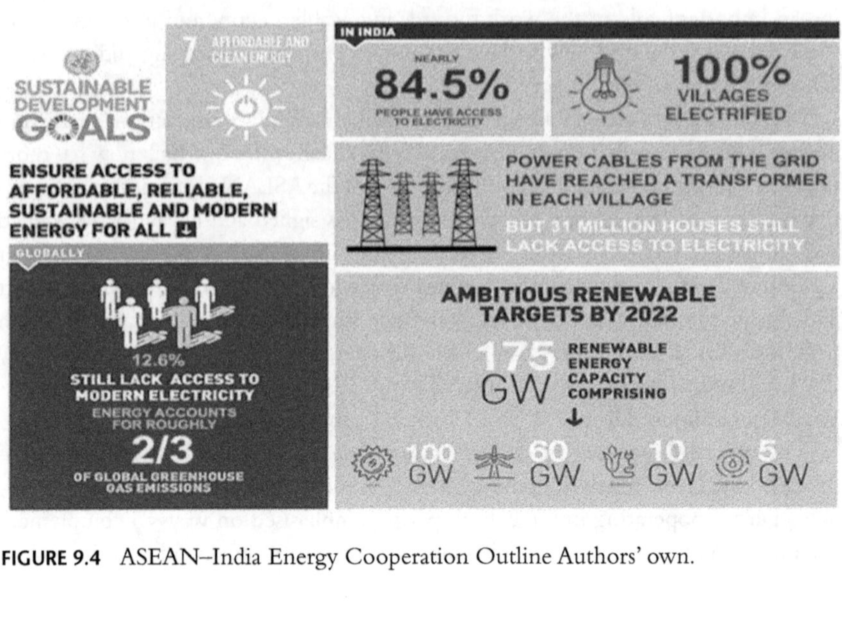

FIGURE 9.4 ASEAN–India Energy Cooperation Outline Authors' own.

Promotion of the cross-border electricity exchange and trade between ASEAN and India would optimise usage of the regional resources for electricity generation. India already has grid interconnections with Nepal and Bhutan but more energy market integration would take place it extended to ASEAN countries through Myanmar.

India can possibly engage in regional and sub-regional cooperation with SAAR, BIMSTEC and ASEAN. For instance, the BIMSTEC region is abundant in energy resources such as hydropower, hydrocarbons and renewable energy. Also, Bangladesh and Myanmar have large gas reserves, which can be explored as alternate sources of gas supply. Similarly, Nepal and Bhutan have immense potential for hydropower, which is untapped due to the absence of a market that can create demand of this magnitude. The energy demand–supply sectors in Bangladesh, India, Myanmar, Sri Lanka, Thailand, Nepal and Bhutan offer a potential for regional resource cooperation, which could go beyond export-import trade relations and link the region in a Bay of Bengal Energy Community and thus contribute to the process of regional integration.[34]

While moving towards a low-carbon growth path, trade in clean/green energy is essential. Therefore, India and ASEAN shall strengthen energy cooperation for trade in clean energy products. Here, India may consider leading the integration process. India's oil companies such as Indian Oil (and other oil companies) have to initiate the integration process with ASEAN. India may develop a structure for a regional energy exchange along with their operational procedures and regulatory and commercial requirements for cross-border trade with ASEAN.

Both ASEAN and India shall identify the technically and economically feasible cross-border interconnections. Besides, India and ASEAN shall improve the investment environment for both electricity generation and transmission. ASEAN and India may consider harmonising legal and regulatory frameworks dealing with cross-border trade along with an Energy Charter Treaty for greater security for cross-border energy transfer related investments and transactions. There are several investment opportunities in energy pipelines and energy-related infrastructure, thereby showing the scope of further P2P collaboration between ASEAN and India.

ASEAN countries and India may undertake projects to support sustainable energy and livelihood. Energy cooperation between India and Myanmar in the border areas can be taken up on a priority basis. Cooperation in the renewable energy sector shall cover followings: (i) energy efficiency; (ii) technology cooperation; and (iii) joint research and development.

Training and capacity building is another field that offers immense learning opportunities, particularly in the renewable energy sector. India could be a major source of training and capacity building in energy services for ASEAN countries. ASEAN and India may consider starting a secretary-level annual dialogue in energy cooperation and also between the energy think tanks of ASEAN and India. Setting up the ASEAN–India Network of Energy Think Tanks may pave the way in generating knowledge products and new ideas.

Notes

1 Delhi Declaration. 'Delhi Declaration of the ASEAN-India Commemorative Summit to mark the 25th Anniversary of ASEAN-India Dialogue Relations.' Ministry of External Affairs (MEA), Government of India, 2018. Assessed 14 September 2019. www.mea.gov.in/bilateral-documents.htm?dtl/29386/Delhi_Declaration_of_the_ASEANIndia_Commemorative_Summit_to_mark_the_25th_Anniversary_of_ASEANIndia_Dialogue_Relations
2 ASEAN Secretariat. ASEAN-India Plan of Action (POA) 2016–2020 outlines the energy cooperation between ASEAN and India. 2015. Assessed September 2019: https://asean.org/wp-content/uploads/images/2015/August/POA_India/ASEAN-India%20POA%20-%20FINAL.pdf
3 IRENA. 'Renewable Energy Outlook for ASEAN', ASEAN Centre for Energy, ASEAN Secretariat, Jakarta, 2016, pp.1–108. Accessed 14 September 2019. www.indiaenvironmentportal.org.in/files/file/Renewable%20Energy%20Outlook%20for%20ASEAN.pdf.
4 'SDG 7: Affordable and Clean Energy.' United Nations. United Nations, 2020. https://in.one.un.org/page/sustainable-development-goals/sdg-7/. Also see: Gielen, D., Francisco Boshella Deger Sayginb Morgan D. Bazilianc Nicholas Wagnera Ricardo Gorinia. 'The role of renewable energy in the global energy transformation' *Energy Strategy Reviews*, 24 (2019), pp. 38–50.
5 'ADB Energy Database.' Asian Development Bank, n.d. www.adb.org.
6 Ibid
7 Kumar, Ankush. 'Electricity Trade in South Asian Could Grow up to 60,000 Mw through 2045.' *ET Energy World*. 2 November 2018. https://energy.economictimes.indiatimes.com/news/power/electricity-trade-in-south-asian-could-grow-up-to-60000-mw-through-2045/66477793.
8 IRADe. 'Cross-Border Trade in South Asia: Challenges and Investment Opportunities.' South Asia Investor's Workshop on 'Cross-Border Electricity Trade' 24–25 September 2014, New Delhi, India. Accessed 14 September 2019. https://irade.org/CBET-in-SA-Challenges-and-Investment-Opportunities-Sept-2014.pdf.
9 See endnote 8.
10 Ibid.
11 Ibid.
12 'India, Nepal Open First Cross-Border Pipeline in South Asia.' The Times of India. 11 September 2019. https://timesofindia.indiatimes.com/india/india-nepal-open-first-cross-border-pipeline-in-south-asia/articleshow/71072041.cms.
13 Mahmud, Khizir. 'Power Grid Interconnections of South Asian Region to Retain Sustainable Energy Security and Figure out the Energy Scarcity.' *Global Journal of Researches in Engineering Electrical and Electronics Engineering*, 12, 10 (2018), pp. 14–19.
14 'Social Security Scheme for Indian Workers Launched in UAE.' The Tribune. Accessed 31 October 2020. www.thetribuneonline.com/foreign-archives26.html.
15 'India Plans to Set up LNG Terminal in Myanmar.' Mint, 3 August 2018. Accessed 31 October 2020. www.livemint.com/Politics/ckXNRlKEAXlkxEgx7cQ3nI/India-plans-to-set-up-LNG-terminal-in-Myanmar.html.
16 Independent Power Producers Association of India Publications (IPPAI). *New Paradigms for India's Regional Energy Trade*. IPPAI, 2011.
17 AIC-RIS. 'Chapter 8: Energy Market Integration and Cooperation.' In *ASEAN-India Development and Cooperation Report 2015* edited by AIC-RIS. New Delhi: Routledge, 2015.

18 Petroleum Planning and Analysis Cell [PPAC]. Petroleum Planning and Analysis Cell homepage. Ministry of Petroleum and Natural Gas, Government of India. 2012. Available at: https://www.ppac.gov.in/
19 EXIM. 'Strengthening ASEAN-India Partnership: Trends and Future Prospects.' 2018, pp. 1–100. Accessed 14 September 2019. www.eximbankindia.in/Assets/Dynamic/PDF/Publication-Resources/ResearchPapers/88file.pdf
20 ACE 'ASEAN Plan of Action for Energy Cooperation (APAEC) 2016–2025' ASEAN Secretariat, 2015, pp. 1–-60.
21 The first APAEC (1999–2004), the second APAEC (2004–2009) and the third APAEC (2010–2015) have been phased to support the energy cooperation agenda under the ASEAN Vision 2020.
22 See endnote 20.
23 Refer to IEA (2014) for the detailed existing and proposed pipeline of the TAGP.
24 Ibid
25 Ibid.
26 Ibid.
27 See endnote 4.
28 'Enhancing Energy Connectivity and Integration in the ASEAN Region.' ASEAN Centre for Energy. Accessed 31 October 2020. https://www.aseanenergy.org/.
29 Post 1997–98 financial crisis, ASEAN countries started meeting regularly with Northeast Asian countries, as called as ASEAN+3 grouping which include ASEAN and Japan, South Korea and China.
30 ACE. 'ASEAN Energy Cooperation Report 2017.' ASEAN Secretariat, Jakarta, 2017, pp.1–46.
31 For more details, Nicolas, Francoise. 'ASEAN Energy Cooperation: An Increasingly Daunting Challenge.' The Institut Francais des Relations Internationales (IFRI), 2009, pp.1–28. Accessed 31 October 2020. https://inis.iaea.org/collection/NCLCollectionStore/_Public/42/050/42050163.pdf
32 Down To Earth. 'India Could achieve it 2030 climate targets.' 2017. Accessed 14 September 2019 www.downtoearth.org.in/news/climate-change/-india-could-achieve-its-2030-climate-targets--59067.
33 So far 79 countries have signed among which 57 countries have been ratified the ISA framework Agreement until November 2016.
34 RIS. 'Future Directions of BIMST-EC: Towards A Bay of Bengal Economic Community (BoBEC)' Research and Information System for Developing Countries (RIS), No. 12, 2004, February, pp. 1–4. Accessed 15 September 2019. http://ris.org.in/images/RIS_images/pdf/pbno12.pdf?cv=1

PART III

India–China

Geo-politics of energy cooperation

10

DECONSTRUCTION OF REGIONS

Emerging role of subregional cooperation in Asia

*Takaaki Oiwa**

Introduction

The Asian Development Bank (ADB) defines a subregion as "any subgrouping of countries within a region."[1] However, this definition has several anomalies, including the ADB's own Greater Mekong Subregion (GMS).[2] Nowadays, a subregion may be considered a subgrouping of countries either within a region or across regions. This chapter focuses on this latter's subregion, the subgrouping of countries across regions. By focusing on subregional cooperation, this chapter is expected to reveal the deficiencies of broad regional frameworks, irrespective of whether they are regional, interregional, or super-regional. This is equivalent to clarify the reason why subregions should be created even when there are regional level institutions and whatever original intent of subregional cooperation, it tends to induce deconstruction of existing regional frameworks, which were institutionalized after the World War II under the auspices of the US hegemony.

In this chapter, I first discuss the GMS and briefly explain the significance of this subregional cooperation program. I believe that the superimposition of other subregional cooperation schemes on GMS will generate new insights into broader regional frameworks, such as the Association of Southeast Asian Nations (ASEAN), interregion across East Asia and South Asia (SA), Belt and Road Initiative (BRI), and Indo-Pacific vision.

Focusing on the Greater Mekong Subregion

In 1992, the GMS Economic Cooperation Program was established under the ADB's initiative with six member countries, Cambodia, Lao People's Democratic

* All views expressed in this article are my own and do not represent the opinions of any entity whatsoever with which I have been, am now or will be affiliated.

Republic (Lao PDR), Myanmar, Thailand and Vietnam, and the People's Republic of China (particularly, Yunnan Province and Guangxi Zhuang Autonomous Region), that is, mainland ASEAN countries and China, which share the Mekong River, although Cambodia, Lao PDR, Myanmar, and Vietnam (i.e., the CLMV countries) were not the members of the ASEAN at the time of establishing the program. The development of GMS was accelerated after its first summit was conducted in the year 2002. Since then, the summit has been held every three years as the highest decision-making body, and this arrangement enabled the further involvement of the Chinese central government, along with certain provinces, in the GMS process. The GMS also has institutionalized its annual ministerial conference, and its secretariat is placed within the ADB headquarters.

This economic cooperation program covers the domains of agriculture, energy, environment, health and human resource development, information and communication technology, tourism, transport, transport and trade facilitation, and urban development[3] with the support of external donors, such as Japan, Australia, and others, as well as the contributions of the ADB and its member countries, particularly those of China.

Since the eighth GMS Ministerial Conference (1998) endorsed the concept of economic corridors to stimulate growth, the development of such cross-border economic corridors has become the main vehicle of GMS development, as shown in Figure 10.1. These corridors mainly comprise the North–South Corridor, vertically linking China and mainland ASEAN countries, and the East–West and Southern Corridors, horizontally linking mainland ASEAN countries. Besides, all six countries have completely ratified the main agreement of the Cross-Border Transport Agreement (CBTA)[4] and, as a part of the Early Harvest Implementation of CBTA, all GMS countries, except Myanmar, allowed the eradication of intermediary stops at the borders from June 2018 onward, although some limitations remain.[5]

Due to the increased physical and institutional connectivity among the member countries brought about by the GMS program, the ASEAN Economic Community (AEC) and ASEAN–China Free Trade Agreement (FTA), and increased inflow of Foreign Direct Investment (FDI) along the recent trends of China plus one and Thailand plus one, many CLMV countries have achieved approximately 7 percent annual gross domestic product (GDP) growth rate, which is among the highest rates in ASEAN countries for the current decade (Figure 10.2). Further, this reduces the traditional ASEAN divide between advanced ASEAN countries and latecomer CLMVs in terms of per capita GDP. With these achievements, the GMS may be considered one of the most successful subregional cooperation programs.

Land bridge connecting Southeast Asia and South Asia

Several historical initiatives have connected Southeast Asia (SEA) and SA through land bridges, such as the Asian Highway and Trans-Asian Railway advocated by the present-day United Nations Economic and Social Commission for Asia and the Pacific.[6] However, recently, attention has been renewed and new initiatives have been proposed by several countries and organizations for this sake, particularly since the opening up of Myanmar.

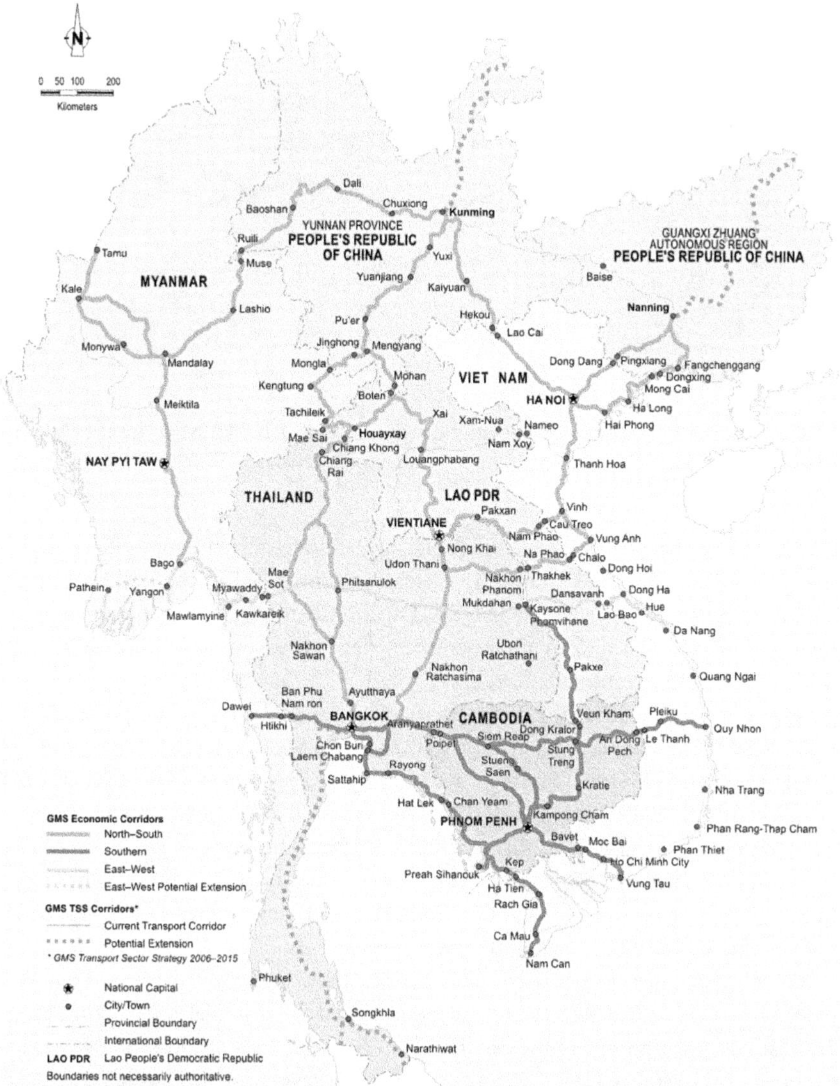

FIGURE 10.1 Economic corridors in the Greater Mekong Subregion. "Economic Corridors in the Greater Mekong Subregion." Accessed November 2, 2020. https://greatermekong.org/content/economic-corridors-in-the-greater-mekong-subregion

The first initiative is a natural extension of the GMS economic corridors from Myanmar to India proposed by the ADB.[7] Specifically, the North–South corridor and East–West corridor through the Western corridor are to be extended to India's northeast region. Second, the Bangladesh-China-India-Myanmar (BCIM) Regional Forum, which is attended by an intermingled representation of track 1 and track 2 levels,[8] first proposed the BCIM Economic Corridor (EC) in 2011 to

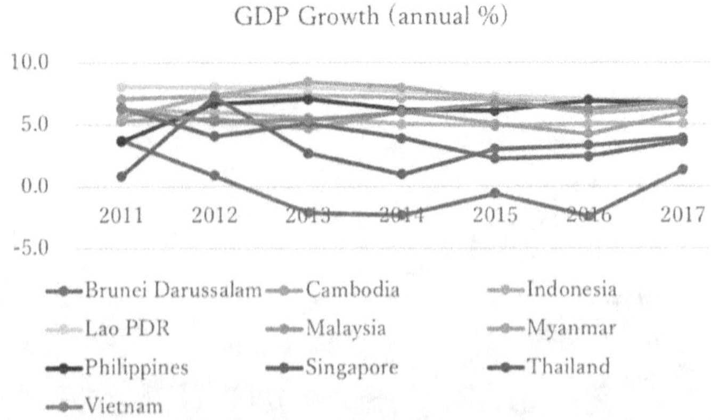

FIGURE 10.2 Achievement of the highest growth rates by CLMVs in the ASEAN region. World Bank. World Development Indicators Database.

link Kunming–Mandalay–Dhaka–Kolkata and, subsequently, the Joint Statement on the State Visit of Chinese Premier Li Keqiang to India 2013 proposed establishing a joint study group (JSG) on BCIM-EC. During the third JSG meeting, which was held in April 2017, the four member countries agreed on upgrading BCIM-EC talks to the intergovernmental level.[9]

The third initiative is the Indo-Pacific Economic Corridor proposed by the United States; it was advocated by the then State Secretary John Kerry through Remarks on the US–India Strategic Partnership 2013.[10] This initiative is explained as an extension of the New Silk Road proposed by the US government, connecting Central Asia, through Afghanistan and Pakistan, to India.[11] The Indo-Pacific Economic Corridor is expected to link the economies of India, Bangladesh, and SEA[12] by "fostering these types of connections—physical infrastructure, regulatory trade architecture, and human and digital connectivity."[13]

Fourth, Japan initiated the Economic Research Institute for ASEAN and East Asia (ERIA), which is the research institute established by a formal agreement among 16 heads of government at the 3rd East Asia Summit in Singapore on November 21, 2007 and submitted the Comprehensive Asia Development Plan (CADP) 2.0[14] at the 10th East Asia Summit in 2015. Compared to original CADP,[15] version 2.0 added the land bridge connecting SEA to India and Bangladesh, in addition to the maritime connectivity between SEA and India, such as the Mekong–India Economic Corridor (Figure 10.3). The inclusion of this land bridge is a result of the adoption of the Bay of Bengal Initiative for Multi-Sectoral Technical and Economic Cooperation (BIMSTEC)[16] as one of eight scenarios for economic corridor development and subregional development in CADP 2.0.

The fifth initiative comprises several BIMSTEC initiatives. The latest update of the Transport Infrastructure and Logistics Study conducted by the ADB dedicated to BIMSTEC[17] recommended, as high-priority road policies and strategies, upgrading access roads to the main BIMSTEC border crossings and to enhance arterial

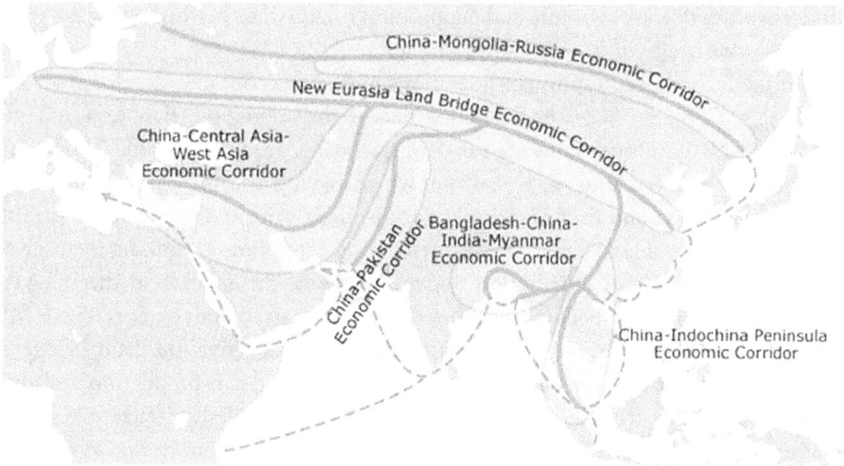

FIGURE 10.3 Economic corridors proposed by BRI. Hong Kong Trade Development Council. Accessed December 9, 2020. https://home.hktdc.com

links to borders. Further, the study recommended coordinating road programs among member states, including the development of the India–Myanmar–Thailand Trilateral Highway connecting Moreh, India, and Mae Sot, Thailand, through Myanmar, that is, from the east end of India to the west end of Thailand.

In the aforementioned initiatives, I discussed subregional initiatives, and among those except for the US proposal the initiatives were proposed by subregional institutions. However, behind the scenes, great powers in Asia and the United States seemed to influence these processes. There is a similarity between these initiatives pertaining to land bridges and the GMS in that all of them focus on economic corridor development among GMS member states. This corridor development, however, has been affected by contending initiatives by the member countries and outside actors as suggested below. Focusing on economic corridor development in GMS, whereas contribution to the North–South Corridor is dominated by China, for East–West Corridor and Southern Corridor development, external donors, including Japan and Australia, support the initiatives of mainland ASEAN countries to strengthen the horizontal connectivity among themselves. Further, this horizontal process is expected to extend to SA, in general, and India, in particular, first through maritime connectivity, such as the Mekong–India Economic Corridor in the original CADP, and then, following the opening up of Myanmar in 2011, through the appearance of the land bridge in CADP 2.0 and the US Indo-Pacific Corridor proposal. This horizontal process is further reinforced by India's Look East and Act East policies, which aim to strengthen the ties between India and SEA, and beyond.

Coincidentally, this land bridge can be considered an extension of the North–South Corridor of the GMS that links China, Myanmar, and Bangladesh and further vertically down to India. Considering China's strategic interests to buffer the Malacca dilemma and assert influence in the Indian Ocean, as well as SEA, we can understand both the economic and geopolitical calculations performed by the great powers to vertically or horizontally assert influence.

Certainly, both economic considerations and socioeconomic development are the original objectives of the establishment of the subregion. East Asia, including Japan, NIEs (Hong Kong, South Korea, Singapore, and Taiwan), China, and advanced ASEAN countries, is well-known as having the most advanced cross-border production and distribution network in the world, and the countries in the region have been able to achieve high-performing economies by linking themselves to this production and distribution network.[18] Now, we understand that CLMV countries are posing to become a part of this network to various extents. The GMS is a mechanism that supports this aim. From this perspective, the land bridge is expected to contribute to the enlargement of the East Asian production and distribution network to SA,[19] particularly India and Bangladesh, similar to CLMV countries, since both the countries are considered ready to join the network after gaining the middle-income country status. Particularly for India, once the Regional Comprehensive Economic Partnership is concluded, this would become most realistic reach together with its own Make in India policy.[20]

If this enlargement is realized, we might identify another type of similarity between the GMS and enlarged East Asia, that is, East Asia plus Eastern South Asia, in the near future. As explained earlier, Lao PDR is currently enjoying an annual economic growth rate of approximately 7 percent, although its economic development is limited by its landlocked nature. This is similar to the Indian Northeast, which is a landlocked region as well. This region has a strategic location at the forefront of India and faces Southeast and Northeast Asia. Today, the Laotian government confidently asserts that Laos is not a landlocked country, but a land-linked country; we hope that the Indian Northeast might be able to share the same conviction.

GMS and BRI

Reportedly, China identifies three neighborhood categories, which are immediate, middle-range, and wider neighborhoods.[21] Whereas the immediate neighborhood, similar to the Indian concept of immediate neighborhood, encompasses the countries that directly share national borders, the middle-range neighborhood covers four regions immediately adjacent to China, such as Northeast Asia, SEA, SA, and Central Asia. Further, the immediate neighborhood basically entails avenues of bilateral relationships, whereas the middle-range neighborhood provides opportunities to further multilateral diplomacy.

It is believed that China started its immediate neighborhood diplomacy initiatives at the beginning of the 1990s to alleviate the harsh international environment that resulted from the Tiananmen Square incident in 1989. Further, during the latter half of the 1990s, China gradually initiated its middle-range neighborhood diplomacy efforts, such as starting the Shanghai Five (predecessor of the Shanghai Cooperation Organization) process (1996) for Central Asia, China ASEAN FTA (which was proposed in 2000) and first GMS summit (2002) for SEA, and six-party talks (from 2003 onward) for Northeast Asia and gaining observer status in the South Asia Association for Regional Cooperation (2005).

In 2013, the BRI was announced at separate occasions for the Belt and the Road with the intention of covering Asia and beyond. The wider neighborhood, which is the third and largest Chinese neighborhood concept, is believed to cover the entire Asian continent. However, it might be revised to cover Eurasia if we consider intended coverage of BRI.

The main vehicle of the BRI is the development of economic corridors connecting China and Europe by land and sea both strategically and economically. The overland Silk Road and maritime Silk Road are to be interconnected by supplementary economic corridors, such as the Indochina Peninsula EC, BCIM EC, China–Pakistan EC, and Central Asia–West Asia EC (Figure 10.4). Based on this basic nature of BRI, the GMS should be considered an important precedent for BRI. The GMS was initiated in 1992 at a time when China was yet to undertake even middle-range neighborhood diplomacy, which emphasizes the significance of economic corridor development in 1998, and the first summit was conducted in 2002.

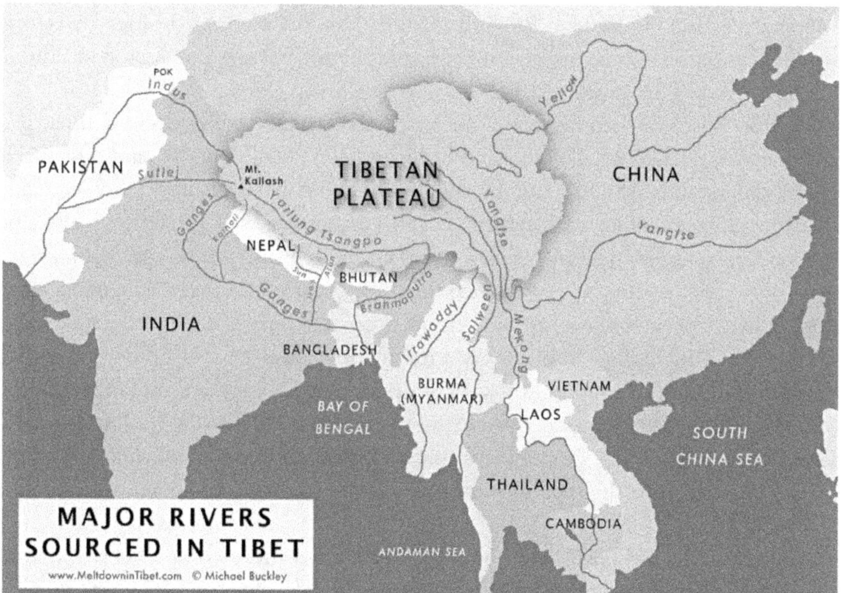

FIGURE 10.4 Depiction of China as the upper riparian country of many transboundary rivers. Source: Daming H., Ruidong Wu, Yan Feng, Yungang Li, Chengzhi Ding, Wenling Wang, and Douglas W. Yu. “China’s Transboundary Waters: New Paradigms for Water and Ecological Security through Applied Ecology”. *Journal of Applied Ecology* (2014), 51, 1159–1168, Fig. 1. Distributions of transboundary river basins and biodiversity conservation priorities on the borders of China and riparian countries.

Moreover, it is noted that the GMS would be an appropriate avenue to further the Indochina Peninsula EC and BCIM EC of BRI if BRI intends to connect regions using economic corridors. However, China rushed to establish Lancang–Mekong Cooperation (LMC), as mentioned in the following section, which seemed to be an intrinsic competitor of the GMS.

Establishment of the Lancang–Mekong Cooperation

The LMC framework was officially launched in March 2016.[22] This new subregional mechanism was rapidly institutionalized. Although the member countries of the LMC are the same as those of the GMS, the LMC secretariat role is apparently assumed by the Chinese government, at least until the establishment of an international secretariat. As observed in this section, China has assumed complete leadership of this framework.[23]

The first step in establishing the LMC pertains to Thailand's earlier initiative for the Conference on Sustainable Development in the Lancang–Mekong Subregion held in January 2014. However, according to Busbarat,[24] China intended to institutionalize the framework and announced its own plan during the 17th China–ASEAN Summit in November 2014. In November 2015, the first LMC Ministerial Meeting was held in Yunnan Province, China. The first summit (Leaders' Meeting) was held in Sanya, China, in March 2016, and the second was conducted in Phnom Penh, Cambodia, in January 2018.

Within this limited time frame, the first Ministerial Meeting decided three priority areas for LMC: (1) Political and Security Issues; (2) Economic and Sustainable Development; and (3) Social, Cultural, and People-to-People Exchanges.[25] Subsequently, the first summit decided to conduct the general summit once every two years[26] and the foreign ministers' meeting once a year. The three priority areas agreed on by the first Ministerial Meeting were renamed the three cooperation pillars and, under these three pillars, five priority areas were decided on for the period of the initial stage of the LMC, including connectivity, production capacity, cross-border economic cooperation, water resources, and agriculture and poverty reduction. Further, at the occasion of the first summit, China announced setting up an LMC Fund to provide concessional loans, special loans, and technical cooperation to member countries.[27] Furthermore, the second summit launched the Five-Year Plan of Action for 2018–2022.

Compared to the GMS, the LMC is considered a more comprehensive framework that covers not only economic and sustainable development but also the other two pillars of politico security and sociocultural issues; therefore, the three pillars of the LMC are nearly similar to those of ASEAN. Further, the fundamental dilemma posed by the LMC is the significant power asymmetry between China and other member countries, particularly without any opportunities of engagement by external actors such as the ADB and other traditional donors to the subregion. This power asymmetry is further strengthened by the argument of hydro-hegemony, which is mentioned here.

Partly due to the emergence of LMC, attention on the ASEAN divide has been renewed. As mentioned earlier, the traditional divide is the significant income gap between advanced ASEAN countries and latecomer CLMVs. However, currently, two additional dimensions of possible divide between mainland and maritime ASEAN countries have been clearly identified. The first dimension is the security divide centered on the crucial difference between countries that have territorial disputes with China in the South China Sea and those that do not have any dispute. In this sense, Vietnam is the crucial exception among all mainland ASEAN countries.

The second dimension is the developmental divide between countries.[28] Even the GMS by itself has expressed concern regarding the possible divide in developmental orientations between mainland and maritime ASEAN countries.[29] Since it has a more solid and exclusive institutional framework than the GMS, the LMC will be able to enhance this tendency. The consequence of LMC institutionalization might not be limited to the development dimension alone.

Another remarkable aspect of the LMC is that it covers water resources as a key priority area. Although hydropower generation is a part of the GMS program, the GMS's energy and environment programs consider limited issues pertaining to river basin managements, rather than water resources management per se.[30]

A plausible explanation of why downstream riparian countries joined the LMC is that the LMC is the first and only organization with water resource management as one of the topics in its main agenda and enjoys the participation of all riparian countries along the Mekong River. The downstream riparian countries have long attempted to involve China in establishing governance on the allocation and utilization of the Mekong River's water. Although the Mekong River Commission was established in 1995 with the aforementioned objective, only four downstream riparian countries have joined this organization and China as well as Myanmar has refrained from becoming the member countries and remained as the official dialogue partner status up to now.

Control over the allocation and utilization of the Mekong River's flow is very important to riparian countries, since this ultimately implies control over access to food and, thereby, the livelihoods of tens of millions of people in the downstream riparian communities.[31] In addition, to mitigate disasters, such as floods and droughts, the countries require access to information on upper stream river flow.

In this respect, "China's unique position as the only country in the region which is completely upper riparian, lends it an unparalleled advantage and power to influence the flow of water to nations downstream."[32] Accordingly, China enjoys a hydro-hegemony status.[33] Taking into account this hydro-hegemony argument, the power asymmetry between China and other LMC members should be enhanced further.

However, this issue is not confined to Mekong River basin countries alone. China is a completely upper riparian country from the perspective of not only mainland ASEAN countries but also South Asian nations, since the Tibetan Plateau, which is dominated by China, has its origins in not only Mekong River but also the Ganges-Brahmaputra-Meghna and Indus river basins.[34]

Time for the Mekong–Ganga Cooperation?

One of the possible ways of coping with the hydro-hegemony argument discussed in the previous section is ensuring collective securitization and solidarity among downstream riparian countries in all regions that have the same concern. One plausible platform for this effort is the Mekong–Ganga Cooperation (MGC), which comprises five downstream Mekong River riparian countries and India and is referenced by the names of two rivers sharing the same concern.[35] However, on scrutinizing this organization, we find that it does not consider the water management issue a priority cooperation area.[36]

On further considering the nature of commons of the Tibetan Plateau or the region encompassing the Himalaya–Hindu Kush mountain range and the Tibetan Plateau as the third pole, rather than the origin of more than 11 cross-border rivers, since their ice fields contain the largest reserve of freshwater outside the polar regions,[37] an area-based framework surrounding this region might suit the demand. However, the existing mechanisms of formal institution to overcome the issues are rather weak[38] and tend to exclude downstream riparian countries, such as mainland ASEAN countries.[39] To overcome the issues, parallel approaches, such as river-basin and area-based approaches, that consider existing institutional settings could provide solutions by renovating and renewing existing institutions.

Conclusions: Prospects for the Indo-Pacific super-region

Buzan and Wæver opined that East Asia and SA form the Asia supercomplex because of the significant interplay between East Asia and SA in terms of security, as well as the weakened role of Myanmar as an insulator separating the two regions.[40] Further, Buzan envisaged that once the economic interplay between East Asia and SA is significantly increased and securitized, the two regions could merge into one region, that is, the Asia regional security complex (RSC) comprising the previous East Asia RSC and SA RSC.[41]

As pointed out somewhere in this chapter, many initiatives and subregional cooperation efforts aim to link two regions economically and strategically, and the resulting connectivity between regions is expected to contribute to the expansion of East Asian production and distribution network to SA. This could function as a crucial effort to integrate Asia.

As discussed through earlier sections, several subregional cooperation schemes exist beyond the current regional borders and interplay among these subregional initiatives. To understand the implications of the constellation, I have focused on the GMS and examined how by superimposing GMS with other subregions we obtain several insights into wider regional frameworks, such as ASEAN, the interregion of East Asia and SA, and BRI. Concurrently, we identified the inextricably interwoven interplay in terms of not only security but also economy and provision of international public goods and the existential significance of such interplay between regions across Asia.

The resulting integrated Asian region centering on the combined region of East and South Asia will form a core for any wider regional perspectives, such as the

Indo-Pacific vision and BRI. The Asian region includes several great powers having the ability to intervene in regions outside Asia,[42] such as the Indian Ocean, the Pacific Ocean, and Central Asia and beyond. Further, we should consider the involvement of the United States as the only superpower having the ability and interest to intervene in the regional and interregional affairs of Asia.

Whereas Buzan refers to the term super-regions as a strategy of the United States to legitimize its intrusions into them (super-regions)[43] and provide itself some leverage against the formation of regional groups excluding it,[44] Medcalf identified that it is understandable to prescribe the Indo-Pacific as a new super-region and this super-region's core is clearly Asia, although it is difficult to define the region's outer frame and inner subregions.[45] Further, he opined that this scale of super-region "dilutes the ability of any single country to unilaterally shape the strategic order."[46]

The Quad[47] (Australia, India, Japan, and the United States), as well as Indonesia, advocated their own Indo-Pacific initiatives. Whereas India and Indonesia consider the Indo-Pacific to extend from the eastern shore of the African continent to the western shore of the Americas,[48] Australia and the United States define the Indo-Pacific as extending from the western shore of India to the western shore of the United States,[49] which corresponds with the geographical coverage of the Indo-Pacific command of the US military regional command system. However, Japan's definition is even more ambiguous. Yet, the important aspect of the Indo-Pacific is not the definition of its geographical coverage. It provides a stage for observing the interplay among a superpower and some great powers and emerging powers centered in Asia; however, such interplay definitely tends to spill out of Asia.

We also observe that ASEAN is in the process of establishing its own Indo-Pacific concept. According to a commentary, ASEAN has already agreed to set five principles on its own conception of the Indo-Pacific, such as openness, transparency, inclusivity, a rules-based approach, and ASEAN centrality,[50, 51] which are nearly the same as Indian Prime Minister Modi's Indo-Pacific principles.[52]

ASEAN is located in a strategic place as the linchpin connecting two oceans. Its proactive initiatives to define the Indo-Pacific concept helps establish a more inclusive regional identity for itself and overcome the ASEAN divides mentioned previously.

Currently, we are expecting the emergence of the Indo-Pacific super-region centered on Asia.[53] How to materialize this super-region still remains as our responsibility and this promised and vast space will be the center stage of global events in the coming decades.

Notes

1 ADB. "Thematic Evaluation Study: ADB Support for Regional Cooperation and Integration, Linked Document 1." 2015. Accessed November 2, 2020. www.adb.org/documents/thematic-evaluation-study-adb-support-regional-cooperation-and-integration

2 As explained in a later part of this chapter, the GMS includes mainland ASEAN countries and China. See: endnote 2. op. cit. It explains "subregion" as a subgroup of countries

and economies within any of the ADB's regional departments, such as the East Asia Department, Southeast Asia (SEA) Department, and South Asia (SA) Department.

3 "Overview of the Greater Mekong Subregion Economic Cooperation". Accessed March 27, 2019. https://greatermekong.org/overview.

4 To date, Thailand and Myanmar have not ratified several annexes and protocols.

5 "GMS countries sign new deal, boost transport connectivity". *Khmer Times*. March 19, 2018. Accessed April 8, 2019. www.khmertimeskh.com/114649/gms-countries-sign-new-deal-boost-transport-connectivity/.

6 "Transport". UNESCAP. Accessed April 8, 2019. www.unescap.org/our-work/transport.

7 Asian Development Bank. "Review of Configuration of the Greater Mekong Subregion Economic Corridors." Metro Manila, Philippines: ADB, 2018.

8 Yhome K. "The BCIM Economic Corridor: Prospects and Challenges". 2017. Accessed April 8, 2019. www.orfonline.org/research/the-bcim-economic-corridor-prospects-and-challenges/. According to Yhome, whereas the representatives of China and Myanmar were at track 1 level at the outset, India and Bangladesh dispatched track 2 level for attendance in the first forum meeting.

9 "Tapping potential of connectivity through BCIM-EC". *Belt & Road News*. 2019. Accessed April 8, 2019. www.beltandroad.news/2019/02/18/tapping-potential-of-connectivity-through-bcim-ec/.

10 Kerry, John. "Remarks on the US-India Strategic Partnership". New Delhi, India, June 23, 2013.

11 Clinton, Hillary R. "Remarks on India and the United States: A Vision for the 21st Century". Chennai, India, July 20, 2011. Also, by combining these two initiatives, Kerry. 2013 (see endnote 11) referred to "rail links that go from the Caspian Sea to the Gulf of Thailand."

12 This is based on the remarks made by the Under Secretary of the US Department of State. Hormats, Robert D. "US Economic Engagement with the Asia Pacific". Washington, DC, June 12, 2013.

13 This remark was made by the Deputy Assistant Secretary of the US Department of State. Sumar, Fatema Z. "Shaping the Future of Trade and Connectivity in the Indo-Pacific". Kolkata, India. May 8, 2014.

14 ERIA. "The Comprehensive Asia Development Plan 2.0 (CADP 2.0)". ERIA Research Project Report, No. 4, 2014.

15 ERIA. "The Comprehensive Asia Development Plan". ERIA Research Project Report. 2010.

16 The BIMSTEC is a regional organization comprising seven member states lying in the littoral and adjacent areas of the Bay of Bengal; it was established in 1997. Currently, the seven member states include five countries from SA, that is, Bangladesh, Bhutan, India, Nepal, and Sri Lanka, and two from SEA, that is, Myanmar and Thailand.

17 ADB. "Updating and Enhancement of the BIMSTEC Transport Infrastructure and Logistics Study Final Report." Metro Manila, Philippines: ADB 2018.

18 Kimura, F. "International Production and Distribution Networks in East Asia: Eighteen Facts, Mechanics, and Policy Implications". *Asian Economic Policy Review*, 1, 2006, 326–344.

19 Nehru, V. "The Rebalance to Asia: Why South Asia Matters". Congressional Testimony, House Committee on Foreign Affairs, Subcommittee on Asia and the Pacific, US Congress, March 13, 2013.

20 Although India has announced that it is pulling out of RCEP negotiations, another initiative to link SA and East Asia has emerged in order to enhance the resiliency of supply chains in the Indo-Pacific region advocated by three countries of Australia, India and

Japan. See: "Australia-India-Japan Economic Ministers' Joint Statement on Supply Chain Resilience". September 1, 2020.

21 Aoyama, R. "Chugoku no Asia Gaiko (Chinese Asian diplomacy)". University of Tokyo Press, 2013. Explanation in this paragraph and next one basically refer to her writings.

22 Accessed April 2, 2019. www.lmcchina.org/eng/gylmhz_1/jj/t1519110.htm.

23 Busbarat, P. "Grabbing the Forgotten: China's Leadership Consolidation in Mainland Southeast Asia through the Mekong-Lancang Cooperation," *ISEAS Perspective*, No. 7, Singapore, 2018.

24 Busbarat, P. "Grabbing the Forgotten: China's Leadership Consolidation in Mainland Southeast Asia through the Mekong-Lancang Cooperation," ISEAS Perspective, 2018 No. 7, Singapore, 2018.

25 Lancang-Mekong Cooperation China Secretariat. "Joint Press Communiqué of the First Lancang-Mekong Cooperation Foreign Ministers' Meeting". 2015. Accessed April 2, 2019. www.lmcchina.org/eng/zywj_5/t1514151.htm

26 The GMS summit is held once every three years.

27 Lancang-Mekong Cooperation China Secretariat. "Sanya Declaration of the First Lancang-Mekong Cooperation (LMC) Leaders' Meeting". 2016. Accessed April 2, 2019. www.lmcchina.org/eng/zywj_5/t1513793.htm.

28 Shiraishi, T. "Japan's Indo-Pacific Policy". 2016. Accessed April 3, 2019. https://carnegieendowment.org/2016/03/01/japan-s-indo-pacific-policy-pub-62929. Also see: Asanuma, S. "Ittai ichiro no yuwaku: Tounan Asia no shiten kara (Allurement of BRI: From the Southeast Asian Perspective)." SRID Journal SR-016-2019-01, 2018. Also see endnote 28.

29 Nearly a decade ago, I wrote a comprehensive report dedicated to the Japan International Cooperation Agency (JICA) on how to support ASEAN through developmental cooperation, in which I indicated this concern and discussed measures to alleviate this possible divide. JICA. "A Report from the Study Group on Assistance to the Southeast Asian Region". Institute for International Cooperation, Tokyo, Japan: JICA 2017.

30 Sunchindah, A. "The Lancang-Mekong River Basin: Reflections on Cooperation Mechanisms Pertaining to a Shared Watercourse," No. PO13-01, the Centre for Non-Traditional Security Studies, S. Rajaratnam School of International Studies, Nanyang Ave, Singapore, 2013.

31 Brennan, E. "China Eyes Its Next Prize—the Mekong". 2018. Accessed June 7, 2018. www.lowyinstitute.org/the-interpreter/china-eyes-its-next-prize-mekong.

32 Bhattacharya, S. "China's Hydro Ambitions and the Brahmaputra," IDSA Backgrounder. New Delhi, India: Institute for Defence Studies & Analyses, 2018.

33 Hydro-hegemony refers to hegemony at the river basin level; it is realized through water resource control strategies, such as resource capture, integration, and containment.

Zeitouna, M. and Jeroen Warner. "Hydro-Hegemony—a Framework for Analysis of Trans-Boundary Water Conflicts". *Water Policy*, 8 (2006) 435–460.

34 Albert, E. "Water Clouds on the Tibetan Plateau". 2016. accessed March 14, 2019. www.cfr.org/backgrounder/water-clouds-tibetan-plateau. The Irrawaddy River originates from sources in the Himalayan glaciers of Upper Myanmar.

35 Further, the Salween River, which extends to China, Myanmar, and Thailand, can be considered a trans-boundary river sharing the same concern.

36 The MGC comprises India and five mainland ASEAN countries, that is, Cambodia, Lao PDR, Myanmar, Thailand, and Vietnam. It was launched in 2000 to ensure cooperation among countries in the domains of tourism, culture, education, and transport and communications.

37 Hilton, Isabel and thethirdpole.net editorial team. "Exploring the Third Pole, Part 1". 2012. Accessed April 7, 2019. https://thethirdpole.net/wp-content/uploads/sites/3/2012/06/Part-1-Final1.pdf.

38 Scott, C. A., Fan Zhang, Aditi Mukherji, Walter Immerzeel, Daanish Mustafa, and Luna Bharati. "Water in the Hindu Kush Himalaya". In *The Hindu Kush Himalaya Assessment,* edited by Wester P., Mishra A., Mukherji A., Shrestha A. Springer, Cham, ICIMOD, 2019.

39 An area-based mechanism involves the International Centre for Integrated Mountain Development (ICIMOD), which is a regional intergovernmental learning and knowledge sharing center that serves the interests of the eight regional member countries of the Hindu Kush Himalayas: Afghanistan, Bangladesh, Bhutan, China, India, Myanmar, Nepal, and Pakistan.

40 Buzan, B. and Ole Wæver. *Regions and Powers: The Structure of International Security*. New York: Cambridge University Press, 2003. This book defines supercomplexes as a "strong interregional level of security dynamics arising from great power spillover into adjacent regions."

41 Buzan, B. "Asia: A Geopolitical Reconfiguration". *Politique étrangère*, 77, 2, summer 2012. The RSC is defined as "a set of units whose major processes of securitisation, desecuritisation, or both are so interlinked that their security problems cannot reasonably be analysed or resolved apart from one another" (Buzan B. and O. Wæver 2003. op. cit.).

42 Buzan B. and O. Wæver. 2003. op. cit. described that the great powers are usually capable of operating in more than one region.

43 The parenthetical text was added by the author of this chapter. Buzan exemplified the Atlantic, Asia-Pacific, and Americas as super-regions.

44 See endnote 41.

45 Medcalf, R. "Australia's New Strategic Geography: Making and Sustaining an Indo-Pacific Defence Policy," Chapter 1. In *New Regional Geopolitics in the Indo-Pacific: Drivers, Dynamics and Consequences*" edited by Chacko, Priya. Routledge Contemporary Asia Series, Routledge. 2016.

46 Medcalf, R. "Reimagining Asia: From Asia-Pacific to Indo-Pacific." 2015. Accessed July 10, 2018. www.theasanforum.org/reimagining-asia-from-asia-pacific-to-indo-pacific/,.

47 The Quadrilateral Security Dialogue.

48 For India, Modi, N. "Prime Minister's Keynote Address at Shangri La Dialogue," June 01, 2018. For Indonesia, Marsudi, R. L. P. "2018 Annual Press Statement of the Minister for Foreign Affairs of the Republic of Indonesia," January 11, 2018.

49 For Australia, Department of Foreign Affairs and Trade of Australia. "The Commonwealth of Australia's 2017 Foreign Policy White Paper". 2017. For the United States, White House. "National Security Strategy of the United States of America." 2017.

50 Chongkittavorn, K. "Watch Out for ASEAN's New Indo-Pacific". 2018. Accessed March 10, 2019. www.bangkokpost.com/opinion/opinion/1587206/watch-out-for-aseans-new-indo-pacific.

51 ASEAN officially disclosed its own "ASEAN OUTLOOK ON THE INDO-PACIFIC" at the occasion of the 34th ASEAN SUMMIT on June 23, 2019 along the lines mentioned here.

52 Modi, N. 2018. op. cit. (See endnote 48).

53 It is possible to imagine another super-region or super-continent, such as Eurasia, because of BRI. However, as I mentioned *A World of Regions and Indo-Pacific – How will the new map be drawn?* (see Oiwa, Takaaki, forthcoming, *A World of Regions and Indo-Pacific – How will the new map be drawn?*(in Japanese), (Chapter 3, Yamamoto, Katsuya ed. Economic Development and Regional Cooperation in South Asia, Ashi Publishing), the most economically and strategically important regions, even for China, are East Asia and SA and the important concern is coping with the United States.

11

CHINA'S ENERGY COOPERATION WITH SOUTHEAST AND SOUTH ASIA

Srikanth Kondapalli

China's energy context

China's comprehensive rise in the last four decades catapulted China on to the global stage with its attendant long-term implications to the global power structure. As the second largest economy in the world in 2010 (displacing Japan and previously Germany), possessing the largest foreign exchange reserves (of more than $3 trillion), becoming the second largest energy consumer in 2003 (after the United States and displacing Japan) and vying to be potentially the largest investor in the energy sector in the world, China had indicated that indeed it had come to the world stage. However, China's GDP – which used to be in double digit figures – contracted to its slowest in 24 years at 7.4 per cent in 2014. Premier Li Keqiang's Work Report on 5 March 2015 fixed the growth rate at 7 per cent for 2015, while the International Monetary Fund had scaled down its estimates for China by 6.8 per cent for 2015, further reducing this to 6.4 per cent for 2016 and 6.6 in 2018.[1]

China's rise also led to importing huge energy resources – primarily from West Asia and Africa – for fuelling such a rise.[2] China used to be an oil exporting country, although it did not join the OPEC (like Russia). However, the economic rise in the 1990s coincided with China becoming a net importer of energy resources by 1993. China's oil import volume increased to 181 million tonnes in 2006. In 2010, China overtook the United States as the largest energy consumer. In 2012 China retained its position as the largest energy consumer with nearly 22 per cent of the global total energy demand.[3] Predictions by British Petroleum for the long-term perspective indicate further upward projections – China is to overtake the United States as the largest oil consumer by 2025 and Russia by 2027 as the second largest gas consumer.[4] Indeed, by October 2013, China became the largest importer of oil, surpassing that of the US imports.[5]

TABLE 11.1 China's energy forecasts, 1995–2020

Year	*Annual consumption (10,000 tonnes)*	*Production (10,000 tonnes)*	*Import (10,000 tonnes)*	*Import dependence (% age)*
1995	15,749.96	14,901.96	848	5.4
2000	23,300	16,300	7,000	30
2005	28,000	18,000	10,000	35.7
2010	34,000	19,500	14,500	42.6
2015	39,800	19,000	20,800	52.3
2020	48,400	18,500	30,000	62

Source: Wang Zhangbao's estimates as cited in the MA dissertation of Yi Yasi. '中国与中亚国家石油贸易' [China and petroleum trade with Central Asian countries]. M.A. Dissertation submitted to **Jilin University,** April 2007, p.8.

The amount of oil imported by China in 2005 accounted for 6.8 per cent of the total in the world, ranking third place after the United States and Japan. In 2007, China displaced Japan to become the second largest importer of oil. China imports about 56.2 per cent of its oil from the Middle East, 22.5 per cent from Africa, 14.4 per cent from the Asian region and from Eurasia about 6.9 per cent. Of this, nearly 93 per cent of the oil is transported through maritime areas.[6] With several of these countries China had initiated veritable interactions ranging from political, diplomatic, economic, or even military and strategic links. The table below provides data related to annual consumption and production, import and import dependence of China that necessitated bigger plans for the energy sector (Table 11.1).

To enhance its energy security China had initiated several measures, viz, diversification of the energy basket to renewable sources, construction of oil/gas pipelines, strategic oil reserves, investing in overseas energy resources, making efforts to enhance energy diplomacy, secure sea lanes of control through despatch of naval contingents (29 so far between 2008 till early 2019), construction of harbours and ports in Asia, Africa and South America, in addition to contracts at Piraeus in Greece, or other strategies.

Official blessing for the Chinese external activities in the energy are forthcoming from the leadership from the early 1990s. More concretely, the 16th Communist Party Congress advocated a 'Go West' strategy by the Chinese government for the purpose of fostering economic ties with its Central Asian neighbours. China had also initiated 'going out' [*zou chuqu*] policy of outward Chinese investments in the oil drilling and transportation sectors and also inviting investments into the country.[7] The 2013–2014 Silk Road initiative and the Asia Infrastructure Investment bank (AIIB) triggered further investments abroad. The inward and outward FDI flows – with China receiving over $120 billion and investing over $100 billion abroad in 2014 increasing to $170 billion in 2018 – has been a new phenomenon recently.

As a result, today, China has oil stakes in 70 projects in 30 countries ranging from Asia, Australia, Africa, Russia and Americas. With the backing of the Chinese state, these ventures abroad received a further fillip to make Chinese investments noticeable – and often controversial – in the world. Successive Chinese leaders such as Jiang Zemin, Hu Jintao, Li Peng, Zhu Rongji, Wen Jiabao, Xi Jinping and Li Keqiang had conducted extensive visits abroad to promote energy diplomacy with several states. Reflecting the importance of the energy issues in China, the 3rd Plenum of the 18th party Congress in 2013 had called for further privatisation of the State Owned Enterprises, including in the energy sector. Also, in 2006 the Central Small Leading Group on Energy (中央能源工作领导小组) was also formed with China's premier in the chair, indicating the importance of the subject. In 2008, the State Council of China had set up an Energy Commission with the then Premier Wen Jiabao as the head and vice Premier Li Keqiang as the deputy along with 21 members, including one lieutenant general from the armed forces.[8]

To secure energy interests China had been following a concerted strategy of securing supply lines. However, as supplies from West Asia and Africa – passing through Indian Ocean Region and Straits of Malacca – can be interdicted by the US over issues such as Taiwan or other disputes. To address this issue, China is planning to divert energy supplies through the Caspian Sea, Kazakhstan, Turkmenistan, Russia and other overland routes.[9] While such land bridges are expensive and can also be interdicted by non-state actors, China nevertheless spent, huge diplomatic, technological, human and financial resources in this regard.

Terming its role in the international energy spheres as 'constructive', China's government stated its outward policy as 'China works sincerely and pragmatically with international energy organizations and other countries on the principle of equality, mutual benefit and win-win to improve the mechanism, expand the fields of cooperation and safeguard international energy security and stability'. It also states that 'Energy issues should not be politicized, and triggering antagonism as well as the use of force should be avoided.'[10] Thus, given the increasing dependence of China on the external energy markets, its position has been moderate and forthcoming. Also, given the conflict situation in West Asia (including the Iraq wars, spread of Islamic State and others), while indirectly criticising the United States role, China is gearing up actively to expand its footprint in the region, including measures to protect its energy interests. Thus by 2015, it had set up a naval base at Djibouti and expanding plans for similar bases elsewhere. Through the Belt and Road Initiative projects, in addition to the 'twin track' pipelines connecting to Central Asia, China also began constructing the China–Pakistan Economic Corridor and China–Myanmar Economic Corridor – both converging in the Indian Ocean Region through the Arabian Sea and the Bay of Bengal.

However, in the economic filed, as a percentage of global investments in the energy sector, China's position has been relatively low compared with the United States or other European countries. This has been the same for mergers and acquisitions and green field investments. In the overall Southeast Asian and South Asian contexts, China's role in the above three categories is still low, but has recently been emerging.[11]

Southeast Asia

Although China's energy dependence on Southeast or South Asia is minimal compared to imports from other regions, with West Asia and Africa constituting major areas of China's imports of energy, these regions nevertheless straddle important sea lines of communications and choke points.[12] China is also making efforts to link with Vietnam, Laos, Myanmar, Thailand and Cambodia in a regional power grid.[13] Also, Vietnam constituted about 5.6 per cent and Indonesia about 4.4 per cent of Chinese oil imports in 2001. The trend increased in the coming years to include Malaysia and Laos as well.[14] In addition, China had laid down an oil pipeline in Myanmar from Sittwe to Yunnan province with a view to not only enhancing energy availability but also to reduce vulnerabilities associated with over-dependence on the Strait of Malacca's. Southeast Asia is thus significant for China's energy considerations as it astrides crucial sea lanes of communications.[15] As a consumer of several energy projects in terms of hydro-electricity, coal-based thermal stations, solar power plants, re-export of excess power generated in the region to the demand areas in China, LNG imports from the region, energy pipelines (such as in Myanmar), investments in natural gas fields (such as in Natuna), plans to build alterative sea routes for sustainable energy supplies such as at Kra Isthmus are some options for China. In 2002, a strategic energy partnership agreement was signed with the ASEAN that provided a framework for expanding energy cooperation.

According to a recent long-term estimate of PriceWater Coopers based on market exchange rates, Indonesia is expected to increase its GDP from $856 billion to $2.6 trillion in 2030 to $8 trillion in 2050. Four other Southeast Asian countries that are expected to join the trillion dollar club include Thailand from $380 billion to $990 billion in 2030 and $2.6 trillion in 2050; Malaysia from $337 billion to $930 billion in 2030 and $2.6 trillion in 2050; Philippines from $290 billion to $848 billion in 2030 to $2.7 trillion in 2050; Vietnam from $188 billion to $685 billion in 2030 and $2.5 trillion in 2050.[16] With economic growth rates expected to increase by various estimates, Southeast Asian region's demand for energy is also expected to increase substantially from the current 240 to 565 GW by 2040. Myanmar's 15-year power development plan forecasts a more than six-fold increase from only 4,581 megawatts (MW) in 2014, to over 29,000 MW by 2031; in Vietnam, the government predicts the demand will triple to 69,500 MW by 2020.[17] China sells electricity three times the cost of the distributed electricity in the domestic market of Vietnam, in addition to other conditions such as penalties if Vietnam does not import a specified amount of electricity.[18] While much of this energy demand is expected to be met by coal-based systems, there is a growing awareness and interest in the renewable sources specifically as prices of the latter are becoming more affordable.[19] This provides an opportunity for India and China to enter the Southeast Asian markets with concrete proposals.[20]

Below are details of a few initiatives in the energy cooperation between China and Southeast Asia based on scattered press reports. According to Jessica Liao's estimates compiled from 2000 to 2016, China had invested in a total of 42 projects in oil and gas in Southeast Asia, 119 projects in hydro-electricity, 64 coal-fired projects and 43 in mining.[21] The Comtec Solar System invested $372 million in Malaysia. The manufacturing plant started operation in 2014 with an annual capacity of 300 MW.[22] Kedah 50,000-kW solar plant, assisted by China, is to be commissioned in 2019.[23] With Brunei, China had concluded commercial oil and gas sector cooperation agreements.

China's energy cooperation with Myanmar is extensive in nature. Projects include a total of $14 billion in 56 Chinese-backed projects proposed, under construction, or completed in Myanmar – Synohydro is working on 17 projects. Some projects include Song Bung 4 hydropower project in Quang Nam province; Za Hung and Song Kon 2 hydropower projects; Hatgyi has been proposed as a large 1,350 MW hydropower dam worth $3 billion, to be located in Karen State. There are also the Chinese investment projects such as the Shwe Gas Pipeline Scheme and Letpadaung copper mines but they have been troubled by rising protests since 2012. The $3.6 billion Myitsone project was proposed on the Irrawaddy, and also the Salween River projects such as the $6–8 billion Tasang dam.[24] In addition, China had operationalised the cross-border energy pipeline with Myanmar. It has a capacity to carry 12 bcm and is 771 km long. In November 2017, China launched a 230 kV Nabar-Shwebo-Ohntaw power transmission line and a substation project in the north-western region's Shwebo to supply electricity to households, which was to be completed by 2019.[25]

Since 2004, power lines have been laid by China connecting with Vietnam, Laos and Cambodia. In addition, hydroelectricity projects have also been commissioned in these countries.[26] Half of the global dams have been in operation in China today and it has also exported such capabilities to over 70 countries in the world, including to Southeast and South Asian regions. In Southeast Asia, the prominent projects include an estimated nearly 30 dams in Myanmar, 14 in Laos, 7 in Cambodia and 3 in Vietnam, mainly by state-owned enterprises.[27] According to EIA estimates, between 2006 and 2011, China invested over $6 billion in generating nearly 3,000 MW projects in these countries.[28]

South China Sea

While China has been exploring the regional power market in Southeast Asia, trouble is also brewing in the region mainly due to the acute contestation over the islands/reefs in the South China Sea. The US Energy Information Agency estimates the South China Sea contains 11 billion barrels of oil and 55 trillion cubic feet of gas. On the other hand, China National Offshore Oil Company estimated in 2012 that the South China Sea has 125 billion barrels of oil and 500 trillion cubic feet of gas (i.e. 5 times China's current proven reserves).[29] Energy prospects reports triggered intense sovereignty claims in the region with the Philippines going to the Permanent Court of Arbitration in The Hague whose verdict was boycotted by China, in July 2016 on no historical claims, denial of drawing EEZ from occupied reefs, etc. has become a fact on the ground. More significantly, the United States, Japan, India and

Australia have come together in the Indo-Pacific idea since November 2017 on maintaining the rule of law and freedom of navigation, among others.

In the energy field, nevertheless, China's largest offshore oil producer has completed construction of the country's longest pipeline yet in the South China Sea, which has a length of 195 km. China National Offshore Oil Corporation (CNOOC) completed the undersea pipeline at the Dongfang 13-2 gas fields in the South China Sea using its CNOOC-201, China's first deep water pipe-laying crane ship. The pipeline is one of the special facilities of the Dongfang 13-2 gas fields, which will provide long-term stable energy to Guangdong Province, Hainan Province and Hong Kong. China's first island-based smart power grid was energised on Yongxing Island, the largest of the Paracel Islands in the South China Sea and the site of Beijing's newly created prefecture level city of Shansha, whose jurisdiction covers virtually the entire sea. Reports by Xinhua said that these grids are to power the numerous military installations that Beijing has piled on the islands and atolls reclaimed from the sea with the ultimate goal of encompassing all natural and artificial islands occupied by PLA troops. The power grid increases an island's power supply as much as eightfold and can operate independently or in conjunction with Hainan province's main electrical grid to meet civilian and military needs.

The state-owned China National Offshore Oil Corporation deployed $1 billion-worth oil rig *Haiyang Shiyou* 981 on 2 May 2014 (southeast of Zhongjian Island in the Paracels). This resulted in the deterioration of relations between China and Vietnam. Vietnam claims that this rig is in its 200-nautical mile exclusive economic zone and on its continental shelf while China says the area is about 32 km from the Paracels (Hoang Sa), which it controls but contested by Vietnam and Taiwan. By the first week of June 2014 China completed the first phase of drilling and exploration at this site and by mid-August the second phase. This was marred by anti-Chinese protests across Vietnam that saw four Chinese killed. Subsequently, China again deployed the rig in the same region. China also began claiming portions of the Natuna gas fields under Indonesia. Indonesian forces sank several intruding Chinese vessels in the region. Also, the Indonesian Air Force conducted a massive air exercise in the region as tensions mounted. Nevertheless, China concluded $337 million worth of hydroelectric projects in Indonesian dams in Kalimantan and Sulawesi regions.[30]

South Asia

While South Asia also forms part of China's energy dynamics mainly in the transit aspects, it has also been active in the region in many areas.[31] At the moment, China has been exploring the regional power market and energy infrastructure in South Asia, and has also expressed interest in the trans-regional energy pipelines like India–Pakistan–Iran and Turkmenistan–Afghanistan–Pakistan–India whenever these materialise. China is keen on extending these pipelines to Yunnan and other provinces in its southwestern regions.

In the mid-2000s, China concluded an energy cooperation agreement with India.[32] As the second largest and fourth largest importers of energy resources both China and India suggested that they should come together to explore mutually beneficial outcomes. On 11 January 2006, India and China signed five memoranda on energy cooperation – with four in the commercial field, including upstream exploration, refining, energy efficiency, pipelines, etc.[33] In November 2006, during President Hu Jintao's visit to New Delhi, both also announced they would cooperate in research in the thorium route of the nuclear cycle. Nevertheless, competition, rather than extensive cooperation, besets the bilateral relations in the energy field. Competition is reflected in Chinese energy companies outbidding those from India in Angola, Kazakhstan, Ecuador, Myanmar and others, while the foreign ministry of China makes coercive diplomatic statements on the ONGC Videsh Limited acquisitions in Vietnam-held South China Sea in the 127 and 128 Blocks.

In the rest of South Asia, China's energy cooperation is more concrete and extensive in nature. China initially made efforts in Bangladesh at tapping potential 60 trillion cubic feet of natural gas. However, not much commercial progress was achieved on this front. It involved in a coal-based power plant in Barapukuria.

Given the huge hydro-electricity potential in Nepal, China has been eyeing this sector in recent times. In February 2012, China signed a contract in Nepal with Three Gorges International Corp for 750 MV West Seti dam at a cost of $1.6 billion by 2019. China is also involved in the Trishuli hydro-electricity project. On 3 May 2017 Nepal signed a contract with China Gezhouba Group Corporation to build a storage-type 1,200 MW project at Budhi Gandaki in central Nepal under the engineering, procurement, construction and finance model estimated to be over $2.5 billion. The height of the dam is to be over 263 metres.[34] This Chinese company is already building the 30 MW Chameliya and 60 MW Upper Trishuli projects.[35] In June 2017, a memorandum was signed in this regard. Given the scale and significance of the project, in September 2017, China included the Budhi Gandaki project as a part of the BRI.[36] However, over 20,000 people will be displaced during the construction process. This has generated controversy and former Prime Minister Baburam Bhattarai demanded the scrapping of the project and argued for self-financing and other measures.[37] Finally the agreement was scrapped on 13 November 2017 citing financial irregularities by the Chinese company. Gezhouba company protested the Nepali decision.[38] Other hydroelectricity projects are also behind schedule, including the West Seti and Kulekhani 3 projects.[39] In November 2017, China signed an agreement worth $3 billion for a 1 GW hydro-electricity project in Nepal.[40] Nevertheless, two hydro-electricity projects have come online including the 50 MW Upper Marsyangdi-A and 25 MW Upper Madi in 2016.[41] In June 2018, both signed an energy cooperation agreement.[42]

While Afghanistan has been destabilised with wars, terrorism and conflict, there is a realisation that Afghan reconstruction efforts should include tapping the rich potential – estimated at over $3 trillion worth of resources. In 2011, China National

Petroleum Corporation signed a deal for exploiting energy reserves in Amu Darya Basin with over $2.5 billion in investments.[43]

More concrete energy cooperation exists between China and Pakistan, including in the nuclear energy field as witnessed by the Chashma series of projects for decades. In 2014, China had announced the China–Pakistan Economic Corridor (CPEC) which amalgamates infrastructure projects connecting Xinjiang to Gwadhar in the banks of the Arabian Sea. The prospects for an energy pipeline connecting Gwadhar to Xinjiang are high in the future. The CPEC includes not only roads, railways, etc. but also construction of hydro-electric projects.[44] In January 2017, Three Gorges Dam Company signed a deal with Pakistan worth $6 billion to build a hydroelectricity dam at Karat, including solar power plants. The Gezhouba Group also signed a contract for $1.8 billion for constructing the Suki Kinari 830 MW hydro project. The Matiari to Lahore electricity transmission line is to be built with $1.5 billion in a deal with the State Grid Corporation in January 2017. Another line is to link Matiari (Port Qasim) to Fiasalabad. A $1.5 billion deal was also signed to build a wind power plant in Punjab. However, in November 2017, Pakistan withdrew from the $14 billion Diamer Bhasa dam from CPEC.[45]

Another South Asian country that straddles the important China's sea lanes of communications is Sri Lanka. China invested in Hambantota port (nearly $1.5 billion), and in Colombo South Harbor. There are also other plans including Norochcholai power plant – 900 MW of thermal power ($1.3 billion) – to meet 45 per cent of the total demand of the nation's power grid. In December 2017, Sri Lanka handed over Hambantota port to China Merchant Ports Holdings on a 99-year lease arrangement with the intention of transforming the port from a 'trans-shipment port' to that of a 'total logistics hub'.[46] The lease was necessitated after Sri Lanka was unable to repay debt and converted the deal into equity. Under this arrangement China will spend $1.12 billion in lieu of a 70 per cent stake in the port.[47] China is also investing in a deep water terminal port, the Colombo International Container Terminal in 270 hectares with an investment of $1.5 billion.

Conclusions

While China's focus has been mainly on West Asia, Africa, Central Asia and Russia recently in alleviating its energy issues, there has also been steady inroads in Southeast and South Asia mainly in investments in the regional power market, energy infrastructure and energy pipelines. As the Tibetan-origin rivers flow into Southeast and South Asian regions, there is an obvious Chinese initiative in hydro-electricity projects in Laos, Cambodia, Myanmar, Nepal and Pakistan – thus contributing to the renewable sources of energy, although a more focused regional power market is yet to emerge. China has also been pushing through other energy mixes, prominently in the nuclear field in Pakistan through the Chashma series of projects in what was termed as 'grandfathering' of such projects. However, a 2006 resolve to cooperate with India has not yet materialised. Nevertheless, solar power offers huge opportunities with the photovoltaic cell market booming in both Southeast and South

Asian markets. Indeed, with India taking the responsibility for the International Solar Energy Initiative, one could expect China's role to increase in this sector. On the other hand, in the traditional energy sectors such as oil, there are both cooperative and competitive trends for China in these two regions. As the 2nd largest importer of oil in the world, mainly from West Asia and Africa, China has been concerned about the supply routes and began securing these through energy pipelines in Myanmar, port construction in Sri Lanka and other such measures. This measure also elicited competitive posturing in the background of Chinese submarine visits to Colombo and Karachi. In the South China Sea, the dispute over the islands/reefs – and in the background of The Hague tribunal ruling in July 2016 – have led to militarisation of the region by China and contested by other claimants and others such as the United States in the Quadrilateral Security Dialogue intending to preserve the maritime order and rule of law.

In relation to India, China's energy tie-up with Southeast and South Asian region brought forth both cooperative and competitive elements, although increasingly veering towards competition between these two largest imports of energy resources. As two 'simultaneously rising' countries, their energy dependence is increasing. In Myanmar, China's companies have replaced Indian oil blocks in Rakhine state. Likewise, in Nepal, subtle competition persists in the hydro-electricity sector. In the case of the South China Sea, where India's public sector unit had invested billions in the energy sector, such equations have been upgraded to near conflict levels. India has over half of its trade passing through the South China Sea, suggesting the vital nature of these seas for India's rise. It also has several energy interests in the region. In October 2011, India's ONGC Videsh Limited (OVL) invested $2.2 billion in oil and gas exploration projects in the South China Sea by signing a joint venture with Petro Vietnam.[48] OVL also has a Block 06.1 in the Nam Con Son basin off Vietnam's south coast – in a joint venture with TNK-BP and PetroVietnam. China did not protest these contracts. However, the OVL entered into a contract in 2006 with PetroVietnam to jointly explore Blocks 127 (abandoned due to hard rock) and 128 in the Phu Khanh basin further north after Vietnam stated that it is well within 200 nm of its claimed area. China protested these and warned 'all foreign companies' to withdraw from its 9-dash claim line in the region. An Indian company, Essar Group, also has a production-sharing contract for a petroleum block off Vietnam's coast, although not in the 9-dash claim line. Nevertheless, in other areas, India and China have had energy cooperation agreements since 2006, although the pace of such cooperation is slow.

Notes

1 Keqiang, Li. 'Report on the Work of the Government.' Gov.cn 16 March 2019. Accessed 2 April 2019. http://english.gov.cn/premier/speeches/2019/03/16/content_281476565265580.htm; Tang, Frank. 'China's 2019 gross domestic product forecast cut to 6.2 per cent by World Bank under "Darkening Skies".' *South China Morning Post*. 9 January 2019. Accessed 6 February 2019. www.scmp.com/economy/china-economy/article/2181339/chinas-2019-gross-domestic-product-forecast-cut-62-cent-world.

2 Huaming, Zhang. 能源经济理论与实践 [Energy Economic Theory and Practice]. Beijing: Beijing Book Co. 2016.

3 See: 'BP Statistical Review: China in 2012.' British Petroleum. Accessed 20 December 2013. www.bp.com/content/dam/bp/pdf/statistical-review/Country%20reports/BP-Statistical-Review-China.pdf

4 See: 'BP Energy Outlook- China Insights.' British Petroleum. Accessed 20 December 2013. www.bp.com/content/dam/bp/pdf/statistical-review/EnergyOutlook2030/Country-insights/China_Fact_Sheet.pdf. See also Finlay, Mark 'The Oil Market to 2030 – Implications for Investment and Policy.' Economics of Energy & Environmental Policy, Vol. 1, No. 1. Accessed 20 December 2013. www.bp.com/content/dam/bp/pdf/statistical-review/The_Oil_Market_2030.pdf. Finlay predicted that China's consumption of oil will grow from 8 million barrels per day to 17.5 Mbd by 2030.

5 Jia, Chen. 'China is No 1 oil importer.' *China Daily*. 18 October 2013. Accessed 20 October 2013. http://usa.chinadaily.com.cn/business/2013-10/18/content_17041824.htm.

6 These figures are from Yueting, Zhang. '中国石油安全的国际政治经济学分析' [An analysis of the international politico-economic aspects of China's oil security]. M.A. dissertation submitted to Nanjing Aeronautical and Astronautics University, March 2007 pp. 17 and 19.

7 On the 'go out' and 'good neighbourliness' policies of China in Southeast Asian energy and mining sectors, see Liao, Jessica C. 'A Good Neighbor of Bad Governance? China's Energy and Mining Development in Southeast Asia' *Journal of Contemporary China*, December 2018. Accessed 4 January 2019. https://doi.org/10.1080/10670564.2018.1557947>.

8 See Kuangrong, Tao. '中国对中亚的能源外交研究' [China's energy diplomacy towards Central Asia]. MA Dissertation submitted to Xinjiang University, November 2011, pp. 19.

9 See Sen, Tan. '浅析中国与中亚能源合作的重要性与对策' [Analysis of the importance of China-Central Asia energy cooperation and countermeasures], 商[Business], January 2013, pp. 59–60.

10 Information Office of the State Council of the People's Republic of China. 'China's Energy Conditions and Policies.' December 2007, pp. 13, 39 and 43 and NDRC. 'Statement on energy cooperation in the 21st century.' 24 January 2005 Accessed 20 December2013. http://en.ndrc.gov.cn/newsrelease/200506/t20050620_8220.html.

11 Andrews-Speed, Philip, Mingda Qiu and Christopher Len. 'Chinese engagement in Southeast Asian energy and mineral resources: motivations and outlook.' *Eurasian Geography and Economics*, vol. 57, issue 3 (2016), pp. 316–42. Accessed 4 January 2019. https://doi.org/10.1080/15387216.2016.1211025

12 See Andrews-Speed, Philip, Mingda Qiu, and Christopher Len. 2016.

13 Songwanich, Suwitchai. 'China's ambitious plans to power Southeast Asia.' *The Nation*. 24 July 2018 Accessed 4 January 2019. www.mekongeye.com/2018/07/24/chinas-ambitious-plans-to-power-southeast-asia/.

14 This is based on Juan, Qian and Fan Ruijie. '*Zhongya yu Dongnanya: Zhongguo shiyou anquan de diyuan zhanlue xuanze*' [Central Asia and Southeast Asia: Geo-strategic choices of China's oil security] *Xinjiang Daxue Xuebao* [Xinjiang University Journal], 2007, 2. p.93. Qian and Fan belong to the Zhenjiang Naval Vessel College in Jiangsu Province and Xiangfan College of Military Economics in Hubei, respectively.

15 Xuegang, Zhang. 'China's energy corridors in Southeast Asia.' *Jamestown Foundation China Brief*, Volume: 8 Issue: 3 (4 February 2008). Accessed 4 January 2019. https://jamestown.org/program/chinas-energy-corridors-in-southeast-asia/.

16 PriceWater Coopers. 'The world in 2050 – will the shift in global economic power continue?.' February 2015, pp. 40–41. Accessed 4 January 2019. www.pwc.com/gx/en/issues/the-economy/assets/world-in-2050-february-2015.pdf. For an estimate a decade

ago, see Symon, Andrew. 'Fuelling Southeast Asia's Growth: The Energy Challenge.' *ASEAN Economic Bulletin,* 21(2) (August 2004), pp. 239–248.

17 Lamb, Vanessa and Nga Dao. 'Perceptions and practices of investments: China's hydropower investments in mainland Southeast Asia.' May 2015. Accessed 4 January 2019. www.eur.nl/sites/corporate/files/CMCP_21-_Lamb_Dao_0.pdf.

18 See endnote 17, p. 7

19 Weatherby, Courtney. 'It's decision time for Southeast Asia as power demand soars.' *China Dialogue*. 14 January 2019. Accessed 16 February 2019. www.chinadialogue.net/article/show/single/en/11024-It-s-decision-time-for-Southeast-Asia-as-power-demand-soars.

20 Andrews-Speed, Philip. 'Mixed motivations and mixed blessings: Chinese investments in Southeast Asian energy and mineral resources.' *ISEAS Perspective*, no. 40 (6 May 2015). Accessed 16 February 2019. https://ssrn.com/

21 See endnote 7, p. 6.

22 Gopal, Sucharita et al. 'Fueling global energy finance: The emergence of China in global energy investment.' *Energies* vol. 11, no. 2804 (2018). Accessed 16 February 2019. www.mdpi.com/journal/energies. They argue that while energy accounts for nearly 25 per cent of all FDI, it only accounts for 4.82 per cent of total M&A activity in the period 1996–2016. Thus, the proportion of global M&A and GF FDI in the energy sector is 5:1 in the period 2003–2016.

23 Gnanasagaran, Angaindrankumar. 'China's energy ambitions in Southeast Asia.' *The ASEAN* Post. 17 August 2018. Accessed 16 February 2019. https://theaseanpost.com/article/chinas-energy-ambitions-southeast-asia.

24 Chellaney, Brahma. 'China's dam problem with Myanmar.' *The Myanmar Times.* 14 September 2016. Accessed 21 September 2016. www.mmtimes.com/opinion/22517-china-s-dam-problem-with-myanmar.html

25 See endnote 23.

26 Government of PR China, National Development Reform Council. 'Country report on China's participation in Greater Mekong Subregion Cooperation.' 30 April 2008. Accessed 16 February 2019. http://en.ndrc.gov.cn/newsrelease/200804/t20080430_208063.html

27 Mathews, Nathanial. 'Chinese hydropower electrifies southeast Asia, but at a cost.' The Conversation. 14 November 2013. Accessed 16 February 2019. http://theconversation.com/chinese-hydropower-electrifies-southeast-asia-but-at-a-cost-20275.

28 'Chinese investments play large role in Southeast Asia hydroelectricity growth.' Energy Information Agency. 16 August 2013. Accessed 16 February 2019. www.eia.gov/todayinenergy/detail.php?id=12571.

29 Hong, Zhao. 'Energy security concerns of China and ASEAN: Trigger for conflicts or cooperation in the South China Sea?' EAI Working Paper, No. 159 (2011). Accessed 16 February 201. www.eai.nus.edu.sg/publications/files/EWP159.pdf.

30 See endnote 23; Springer, Cecilia. 'The China-Indonesia energy entanglement moves in a new direction.' ISEAS. 18 March 2016 no. 13. Accessed 22 April 2016. www.iseas.edu.sg/images/pdf/ISEAS_Perspective_2016_13.pdf.

31 There is also the concern in the backdrop of the United States and Indian naval cooperation, that the Indian Ocean Region could pose a challenge to the sustainable supplies of China. See Li, Zheng. '*Yindu de haiyang anquan zhanlue yu YinMei de hezuo yu maodun- Yi Yindu yang wei zhongxin*' [India's Ocean Security Strategy and India-US cooperation and contradictions – Focus on Indian Ocean]. Master's thesis submitted to Sichuan University, 2006 Chengdu 49 pp.

32 Müller-Kraenner, Sascha .'China's and India's emerging energy foreign policy' Yale 2008. Accessed 22 January 2009. http://worldfellows.yale.edu/.../DIEChinaandIndiasEmergingEnergyForeignPolicy.pdf.

33 'China, India sign five memoranda on energy cooperation.' Xinhuanet. 12 January 2006. Accessed 24 January 2006. http://in.chineseembassy.org/eng/ssygd/zygx/zysj/llds/t230899.htm.

34 'China Gezhouba wins Nepal hydropower project contract.' Nepal Energy Forum. Accessed 16 February 2019. www.nepalenergyforum.com/china-gezhouba-wins-nepal-hydropower-project-contract/. This report suggests that the Budhi Gandak project could overcome the 600 MW shortage that the country is facing. Nepal also has plans to generate 10,000 MW of electricity from the current 760 MW by 2025.

35 'China's Gezhouba lands Budhi Gandaki contract.' Nepal Energy Forum. 24 May 2017. Accessed 16 February 2019. www.nepalenergyforum.com/chinas-gezhouba-lands-budhi-gandaki-contract/.

36 'Budhi Gandaki listed as component of BRI.' Nepal Energy Forum. 5 September 2017. Accessed 16 February 2019. www.nepalenergyforum.com/budhi-gandaki-listed-as-component-of-bri/.

37 'Scrap Budhi Gandaki deal with Chinese firm: Ex-PM to Nepal govt.' Nepal Energy Forum. Accessed 16 February 2019. www.nepalenergyforum.com/daily-news-analysis-scrap-budhi-gandaki-deal-with-chinese-firmex-pm-to-nepal-govt/.

38 'Chinese state firm criticises Nepal over decision to scrap US$2.5bn dam contract.' *South China Morning Post*. 1 December 2017. Accessed 16 February 2019. www.scmp.com/news/china/diplomacy-defence/article/2122475/chinese-state-firm-criticises-nepal-over-decision-scrap]

39 'Chinese infrastructure projects in Nepal running way behind schedule.' Republic World. 31 August 2017. Accessed 16 February 2019. www.republicworld.com/s/6070/chinese-infrastructure-projects-in-nepal-running-way-behind-schedule.

40 Timperley, Joselyn. 'China leading on world's clean energy investment, says report.' *Carbon Brief*. 9 January 2018. Accessed 16 February 2019. www.carbonbrief.org/china-leading-worlds-clean-energy-investment-says-report.

41 'China-invested hydropower plant starts operation in Nepal.' China.org. 31 December 2016. Accessed 16 February 2019. www.china.org.cn/world/2016-12/31/content_40017213.htm.

42 'Nepal to hold talks with China on energy cooperation.' *Business Standard*. 22 August 2018. Accessed 16 February 2019. www.business-standard.com/article/news-ians/nepal-to-hold-talks-with-china-on-energy-cooperation-118082200224_1.html.

43 Jin, Wang. 'The US withdrawal and One Belt One Road: Chinese concerns and challenges in Afghanistan.' *Strategic Assessment*, vol. 19, No. 3 (October 2016). Accessed 16 February 2019. www.inss.org.il/he/wp-content/uploads/sites/2/systemfiles/SystemFiles/adkan19-3ENG_3_Wang%20Jin.pdf

44 Christopher, Venita. 'CPEC and Pakistan-China energy cooperation.' *Modern Diplomacy*. 16 July 2018. Accessed 16 February 2019. https://moderndiplomacy.eu/2018/07/16/cpec-and-pakistan-china-energy-cooperation/.

45 'Pakistan stops bid to include Diamer-Bhasha dam in CPEC.' *Tribune*. 15 November 2017. Accessed February 16, 2019. https://tribune.com.pk/story/1558475/2-pakistan-stops-bid-include-diamer-bhasha-dam-cpec/.

46 'Sri Lanka joins China's Belt and Road with operations of Hambantota Port: PM.' *Xinhua*. 9 December 2017. Accessed 16 February 2019. www.xinhuanet.com/english/2017-12/09/c_136813766.htm.

47 Sri Lanka has been facing acute debt repayments issue with over 95 per cent of government revenue going towards debt servicing. See Mendis, Patrick and Joey Wang, 'Belt and road, or a Chinese dream for the return of tributary states? Sri Lanka offers a cautionary tale.' *South China Morning Post*. 9 January 2018. Accessed 16 February 2019.

www.scmp.com/comment/insight-opinion/article/2127415/belt-and-road-or-chinese-dream-return-tributary-states-sri.

48 See for these events ONGC website. Accessed 16 February 2019. www.ongcvidesh.com/Assets.aspx?AspxAutoDetectCookieSupport=1 ; 'India pulls out of choppy oil block in Vietnam' *India Today*. 13 May 2012. Accessed 18 May 2012. http://indiatoday.intoday.in/story/india-pulls-out-of-choppy-oil-block-in-vietnam/1/188568.html; 'India affirms continued oil and gas exploration with Viet Nam.' Bien Gioi Lanh Tho. 15 September 2012. Accessed 16 February 2019. http://biengioilanhtho.gov.vn/eng/indiaaffirmscontinuedoilandgas-nd-48281f0e.aspx and Parashar, Sachin 'Any use of force in South China Sea not acceptable to India: Salman Khurshid.' *The Times of India*. 1 July 2013. Accessed 12 July 2013. http://articles.timesofindia.indiatimes.com/2013-07-01/india/40306919_1_salman-khurshid-south-china-sea-navigation.

12

FACTORING NORTHEAST ASIA IN INDIA'S ENERGY SECURITY

Sharad K. Soni

Introduction

Although energy security is a complex term, today it largely implies to ensuring the security of energy supply. The most widely used definition of energy security has been specified in a policy document of the International Energy Agency which defines the term as the availability of an 'adequate supply of energy at a reasonable cost'.[1] That is to say that the sustainable economic growth of a country significantly depends on the long-term availability and uninterrupted supply of energy from multiple sources but at a reasonable cost. In this vein, it would be pertinent to concur with the theory that there are direct links between energy supply and economic growth which, for quite some time now, have pushed the issue of energy security at the core of the policy debate. Over the last few years, India has also been involved in exploring multiple energy policy options, both domestic and external, multiple fuels, and multiple suppliers. The sole purpose of doing so is to tap the renewable and non-renewable energy, which also demands India that reconnoitre its participation in transnational natural gas pipeline projects. No wonder then that resource-rich individual countries and regions are looked upon by India as potential partners in its quest for energy security. One such region, which over the past 30 years or so has been one of the fastest growing energy markets, is Northeast Asia.

A subregion of East Asia and having an enormous geo-strategic significance in the current context, Northeast Asia is positioned at a crucial juncture of energy supply chain and hence figures prominently in terms of energy cooperation initiatives. Both the energy-consuming as well as energy-supplying countries make this region an important entity connecting a network of growing supplies and markets. The term 'Northeast Asia' appeared in academic discourses in the 1930s after it was introduced by an American historian and political scientist Robert Kerner, who taught at the University of California.[2] In Kerner's description, 'Northeast Asia' covered the Korean Peninsula, the Manchurian Plain, the Mongolian Plateau, and the mountainous regions of Eastern Siberia, extending from Lake Baikal to the Pacific Ocean. However, the present positioning of states, nations, and borders in Northeast Asia emerged only very recently, which includes several important powers like China, Japan, the two Koreas (South and North), Russia and Mongolia.[3] Being home to the world's great consumers, Northeast Asia often confronts energy security issues given that China has increased its energy imports to meet the mounting demand, while Japan and South Korea remain highly dependent on energy supply due to the lack of indigenous energy sources. China, Japan and South Korea are all on the list of the world's top ten oil consumers with a share of 14 per cent, 4 per cent and 3 per cent respectively in the total global oil consumption in 2017.[4] As of 2019, oil remained the world's leading fuel, accounting for 33.1 per cent of primary energy consumption, while coal came in as the second-largest fuel with a share of 27 per cent followed by natural gas with its share standing at 24.2 per cent.[5] China continues to be the world's biggest importer of oil since it replaced the US in 2015, while Japan and South Korea are the two biggest importers of coal and LNG.

As Japan's nuclear reactors were shut down after the Fukushima Daiichi accident in 2011, Japan once again found itself resource poor country. Like China and Japan, South Korea is also looking for reliable energy supplies. Fortunately, Russia and Mongolia are now presented as the new sources of supply to the Northeast Asian states. While Russia as the world's largest natural gas and second largest oil exporting country has become a key strategic country for the reasonable energy solution to Northeast Asia, Mongolia too possesses large fuel and energy potential due to having a very significant natural resources. This makes Northeast Asia an important region, which is critical to India's 'Act East' policy for not only boosting its strategic presence in the region but also to a large extent ensuring its energy security demand. India, for quite some time now, has been trying to intellectually invest and take part in multilateral cooperation initiatives to enhance its Northeast Asia outreach in its quest for energy security. Today most of India's allies in Northeast Asia are formal or informal partners of the United States which has a strong presence in the region. Not only the United States but also Japan, Mongolia and South Korea consider India as a potential player that has the capability to alter the dynamics of the region in the face of China's domineering posture.

It is in this context that this chapter not only seeks to understand the energy domain of Northeast Asia but also examines the prospects for India's energy cooperation in this rising energy region that factors critically in New Delhi's quest for energy security. It argues that the Russian Far East and Mongolia being components of Northeast Asia with potential sources of energy supply, may provide an extra edge to India in fulfilling the gaps in its energy demands through cooperative mechanisms. However, the overall focus sticks to analysing the Northeast Asian factor in India's eastward energy engagements despite facing external hurdles vis-a-vis the growing Chinese influence in the region.

Energy outlook of Northeast Asia

Accounting for almost one-fifth of the world economy, Northeast Asia is considered to be a rising energy region with strong complementarities between energy-consumer countries (China, Japan and South Korea) and energy-producer countries (Russia and Mongolia) belonging to the region. This region has become a prime operator in the world energy markets mainly due to incredible growth in China's energy demand. In the last decade, as the gap widened between consumption and production levels in Northeast Asia, the region's economic powers became increasingly concerned about their energy security, because the fear abounds that tight supplies and ensuing high prices could result in jeopardizing economic growth.[6] Such a scenario could only result in developing a competitive atmosphere not only for securing energy supplies but also pushing for economic growth in the whole region. Furthermore, as the global demand for energy has been projected to increase by 80 per cent in 2050 over what was the consumption in 2010,[7] Northeast Asia is being seen as a hotbed for the energy-driven regional cooperation so as to become a significant contributor to the supply-demand chain. Of late, the importance of such cooperation among Northeast Asian countries has constantly been highlighted to deal with uncertainties in the global energy market and to avoid potential conflicts with regard to energy supply among consumer countries.[8] However, the actual execution of energy cooperation with the aim of sharpen the edge of regional integration has reflected stiff competition among major energy-consuming countries of the region, i.e., China, Japan and South Korea.

The background of this competition can be traced back to the middle of the last decade when the competing powers began adopting new resource security strategies by means of 'resource diplomacy', i.e. energy-consuming countries' foreign policies aimed at enhancing bilateral links with key supplier states. The idea behind adopting new resource security strategies by these three import-dependent Northeast Asian countries developed due to 'a global resources boom' or what was described as 'a resource crisis' from the consumer's viewpoint that began in the mid-2000s.[9] All this added much to resource politics in the region in terms of securing access to foreign resource supplies, though many quarters would agree that constant development of cooperative and multilateral mechanisms can prove to be a meaningful approach to overcome resource insecurity in the long run. Considering the ever-increasing dependence of the Northeast Asian countries on energy import and export, especially of oil and natural gas, it appears that the energy sector of China, Japan, the two Koreas, Russia and Mongolia can become a driving force in the regional integration of these economies so as to address the issues of resource insecurity.[10] Yet, the prevailing situation suggests that with its vast proven energy reserves and relative geographic proximity to the Northeast Asian markets, the Russian Far East has become a theatre for competition between energy consuming countries of Asia in general and Northeast Asia in particular.[11] Besides, it has been largely due to China's rapid rise that 'energy projects such as Sino-Russian pipelines and energy exploration in the East and South China Sea have intensified geopolitical competition as well as regional rivalries'.[12] Particular mention may be made of escalating rivalries within the Northeast Asian region 'between China and Japan over access to Russian gas, a scramble for Mongolian coal and potential oil reserves, and rival claims for off shore oil or gas reserves'. Even concerns for growing resource nationalism on the part of Russia which has already made a shift to globalism raise questions if 'Moscow will seek to use its energy endowment for political ends'.[13] It, therefore, needs to be examined if resource security strategies on the part of consuming countries have paid off and created grounds for the successful implementation of regional energy cooperation in Northeast Asia.

Notwithstanding the adoption of some unilateral strategies for resource security at individual country level in the last two decades or so, the ground reality across Northeast Asia is indicative of the common energy security challenges that the region is still facing. Northeast Asia is currently the world's third-largest energy-consuming region, but by 2030 its primary energy consumption has been projected to surpass both North America and Europe, thus posing challenges to region's energy security.[14] With China, Japan, and South Korea being the world's leading consumers and importers of fossil fuels, especially the oil and natural gas, such challenges have given a jolt to intensify the competitive atmosphere over access to imported energy. While China has pursued 'an aggressive *going abroad* energy policy' to find overseas sources of crude oil since its becoming a net importer of oil in 1993, Japan and South Korea have also pitched in 'the mercantilist competition' to procure their own energy sources, both within and beyond Northeast Asia.[15] This is more so because Japan and South Korea remain almost totally dependent on imported energy in spite of a slight decrease in their energy demand in recent years. China, on the other hand, is a significant producer of oil and natural gas, but its energy demand has outstripped domestic production.[16] Moreover, not only the energy outlook but also the challenges to energy security vary among the three countries: 'Japan does not maintain any gas grid; hence, pipeline gas from mainland China or even Russia may matter less for Japan than it does for South Korea, which maintains a rather well developed gas grid.'[17] In the past few years, rapid economic growth has brought China to an unprecedented resource vulnerability, particularly in the energy sector, which constantly threatens the sustainable development of the country.[18] By 2035, China has been projected to consume 68 per cent more energy than the United States, with the International Energy Agency (IEA) speculating that energy consumption may reach at 6.5 btce by 2050.[19]

In Japan, although there has been a slight decrease in energy demand due to a maturing economy and declining population, it is still expected to grow a little to reach 22.2 quadrillion BTU in 2040 compared to 22.1 quadrillion BTU in 2010. Under the current energy plan of Japan, the fossil fuels (i.e. coal, oil and gas) account for 56 per cent of the energy mix that is expected to prevail even in 2030.[20] Since Japan depends on overseas suppliers for meeting most of its demand for fossil fuels, its strategies for securing a stable supply of energy need a periodic review given that ratios of its dependence on imports for fossil fuels in 2018 were 99.7 per cent for oil, 97.5 per cent for LNG (Liquefied Natural Gas) and 99.3 per cent for coal.[21] However, in order to deal with resource security challenges, the basic guiding principle of Japan's future energy policy has been code-named as '3E+S' (Energy Security, Economic Efficiency and Environment + Safety). This principle puts emphasis principally on ensuring energy security while simultaneously improving economic efficiency and environmental protection with safety as a basic proposition. Based on this principle, Japan's 2030 National Energy Plan, the fifth such plan, was approved in 2017, which aims at creating 'a multi-layered energy supply-demand structure whereby each energy source delivers maximum strength and compliments the weaknesses of the others'.[22] The energy supply-demand structure is also called 'energy mix' implying the necessity to combine various energy and power sources to achieve maximum efficiency.

South Korea, the eighth-largest energy consumer in the world, is an 'energy-poor' country depending extensively on imports from overseas for its energy supplies including crude oil, natural gas, coal, and uranium. At present, over 95 per cent of its energy consumption is imported, which leaves its national economy highly vulnerable to external shock.[23] In 2018, US$1,459 billion was spent on importing energy and resources equivalent to almost 27.3 per cent of the total amount of imports.[24] With such a heavy dependency on energy imports, the energy security issue remains high on the agenda as the country is 'vulnerable to changes in the global energy market, including a rise in prices and a supply-demand imbalance'.[25] The issue of energy security, therefore, demands concerted efforts, especially at a time when South Korea's total energy consumption is projected to show an increasing trend to reach 15.9 quadrillion BTU in 2040 in comparison to the 2010 figure of 10.8 quadrillion BTU.[26] However, in order to promote its energy security through a stable gas and electricity supply, the country continues to support the construction of gas pipelines and super grids in Northeast Asia. The Northeast Asian Super Grid, in particular, aims at electricity generation in Russia and Mongolia, from where the electricity would be transmitted to South Korea, China and Japan through an international electricity grid.[27]

Energy potential of Russia's eastern region

Right from the hunt for Siberian fur in the sixteenth to seventeenth century to large-scale development of Siberian, Arctic and Far Eastern oil, gas and uranium in the twenty-first century, Russia has remained socially and economically dependent on the natural resource extraction as well as raw material production.[28] Today Russia has come a long way in becoming an energy giant as it produces a total of 1,370 million tons of energy yearly, of which almost half is consumed in the country, while the rest is exported to other countries. In recent years, the share of natural gas has increased significantly in the energy mix, thus accounting for half of the overall energy consumption in Russia, while oil fulfils around one-fifth of domestic energy demand, coal a little less than 20 per cent, nuclear 6 per cent, hydropower and renewables between 1 and 2 per cent, though hydropower and nuclear power constitute one-third of domestic electricity production, with each contributing to

15 per cent.[29] Russia's energy sector, thus, accounts for more than a quarter of its gross domestic product (GDP), almost two-thirds of the Russian export market and roughly 30 per cent of the country's budget. In addition, being the world's largest exporter of energy resources, Russia's energy exports including rents coming from exports of oil, gas, coal, uranium and nuclear technologies constitute half of the country's entire budget with 'oil and gas still account for 60 per cent of exports'.[30] Of the total yearly production of 1,370 million tons of energy, 640 million tons are exported.[31] Breakup wise, Russia exports 75 per cent of the 550 million tons of produced oil with 50 per cent share of crude oil and 25 per cent share of refined oil products. Contrary to this, nearly three-quarters of the 650 billion cubic metres (bcm) of gas produced is consumed domestically, which provides only about 15–20 per cent of budget income flow. Hence, there is no exaggeration to say that 'these flows of energy within Russia and especially out to the global markets mean that Russia's energy industry accounts for 25–30 per cent of GDP'.[32]

Considered as a 'petro-economy', Russia has seen a sharp growth in its energy profile with production of oil increasing from 6 million barrels a day (m b/d) in 1999 to more than 11 m b/d in 2018 and gas from 52 billion cubic feet a day (bcf) to 65 bcf during the same period.[33] At the export front in 2018, oil constituted over 9 m b/d, while the share of natural gas accounted for close to 250 bcm.[34] Given the revenue earnings from the energy sector, it has always been part of policy formulation in Russia for both the internal as well as external affairs. More specifically, energy has been the key dominant factor that motivated Russia in evolving its policy towards Northeast Asia. It is so because a strong, sustainable and resource-rich Russia 'has the potential to exploit its energy resources, mainly oil and natural gas, both for its economic development as well as helping the country for its strategic positioning in the Northeast Asian region and beyond'.[35] The increasing demand for energy in Northeast Asia, triggered by consumers like China, Japan and South Korea created a new opportunity for Russia to exploit new energy markets by making most of potentially huge, yet still underdeveloped oil and natural gas resources lying in the eastern region.[36] In particular, Russia holds the world's largest known reserves of natural gas, much of which are located in the Russian Far East. Due to a high reliance on coal, especially in the Far East region, the national gas distribution programme, *Gazifikatsiya Rossii* (Gasification of Russia), has been implemented not only to step up gas supply in the peripheral areas of European Russia to fulfil the gaps in the energy demand, but also to connect Siberian and Far Eastern regions to 'mainland' Russia. This connectivity is considered to be crucial 'both in maintaining central control over these far-away regions, and subsequently impeding Chinese influence in this region that Moscow views with a geopolitical glance: as a potentially separatist region'.[37]

Russia's ability to use the energy resources of East Siberia and the Far East to foster large-scale cooperation with Northeast Asia began with an interest in diversifying its energy exports as well as opening a great energy 'window' to East Asia that could create additional elements for energy stability in the whole Asia-Pacific.[38] In this vein, a document entitled *Energy Strategy of Russia for the Period up to 2030* has already unveiled Russia's very ambitious energy export goals. According to the document, taking 2008 as the base year the target has been set to increase exports in oil in the Asia-Pacific region from 8 per cent to 22–25 per cent and natural gas from 0 per cent to 20 per cent by 2030.[39] In order to achieve such an energy exports target, Russia's 'energy diplomacy' is the mainstay in its Asia-Pacific policy in general and Northeast Asian policy in particular. And there is little doubt that the potential of East Siberia and the Russian Far East has driven Russia to become an emerging seller of energy to Northeast Asia. A significant contribution has been made by the three state-owned energy companies, Gazprom, Rosneft and Rosatom who are the main actors in terms of defining Russia's energy policies in Northeast Asia. Moreover, East Siberia and the Russian Far East region is the second most important oil and gas province in Russia after West Siberia, with the Russian Far East having land borders with China and North Korea and sea borders with Japan and the USA.[40] Today Russian interests include the development of the territories in East Siberia and the Russian Far East mainly due to the necessity to cooperate with the Northeast Asian countries needing energy resources, so that regional integration could be realised, which will enable these countries to overcome their contradictions and start mutually beneficial cooperation for ensuring their energy security.[41] Surplus oil extracted from new oilfields in Eastern Siberia and Sakhalin in the Russian Far East is now the Russian priority to sell it to the Northeast Asian energy consuming countries (i.e. China, Japan and South Korea), which are located closest to these regions. This would also be cost-effective for the countries of Northeast Asia in terms of low transportation costs.

Although oil continues to be the primary global fuel source, the importance of natural gas has increased tremendously due to changes in energy consumption and growing efforts to find alternatives to both oil and coal.[42] In comparison to oil, gas is a much less fungible commodity because it cannot be easily stored or transported over long distances. However, gas can be most easily and cheaply transported through a mature technology of overland pipelines. Of late, a surge in the use of liquefied natural gas (LNG) and advancement in pipeline technology have converted gas from being a local commodity into becoming a multinational business. With remarkable foreign investment, improvements in production capacity, and the construction of pipelines and other infrastructure, Russia appears to be able to respond to growing demand for natural gas. It has been working seriously for the delivery of surplus gas acquired from new fields in Eastern Siberia, the Far East and the Arctic region, to not only Northeast Asia but also the United States and perhaps even South Asia, India in particular. Three main gas-bearing regions: Yakutiya in Eastern Siberia, Kovytka near Lake Baikal, and Sakhalin Island are considerably well located to serve Northeast Asia.[43] A 3,000-km 'Power of Siberia' gas pipeline taking gas from Russia's eastern Siberia to northeastern China was already inaugurated in December 2019.[44] The pipeline as the first direct Russia–China gas link, when fully become operational in 2025, will export 38 bcm of gas annually, though Russia's Gazprom has been considering with Chinese partners increasing the capacity to 44 bcm annually.[45] Scholars argue that, on the one hand, Russia is striving to make use of its eastern region's energy potential as an instrument of bilateral foreign policy as well as a means to become a 'global energy power', while, on the other hand, access to Russian resources seems to be becoming a way for improving energy security for China, Japan and South Korea.[46] No wonder then that 'energy has become one of the essential parts of Russia's identity in the world,'[47] but it is indeed the natural gas that is fast emerging as Russia's energy future. The energy potential of Russia's eastern region has encouraged India also in recent times to find its own niche there as part of New Delhi's Northeast Asian outreach in its quest for energy security. East Siberia and the Russian Far East, in addition to Mongolia, have considerable energy resources to offer that could be explored within the framework of India's 'Act East' policy.

Mongolia's energy scenario and potentiality

Despite the fact that Mongolia is strategically positioned at the cross-junction of Central Asia, Northeast Asia, Far East, China and Russia,[48] its regional identity as Northeast Asian country emerged only in the early 1990s following the attainment of 'real independence' after remaining under Soviet protection for almost seven decades.[49] Alignment with Northeast Asia within the political and intellectual circle was recognized as the key to Mongolia's economic growth, national security, and integration into the global economy given that the country possesses natural resources in abundance. Mongolia is now believed to be playing its own 'Great Game' in Northeast Asia by changing the rules for the development of its minerals and energy security.[50] It is indeed the mining sector that is one of the key drivers of export revenue for Mongolia and is often referred to as the 'engine of the economy'.[51] Having significant reserves of thermal and coking coal, uranium, oil, copper, gold, silver, iron ore, tungsten, rare earth metals as well as a huge potential for renewable energy development of both wind and solar power, Mongolia remains an attractive destination for foreign investors. In order to attract new foreign investments, in November 2017, the Mongolian Parliament approved changes to the country's 2006 Minerals Law including mechanism for obtaining new exploration licences by moving to an open tendering system. Several other changes even in the Energy Law of Mongolia concerning both the conventional as well as renewable resources have also been made after Mongolia realized that 'Northeast Asia's economic growth requires secure energy resources and sees its own mineral deposits … as motivation for regional actors to implement an 'infrastructure linkage strategy' for Mongolia to build up its poor rail and pipeline infrastructure'.[52] At the same time, Mongolian policymakers consider Northeast Asia as home to four of the world's major powers – the United States, Russia, China and Japan – and hence, Mongolia's Northeast Asian identity gives it extra mileage to intermingle with these powers.

Foreign investment is a major concern in Mongolia's energy sector, which is almost entirely fossil fuel-based and is dominated by coal, which accounts for 60 per cent of primary energy and 95 per cent of secondary energy, besides being the sole resource available at affordable cost in the country.[53] According to a report dated February 2018 provided for the ADB project in Mongolia, the coal resource deposit is estimated at 179 billion tons in 15 coal basins, which could potentially generate 285,741 terawatt-hours of electricity to meet the total electricity demands in China, Japan and South Korea for the next 20 years.[54] Mongolia is one of China's biggest suppliers of coking coal, exporting a total of 2.44 million tons in January–February 2020, which is in fact down by 30.7 per cent a year earlier due to sluggish Chinese demand.[55] In fact, China is inclined to purchase all of Mongolia's energy exports, and Russia is able to supply Mongolia with the energy products it badly needs, including refined petroleum products, electricity and natural gas.[56] Currently, almost 95 per cent of Mongolia's petroleum and energy needs are served by Russia, while China buys more than 90 per cent of the country's mining exports, mainly coal and copper. Domestically, petroleum exploration and production are executed exclusively under Public Sector Companies (PSCs) contracted over each petroleum block between the investor and the Mongolian Government. On the basis of data obtained from Mineral Resources and Petroleum Authority of Mongolia, Mongolia Extractive Industries Transparency Initiative, and Ministry of Mining and Heavy Industry of Mongolia, Petro Matad, a Mongolia-based oil exploration company confirms that as of 2020, out of a total of 33 petroleum blocks, three blocks have advanced to production, while exploration is being conducted on 17 blocks under 18 PSCs.[57] Between 1996 and 2019, 65 million barrels of oil have cumulatively been produced in Mongolia, of which 62 million barrels have been exported to China between 1998 and 2019.[58] Since there is no in-country refinery under operations, the produced oil is exported, while all the domestic consumption of refined oil products is satisfied by imports. But in order to reduce its dependence on imports, Mongolia has commenced the construction of country's first ever petrochemical refinery, supported by a US$1.236 billion soft credit line from India coming in the backdrop of China's Belt and Road Initiative (BRI).[59] After completion of its construction in 2022, the refinery with an initial capacity of 1.5 million metric tonnes per annum will produce diesel and gasoline as the primary products and liquefied petroleum gas (LPG), fuel oil and aviation fuel as secondary products. Expressing satisfaction on the progress of the project, India's Minister for Petroleum and Natural Gas, Dharmendra Pradhan, has been quoted as saying, 'the refinery will meet almost the domestic Mongolian requirement of petroleum products, help enhance Mongolia's long-term energy security and economic development and also promote development of ancillary industries related to refinery and pipeline operations'.[60]

In addition, Mongolia can find its strategically important uranium deposits useful for producing energy with the help of its 'third neighbours' like India and Japan to reduce its high dependency on oil and gas imports from Russia and its energy supply commitment to China. According to the Nuclear Energy Authority, a total of nine uranium deposit mines have been identified in Mongolia with 68,500 tons of proven uranium.[61] However, according to the Japan Oil, Gas and Metals National Corp, 'the country has untapped areas that may contain as much as 1.39 million tons, which would make it the world's largest source of the Uranium ore'.[62] Mongolia, indeed, has the potential to play a more important role as a supplier of energy for the Northeast Asian region besides serving as a potential corridor for Russian energy exports to China and supplying renewable energy and coal to South Korea and Japan.[63] Already in a meeting of the Eastern Economic Forum (EEF) on 12 September 2018 in Vladivostok, Russia and Mongolia together with China, Japan and South Korea, had agreed to a number of hydrocarbon production and supply initiatives aimed at expediting the development of regional energy supply infrastructure in Northeast Asia. Mongolia also proposed, as part of Mongolia's initiative in 'China–Mongolia–Russia Economic Corridor',[64] that 'Russia build a natural gas pipeline to China via Mongolia as well as construct an Asian Super Grid to help balance the regional electricity peak load'.[65] The importance of trans-Mongolian route lies into fact that construction of a Russia-China gas pipeline from East Siberia through Mongolia will be faster and easier than the western route through the Altai Mountains into Xinjiang. Mongolia's proactive posture has recently resulted in the launch of a second Russia–Mongolia–China gas pipeline 'The Power of Siberia 2' which 'underscores Mongolia's increasing geopolitical significance in East Asia, especially as competing hubs like Xinjiang grow increasingly unstable'.[66] This mega-project could be a game-changer in the supply of gas to Northeast Asia, thus enhancing the status of Mongolia also both as an energy supplier country as well as a participant in regional energy cooperation. While India is moving eastward to seek its energy opportunities, Mongolia may serve well given that in recent years this tiny populated but resource-rich country has raised its energy profile

> through its emergence as a coal exporter and through proposals for a number of large energy projects in the country, including major expansions of coal production, coal-fired electricity exports, coal gasification and coal to liquids, uranium mining, renewable energy schemes, and cross-Mongolia oil and natural gas pipelines and electricity transmission lines.[67]

India's energy engagements in Northeast Asia

In order to understand India's objectives in its energy engagements in Northeast Asia, it is important to understand its energy policies within the foreign policy framework. In the energy field, India has two overriding concerns: first, the country seeks to increase its domestic energy capabilities to help boost economic growth and second, to ensure its access to imported energy supplies as well as new energy technologies. In this regard, the energy agenda in India has been set to be inclusive, market based and climate-sensitive. The whole issue of energy was elaborated by the Indian Prime Minister Narendra Modi back on 5 December 2016 during his inaugural address to the Petrotech-2016 Exhibition, held in New Delhi, where he unveiled four pillars of his vision for India's energy future: energy access, energy efficiency, energy sustainability and energy security.[68] In order to realise this vision, varied opinions among the experts on energy issues have come to light including a call for more initiatives abroad by competing and cooperating more intensely in the international arena through 'enlightened diplomacy and negotiations'.[69]

India's energy policies abroad are suitable to follow its general foreign policy path of 'enlightened self-interest' and diversified options.[70] This strategy will not only move India to act cooperatively when it suits its interests, but also act competitively when it needs to be, particularly in acquiring assets or pursuing partners. Does this mean the same so far as India's quest for energy engagements in Northeast Asia is concerned? In fact, with the initiation of the 'Act East' policy in November 2014, a more action-oriented policy towards East Asia – in contrast to India's original 'Look East' policy – Northeast Asia has come to occupy an important place in India's foreign policy in general and energy policy in particular.

Within the framework of the 'Act East' policy India has been able to engage both Russia and Mongolia as the new destinations of energy sources. In June 2015, Mongolia was dubbed by Modi as 'an integral part of India's 'Act East' Policy' during his first-ever Prime Ministerial visit to Mongolia where he announced a US$ one billion line of credit to help develop infrastructure in the energy sector.[71] A few years later in September 2019, as the Chief Guest of the 5th Eastern Economic Forum (EEF) Modi's visit to Vladivostok, the first by an Indian Prime Minister to the Russian Far East region, saw India extending its 'Act East' Policy to 'Act Far East' Policy with the announcement of a line of credit worth US$ one billion for the development of the resource-rich region located in Asiatic Russia.[72] This new dimension of India's foreign policy together with first region-specific line of credit that India has extended to any country, ensures not only India's energy engagements with Russia but also marks New Delhi's presence in the Russian Far East right in the vicinity of China's immediate neighbourhood. India's investments in developing energy infrastructure as well as acquiring assets in oilfields located in Mongolian and Russian Far East regions have already started, though more areas for such engagements need to be explored. In the past, India has already made a huge energy investment in Russia with Indian state-owned firms having spent close to US$10 billion in acquiring stakes in oilfields such as Sakhalin-1, Taas-Yuryakh and Vankor, while cooperation with Russia's oil giant Rosneft to invest in Far East Russian cluster for ensuring India's energy security is currently in the pipeline.[73] Last year in September 2019, India pitched for its stake in vast oil and gas fields as well as liquefied natural gas (LNG) terminals in the Arctic region of Far East Russia in addition to other oil fields including Sakhalin-3 with the aim of sourcing one million barrels per day of oil and oil-equivalent gas from Russia.[74] In Mongolia, besides being involved in the development of Mongolian oilfields India already has a bilateral civil nuclear agreement for supply of uranium to India as well as an agreement on cooperation in renewable energy sector.

Exploring new avenues of India's energy cooperation with the energy-consuming countries of Northeast Asia like Japan and South Korea is a continuous process. India already has Civil Nuclear Energy Cooperation deals with Japan and South Korea. India and Japan are involved in further strengthening of their cooperation in the energy development of both countries, besides contributing to worldwide energy security. However, a geopolitical competition in Northeast Asia and the emerging strategic geometry in the larger Indo-Pacific region adds more complexities to an existing competitive and often conflicting India–China relationship. In such a situation, despite external hurdles like potential Chinese resistance to India's outreach in the region, a tactful energy policy will go a long way in exploring and executing energy cooperation with other regional stakeholders. It is more so because India's energy demand in the coming years will speed up further as India plunged into 'manufacturing through Modi Government's much vaulted 'Make in India' programme, developmental projects and access to electricity to all'.[75] In the last few years, India's renewable energy sector has flourished tremendously with the country being fourth most attractive renewable energy market in the world.[76] Ranked fourth in wind power, fifth in solar power and fifth in renewable power installed capacity in 2018, 'India has been leading the world in its pursuit of enhanced solar energy capacity through International Solar Alliance [ISA]'.[77] India's re-election as President of ISA recently in October 2020 further increases its responsibility to galvanise investments worth US$1 trillion for harnessing solar energy as per ISA's plan for 2030, when solar is expected to become most important source of energy for electricity production.[78] India's own capacity as well as cooperation with Northeast Asian partners in the field of renewable energy will go a long way in benefitting all stakeholders in terms of ensuring access to clean energy.

It needs to be pointed out that ever since India emerged as the world's third largest energy consumer country after China and USA in 2012, it has been continuing to hold the same rank with its demand for energy going up. Between 1990 and 2018, India's primary energy consumption has almost tripled reaching the figure of an estimated 916 million tons of oil equivalent. In 2018, coal continued to have largest share of 45 per cent in India's total energy consumption, followed by petroleum and other liquids with 26 per cent share, and traditional biomass and waste with 20 per cent share.[79] Other renewable fuel sources constitute a small portion of primary energy consumption, though several of these resources, such as solar, wind, and hydroelectricity have significant potential of capacity. Diesel remains the most-consumed oil product in India, accounting for 39 per cent of the total consumption of petroleum products in 2019, hence the country's crude oil imports reached at 4.4 million b/d.[80] The same year, India became the world's fourth-largest LNG importer, receiving approximately 1.2 trillion cubic feet (tcf) or 7 per cent of the global trade. Although natural gas accounts for 6 per cent of the country's energy consumption, India plans to increase the natural gas market share to 15 per cent by 2030 as part of efforts to reduce air pollution and use cleaner-burning fuels. Given the projection by International Energy Agency that India's energy demand will more than double from 898 million tonnes of oil equivalent (mtoe) in 2017 to 1880 mtoe in 2040,[81] energy security issues remain a challenge where reframing the relationship with energy suppliers as one of interdependence would help bring relief to a large extent in ensuring continuous energy flow. The opportunities the Northeast Asian countries, particularly the energy producing countries, have offered to India are indeed in the interest of India's quest for energy security. In future too, India must explore such opportunities to engage itself in the regional energy bonding both at the bilateral as well as multilateral level.

Conclusion

Being a region comprising the energy producing, consuming and transit countries Northeast Asia is of vital importance in India's eastward expansion for its quest for energy security. But the energy outlook of the region suggests that the prevailing scenario in China, Japan and South Korea is indicative of the fact that stable energy supplies are necessary for these consumer countries to ensure energy security in Northeast Asia. In this regard, Russia's eastern region (East Siberia and Russian Far East) and Mongolia have much to offer in terms of energy supplies as well as promoting energy cooperation in the region. But it is competition rather than cooperation that appears to be the existing phenomenon despite some initiatives to create an energy security regime. The challenges of energy security and achieving more sustainable use of energy resources call for renewed and more effective intra-regional and inter-regional cooperation, including a multilateral mechanism that can help facilitate dialogue and cooperation on various proposals on interconnection.[82] In this vein, India's Northeast Asian outreach through bilateral and multilateral cooperative mechanisms within the ambit of the 'Act East' and 'Act Far East' policies may be a game changer in creating mutually beneficial sustainable partnerships for energy access and security both in terms of conventional as well as renewable energy. This is more so because India's energy bonding is slowly but steadily growing with almost all the energy producing, consuming and transit countries belonging to Northeast Asia.

In addition, India's energy policy abroad including in East Asia is being pursued in a much more inclusive manner to address its fast-growing energy demand in an environment where competition remains to be the catch-phrase. China, for obvious reasons, poses a major challenge to India, which is a relatively new player in the Russian Far East and Mongolia in terms of joint ventures and equity investments for developing energy infrastructure. In spite of China being a dominant external actor in the Far East and Mongolia, India's scope of its bold presence there cannot be ruled out. With 50 business agreements concluded between Indian and Russian entities on the side-lines of the 5th Eastern Economic Forum in 2019 that will lead to several billions of dollars of investment, India's stake in the Russian Far East is going to be impressive.

If Russia, as a major energy producer, develops a strategic understanding with India and China, both major energy consumers, this may produce a concrete result within the Russia–India–China (RIC) trilateral framework, where energy is an agreed area of cooperation. India is currently negotiating with Russia and Mongolia to import coking coal, a raw material for making steel, in order to reduce its dependence on Australia. Mongolia can also be a stable supplier of nuclear fuel for India due to having significant deposits of uranium. However, experts on energy issues believe that rather than competition and conflict, 'confidence-building and improving mutual trust should be the goal' as 'in a globalized energy market, no country can achieve energy security unilaterally … Multilaterally, the region should have a goal of bringing China and India more directly into the global institutions such as the IEA [International Energy Agency]'.[83] Only time will tell how much improvement comes in the competitive environment of energy security concerns. Until then India must continue with constructive engagements in Northeast Asia in its quest for energy security despite the prevalent hurdles in the face of growing Chinese influence in the region.

Notes

1 International Energy Agency. *Energy Technology Policy.* Paris: OECD/IEA, 1985, 29.
2 Narangoa, Li and Robert Cribb. *Historical Atlas of Northeast Asia, 1590–2010: Korea, Manchuria, Mongolia, Eastern Siberia.* New York: Columbia University Press, 2014. Accessed 29 July 2020. www.jstor.org/stable/10.7312/li--16070.
3 Ibid., pp. 3.
4 'What Countries Are the Top Producers and Consumers of Oil?.' US Energy Information Administration. 1 April 2020. Accessed 6 October 2020. www.eia.gov/tools/faqs/faq.php?id=709&t=6.
5 *BP Statistical Review of World Energy 2020.* London, 2020, 4. Accessed 6 October 2020, www.bp.com/content/dam/bp/business-sites/en/global/corporate/pdfs/energy-economics/statistical-review/bp-stats-review-2020-full-report.pdf
6 Kim, Suk Hi, Junhua Jia and Michael Whitty. 'The Northeast Asian Energy Situation and the North Korean Factor.' *North Korean Review* 7, no. 1 (2011): 80.
7 OECD. *The OECD Environmental Outlook to 2050: The Consequences of Inaction.* Paris: OECD Publishing, 2012, 60. Accessed 28 July 2020. http://dx.doi.org/10.1787/9789264122246-en
8 Jae-Seung Lee. 'Energy Security and Cooperation in Northeast Asia.' *Korean Journal of Defense Analysis* 22, no. 2 (2010): 217.
9 Wilson, Jeffrey D. 'Northeast Asian Resource Security Strategies and International Resource Politics in Asia.' *Asian Studies Review* 38, no.1 (2014): 20.
10 Voropai, Nikolai et al. 'Development of Electric Power Cooperation in Northeast Asia.' *Global Energy Interconnection* 2, no.1 (February 2019):1. Accessed 28 July 2020. https://doi.org/10.1016/j.gloei.2019.06.001
11 See endnote 6.
12 Oh, Miyeon. 'Korea's Role in Asian Energy Cooperation.' In *The Korean Pivot: The Study of South Korea as a Global Power* edited by Victor D. Cha and Marie Dumond. Washington DC: Center for Strategic and International Studies, 2017. Accessed 20 October 2020. https://csis-website-prod.s3.amazonaws.com/s3fs-public/publication/170718_Cha_KoreanPivot_Web.pdf
13 Freeman, Carla P. 'Building an Energy Cooperation Regime in Northeast Asia.' In *Energy Security Cooperation in Northeast Asia* edited by Bo Kong and Jae Ku. London: Routledge, 2015, 158.
14 Lee, Songsoo. 'Rising Energy Demand in Northeast Asia.' *Eppen*. 3 July 2016. Accessed 2 August 2020, https://isdp.eu/publication/rising-energy-demand-northeast-asia/
15 Ibid.
16 Ibid., p. 58.
17 Kim, J. James, Park Jiyoung and Choi Hyeonjung. 'Towards a Framework for Energy Cooperation in Northeast Asia: Challenges and Opportunities.' *The Asan Institute for Policy Studies*, Issue Brief 2014–20, 22 July 2014, 3. Accessed 25 August 2020. https://en.asaninst.org/contents/towards-a-framework-for-energy-cooperation-in-northeast-asia-challenges-and-opportunities/

18 Zhao, Suisheng. 'China's Global Search for Energy Security: Cooperation and Competition in Asia-Pacific.' *Journal of Contemporary China* 17, 55 (May 2008): 208.
19 See endnote 14.
20 Gerretsen, Isabelle. 'Japan Net Zero Emissions Pledge Puts Coal in the Spotlight.' *Climate Home News*. 26 October 2020. Accessed 28 October 2020. www.climatechangenews.com/2020/10/26/japan-net-zero-emissions-pledge-puts-coal-spotlight/
21 Japan, Agency for Natural Resources and Energy. *2019 – Understanding the Current Energy Situation in Japan (Part 1)*. Tokyo: Ministry of Economy Trade and Industry, 13 August 2020. Accessed 28 October 2020. www.enecho.meti.go.jp/en/category/special/article/energyissue2019_01.html
22 Ibid.
23 Hong, J. H. et al.. 'Long-Term Energy Strategy Scenarios for South Korea: Transition to a Sustainable Energy System.' *Energy Policy* 127 (2019): 426. Accessed 25 August 2020, https://doi.org/10.1016/j.enpol.2018.11.055
24 Republic of Korea, Ministry of Foreign Affairs. *Policy Information: Energy*. Seoul: Ministry of Foreign Affairs. Accessed 28 September 2020. www.mofa.go.kr/eng/wpge/m_5657/contents.do
25 Ibid.
26 See endnote 14.
27 See endnote 23, p. 427.
28 Tynkkynen, Veli-Pekka. *The Energy of Russia: Hydrocarbon Culture and Climate Change*. Cheltenham: Edward Elgar Publishing, 2019, 3-4. Accessed 31 October 2020. www.elgaronline.com/view/9781788978590/9781788978590.xml
29 Ibid., pp. 9.
30 Butler, Nick. 'Moscow Is Being Forced to Change Its Energy Strategy.' *Financial Times*. 9 December 2019. Accessed 1 November 2020. www.ft.com/content/bd2f93f2-1685-11ea-8d73-6303645ac406.
31 See endnote 28, p. 11.
32 Ibid., pp. 2–3.
33 See endnote 30.
34 Ibid.
35 Soni, Sharad K. 'Russian Policy towards Northeast Asia: The Mongolia Factor.' *The Mongolian Journal of International Affairs*, 19 (2014): 37.
36 . Shoichi Itoh. *Russia Looks East: Energy Markets and Geopolitics in Northeast Asia*. Washington, DC: Centre for Strategic and International Studies, 2011, vii.
37 See endnote 28, p. 10.
38 Lousianin, Sergey G. 'Russia's View on the Northeast Asia Security Landscape – the Mongolian Aspect.' *The Mongolian Journal of International Affairs*, 13 (2006): 26–27.
39 Ministry of Energy of the Russian Federation. *Energy Strategy of Russia for the Period up to 2030*. Moscow: Institute of Energy Strategy, 2010, 140–141. Accessed 26 June 2020. www.energystrategy.ru/projects/docs/ES-2030_%28Eng%29.pdf
40 Dyomina, Olga and Alexander Izhbuldin. 'Energy Sector Current Status, Recent Changes, and Energy Policies in the Russian Far East (RFE).' *NAPSNet Special Reports*. 28 August 2020. Accessed 27 October 2020, https://nautilus.org/napsnet/napsnet-special-reports/energy-sector-current-status-recent-changes-and-energy-policies-in-the-russian-far-east-rfe/
41 Voropai, Nikolai et.al. 'Development of Electric Power Cooperation in Northeast Asia.' *Global Energy Interconnection* 2, 1 (February 2019):1. Accessed 23 August 2020, https://doi.org/10.1016/j.gloei.2019.06.001

42 Fiona Hill. 'Russia: The 21st Century's Energy Superpower?.' *Brookings*, 1 March 2002. Accessed 28 October 2020. www.brookings.edu/articles/russia-the-21st-centurys-energy-superpower/
43 Ibid.
44 'Russia Opens Power of Siberia Gas Pipeline to China.' *The Economist Intelligence Unit*. 10 December 2019. Accessed 30 October 2020. www.eiu.com/industry/article/348791418/russia-opens-power-of-siberia-gas-pipeline-to-china/2019-12-10
45 Elliot, Stuart. 'Russia's Gazprom Mulls Power of Siberia Capacity Expansion to 44 Bcm/year.' S&P Global. 26 June 2020. Accessed 30 October 2020. www.spglobal.com/platts/en/market-insights/latest-news/natural-gas/062620-russias-gazprom-mulls-power-of-siberia-capacity-expansion-to-44-bcmyear
46 Wyciszkiewicz, Ernest. 'Prospects for Energy Cooperation in North-East Asia.' *PISM Research Papers*, 2 (August 2006): 41. Accessed 12 September 2020. www.files.ethz.ch/isn/93294/2006_2.pdf.
47 Akaha, Tsuneo. 'A Distant Neighbor: Russia's Search to Find Its Place in East Asia.' *Global Asia* 7, 2 (Summer 2012): 2. Accessed 28 October 2020. www.globalasia.org/v7no2/cover/a-distant-neighbor-russias-search-to-find-its-place-in-east-asia_tsuneo-akaha.
48 Stobdan, P. 'India and Mongolia: Modi on Ashoka's Path.' IDSA Comment, 13 May 2015. Accessed 16 August 2020. https://idsa.in/idsacomments/IndiaandMongolia_pstobdan_130515.
49 Soni, Sharad K. 'India-Mongolia Relations: Implications for Regional Cooperation in North East Asia.' *Mongolian & Tibetan Quarterly* 18, 2 (June 2009): 60–64.
50 Campi, Alicia Campi. 'Mongolia's Turn at the "Great Game".' *Asia Pacific Bulletin*, 184. 1 November 2012. Accessed 12 September 2020. www.eastwestcenter.org/sites/default/files/private/apb_184_0.pdf
51 Melville, Christopher and Erdenedalai Odkhuu. 'Mining in Mongolia: Overview.' *Thomson Reuters Practical Law*. 1 August 2020. Accessed 3 November 2020. https://uk.practicallaw.thomsonreuters.com/w-017-7372?transitionType=Default&contextData=(sc.Default)&firstPage=true
52 See endnote 50.
53 ADB. 'Sector Assessment: Energy.' *Ulaanbaatar Air Quality Improvement Program: Report and Recommendation of the President*. RRP Mon 51199, Manila: Asian Development Bank, 2018, 1. Accessed 3 November 2020, www.adb.org/sites/default/files/linked-documents/51199-001-sd-01.pdf
54 Ibid.
55 Wong, Dylan. 'Mongolia Resumes China Coal Exports.' Argus. 1 April 2020. Accessed 3 November 2020. www.argusmedia.com/en/news/2092461-mongolia-resumes-china-coal exports#:~:text=Mongolia%20is%20one%20of%20China's,30.7pc%20a%20year%20earlier
56 Krusekof, Charles. 'Mongolian Perspectives on Northeast Asian Energy Security Cooperation.' In *Energy Security Cooperation in Northeast Asia* edited by Bo Kong and Jae Ku. Routledge, 2015, 100.
57 'Oil in Mongolia.' Petro Matad. Accessed 3 November 2020. www.petromatadgroup.com/mongolia/oil-in-mongolia/
58 Ibid.
59 Erdenejargal, E. 'State visit enhances Mongolia-India strategic partnership.' *Montsame*. 30 September 2019, Accessed 17 October 2020. https://montsame.mn/en/read/202211

60 'Pradhan Meets Mongolian Delegation, Discusses Ways to Enhance Economic Cooperation.' Outlook. 10 January 2020. Accessed 3 November 2020. www.outlookindia.com/newsscroll/pradhan-meets-mongolian-delegation-discusses-ways-to-enhance-economic-cooperation/1705424

61 'New Uranium Mining Projects – Mongolia.' Wise Uranium Project. 30 July 2020. Accessed 7 November 2020. www.wise-uranium.org/upmn.html

62 'Mongolia Talks Slated to Secure Uranium as Competition Soars.' 7 October 2008. Accessed 4 November 2020. www.japantimes.co.jp/news/2008/10/07/business/mongolia-talks-slated-to-secure-uranium-as-competition-soars/.

63 See endnote 56, pp. 100.

64 Soni, Sharad *K.* 'China-Mongolia-Russia Economic Corridor: Opportunities and Challenges.' In *China's Global Rebalancing and the New Silk Road* edited by B. R. Deepak. Singapore: Springer, 2018, 101–117.

65 Campi, Alicia J. 'Mongolia Links Gas Transit Pipeline to Asian Super Grid Negotiations.' *Eurasia Daily Monitor* 15, 145 (October 2018). Accessed 25 August 2020. https://jamestown.org/program/mongolia-links-gas-transit-pipeline-to-asian-super-grid-negotiations/

66 Sobolik, Michael. *Indo-Pacific Monitor*, 4, 17 January 2020. Accessed 7 November 2020. www.afpc.org/publications/bulletins/indo-pacific-monitor/indo-pacific-monitor-no.-4

67 See endnote 56, p. 100.

68 'PM's Address at the Inaugural Session of PETROTECH – 2016 Exhibition.' PMINDIA. 5 December 2016. Accessed 3 November 2020. www.pmindia.gov.in/en/news_updates/pms-address-at-the-inaugural-session-of-petrotech-2016-exhibition/

69 Raj, Parimal, Arpit Saxena and Shashank Gupta. 'Energy Security an Indian Perspective: The Way Forward.' Paper presented at the *8th Biennial International Conference and Exposition on Petroleum Geophysics, Hyderabad, 2010*, 6. Accessed 3 November 2020. www.spgindia.org/2010/137.pdf

70 Madan, Tanvi. *The Brookings Foreign Policy Studies, Energy Security Series: India*. Washington, DC: The Brookings Institution, November 2006. Accessed 5 November 2020. www.brookings.edu/wp-content/uploads/2016/06/2006india.pdf

71 Soni, Sharad K. 'Emerging Dimensions of India-Mongolia Relations.' *Indian Foreign Affairs Journal* 11, 1(2016): 54.

72 Chandrasekhar, Balasubramanian. 'Act Far East Policy: India's Bear Hug' *The Geopolitics*. 24 October 2019. accessed 3 November 2020, https://thegeopolitics.com/act-far-east-policy-indias-bear-hug/

73 'India in Talks with Rosneft to Invest in Far East Russian Cluster: Pradhan.' Energyworld.com. 18 December 2019. Accessed 3 November 2020.
https://energy.economictimes.indiatimes.com/news/oil-and-gas/india-in-talks-with-rosneft-to-invest-in-far-east-russian-cluster-pradhan/72862503

74 'India Pitches for Stake in Far East Oilfields, Higher Imports of Oil From Russia.' *BloombergQuint*. 17 September 2020. Accessed 7 November 2020. www.bloombergquint.com/business/india-pitches-for-stake-in-far-east-oilfields-higher-imports-of-oil-from-russia.

75 Sharma, Ashok. 'India's Quest for Energy Security.' *The Pioneer*. 23 February 2020. Accessed 17 August 2020, www.dailypioneer.com/2020/sunday-edition/india---s-quest-for-energy-security.html.

76 'Renewable Energy Industry in India.' India Brand Equity Foundation. 21 October 2020. Accessed 7 November 2020. www.ibef.org/industry/renewable-energy.aspx

77 'Cabinet Approves India's Approach to UN Climate Change Conference to Be Held in Spain Next Week.' PIB Delhi. 27 November 2019. Accessed 3 October 2020. https://pib.gov.in/PressReleaseIframePage.aspx?PRID=1593665

78 'India re-elected as president of International Solar Alliance.' *The Hindu*. 15 October 2020. Accessed 5 November 2020, www.thehindu.com/news/international/india-re-elected-as-president-of-international-solar-alliance/article32859827.ece
79 US Energy Information Administration. *Country Analysis Executive Summary: India*. Washington, DC: EIA, 30 September 2020. Accessed 7 November 2020. www.eia.gov/international/content/analysis/countries_long/India/india.pdf
80 Ibid.
81 Gupta, Uma. 'India's Energy Demand Will More than Double by 2040 – IEA.' *PV Magazine*. 13 November 2018. Accessed 4 November 2020. www.pv-magazine-india.com/2018/11/13/indias-energy-demand-will-more-than-double-by-2040-iea/.
82 United Nations Economic and Social Commission for Asia and the Pacific (ESCAP). *Unlocking the Potential for East and North-East Asian Regional Economic Cooperation and Integration*. 2017, vii. Accessed 7 November 2020. www.unescap.org/sites/default/files/publications/Unlocking%20the%20Potential%20for%20East%20and%20North-East%20Asian%20Regional%20Economic%20Cooperation%20and%20Integration_0.pdf
83 Herberg, Mikkal E. 'Energy Competition and Energy Cooperation in Northeast Asia.' In *Energy Security Cooperation in Northeast Asia* edited by Bo Kong and Jae Ku. London: Routledge, 2015, 28.

13

THE 'BELT AND ROAD INITIATIVE' AND INDIA–CHINA ENERGY COOPERATION AND COMPETITION

B. R. Deepak

On 7 September 2013, Chinese President Xi Jinping proposed a concept linking Eurasia by building a Silk Road Economic Belt during his speech at the Nazarbayev University, Kazakhstan. A month later, he proposed the twenty-first-century Maritime Silk Road, which envisages building hard and soft infrastructure from the Indo-Pacific to Africa, including transport, energy, water management, communication, earth monitoring, economic and social infrastructure, thus turning the concept into a 'Belt and Road Initiative' (BRI). In 2015, during the Bo'ao Forum for Asia in Sanya, Hainan, China rolled out an action plan that enunciated five major goals of the vision in terms of promoting policy coordination, facilitating connectivity, uninterrupted trade, financial integration and people-to-people exchanges. In order to facilitate these 'five connectivity goals', China identified six major economic corridors along the BRI for a new type of regional development model. These are Bangladesh, China, India, Myanmar Economic Corridor (BCIM); China Pakistan Economic Corridor (CPEC); New Eurasia Land Bridge; China, Mongolia, Russia Economic Corridor; China Central Asia Economic Corridor; and China, Indochina Peninsula Economic Corridor. Of these China has committed US$73 billion to the CPEC, which has been termed as the pilot and flagship of the BRI projects. Owing to India's opposition to the BRI, China dropped BCIM from the BRI during the second BRI Forum in April 2019 and replaced it with China–Myanmar Economic Corridor (CMEC), which was signed on 9 September 2018 according to a statement issued by China's National Development and Reform Commission (NDRC). This would be the second bilateral economic corridor after the CPEC and perhaps another flagship as far as connectivity in Southeast Asia and South Asia is concerned.

Given China's economic growth trajectory in the last 40 years since reforms, the greater demand for energy resources is the natural outcome. Although China is now the world's fifth largest oil producer, the country has been a net oil importer since 1993. Since 2017, China has trounced the United States as the largest importer of crude oil; in 2018, China's import reached 9.2 mb/d of crude oil, of which more than half came from the Middle East. Besides economic growth, which has slumped of late, falling domestic output and the ongoing strategic storage are the main reasons for growing imports.[1] Though China is the largest consumer and importer of oil and gas, China's dependence on oil and natural gas in 2016 was 65.5 per cent and 36.6 per cent, respectively. It is expected that this percentage will remain so in the future too, despite China making headways in renewable energy mix. In this context, the countries along the 'Belt and Road' are crucial in guaranteeing China's oil and gas security.

Energy security strategy along the BRI countries

The BRI countries have abundant oil and gas reserves and their capacity to export is huge. It has been reported that by the end of 2016, the proven oil and gas reserves of the BRI countries were 139 billion tons and 143.4 trillion cubic metres, accounting for 57.75 per cent and 76.85 per cent of the global total, respectively.[2] In 2018, although out of 15 top exporters of crude oil to China, 10 were from the BRI countries, and if Latin America is included, it takes the tally to 13, leaving out the US and the UK, however, the dependence on a few countries like Russia, Saudi Arabia, Angola, Oman, Iraq and Iran is huge and accounts for almost 60 per cent of its total oil import. It is also owing to the fact that almost half of the oil reserves are found in the region, moreover the proximity to China also makes it viable as far as transportation cost is concerned. Nevertheless, this is also a cause for concern as both the Middle East and Africa are extremely volatile regions and the transportation through various choke points subjects the imports to various risks.

China's natural gas imports are less diversified comparing its oil imports. Though China imports gas from Australia, Qatar, the United Arab Emirates, the United States, Myanmar and Indonesia, however, Turkmenistan remains China's largest exporter of natural gas. The China–Turkmenistan gas pipeline was China's first transnational gas pipeline.

China is of the view that at present its energy security is highly dependent on cooperation with the US rather than the competition. Nevertheless, there is a general feeling in China that the US has been aggressively containing China not only in its backyard, i.e. the South China Sea and Taiwan, but also in the Middle East by exercising its control on the region's energy resources. Therefore, from an energy security point of view, China considers the US as a major threat. Although China is hedging the US threat by investing beyond the Middle East including Latin America and Africa, clearly Russia, the Central Asian Republics and Myanmar have emerged as the new guarantors of China's energy security, which in turn may offer potential opportunities for energy cooperation between China and other countries in the vicinity including India.

The six economic corridors that China is building along the BRI countries have been projected as connectivity projects offering a smooth flow of public goods and services, connecting civilisations and peoples alike, thus integrating regions economically and endeavouring towards realising the goal of shared future. Securing energy security is an extremely important component of the BRI. It is not only the external connectivity but also inter-provincial connectivity that has been integrated into the larger framework of the BRI. In this context, China has planned to connect half of its provinces with Asia, Africa and Europe. For example, Yunnan has become a hub connecting China to Southeast Asia and South Asia. Kunming, the capital city of Yunnan would be connected to various transport corridors, the most ambitious of these – the Trans-Asia Railway (TAR) to be completed by 2020, connecting Kunming to Singapore. In the same vein, Xinjiang is turning into a hub for connecting China with Central Asia and South Asia, and Fujian is poised to become a new fulcrum for the twenty-first-century Maritime Silk Road. It has been reported that by 2020, China will build 172 major water conservancy projects with an investment of $87.6 billion, and by 2030, 1,600 airports with an investment of $23.3 billion would be constructed.[3] Therefore, there is a new wave of competition amongst Chinese provinces for the BRI projects inside as well as outside China. Externally, China has built the A, B and C lines of the Central Asian natural gas pipeline, namely Sino-Kazakhstan crude oil pipeline, Sino-Russian crude oil pipeline, and Sino-Myanmar oil and gas pipeline. The crude oil transportation capacity of these lines has reached 35 million tons/year and the natural gas transmission capacity of 67 billion cubic metres/year.[4] As China treats India as one of the BRI countries, this chapter looks into the issue of energy security between India and China, primarily in Myanmar, Central Asia and Africa, and explores if a mechanism for cooperation could be established or not.

Securing energy through China–Myanmar Economic Corridor

With its rich oil and gas reserves, Myanmar has emerged as a reliable source of energy for India and China. Both have pursued aggressive energy diplomacy and strengthened their energy cooperation with Myanmar. As far as China's cooperation with Myanmar is concerned, currently PetroChina, China National Offshore Oil Corporation (CNOOC) and SINOPEC have signed agreements for the development of 15 oil and gas fields in Myanmar. Of these, CNOOC Limited has obtained six oil and gas field mining contracts; SINOPEC received the PSC-D oil and gas field in the Mahudang area, and PetroChina obtained three oil and gas fields AD-1,6,8 in Rakhine area; RSF-2 of Tuyuan and RSF-3 oil and gas fields of Gowejo; IOR-3 oil and gas fields of Dema and IOR-4 of Mahudang as well as PSC-F oil and gas fields in Naraydiwin.[5] However, since the open tender process initiated in 2011, a large number of Western (Italy, France, Australia, etc.) and Asian (Thai, Malaysia, South Korea, India, etc.) energy companies have begun to enter Myanmar's energy market, posing a huge challenge to Chinese energy companies. Although China has obtained 15 of the 38 oil and gas fields, however, most of these were not obtained through open bidding, but through government to government agreements. According to Dadwal, when open bids were invited in 2013, only one Chinese company could make it to the bidding list comparing seven companies from India.[6] Therefore, it could be discerned that China is facing huge competition in the energy market of Myanmar, asserts Peng.[7]

As far as oil and gas pipelines are concerned, China and Myanmar signed an energy cooperation plan for the construction of a $2.5 billion China–Myanmar oil and gas pipeline in June 2009. PetroChina has a 50.9 per cent stake whereas the rest is held by Myanmar Oil and Gas Enterprise, South Korea's Daewoo International, and India's ONGC Videsh Ltd (OVL) and GAIL. The total length of the pipeline is 2,402 kilometres. The pipeline originates in Madeira on the west coast of Rakhine, passes through Mandalay, Mujie, Ruili, Kunming and Guiyang, and finally arrives in Guigang, Guangxi. The gas and oil pipelines became operational in 2015 and 2017 respectively, and as reported in July 2018 by various Chinese news reports, the pipeline has unloaded a record 10.98 million tons of crude oil. As of September 2018, the cumulative transportation volume has been recorded at 21.426 billion cubic metres, of which 18.715 billion cubic metres was shipped to China.[8]

Last year on 19 November, China's Ministry of Foreign Affairs revealed that during his meeting with the State Counsellor and Foreign Minister Aung San Suu Kyi in Nay Pyi Taw, Foreign Minister Wang Yi proposed the establishment of the China–Myanmar Economic Corridor (CMEC) which will connect China's southwestern province of Yunnan to Mandalay in central Myanmar, and then east to Yangon and west to the Kyaukpyu Special Economic Zone (SEZ) forming an equation of three-terminal support (*sanduan zhicheng*) and three-legged cooperation (*sanzu dingli*). Wang Yi pointed out that the CMEC will open up new vistas for building the 'Belt and Road Initiative' between China and Myanmar. The CMEC envisages to have the Kyaukpyu deep sea water port ($1.3 billion) with two berths in its initial phase including Kyaukpyu SEZ ($2 billion); China–Myanmar oil and gas pipeline ($5 billion); Mandalay Yida Economic and Trade Cooperation Zone ($4 billion); Tagaung Taung (*Dagongshan*) Nickel Industry Development Project ($820 million); Letpadaung copper mine project ($1 billion); Kunming–Kyaukpyu railway line; Mandalay–Tigyaing–Muse expressway and Kyaukpyu-Nay Pyi Taw highway projects etc. Though the CITIC Myanmar CEO Yuan Xibin argues that China didn't want to have the present 70 per cent stake in the Kyaukpyu port, it is widely believed that China wanted to have a between 70 and 85 per cent stake owing to the aborted, $1.5 billion Myitsone dam project, where China suffered huge economic losses. Also, owing to the debt trap issues, Myanmar cut to size an originally conceived ten berth port worth $7.5 billion to the present scale of investment. Many of these projects predate the BRI and were negotiated by China taking the so called 'aerial route'. The port is of great strategic and economic significance to China as it will give it access to the Bay of Bengal, diversify its energy routes, and cut short almost 5,000 kilometres of the sea route, thus getting rid of the so-called Malacca dilemma. China would be able to stock its energy and other imports from the Middle East, Europe, Africa, India etc., and countries in Kyaukpyu, and transport these to China through already functional pipeline, roads and the proposed rail connectivity.

India too has strengthened its energy cooperation with Myanmar. In 1998, GAIL signed a memorandum of understanding with Myanmar for the transportation of

280,000 cubic metres of natural gas/day to be used by West Bengal, Orissa and Mizoram. On 23 September 2007, OVL acquired three offshore deep-water exploration Blocks AD-2, AD-3 and AD-9. In 2014 biddings, the RIL won shallow-water blocks M-17 and M-18, while OIL and its partners got blocks M-4 and YEB.[9] In August 2018, it was revealed by the Indian Minister of Petroleum that Indian Oil Corp (IOC) is also working with Myanmar companies in setting up LPG storage facilities and Petronet LNG is working on setting up an LNG terminal there. Peng posits that India is a latecomer in Myanmar's energy market. It is in a relatively disadvantageous position vis-à-vis China, for of the 38 oil and gas fields that have been tendered in Myanmar, India has only gained about 8.[10]

Nonetheless, neither China nor India can squeeze each other out of Myanmar's energy market. In the words of Peng the relative advantageous/disadvantageous position of China and India in Myanmar's energy market makes it possible for China and India to compete as well as cooperate in Myanmar's energy market.[11] Moreover, multilateral cooperation as regards co-development of energy resources will mitigate investment risks, generate high profits, as far as production, processing, marketing and distribution of resources is concerned.

Energy security and China Central Asia economic corridor

The BRI Action Plan defines Xinjiang as a core area both politically and geographically. China considers Xinjiang as a window to the west and central, south and west Asia. Both the medium and long-term goals have been in place to realize the BRI. The medium-term goals are aimed at completing railway and road connectivity between China and Pakistan within 5–10 years, whereas the long-term goals are set to be achieved by the year 2049; these goals are Three Channels, Three Bases and Five Centres in Xinjiang. Three Channels include North–Central–Southern Channels; Three Bases comprise oil and gas, coal and wind power bases; Five Centres are healthcare, traffic, culture, logistics, and education. [12]

The CPEC will link the Pakistani city of Gwadar to China's Xinjiang via a vast network of highways, railways and oil and gas pipelines. It has been reported that a pipeline will also be built from Gwadar to Kashgar to transport oil from the Persian Gulf and Iran. From the Gulf, one million barrels would be exported to China, as it is getting ready to shift 17 oil exports from the Gulf via Gwadar. The Gwadar-Kashgar pipeline is expected to be completed by 2021. According to Malik Senior Research Fellow, Institute of Strategic Studies, Islamabad, 'when more oil would be exported to China via the Gulf and Iran, a major source of Chinese oil imports, could also boost Pakistan's trade invariably'.[13] The emerging Pakistan under the CPEC would be a 'gateway' to China and Central Asia. The pipeline is not without vulnerability, as the Chinese investment in Gwadar, a port in Baluchistan, has been opposed by the Baluchistan Liberation Army, a separatist group seeking independence from Pakistan. This together with internal terror outfits within Pakistan has forced Pakistan to raise an army division to protect the Chinese investment.

As regards the Central Asian Republics (CARs), China is relatively a new player; however, in a short span of time, it has upstaged Russia as a dominant trade partner of the region since 2009. In 2014, China's trade with the five CARs crossed $45 billion compared with Russia's less than $35 billion.[14] The divers behind this growth have been energy exports and other natural resources, especially with Kazakhstan and Turkmenistan. The first investment China National Petroleum Corporation (CNPC) made in Kazakhstan was in 1997 when it purchased a 60.34 per cent stake in AktobeMunaiGas. The CNPC AktobeMunaiGas (CNPC AMG) now owns five oilfields, two gas fields and one oil exploration block in Kazakhstan.[15] Since then, CNPC has signed six more deals. According to the statistics, there were a total of 2,749 Chinese companies in Kazakhstan by the end of 2015. So far, China has invested nearly US$43 billion in Kazakhstan, and Kazakhstan has become China's largest investment destination along the Belt and Road routes.[16] The 2,833-kilometre-long China–Kazakhstan crude oil pipeline runs from Atyrau in Kazakhstan to Petro China Dushanzi Petrochemical Company via the Alataw Pass in China's Xinjiang Uygur Autonomous Region. Oil imports through this pipeline has reached the 100-million-ton mark in 2017.

The A and B lines of the Central Asian natural gas pipeline are designed to have an annual gas transmission capacity of 300×108 cubic metres. The starting point is the border between Turkmenistan on the right bank of the Amu Darya, passing through Uzbekistan and Kazakhstan, and entering China in Ergos, Xinjiang. After entering the Alashankou, it is connected to the second line of the West–East Gas Pipeline. The Central Asian natural gas pipeline C line starts from Gdaim, on the border of Tuwu, and enters the Khorgos port of Xinjiang via Uzbekistan and Kazakhstan. It is connected to the third line of the East-West Gas Pipeline. In May 2017, the natural gas pipeline project on the southern line of Kazakhstan was completed. Kazakhstan officially implemented the gas supply agreement with China on 13 October 2017.[17] It is believed that if the agreement is successfully implemented, the amount of natural gas imported from Kazakhstan will reach 5 billion cubic metres.[18] In terms of natural gas, China's main partner is Turkmenistan. In 2016, Turkmenistan's proven natural gas reserves were 17.5 trillion cubic metres, ranking fourth in the world. In 2016, China imported 29.4 billion cubic metres of natural gas from Turkmenistan, accounting for 35.8 per cent of the total imports.

Since India has boycotted the Belt and Road Forum for International Cooperation (2017 and 2019) initiated by China owing to India's territorial concerns in union territories of Kashmir and Ladakh, India's cooperation with China on the CPEC is ruled out, albeit there is a possibility if it is rerouted through the CARs and Afghanistan, given the dynamics of Sino-Pak entente cordiale, the possibility is remote. There is another view that India could reserve its territorial difference and be a stakeholder as far as investment in the disputed territory is concerned on the Russo-Japanese model of investments in Kuril Islands.[19] However, Pakistan may not support such an investment and joint development of the disputed territory under its jurisdiction. Given China's military posturing and bloody clashes between India and China at Galwan in the Western Sector, the possibility of such a cooperation is slim.

Energy security and Africa

China has invested more than $34 billion in the energy sector in Africa. Presently, Africa has emerged as China's second largest source of oil imports after the Middle East, accounting for about 20 per cent of China's total oil imports.[20] It has signed a 'loan-for-oil' agreement with Angola, and its oil and gas cooperation with Nigeria, Equatorial Guinea and other countries is on solid ground. In the field of natural gas, PetroChina spent $4.21 billion in 2013 to buy a 28.75 per cent stake in Italy's Eni East Africa,[21] which indirectly obtained a 20 per cent interest in the Block 4 project in Rovuma Basin of Mozambique, marking the beginning of cooperation between Chinese oil and gas companies and African countries in the natural gas sector. In April 2016, CNPC, Mozambique and South Africa signed a joint development agreement for the Mozambique-South Africa gas pipeline project.[22]

As far as India is concerned, almost 26 per cent of its total oil imports comes from Africa. Therefore, energy security with Africa remains an important link in India's overall relationship with African countries, which has been strengthened and consolidated by holding India-Africa Forum Summits (IAFS) in places like New Delhi (2008, 2015) and Addis Ababa (2011). Countries such as Nigeria, Angola, Sudan, Equatorial Guinea and Gabon have emerged as partners in India's energy cooperation. It is generally believed that if China has an advantage over India in terms of crude oil, India is better poised as far as natural gas cooperation with Africa is concerned. According to the British Petroleum (BP) World Energy Statistical Yearbook (2017), Africa's crude oil exports to India were only one-third of the EU's, and Africa's natural gas exports to India were just half of the EU.[23]

Given the posturing of India and China in the African energy market, it is perhaps futile for both to compete for each other's share in the market, nor can both afford to follow a strategy to force each other out of the African market. Therefore, there will be an element of competition, but also a room for cooperation. Some of the Chinese scholars believe that India is more competitive than China in the African energy market, for it has both the historical as well as geographical advantages, and hence energy competition between China and India in Africa will be very intense. Nevertheless, Chinese scholars also posit that China will cooperate with India to obtain a corresponding right to discourse in the international energy market dominated by the developed countries. They say China is willing to cooperate with India in overseas energy markets, especially in countries like Iran, Syria and Sudan, which are at loggerheads with the United States.[24] This, at times, seems possible; however, in the face of the US pressure, it is unlikely that India would be ready for such a cooperation.

Exploring possibilities for cooperation amidst competition

If China's dependence for energy sources on the Middle East is over 50 per cent, India's dependence is over 60 per cent. The scarcity of oil and gas, and importance of energy resources for economic growth make the competition between the two inevitable. Therefore, energy diplomacy remains integral to their foreign policy. Their overlapping interest in Iran, Myanmar, Russia, Kazakhstan, Nigeria and Venezuela, etc. has intensified the degree of competition. For example, Myanmar, with abundant natural gas reserves, has received economic assistance worth $84 million from China. In the same vein, India and Myanmar signed a $1.35 billion oil and gas development agreement in 2010 and invested in Myanmar's offshore A1 and A3 oilfield blocks.[25] In June, the same year, the China–Myanmar oil and gas pipeline project took off. Second, the state-owned monoliths of India and China competed in the international energy markets, and obviously owing to the deep pockets of the Chinese companies, India lost due to the higher bids offered by the Chinese companies. For example, in 2005, they competed for a Canadian company's oil and pipeline assets in Ecuador; in 2008, both competed for the Russian Imperial Energy listed in London stock; India's $600 million bid in Angola was trounced by China's $2 billion; India's $3.9 billion bid in Petrokazakhstan was outclassed by China's $4.2 billion.

In the view of such a scenario, in 2005, during Chinese Premier Wen Jiabao's India visit, both sides in the Joint Statement expressed their intention to cooperate in the field of energy security and energy conservation. In the same year, both countries, for the first time jointly acquired a 38 per cent stake in Petro-Canada's Afulat oil field in Syria for $573 million; in 2006, both jointly acquired a 50 per cent stake in Colombian oil company Omimex de Colombia, each holding 25 per cent of the share. At the same time, China Petroleum Pipeline Bureau (CPP) undertook the construction of the East-West Gas Pipeline Project in India. The project starts from the city of Kakinada in Andhra Pradesh and ends in the city of Baruch in Gujarat covering a distance of about 1,366 km. It is the largest energy cooperation project between the two countries to date.[26]

In 2006, relevant departments of the two countries signed the Memorandum on Strengthening Oil and Gas Cooperation, and proposed the establishment of a Joint Working Committee for institutionalised dialogue. In 2007, India and China held an international seminar on 'China-India Energy Dialogue' in Shanghai. The next year when Indian Prime Minister Manmohan Singh visited China, he emphasized overseas energy cooperation between the two countries. Undoubtedly, there was some progress in the areas of government consultation, joint bidding, and development; however, the actual cooperation between the two is still limited. It is in this context that the BRI offers some opportunities that could overcome some constraints and pave way for bilateral energy cooperation. According to Chinese scholars,[27] the aim of the BRI is to create a new regional order where there would be implied 'distribution of power, benefits, ideas, and responsibilities'. The 'Five Connectivity and Three Commons' (*wutong/santong*), especially the latter that advocates building the community of shared interest, future and responsibility will pave the way for energy as well as cooperation in other domains.

What are India's options vis-à-vis China in the CARs and Southeast Asia, especially Myanmar? Even if India does not have a direct land border with the CARs, India has been talking about the 'ancient roots'. India has remained disenchanted with Central Asia (CA), which is why it is a player at the margins. Its trade with CA stands at a poor $700 million. It appears that Modi's foreign policy is poised to 'go global' and has shown interest in the region's energy, trade and investment as well as dialogue on counterterrorism, etc. issues. More importantly, as we see the congregation of major powers in the region, it is time for India to unfold a pragmatic and positive policy and be an insider rather than an outsider in the region. India would be welcomed by the CARs, as they would neither like to see the Russian nor the Chinese domination in the region. If the US prefers China over Russia in the region, India will be supported both by the US and Russia, for the Indian engagement in the region will offset some of the Chinese influence, thus becoming another pillar in the region.

Can India mend and consolidate its ties with Iran to the extent of a pivot or near pivot country? Construction of the Chabahar Port needs to be carried out at a feverish pace, which will serve India's strategic as well as economic interest in the region. This would be extremely important if India wants to secure energy supplies from the CARs and Russia. Both overland transportation, i.e. Turkmenistan–Afghanistan–Pakistan–India Pipeline (TAPI), and Iran–India–Pakistan Pipeline, and sea routes need to be explored, albeit there are concerns about the overland routes given the volatility in the Af–Pak region and the morbid state of India–Pak relations. China, on the other hand, is quick to exploit discordance between the US and Iran. If the reports are to be believed, China is negotiating a $400 billion deal with Iran for a period of 25 years, which would get China a substantial discount on Iranian oil. In return, Beijing will invest the said amount in Iran's industrial sectors including infrastructure and telecom.[28]

Second, since China has invested heavily in the upstream as well as downstream energy infrastructure in the CARs, especially in Kazakhstan and Turkmenistan, China controls around 1/3 of Kazakhstan's oil and most of Turkmenistan's gas exports. As discussed in the preceding sections, China has connected Xinjiang to Kazakhstan and Turkmenistan through a network of oil and gas pipelines making it a major hub of connectivity. India may consider opening Ladakh and Kashmir, especially the Ladakh region for linking it to Xinjiang, which would be cost-effective comparing the land and sea options from the west. A similar approach could be explored through the BCIM region. Here again, given the frequency of Chinese transgressions and military standoffs in the area, such a possibility seems remote. The Galwan fatalities on 15 June 2020 have ruled out such a cooperation perhaps for a long time to come.

Third, in the BCIM countries, an oil and gas pipeline network can be built, which can be a hub for energy supply between India and China as well as other Asia–Pacific countries. Sino-Myanmar oil and gas pipelines has played a crucial role in alleviating natural gas shortage, providing 450 million cubic metres of gas to Yunnan. Under the framework of the BCIM, Myanmar has the potential to become a key area to promote Sino-Indian energy cooperation through land and sea. India has been undertaking the 2,600-kilometre Jagdishpur–Haldia and Bokaro–Dhamra pipeline under the Pradhan Mantri Urja Ganga project, and the same is being extended from Brauni to Guwahati for connecting other areas of Northeast India with the Indradhanush Gas Grid by way of laying a 1,500-kilometre pipeline. If these could be connected to the Myanmar pipelines, it would be more cost-effective in terms of transmission and laying of the pipelines.

Fourth, investments in renewable energy including solar, wind, biogas, etc. need to be promoted. Though China accounted for about 89 per cent of India's total imports of solar cells in the year 2017–2018, however, localisation of the manufacturing has not happened.

Challenges for China

Since the investment involved is huge, China has been building a risk management and response mechanism in the BRI countries. It has been turning to the global insurance companies and buying options to hedge the risk, diversifying its models of cooperation; however, the following challenges remain.

Geopolitical factors

Chinese scholars[29] posit that risks related to geopolitics along the BRI countries are huge. Risks such as 'Ukrainian crisis and the US–European–Russian rivalry' in the Central Asian region, India's unwillingness to 'accommodate other players in South Asia', and Japan trying to expand its own 'political influence' by undermining the Chinese initiative have thrown challenges to the Chinese investments and diplomacy in these regions. Second, risks from terror outfits, nationalistic sentiments, and piracy, especially when 'Central Asia, South Asia, and the Middle East have limited security capabilities' the transportation of oil and gas faces greater security risks. This remains a dilemma as more than 80 per cent of the Chinese oil transportation takes place through the choke points like Malacca. Third, there are risks related to 'political instability and deep contradictions between political and religious factions'. Some of these risks are synonymous with India's concerns about the BCIM that covers most of India's northeast provinces. Though China has been hedging these risks and institutionalising its energy cooperation by way of its engagement in multilateral forums such Shanghai Cooperation Organization (SCO), Regional Comprehensive Economic Partnership Agreement (RCEP), China–Japan–Korea Free Trade Zone, Asia–Pacific Economic Cooperation (APEC), the Group of 20 (G20), and the BRICS, the challenges remain.

Socio-cultural factors

The regions along the BRI abound in different types of civilizations and religions and have different cultures. Therefore, failing to understand the social and corporate culture of these regions and countries will face many challenges. Shi Ze cites the example of China's construction and operation of the South Su power plant in Indonesia that witnessed disturbances, strikes and even threats of violence.[30]

Localisation drive

It is evident that countries along the BRI are tightening their control over foreign-funded enterprises. They have adopted restrictive measures in the areas of labour licensing, taxation and environmental protection. For example, they are emphasizing localization in terms of procurement of the goods, enlisting engineering services, employing labour, fixing minimum salary and layoff policies have become extremely stringent. Moreover, a series of laws and regulations promulgated in order to attract investment, especially in the Central Asian countries are issued in the form of presidential decrees, which are subject to change, thus affecting the stability of investment.[31]

The ghost of debt trap

Some of the smaller participants of the BRI such as Mongolia, Pakistan, Laos, Sri Lanka, Kyrgyz Republic and Tajikistan are deep in debt. China committing $73 billion for CPEC may be difficult for Pakistan to service the loan; the example of Sri Lanka being forced to swap over $1 billion for Chinese equity is an example often cited to highlight the 'ills' of the BRI. Though the Laos high-speed railway may connect China to Thailand, the cost is too high and Laos may never be able to return the money. In 2018, citing 'tough financing terms' Pakistan cancelled the $14 billion Diamer–Bhasha Dam project; Nepal and Myanmar followed suit by scrapping a $2.5 billion and $3.6 billion hydroelectricity project, respectively. In the same vein, Malaysia too has cancelled the East Coast Rail Link and the Sabah natural gas pipeline projects in August once the new regime under Mahathir Mohamad formed the government. There are other risks related to exchange rate fluctuations and varied technological standards along the BRI.[32]

Conclusion

The BRI and China's energy security remains intertwined. It could be discerned that India and China are fiercely competing for energy resources in Myanmar, the Middle East and Africa, etc. regions and countries. As the BRI spans over the world's major energy production and consumption markets, it creates opportunities for aligning India's energy policy with China in Myanmar, Central Asia and Russia, for the BRI aims to improve the oil and gas investment environment on the one hand and capital, technology and infrastructure conditions for energy cooperation, which could enable cooperation in the fields such as processing, refining, consumption and services on the other.

Since the energy production capacity of India and China has been outpaced by consumption, the energy deficiency is bound to increase in the future. Though both countries have initiated their own domestic, peripheral and external energy strategy, it is pertinent that they cooperate in the international energy markets so as to curb the crude oil prices, bring down the prices of the bids and transportation, and share their experience and technologies to overcome their dependence on developed countries. Furthermore, building sizeable oil reserves would be too expensive for both, it would be sensible to consider co-financing an oil reserve system for mitigating the risks in the international energy market. They could also work together to improve and maintain energy channels and transportation networks in volatile areas to ensure the safety of sea and land transportation. Gong et al. propose four principles, which are flexibility, gradualness, openness and consensus, for building such a mechanism.[33] Besides, they recommend five components for such a mechanism in the form of international multi-faceted coordination mechanism, information exchange and sharing mechanism, forward-looking technical cooperation mechanism, joint bidding mechanism and an energy security channel co-construction mechanism. According to them, the mechanism will greatly promote distribution of benefits and burden sharing between China and India, and encourage China and India to make efforts to achieve collective goals.

Also, since some of the institutions such as Asian Infrastructure Investment Bank promote North–South financial cooperation under the BRI, it would make sense if India makes use of such institutions. However, in order to realise an integrated energy market in Asia, a slew of intergovernmental agreements, including currency swaps, liberalised investment is necessary for the transactions between suppliers and buyers.

In short, as the world's most populous countries and energy-deficient countries, both face various uncertainties in the field of energy security. Of course, there would be a certain degree of competition; however, both must establish and institutionalise a long-term win-win cooperation mechanism for sustainable and stable energy security. The BRI offers a platform to explore such cooperation. At the same time, the border standoff with China and India's growing bonhomie with the US in the Indo-Pacific region may render such a possibility meaningless.

Notes

1 According to the 2017 edition of the *BP World Energy Statistical Yearbook*, by the end of 2016, China's proven oil reserves were only 3.5 billion tons, accounting for 1.5 per cent of the world's proven natural oil reserves; proven natural gas reserves were 5.4 trillion cubic metres. For details see: *BP World Energy Statistical Yearbook*. BP plc. Accessed 1 October 2019. www.bp.com/content/dam/bp-country/de_ch/PDF/bp-statistical-review-of-world-energy-2017-full-report.pdf.

2 Liu, Bin, Zhang Yi, and Zhu Tiantian. 2018. 《中国与'一带一路'沿线国家能源合作问题探究》 'Research on energy cooperation between China and the "Belt and Road" countries.' *Crossroads: Southeast Asian Studies*, 5 (2018): 10. Guangxi Academy of Social Sciences. Another source puts it at 133.8 billion tons and 155 trillion cubic metres respectively, accounting for 57 per cent and 78 per cent of the world's remaining total reserves. It also depends on the number of countries included in the BRI, generally the number has varied between 25 and 30.

3 Liu, Jinsong. 《一带一路'将给工商界带来八大机遇》 '"Belt and Road" will bring eight major opportunities to the business world.' *Dagong Bao*. 19 May 2015. Accessed 26 October 2020. http://news.takungpao.com/mainland/focus/2015-05/3003993.html.

4 Xie, Kechang.《着力推进'一带一路'国际能源合作》 'Focus on promoting the "Belt and Road" international energy cooperation.' *China Science and Technology Enterprise*, (June 2017): 15.

5 Peng, Nian.《中印在海外能源市场的竞合博弈》 'China-India competition and cooperation in the overseas energy market.' *Journal of South Asian Studies*, 2 (2018): 20–27. National Institute for South China Sea Studies.

6 Dadwal, Shebonti Ray. 'Myanmar Opens to Business Opportunities: But it is Sustainable?.' IDSA Comment. 14 June 2013. Accessed 27 October 2020. www. idsa. in/discommends/ MyanmarOpenstoBusinessOpportunities srdadwal 140613. html.

7 See endnote 5.

8 Deepak, B. R. 'Kyaukpyu port construction and China-Myanmar economic corridor.' *Sunday Guardian*. 24 November 2018. Accessed 26 October 3030. www.sundayguardian-live.com/opinion/watch-kyaukpyu-port-china-myanmar-economic-corridor.

9 PTI. 2014. 'ONGC Videsh to get stake in Myanmar oil and gas block.' *The Economic Times*. 8 April 2014. Accessed 26 October 2020. https://economictimes.indiatimes.com/industry/ongc-videsh-to-get-stake-in-myanmar-oil-and-gas-block/articleshow/33448804.cms?from=mdr.

10 See endnote 5.

11 Ibid.

12 Deepak, B. R. 'China's global and civilizational re-balancing and India's options.' *China and the World: Ancient and Modern Silk Road* 1, 2 (2018): 1–16, Singapore: World Scientific.

13 Malik, Ahmad Rashid. 'The China–Pakistan Economic Corridor (CPEC): A game changer for Pakistan's economy.' In *China's Global Rebalancing and the New Silk Road* edited by Deepak, B. R. Springer, 2018.

14 Deepak, B. R. *India and China: Foreign Policy Approaches and Responses*. Delhi: Vij Books, 2016, pp. 27–30.

15 Liu, Mingde, Peng Xia.《全球影响力分析框架下的中哈能源关系研究》 'Research on China–Kazakhstan energy relations under analysis framework of global influence.' *Sino-Global Energy*, 23, no. 8 (2018): 1–9.

16 Zhang, Junmian. 'China, Kazakhstan deepen energy cooperation.' *Belt and Road Portal*. 21 July 2017. Accessed 26 October 2020. https://eng.yidaiyilu.gov.cn/home/rolling/20467.htm.

17 See endnote 15.

18 Wang, Li.《一带一路背景下中国与中亚国家能源合作》 'Sino-Central Asia energy cooperation under the Belt and Road.' *Practice in Foreign Relations and Trade*. 2018, pp. 37–40.

19 See endnote 8, p. 8.

20 See endnote 5, p. 22.

21 OGE [Oil and Gas Editors]. 'CNPC completes buy of stake off Mozambique.' 29 July 2013. Accessed 26 October 2020. www.ogj.com/articles/2013/07/cnpc-completes-buy-of-stake-off-mozambique.html.

22 See endnote 5.

23 *BP World Energy Statistical Yearbook*. BP plc. Accessed 1 October 2019. www.bp.com/content/dam/bp-country/de_ch/PDF/bp-statistical-review-of-world-energy-2017-full-report.pdf

24 See endnote 5, p. 23.

25 Feng, Naikang and Li, Yang.《'一带一路'倡议下中印能源合作前景浅析》 'A preliminary analysis of China–India energy cooperation under the "Belt and Road Initiative".' *Contemporary World*. (November 2015): 50-51.

26 Ibid.

27 Ibid, pp. 52–53.
28 'US exasperated over Iran–China $400 billion pact.' *Eurasian Times*. 13 July 2020. Accessed 26 October 2020. https://eurasiantimes.com/us-exasperated-over-iran-china-400-billion-pact/.
29 Shi Ze.《能源资源合作:共建'一带一路'的着力点》'Energy resources cooperation: focus on building the "Belt and Road".' *Journal of Xinjiang Normal University* (Philosophy and Social Sciences), 36, 1 (2015).
30 Ibid.
31 See endnote 18.
32 Deepak, B. R. 'China's Belt and Road Initiative in unlikely to fail.' *Sunday Guardian*. 28 September 2018. Accessed 26 October 2020. www.sundayguardianlive.com/opinion/chinas-bri-unlikely-failchinas-bri-unlikely-fail.
33 Gong, Qinlin; Yang, Wenwu, and Lu, Penghui.《中印能源共赢性发展互动机制探讨》'Exploring a win-win energy development mechanism for China and India.' *South Asian Studies Quarterly*, 5 (2014): 85–89.

14

GEO-POLITICS OF THE SOUTH CHINA SEA

The energy perspective

Sanjay K. Bhardwaj and Md. Obaidur Rahaman

Background

In recent decades, the South China Sea has become one of the most contested and disputed maritime places in the world.[1] In modern inter-state relations, it occupies a central position in regional and international politics. Most of the South China Sea littoral states compete with oil and natural gas, fisheries and other sea-bed hydrocarbon deposits. They are disputing territorial rights and maritime sovereignty claims in the region. Who controls resources has become a central point of geopolitical discourse in Asia-Pacific.

The South China Sea is delimited by eight politically diverse states such as China, Taiwan, the Philippines, Vietnam, Brunei, Indonesia, Singapore, and Malaysia. It is composed of diverse physiographic features, for example, archipelagos, atolls, rocks, shoal, islets, reef, banks, etc. The Spratly Islands, the Paracel Islands, the Pratas Islands, the Macclesfield Bank, and the Natuna Islands are some most important and controversial archipelagos in the region. However, the Spratly Islands is the most disputed one where almost all the littoral states claimed their territorial sovereignty rights. Thus, the geography and its resource implications are motivating factors for comprehensive and outstanding attention. Besides the littoral states, the geo-strategic significance of the South China Sea also is an imbuing factor extra-regional powers such as the United States, Japan, Russia, India, Australia, etc. for adjusting regional politics in international settings.

However, China believes that the South China Sea dispute is a regional issue and should be resolved bilaterally through consultations and negotiation with other coastal states. However, the other South China Sea coastal states, especially Vietnam and the Philippines, want to solve the conflict through multilateral negotiations at international level. Hence, the extra-regional powers are directly or indirectly involved in this dispute.

The South China Sea has now become a 'new geopolitical node' where the major powers seem to be embroiled in a devious struggle for hegemony. In the American viewpoint, China is trying to assert control over an area covering roughly 80 per cent of the South China Sea despite the objections of other littoral states. In fact, China's 'nine-dash line' of blurred territorial claims in the South China Sea have 'created uncertainty, insecurity, and instability' among its neighbours.[2] The United States is trying to convey to other littoral states that China surreptitiously intends to transform the South China Sea into a 'Chinese Lake'.[3] The United States has warned that China's maritime claims in the disputed waters of the South China Sea could be an effort to gain creeping control of oceans in the Asia-Pacific region. Moreover, China rejected the United States' allegations and accused Washington of exaggerating tensions, deliberately complicated the status quo, and escalating the disputes in the South China Sea. China has also accused the United States that its government officials intentionally used the 'West Philippine Sea'[4] instead of the staid nomenclature of South China Sea.[5] Mira Rapp-Hooper for instance, contends that 'the United States and its allies pit them against China' to counter China's hegemony in the region.[6] Hence, in the process to control the South China Sea, both the coastal states and extra-regional powers are intensifying their naval and military activities in the region. As a result, the South China Sea has become a new 'flash point' in the Asia-Pacific.

In the same tedium, the present narrative strives to zero in upon the contemporary geopolitics in the South China Sea and also examines how oil and natural gas and other hydrocarbon resources influence the political behaviour of regional and extra-regional powers in the twenty-first century. This chapter is intentionally four forked. The first section zeroes in geopolitics of energy resources in the South China Sea. The second fork examines how the geopolitics of marine resources is responsible for the dispute. The third section of the study examines the role of major powers in South China Sea disputes. The last section delves inside at India's role and its interests in the conflict-ridden South China Sea.

Geopolitics of oil and natural gas in South China Sea

In the early phase of the twenty-first century, the South China Sea was a cynosure of all eyes for geographers, economists, political scientists, journalists, international lawyers, and strategists because of its significance in Asian geopolitics. British strategist Spykman describes the South China Sea as the 'Asiatic Mediterranean',[7] and K. M. Panikkar, interestingly considered the sea as the 'True Mediterranean'.[8] The South China Sea has also been strategically comprehended as a 'Geographical Pivot' because of its geographical conditions and sanguine strategic significance. The geographical conditions include its unique physiographic settings, presence of oil and natural gas as well as other seabed hydrocarbons resources. Its diverse fauna and flora, minerals, and metallic elements are regarded as valuable marine deposits. Thus, the strategic significance of the South China Sea comprises its geographical position and sea lines of communications. Mackinder argued that in international politics all the major countries rotate around the 'Pivot State', which is always considered to be great and the actual balance of political power at any given time is a 'product of geographical conditions and other the relative number, virility, equipment, and organisation of the competing people'.[9]

Geographical significance

The South China Sea is akin to a semi-enclosed, sequestered or almost landlocked sea at the intersection between the Pacific and the Indian Ocean. It is situated at the conflict-ridden cusp of the triple junction, namely, the Asian Continental Plate, the Pacific Oceanic Plate, and the Indo-Australian Plate, one of the most geologically complex maritime spaces in the world. It provides amazing surroundings for intensive research on the nature of continental-oceanic and oceanic-oceanic plate interactions and the associated geological processes that control the genesis of ore and hydrocarbons. Indeed, the South China Sea belongs to the 'East Indies Triangle'[10] where modern marine and terrestrial biodiversity reaches a global maximum.[11] It is also ecologically the most homogeneous geographical space where all the island groups, atoll, and islets are covered with brush, grass, coconut palms, mangrove, and swamps. It comprises more than 2,500 species of marine fishes and 500 species of reef-building corals.[12] This is one of the world's diverse mangrove ecosystems. Thus it has become an economically valuable and geopolitically competitive region in the world.

According to geologists, the South China Sea, is one of the richest maritime spaces that abounds in the world. They hypothesized that the sea provides abundant fisheries, oil and natural gas, and hydrocarbon resources. The littoral states of the South China Sea are dependent on fish stocks as fish consumption provides a significant percentage of protein intakes in East Asian countries.[13] It accounts for as much as 10 per cent of the 'fishing catch landed globally'.[14] However, a University of British Columbia study in 2015 unveiled that the sea produces 10 million tonnes of fish or 12 per cent of the global catch each year.[15] Its fisheries also provide an expensive form of protein, food security, and a source of foreign exchange. Rosenberg described the significance of the South China Sea in the following words:

> For centuries, the South China Sea has provided abundant fisheries for its coastal countries. Flushed all year round by several large rivers, the flat and shallow sea beds of the South China Sea are important among the world's most productive fishing grounds. Fisheries are important around the South China Sea as providers of an inexpensive form of protein, means of livelihood, and a source of foreign exchange earnings. A large portion of the coastal workforce is dependent on the marine environment through employment in fishing, marine transportation, offshore exploration and extraction of hydrocarbon and other natural resources, recreation, and tourism.[16]

Fish remains a major industry in the South China Sea littoral states. Borton argues that 'currently the South China Sea accounts for one-tenth of the world's global fisheries catch, and plays host to a multi-billion dollar fishing industry'.[17] Vietnam is one of the world's top five seafood exporters, together with Indonesia and Thailand, and has the world's third-largest fishery production and aquaculture industry after China and India. If farmed species are included, Vietnam exported the US$6.57 billion worth of seafood in 2015.[18] Indonesia is home of the world's largest tuna fishing grounds, which produces more than 100,000 tonnes of tuna a year. However, 90 per cent of the roughly 5,400 local and foreign vessels that ply the Indonesian waters have no permits, putting the sector's losses to poaching at as high as US$25 billion annually.[19] Thus, fisheries continue to play a critical role in regional food security and maritime disputes.

In addition to marine living resources, the South China Sea is also ringed by hydrocarbon resources. For example, the Amoco oil company reported in the mid-1970s that there were about 7,700 million barrels of oils, and another 38,000 million barrels were to be discovered soon in Southeast Asia. There are approximately 11 billion barrels of oil reserves and 190 trillion cubic feet of natural gas reserves in the South China Sea. In 2012, Chinese National Offshore Oil Company estimated that the area holds around 125 billion barrels of oil and 500 trillion cubic feet of natural gas.[20] Due to the presence of abundant oil and natural gas, the South China Sea is also regarded as the new nomenclature of 'Second Persian Gulf' or 'The next Persian Gulf'.[21] However, in recent years competition for oil and natural gas in the South China Sea has triggered standoffs between claimant states, especially between China and Vietnam, and between China and the Philippines. In 2016, the Chinese and the Philippine government have attempted to discuss and build joint development of hydrocarbons at Reed Bank, but unfortunately, it did not work out. Tables 14.1 and 14.2 show estimated hydrocarbon production and proved and probable reserved in the South China Sea (SCS):

Besides the fisheries and hydrocarbon resources, coconut, breadfruit, and tung oil trees have been cultivated on many of the principal islands. In recent years, banana, papaya, and pineapple plantations have been introduced. It is also noted that the reefs, lagoons, and outer waters of these islands offer bountiful supplies of fish,

TABLE 14.1 Estimated hydrocarbon production in SCS (2011)

Country	*Oil (1000 barrels/day)*	*Natural gas (billion cubic feet)*	*Major production area*
Brunei	120	400	Baram Delta
China	250	600	Pearl River Mouth Basin
Indonesia	60	200	Natuna Basin
Malaysia	500	1800	Sabah Sarawak Malay Basin
Philippines	25	100	Palawan Basin
Thailand	N/A	N/A	Gulf of Thailand, Malay Basin
Vietnam	300	300	Cuu Long Basin & Nam Con Son Basin

Source: US Energy Information Administration, 2013.

TABLE 14.2 Estimated proved and probable reserves in SCS (2011)

Country	*Crude oil & liquid reserves (billion barrels)*	*Natural gas reserves (trillion cubic feet)*
Brunei	1.5	15
China	1.3	15
Indonesia	0.3	55
Malaysia	5	80
Philippines	0.2	4
Taiwan	0	0
Thailand	0	1
Vietnam	3	20
Total	11.2	190

Source: US Energy Information Administration, 2013.

cuttlefish, and oysters, and black tuna provides an important fishery for littoral states. Similarly, the Spratly and the Paracel islands are the primordially ideal nesting areas for migratory sea tortoise, the eggs, flesh, and shells of which have been harvested for centuries. Many coastal people are dependent on this marine space for their livelihoods through employment in fishing, marine transportation, tourism, offshore exploration, and extraction of hydrocarbon resources.

However, there are always escalations among coastal states regarding illegal fishing and drilling for oil and gas in disputed islands. For example, an escalation that took place between 'Beijing and Hanoi involved the arrest of 23 Vietnamese fishermen by Chinese officials in March 2012 who were accused of illegal fishing and poaching near the Paracel Islands'.[22] Another escalation occurred in April 2012 with 'Chinese and the Philippines vessels caught up in a stand-off at Scarborough Shoal in the South China Sea. The Philippines naval authorities had exposed several Chinese fishing vessels anchored at the Shoal disputed by both China and the Philippines'.[23] A Philippine navy ship attempted to seize the Chinese fishermen allegedly accused of poaching and unlawful fishing. Dicke and Holbigs describe that China started to drill for oil near the Paracel Islands that are claimed by both Vietnam and China as territorial waters, which led to considerable diplomatic tensions and violent actions against Chinese enterprises in Vietnam.[24] Thus the geography of the South China Sea and its resource implications play a significant role for their outstanding attention as well as major confrontations in the region (Figure 14.1).

Strategic significance

The geographical complexity of the South China Sea is due to the archipelagic nature of its eastern and southern bounds. In the other words, most of its principal entry and exit points for maritime navigation are very narrow and represent 'choke

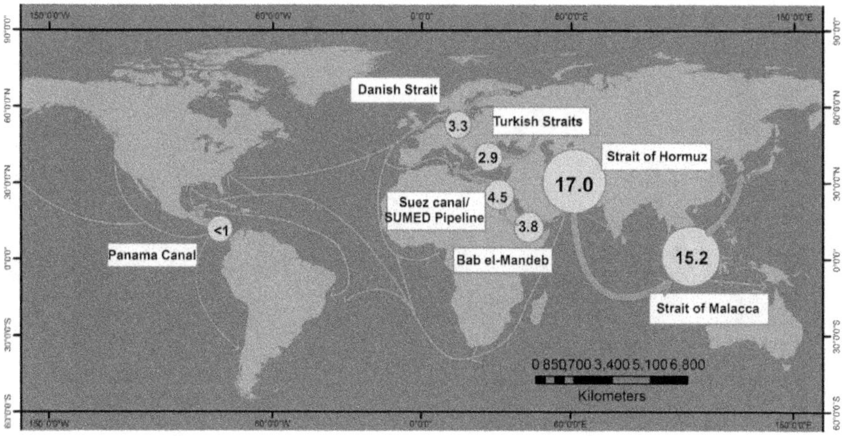

FIGURE 14.1 Strategic significance of South China Sea. Authors, based on data from the US Energy Information Administration, 2013 (million barrels per day of crude oil and petroleum)

points' in terms of maritime security. It is crisscrossed by major shipping routes and divided Southeast Asia into a maritime sphere. Its central location in East Asia ensures its trade and strategic communications. The significance of the strategic position of the South China Sea can be described in the following words:

> As it lies between the Indian Ocean and the Pacific, the South China Sea is a vital strategic area. It acts as a gateway to the outside world for the mainland and the offshore islands of China. The [Paracel and Spratly] archipelagos occupy a central to the shipping lanes connecting Canton, Hong Kong, Manila, and Singapore. [Hence] their geographical position is extremely important.[25]

From geostrategic perspectives, the South China Sea is located at the heart of the Indo-Pacific therefore it is also known as the 'maritime heartland' in the region. Its geographic location between the Pacific and the Indian Ocean ensures its importance for trade and communications.[26] Its central location in East Asia provides its significance for business and strategic communications. Every year, about $1.2 trillion in US trade crosses the South China Sea. China, Japan, and South Korea each import over 80 per cent of their crude oil via the South China Sea.[27] So, the South China Sea has become a major trade route for crude oil. In 2016, more than 30 per cent (15 million barrels per day) of global maritime crude oil passed through the South China Sea. In the same year, the Middle East accounted for more than 70 per cent of total South China Sea crude oil shipments. In 2016, Saudi Arabia recorded the largest (24 per cent) source of crude oil traversing the South China Sea, followed by the United Arab Emirates (11 per cent), Iran, Iraq and Kuwait (8 per cent), Angola,

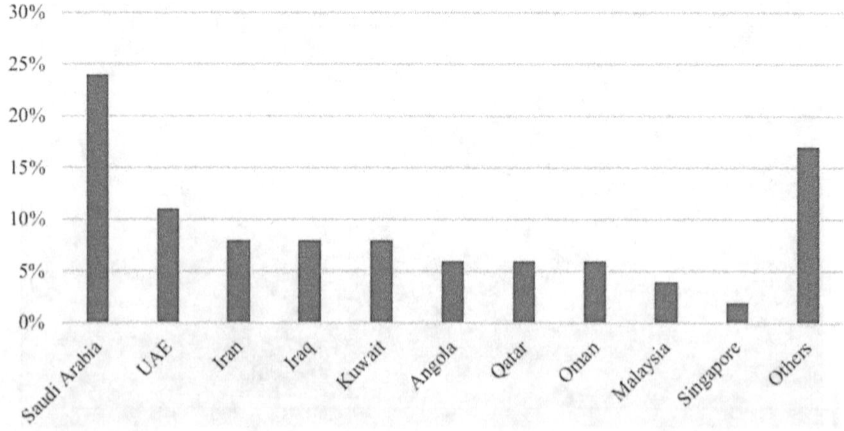

FIGURE 14.2 Exporters (2016). Authors, based on data from the US Energy Information Administration, based on Clipper Crude Data Service, 2016. Accessed 20 October 2020. www.eia.gov/todayinenergy/detail.php?id=36952.

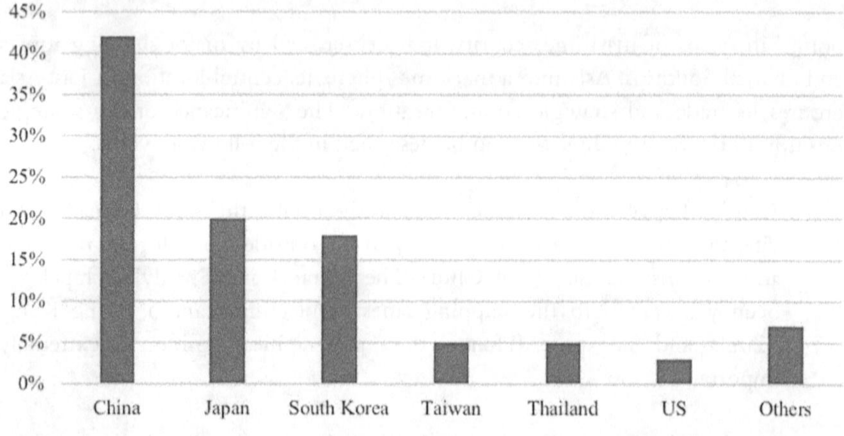

FIGURE 14.3 Importers (2016). Authors, based on data from the US Energy Information Administration, based on Clipper Crude Data Service, 2016. Accessed 20 October 2020. www.eia.gov/todayinenergy/detail.php?id=36952.

Qatar and Oman (6 per cent), Malaysia (4 per cent), Singapore (2 per cent) and others (17 per cent) (Figure 14.2). On the other hand, about 90 per cent of the crude oil is shipped by China, Japan, and South Korea through the South China Sea. China recorded the largest (42 per cent) share of crude oil importer country through the South China Sea in 2016, followed by Japan (20 per cent), South Korea (18 per cent), Taiwan and Thailand (5 per cent), the United States (3 per cent), and others (7 per cent) (Figure 14.3). Figures 14.2 and 14.3 show the South China Sea crude oil flow in 2016.

It is a pertinently plausible theme that the South China Sea occupies a significant geostrategic position across the sea lines of communications (SLOCs) that connect the Middle East energy producers with the Great Asian market in North-East Asia. This maritime heartland not only connects the Indian Ocean with the Pacific Ocean but also provides a seaborne business network from the Middle East countries to the East Asian nations. Some of the most important cities of the world, for example, Shanghai, Tokyo, Singapore, Manila, Hanoi, etc. have already been developed as business hubs around the South China Sea. Thus, the South China Sea has occupied a vital geostrategic position in Asia-Pacific and its strategic position further widened through its business network and sea-borne trades in the region. These characteristics have prompted the conflicts among the claimants' countries, including China, Taiwan, Vietnam, the Philippines, Malaysia, Indonesia, and Brunei to evolve unabated.

South China Sea Dispute

The South China Sea dispute remains the most critical issue in the history of world politics. Since 1945, maritime disputes not only involve contests over territory, islands, reefs, atolls, cays but also over fish, oil and natural gas, and marine sea bedded deposits and these have become an increasingly high profile subject matter in the academicians and policy makers. In fact, the South China Sea is a host of manifold, long-lasting, and the most challenging overlapping territorial and maritime jurisdictional claims. These disputes remain a source of conflicts among claimant states. The overlapping territorial rights and maritime claims and contentions between states are not a new feature of international politics. These are the results of the natural condition of completion among sovereign states.[28] Hence, territorial disputes have always been a common part of global political life. Holsti argued that the interaction between territorial states each pursuing their various conflicting national interests shaped by a continuous struggle for power and territorial disputes has been a primary cause of international conflicts.[29]

Territorial rights

There are disputes of opposing and overlapping territorial claims among littoral states including China, Taiwan, Vietnam, Malaysia, the Philippines, and Brunei. The most contested and overlapping territories claims occurred on the Spratly Islands and the Paracel Islands. The Paracel Islands are contested by China, Taiwan, and Vietnam, whereas China, Vietnam, Malaysia, Brunei, the Philippines, and Taiwan assert their sovereignty right on the Spratly Islands. There are some isolated and contested features in the South China Sea such as Scarborough Shoal, Pratas Islands, and Macclesfield Bank. Although the Paracel Islands are initially claimed by China and Vietnam, China forcibly ejected South Vietnamese troops from the Paracels in 1974.[30] Since 1974, the Paracel Islands have been completely controlled by China and denied the existence of territorial sovereignty dispute over the Paracels. Nevertheless, the islands are a continuing source of tension between China and Vietnam, especially regarding the incarceration of Vietnamese fishing vessels.[31] Scarborough Shoal is another disputed feature in the South China Sea. It is located approximately 124 nautical miles from Zambales province in the Philippines and is claimed by China, the Philippines, and Taiwan. Scarborough Shoal is a large atoll with a lagoon of about 150 square km surrounded by the reef.[32] Scarborough Shoal was the panorama of incidents between Chinese and Philippine vessels for several months in 2012. It is noted that, except for Brunei, all the claimant states have established a military presence in these islands. The long-standing territorial disputes among the complainant states in the South China Sea have become a major security flash point in the Asia-Pacific. As Fang has stated, overlapping claims by six major powers and escalation tensions are the major threats to peace, stability, and prosperity of the region.[33] The Spratly archipelago has become a sensitive flash point in regional and global politics in recent years, and any conflict in the South China Sea jeopardises peace and stability in Asia-Pacific.[34] Hence, the South China Sea is the flash point in the Pacific wherein conflict is most like to break out through misunderstanding and miscalculation.

Maritime sovereignty claims

The overlapping maritime sovereignty claims by littoral states in the South China Sea is another cause of concern in Asia-Pacific. The littoral states are justifying their legitimate claims over maritime sovereignty rights. Besides powerful China, the other littoral states such as Vietnam, the Philippines, Malaysia, and Brunei assert their claims from their coastal areas. Indonesia asserts maritime rights from Natuna Island. However, China bases its maritime rights on its claims to sovereignty over disputed island groups, in addition to the coast of the Chinese mainland. Some experts accept that China's Exclusive Economic Zone (EEZ) claims over the features of Spratly Islands is behaving like an expansionist country. Concerning the Spratly Islands, the primary focus for the South China Sea disputes, while this group 'comprises over 170 named features, scattered over approximately 240,000 square km of maritime space in the southern part of the South China Sea', only '48 features among the Spratlys group are known to rise above water at high tide'.[35] In fact, it covers a larger area of maritime rights than other littoral states and as illegitimate because part of the claims appears to be based on land features that would not qualify as islands under Article 121(3). Moreover, the 'nine-dash line' that appears on Chinese maps of the region creates further ambiguity because, as Storey argues, 'the Chinese government has never defined what this line represents'.[36] Thus, the proximity of neighbouring states, coupled with the geographical reality of the South China Sea as a semi-enclosed sea surrounded by multiple states, means that maritime claims tend to converge and overlap with one another.

However, the maritime sovereignty claims can be examined in the context of the United Nations Convention Law on the Sea 1982 (UNCLOS). This convention regulates internal waters, archipelagic waters, territorial seas, exclusive economic zones (EEZs), continental shelves, contiguous zones, and high seas. It also fixed the territorial sea[37] at 12 nautical miles (nm), a contiguous zone[38] of 24 nm, and the EEZ[39] up to 200 nm. Furthermore, the continental shelf could extend beyond the 200 nm limitation under certain topographical considerations could be claimed up to 350 nm.[40]

All the littoral states claim a territorial sea and an EEZ as well as a continental shelf from their mainland coast. However, Indonesia and the Philippines claim their maritime sovereignty from their archipelagic baselines. Article 121 of the UNCLOS provides for the Regime of Islands, which could be treated in the same manner as 'other land territory' and provides the basis for measuring maritime claims from baselines around them. To constitute an island under the terms of Article 121 of UNCLOS a feature must be 'a naturally formed area of land, surrounded by water, which is above water at high tide'.[41] Article 121(3) of UNCLOS states that: 'Rocks which cannot sustain human habitation or economic life of their own shall have no exclusive economic zone or continental shelf'.[42] There are different holding positions between the United States and China on 'freedom of navigation' under UNCLOS. According to Klein and Hopper, the United States' interpretation of freedom of navigation is that all ships can pass through the 200 nm EEZ and 12 nm territorial sea of a coastal state without obtaining prior permission. This position holds that military vessels can conduct any activity in the EEZ, including military exercises and surveillance.[43] However, the Chinese interpretation of freedom of navigation is the opposite of what the United States thinks. The Chinese believe that 'military vessels cannot conduct exercises or surveillance in the EEZ' within 200 nm and 'military ships need to request permission to enter a coastal state's territorial sea'.[44]

Nine-dash line

The so-called 'nine-dash line' drawn by China is one of the most controversial issues in international politics. China's has claimed Paracel Islands, Spratly Islands, Pratas Islands, Macclesfield Shoal, and their surrounding waters, which has given rise to several criticisms from not only littoral states but also from extra-regional powers. This 'nine-dash line' is also referred to by different names such as 'nine-dash interrupted line',[45] 'nine-dash intermitted line',[46] 'dashed line',[47] 'U-shaped line',[48] 'tongue-shaped line',[49] 'Cow's Tongue',[50] and the line of 'national boundary'[51] as well as 'the Chinese borders.[52] According to Hayton, in the year 1936, Bai Meichu, an ardent nationalist geographer who had earlier created the 'Chinese National Humiliation Map' to educate his countrymen, produced his most memorable map, showing a U-shaped line marked by 11 dashes going around the perimeter of the South China Sea from as far south to as far James Shoal. In 1953, the Chinese government removed two dashes that had cut through the Gulf of Tonkin next to Vietnam, leaving the line with only nine dashes. This 'nine-dash line' showing the border of China's claim has since been presented in 2009 to the UN Commission on the Limits of the Continental Shelf as marking the extent of China's historic waters. China in 2013 added one more dash line in the north-east of Taiwan. Now it has become a ten-dash line and almost all the littoral and extra-regional powers raised the issue by saying that China is trying to control the whole South China Sea based on historical water claims.[53] Many scholars have rejected China's 'historical water' claims, saying they are illegal and invalid. Kondapalli argues, 'China's "nine-dashed line" is illegal and baseless' concerning international laws.[54] Kaplan argues that China's claim is based on historical perspectives. He described that China's forebears discovered the islands in the South China Sea during China's Han dynasty reign in the period of the second century BC. He also explains that during the Song and Yuan dynasty many official and unofficial Chinese accounts indicated that the South China Sea came within China's national boundary just after the Second World War. During that period, China was incorporating the South China Sea as the 'dry-land formation into Chinese territory' including 'U-Shaped Cow's tongue, a historical nine-dashed line'.[55] Thus, China's historical claims do not have any legal backup.

However, Mollman contends that China's nine-dash line was 'in part to counter a claim by Vietnam over an extended continental shelf and sovereignty over the Paracel and Spratly Islands'.[56] He further argues that the Chinese map's accompanying text: 'China has indisputable sovereignty over the islands in the South China Sea and the adjacent waters and enjoys sovereignty rights and jurisdiction over the relevant waters as well as the seabed and subsoil thereof'.[57] This mere statement is a grave flouting of International Law. The United States has highly criticized China's nine-dash line map of 2009. The US State Department stated that China failed to clarify its nine-dash line claims over the South China Sea in a way consistent with international law. The US State Department further asked that unless China clarifies that the dashed-line claim reflects only a claim to islands within that line and any maritime zones that are generated from those land features follow the international law of the sea, as reflected in the LOS Convention, its dashed-line claim does not accord with the international law of the sea. In response to the US State Department's question on China's nine-dashed line claim, Chinese Foreign Ministry Spokesperson Hong Li replied that:

> The US report ignores the basic facts and international legal principles and is contrary to its promises not to take a position or sides. It is not helpful to the resolution of the South China Sea issue and the peace and stability of the South China Sea. We urge the US side to abide by its promises, act and speak cautiously, and objectively and fairly view and deal with the relevant issue.[58]

It is noted that the nine-dash line map has neither coordinate (altitude or longitude) nor specific datum nor the geodetic system. Another puzzle is that no one has ever clearly explained decisively what 'nine-dash line' actually means. Therefore, the United States and its allies assume that China's 'nine-dash line' is based on China's secret strategy to capture the whole South China Sea. Hence, the 'nine-dash line' is purely hypothetical and is based upon China's geopolitical imagination rather than geographical reality.

Major actors in South China Sea

The South China Sea has emerged as a critical maritime theatre that links the Indian and Pacific Ocean. Most of the recent geo-strategists like to call it 'the Chinese Caribbean'. Just as Rome sought control over the Mediterranean and the United States over the Caribbean in pursuit of regional dominance, China to seeks supremacy over the South China Sea. In the words of Fravel, it is the 'new central theatre of conflict' in the world.[59] Kaplan calls the South China Sea 'the 21st century's defining battleground', the 'throat of global sea routes'.[60] China seemingly covets a hegemonic position there, having repeatedly asserted 'indisputable sovereignty' over virtually the entire expanse while conducting itself as though it intends to create a closed sea.[61] China's naval rise is a crucial factor prompting the United States to 'pivot' or 'rebalance' to the western Pacific and the Indian Ocean. However, the Asia-Pacific region has not become a 'geopolitical node; in the world, rather it has happened due to the changing inter-state diplomacy and security dynamics in the region, which can be observed through the lens of the strategic culture of the major actors. This offers an account of strategic cultures and the emergence of more complex security challenges. According to Gilboy and Heginbotham, 'strategic culture is an inherited body of political-military concepts based on shared historical and social experience and often embodied in classic military texts – strategic culture may shape leader's interpretation of international events and preferences for responses'.[62] As per Gray, strategic culture 'provides the milieu within the strategy is debated' and represents a semi-permanent influence on security policy.[63] The strategic culture of the Asia-Pacific illuminates the origins and implications of the difficult issues of the region, from the rise of China and the American pivot to the shifting calculations of the other regional actors.

Today, the policy-makers also face numerous challenges as well as opportunities in the region. The United States has been working to foster a new Trans-Pacific Partnership for a trade and commerce and investment to counter Chinese influence in the Asia-Pacific region. Moreover, it is not only a place of destination for the United States to direct investment for economic growth, rather China remains at the centre of all investment and developments. This is also the most significant region for China to expand its economic dominance in the world. Chinese President Xi Jinping stated that, 'China cannot develop in isolation of the Asia-Pacific, and the Asia-Pacific cannot prosper without China'.[64] However, Oggaard argues, 'China's current national security strategy focuses on limiting the possibilities of violent conflict in its neighbour.' She also pinpoints that 'China has adopted a constructive and continuous dialogue to manage conflicts that have been approved by all littoral parties'.[65] Going by Hooper, the United States' 'desire to maintain a "Modus Vivendi" with China', but 'Washington apparently does not intend to clarify its extended deterrence in the South China Sea'.[66] This is the avowed catch here as US needs to publicly declare that China is a threat to global peace and security and needs to be delimited as part of well defined, 'containment strategy'.

As a major power, Japan has also recently involved itself in a fascinating debate over the South China Sea disputes. Johnson elucidates that the much referred to Japanese submarine (*Oyashio*), destroyers (*Ariake* and Setogiri) including 445 Japanese personnel, and 55 officers arrived in the Philippines for a port call at Subic Bay near disputed waters of South China Sea for the confidence-building exercise 'amid China's growing assertiveness' in the South China Sea and the East China Sea.[67] Lued Lincuna, a Philippines Navy public affairs officer said that the exercise was 'not directed at any other countries' and 'it has nothing to do with China'.[68] However, Hong Lei, China's Foreign Ministry spokesperson stated, 'Beijing was a watchful eye on Tokyo's move in the area'.[69] Talking pithily, it can be asserted that the expanse of the South China Sea has become the most militarised place in Asia-Pacific and its implications could be immense to the international community.

India in the South China Sea

India's primary area of maritime interest is in the Indian Ocean. The South China Sea is the secondary one. But in recent times, it has become an active and the most influential actor in the region. From geographical perspectives, although India is not a littoral state of the South China Sea, it is widely accepted as an important stakeholder in the security affairs of the region. According to Prokhor, being a 'geo-political node' of the earth,[70] the South China Sea also attracts extensive attention in the strategic community of India. Since 2000, India has actively started its maritime activities in the South China Sea. Its maritime strategic interest is primarily motivated by the provisions of oil exploration deal with littoral states and freedom of navigation as per UNCLOS. The Act East policy has further marked a strategic shift of India's vision that accelerated its active participation and involvement in the Asia-Pacific region.

The socio-economic structure, way of living, maritime trade and communication, security, and prospect and prosperity of a country have largely been dependent on the location and position of a country from the distance of the ocean. Thus, the geographical location of India is strategically significant. 'The peninsular character of the country with its extensive and open coastline, and with littoral which is extremely fertile and rich in resources, makes India entirely dependent on the Indian Ocean.'[71] India's sea-trade, energy security, lifeline, and future prosperity are basically dependent on the Indian Ocean. Therefore, the Indian Ocean manifests its past experiences, present status, and future destiny in the global world order. Hence, 'India should be given more importance to the Indian Ocean because it must truly remain Indian'.[72] India's first Prime Minister Jawaharlal Nehru on 28 March 1958 stated that 'Virtue its geography, India is in the "lap of an ocean" and reiterated the importance of the sea to India and India could not afford to be weak at sea'.[73] Nehru further observed, 'Whoever controls the Indian Ocean influences India's trade'.[74] The post-Cold War era had a paradigm shift in the Indian economic policy. Prime Minister Narasimha Rao in 1991–92 launched the 'Look East policy', which was viewed as a strategic shift in India's vision. India's political elite, irrespective of their political affiliations, have enunciated a maritime strategic vision and defined the strategic geography. The then Prime Minister Atal Bihari Vajpayee noted in 2003,

> As we grow in international stature, our defence strategies should naturally reflect our political, economic, and security concerned, extending well beyond the geographical countries of South Asia – Our security environment ranges from the Persian Gulf to the Straits of Malacca across the Indian Ocean, includes Central Asia and Afghanistan in the North West, China in the North East and Southeast Asia. Our strategic thinking has also to extend to these horizons.[75]

Defence Minister George Fernandes has also noted 'India's area of interest extends from the North of the Arabian Sea to the South China Sea'.[76] Similarly, the then Prime Minister Manmohan Singh has also articulated the significance of India's strategic geography as,

> India's growing international stature gives it strategic relevance in the area ranging from the Persian Gulf to the Strait of Malacca. India, has, too exploited the fluidity of the emerging world order to forge new link through a combination of diplomatic repositioning, economic resurgence and military firmness.[77]

In fact, since 2000, India had started its maritime strategic activities beyond the Indian Ocean into the South China Sea. The Indian Maritime Doctrine 2009 clearly mentioned that India's maritime strategic area of interest expands from the north of the Arabian Sea to the South China Sea covering both the Indian Ocean and the Pacific Ocean for maintaining peace, stability, and security in the Indo-Pacific Region.[78] Nevertheless, the entry of India into the South China Sea is a part of an oil and natural gas exploration arrangement. Indian-owned state energy company ONGC and ONGC Videsh Limited, 'has established partnership agreements with Petro-Vietnam'[79] and started hydrocarbon resource exploration activities in different blocks ofVietnam's EEZ. Baruah describes the 'company's historical engagement with Vietnam dates back to 1988 when it acquired its first overseas asset, block 06 and the ONGC Videsh Limited then acquired block 127 and 128 for exploration in 2006'.[80] In 2006, when the ONGC Videsh Limited-Petro Vietnam deal started their joint exploration and production sharing activities in Block 127 and Block 128 in the Phu Kahn basin of the South China Sea, Beijing claimed that ONGC Videsh Limited's activities were illegal as these blocks lay in Chinese waters.[81] However, Manmohan Singh, then Prime Minister of India, vividly clarified at Bali in November 2011, 'India's presence in the South China Sea was purely for economic purposes'.[82]

India's interest in the South China Sea is not only related to the exploitation of oil and hydrocarbon resources, but also to secure its energy assets overseas, maritime trade, secure its ports and shipping, the safety and security of the sea lanes of communication, freedom of navigation, and balance of power in Asia-Pacific. Ranjan Mathai, the former Foreign Secretary assumed that the South China Sea 'remains crucial to our foreign trade, energy, and national security interests'.[83] Manmohan Singh has further pointed out, 'our strategic interest in the South China Sea is related to maintain maritime trade, energy, and economic security and to maintain freedom of the sea'.[84] Pardesi also expresses that India has three basic security-related issues in the region, 'to maintain a stable balance of power, to ensure the security of the Malacca, and to ensure the freedom of navigation in the South China Sea'.[85] Furthermore, Raja Mohan articulates that India's interests in the South China Sea are mainly associated with its 'trade with East Asia, its expanding blue-water ambitions and freedom of navigation, and India is concerned about the danger of Beijing convert the South China Sea into a Chinese Lake'.[86] However, Scott argues that India's interests in the South China Sea are based on its own 'strategic calculations'.[87]

The rise of the Chinese navy in the South China Sea, the Western Pacific, and the Indian Ocean has influenced the Indian navy to rethink its maritime sphere of influence in the Indo-Pacific. According to Brewster, the driving factors for India's interest are the rise of China in the Indo-Pacific and the influence of the United States.[88] In fact, the Act East policy, Malabar exercise, joint naval exercise, and joint patrols in the South China Sea are broadly influenced by the American 'pivot to Asia' doctrine.[89] Nevertheless, India's ambition is to become a maritime power in the arena of regional and global power politics. India wants to correct its past mistakes of ignoring sea power by developing maritime strategic culture, identity, strategic thinking, naval thoughts, naval development, and modernization, etc. India's other ambition is to become a prominent Asia-Pacific power and play a proactive and constructive role in strategically moulding the region by establishing bilateral and multilateral links with the South China Sea littoral states and extra-regional powers.

Over the past 25 years, India has undertaken a concerted effort to direct its foreign, economic, and military policies to East Asia as well. Its expanding role beyond its immediate neighbourhood especially in the Asia-Pacific has been facilitated by increasing ties with Vietnam, Philippines, Brunei, Malaysia, Indonesia, Singapore, United States, Japan, Australia, and South Korea, which helps India to hedge against China's growing assertiveness in the Indian Ocean and South China Sea. India is steadily growing economic partnerships, naval deployments, military training, etc. with key littoral states of the South China Sea. India's global rise as an emerging maritime power in Asia has also brought about more responsibility to play a key role in the South China Sea. So, India has to maintain the balance of power in the South China Sea and the Indian Ocean and foster stability and a peaceful environment in the Indo-Pacific Region. A multipolar political system in both Asia and the world would be in the interest of India.

India's strategic ambitions are to protect its sovereignty, sea lines of communication, and maritime areas of interests. From this perspective, India must play a very significant role in maintaining freedom of navigation in the South China Sea domain without interfering in the disputes. On the other hand, adjacent littoral states of the South China Sea are looking towards India with great expectations that it should create a balance of power and possibly to control China's growing hegemony in the region. India has both the internal as well as external balancing strategies. It has military, naval as well as the strategic relationship with Vietnam, Philippines, Brunei, Malaysia, Thailand, Singapore, Indonesia, and other ASEAN countries, which act as its internal balancing. On the other hand, its military and maritime security links with great powers such as the United States, Australia, and Japan (external balancing) could help India to play a proactive and constructive role to reshape the Asia-Pacific. With this regard, ASEAN welcomed and appreciated India's role in the Asia-Pacific. So, India can play a pro-active and constructive role to reshape the Asia-Pacific region through a military–diplomatic balancing strategy.

Conclusion

The geopolitics of the South China Sea has historical as well as contemporary significance. It can be called a 'maritime heartland' because of its abundant marine resources and strategic position. Constituting the critical maritime basins and access to the Pacific and Indian Oceans, the South China Sea is one of the world's busiest maritime traffic of civilian and naval. It has become a new hotspot where almost all the South China Sea littoral states are in dispute over territorial rights, overlapping maritime sovereignty claims, and rights of exploration and exploitation of natural resources within their EEZ. It has been further complicated because of the intersection of superpower hegemony and power politics.

However, India's balancing acts could create a Sino-Indian rivalry in the Indo-Pacific region. As, China has questioned India's role and intention in the disputed South China Sea. It warns India to abstain from the South China Sea. China argues that the condition of the South China Sea remains stable and peaceful; therefore, no third party will be allowed to intervene in the issue of escalating tensions. On other hand, India has expressed its concern about Chinese assertiveness and freedom of navigation in the South China Sea. It also stated that the disputes should be resolved by the international law of the sea, including the UNCLOS 1982. In response to India's position, China said it enjoys 'indisputable sovereignty' over the South China Sea and its territorial waters. China has expressed that there is no problem with freedom of navigation and over-flight, rather China is committed to safeguarding freedom of navigation in the South China Sea. China accused that India's oil exploration deals with Vietnam in the South China Sea as a geopolitical card for compromising the Sino-Indian border issue. China also alleged that it is the United States that is trying to stimulate the matter of freedom of navigation and building an anti-China coalition in the Indo-Pacific. Therefore, China warned the United

States and its allies not to get involved in the South China Sea issue and said that any anti-China coalition would further escalate tensions, rather than solve the dispute.

Hence, India and China need to adopt a constructive approach and rid the conflicting land claims to solve their bilateral flash points rather than heighten their disputes. A comprehensive policy dialogue between India and China will dexterously facilitate both the countries to ensure an economic development, energy security, better trade and environmental regimes. A resource-sharing approach will guarantee the twenty-first century as the Asian century.

In a nutshell, the South China Sea dispute is a matter of serious concern for the international community. It should be resolved by the effective implementation of the Declaration of Code of Conduct (DOC) and the negotiations on the Code of Conduct (COC), otherwise there will a very limited chance to resolve the disputes over the South China Sea and the dispute may continue in future and could become a dangerous and deleterious battleground in the Asia-Pacific region.

Notes

1 Hiebert, Murray, Phuong Nguyen, Gregory B. Polling. *Perspectives on the South China Sea: Diplomatic, Legal and Security Dimensions of the Disputes.* New York: Rowman & Littlefield, 2014.

2 Sichun, Wu and Hong, Nong. *Recent Development in the South China Sea Dispute: The Prospect of a Joint Development Regime*. New York: Routledge, 2014.

3 Till, Geoffrey. 'The South China Sea dispute: An international history.' In *Security and International Politics in the South China Sea: Towards a Cooperative Management Regime* edited by Sam Bateman and Ralf Emmers. New York: Routledge, 2009; Rahman, Chris and Tsanmenyi, Martin. 'A Strategic Perspective on Security and Naval Issues in the South China Sea.' In *Maritime Issues in the South China Sea: Troubled Waters or a Sea of Opportunity* edited by Nien-Tsu Alfred Hu and Ted L. McDorman. New York: Routledge, 2013; Hiebert, Phuong Nguyen, Gregory B. Polling. *Perspectives on the South China Sea (Note 1).* p. 103.

4 Banyan. 'The Devil in the Deep Blue Detail.' *The Economist*. New Delhi, 4 February 2012. Accessed 21 February 2013. www.economist.com/node/21546033.

5 Shicun, Wu and Valencia, Mark. *UN Convention on the Law of the Sea and the South China Sea*. New York: Routledge, 2016.

6 Rapp-Hooper, Mira. 'Uncharted Waters: Extended Deterrence and Maritime Disputes.' *The Washington Quarterly*, 38, 1 (2015), 127–146.

7 Spykman, Nicholas J. *America's Strategy in World Politics: The United States and the Balance of Power.* New York: Harcourt, Brace and Company, 1942, pp. 46–49.

8 Panikkar, K.M. *Indian and Indian Ocean: An Essay on the influence of Sea Power on Indian History*. London: George Allen & Unwin Ltd., 1945.

9 Mackinder, H.J. 'The Geographical Pivot of History.' *Geographical Journal*, 23, No. 4 (1904), 421–437.

10 Briggs, J.C. 'Coincident Biogeographic Patterns: Indo-West Pacific Ocean.' *Evolution*, 53 (1999), 326–335.

11 Wang, Pinxian and Li, Qianyu. *The South China Sea- Paleoceanography and Sedimentography.* The Netherlands: Springer, 2008.

12 Latypov, Yu Y. 'Coral Communities of the Namsu Islands (Gulf of Siam, South China Sea).' *Marine Ecology Progress Series*, 29 (1986), 216–270. Accessed 6 March 2015, http://dx.doi.org/10.3354/meps029261.

13 Emmers, Ralf. *Resource Management and Contested Territories in East Asia*. London: Palgrave McMillan, 2013.

14 United Nations Environmental Programme. *United National Reports on the Fish Stocks and Habitats of Regional, Global, and Transboundary Significance in the South China Sea*. UNEP/GEF/SCS Technical Publication No. 15, 2007; Kaplan, Robert D. *Asia's Cauldron: the South China Sea and the end of a stable Pacific*. New York: Random House, 2015. Also see endnote 4.

15 Lopez, Leslie. 'South China Sea-Part One: Fish Wars.' *Straits Times*, Kota Kinabalu. 3 March 2016. Accessed 5 March 2016. www.straitstimes.com/asia/south-china-sea-fish-wars.

16 Rosenberg, David. 'Fisheries Management in the South China Sea.' In *Security and International Politics in the South China Sea: Towards a Cooperative Management Regime* edited by Sam Bateman and Ralf Emmers. London: Routledge, 2009.

17 Borton, James. *The South China Sea: Challenges and Promises.* Carolina: Xlibris Corporation, 2015.

18 See endnote 15.

19 Sugandhi, Hendra. Is Indonesia really top global tuna exporter. *The Jakarta Post*, 11 June 2019. Accessed 20 November 2019. http:Is Indonesia really top global tuna exporter? - Opinion - The Jakarta Post.

20 O'Brien, Friderich. *South China Sea Oil, Two Problems and Ownership and Development*. Singapore: Institute of Southeast Asian Studies, 1977.

21 See Kaplan (2015), endnote 14.

22 Emmers, Ralf. *Resource Management and Contested Territories in East Asia*. London: Palgrave Macmillan, 2013.

23 Santos, Tina G. 'PH, Chinese Naval Vessels in Scarborough Shoal Standoff.' *Philippines Daily Inquirer*. 11 April 2012. Accessed 19 August 2013. http://globalnation.inquirer.net/32341/ph-chinese-naval-vessels-in-scarboroughshoal-Standoff.

24 Dicke, Vera and Heike Holbigs. 'Rising Sion-Vietnamese Tensions in the South China Sea.' GIGA Focus, No. 8. 2014. Accessed 18 May 2016. www.gigahamburg.de/en/system/files/publications/gf_international_1408.

25 Samuels, Marwyn S. *Contest for the South China Sea*. New York: Methuen, 1982; Also see Till (2015), endnote 3.

26 Raine, Sarah. 'The South China Sea: A Maritime Hotspot.' 6 June 2012. Accessed 12 October 2013. www.gmfus.org/blog/2012/06/06/south-china-sea-maritime-hotspot.

27 Rahman, Chris and Tsamenyi, Martin. 'A Strategic Perspective on Security and Naval Issues in the South China Sea.' *Ocean Development & International Law*, 41 (2010), 315–333. Doi: 10.1080/00908320.2010.499277.

28 Dey, Alan J. *Border and Territorial Disputes*. USA: Longman, 1982.

29 Holsti, K.J. *International Politics: A Framework for Analysis*. New Jersey: Prentice Hall, 1972.

30 Tonnesson, Stein. 'Why Are the Disputes in the South China Sea so Interactable? A Historical Approach.' *Asian Journal of Social Science*, 30, no. 3 (2002), 570–601.

31 Buszynski, Leszek. 'The South China Sea: Oil, Maritime Claims, and U.S.-China Strategic Rivalry.' *The Washington Quarterly*, 35, No. 2 (2012), 139–156.

32 Keyuan, Zou. 'Scarborough: A New Flashpoint in the Sino-Philippines Relations?.' *IBRU Boundary and Security Bulletin* (summer 1999), pp. 71-81.

33 Fang, Yang. 'South China Sea Dispute: Why China Takes a Pragmatic Stance.' East Asia Forum, Singapore, 26 August 2011. Accessed 19 August 2013. www.eastasiaforum.org/2011/08/26/south-china-seadispute-why-china-takes-pragmatic-stance.

34 Chakraborti, T. and Chakraborti, M. 'South China Sea: Refashioned Conflict and the Road Ahead.' *World Focus*, XXXII, No. 4 (2011), 222.
35 Hancox, D. and Prescott, V. 'A Geographical Description of the Spratly Islands and an Account of Hydrographic Surveys amongst Those Islands.' *Marit Briefings*, 1:6 (1995). Also see Dzurek, D.J. 'The Spratly Islands Dispute: Who's on First?.' *Marit Briefings*, 2, No. 1 (1996), pp. 1–65.
36 Storey, Ian. 'Conflict in the South China Sea: China's Relations with Vietnam and the Philippines.' *The Asia-Pacific Journal*, 6, no. 4 (2008), pp. 1–9.
37 UNCLOS, United Nations Convention on the Law of the Sea, Oceans and Law of the Sea, Division for Ocean Affairs and Law of the sea. 10 December 1982. Accessed 24 March 2013. www.un.org/depts/los/convention_agreements/texts/unclos/
38 Ibid, p. 31
39 Ibid.
40 Ibid.
41 Ibid.
42 Ibid.
43 Klein, Adam and Rapp-Hooper, Mira. 'Freedom of Navigation in the South China Sea: What to Watch For.' *Lawfare*. 23 October 2015. Accessed 25 November 2015. www.lawfareblog.com/freedom-navigation-operations-south-china-sea-what-watch.
44 Ibid.
45 Valencia, M.J. and Ludwig, N.A. *Sharing the Resources of the South China Sea*. Dordrecht: Martinus Nijhoff, (1997), p. 24. also see Keyuan, Z. 'China's U-Shaped Line in the South China Sea Revisited.' *Ocean Development & International Law*, 43, no. 1 (2012), 18–344.
46 Guoxing, Ji. 'China versus South China Sea.' *Security Dialogue*, 29, No. 1 (1998), 101–112. Accessed 29 March 2015. www.prio.org/Publications/Publication/?x=2333. Also see Keyuan (2012), endnote 45.
47 Keyuan (2012), endnote 45. Also see Smith, Robert W. 'Maritime Delimitation in the South China Sea: Potentiality and Challenges.' *Ocean Development and International*, 41 (2010), 224.
48 Latypov, Yu Y. 'Coral Communities of the Namsu Islands (Gulf of Siam, South China Sea).' *Marine Ecology Progress Series*, 29 (1986), 216–270. Accessed 6 March 2015. http://dx.doi.org/10.3354/meps029261. Also see Keyuan (2012), endnote 45, p. 18–34; Miyoshi, M. 'China's U-Shaped Line Claim in the South China Sea: Any Validity under International Law?.' *Ocean Development & International Law*, 43, 1 (2012), pp. 1–17.
49 Dzurek, D.J. 'The Spratly Islands Dispute: Who's on First?' *Marit Briefings*, 2, No. 1 (1996). Also see Keyuan (2012), pp. 18-34.
50 See Kaplan (2015), endnote 14.
51 Lo, Chi-kin. *China's Policy towards Territorial Disputes: The Case of the South China Sea Islands*. London: Routledge (1989), p. 45. Also see Keyuan (2012), endnote 45, pp. 18–34.
52 Keyuan, Z. (2012), endnote 45, pp. 18–34. Also see Buchholz, Hanns J. *Law of the Sea in the Pacific Ocean*. Singapore: Institute of Southeast Asian Studies (1987), p. 43.
53 Hayton, Bill. *The South China Sea: The Struggle for Power in Asia*. London: Yale University Press, 2014.
54 Kondapalli, Srikanth. Personal Interview. New Delhi: Jawaharlal Nehru University, 2016.
55 See Kaplan (2015), endnote 14.
56 Mollman, Steve. 'The line on a 70-years-old map that threatens to set off a war in East Asia.' *Quartz*, 7 July 2016. Accessed 12 July 2016. https://qz.com/705223/where-exactly-did-chinas-nine-dash-line-in-the-south-china-sea-come-from/.
57 Mollman. 'The Line on a 70 years old map (Notes 70).' p. 5.

58 Macaraig, Ayee. 'US: China Failed to Clarify 9-dash Line with Law.' *Rappler*. 9 December 2014. Accessed 27 October 2015. www.rappler.com/nation/us-study-nine-dash-line.
59 Fravel, M. Taylor. 'China's Island Strategy: Redefine the Status Quo.' *The Diplomat*. 1 November 2012.
60 Kaplan, Robert D. 'The South China Sea: Is the Future of Conflict.' *Foreign Policy*, September/October 2011.
61 Xinhua. 'China Opposes Military Intervention in South China Sea.' Beijing, 31 July 2012.
62 Gilboy, George J. and Heginbotham, Eric. *Chinese and Indian Strategic Behaviour: Growing Power and Alarm*. New Delhi: Cambridge University Press, 2012.
63 Gray, Colin. 'National Style in Strategy: The American Example.' *International Security*, 6, No. 2 (1981), 35.
64 Anderlini, Jamil. 'Xi Strikes Strident Tone on Foreign Policy.' *The Financial Times*, Beijing, 29 January 2013. Accessed 12 March 2015. www.ft.com/cms/s/0/13f6b08a-6a21-11e2-a7d2-00144feab49a.html#axzz4EvfaPsw8
65 Oggaard, Liselotte. *China and Coexistence: Beijing's National Security Strategy for the Twenty-First Century*. Baltimore: Johns Hopkins University Press, 2012.
66 See endnote 6.
67 Johnson, Jesse. 'Beijing Opens New Lighthouse on Man-made Islands in the South China Sea.' *Japan Times*. 6 April 2016. Accessed 19 May 2016. www.japantimes.co.jp/news/2016/04/06/asia-pacific/beijing-opens-new-lighthouse-man-made-island-south-china-sea/
68 'South China Sea Theater, This Time Japan Confronts China.' *Japan Times*. 8 April 2016. Accessed 18 May 2016. http://sajeevpearlj.blogspot.com/2016/04/south-china-sea-theater-this-time-japan.html
69 'South China Sea.' *Japan Times*. 8 April 2016.
70 Tebin, Prokhor. 'South China Sea: A New Geopolitical Node.' *Asia Times*. 14 October 2011. Accessed 13 March 2013. https://intellibriefs.blogspot.com/2011/10/south-china-sea-new-geopolitical-node.html
71 See endnote 8.
72 Ibid.
73 Singh, Satyindra. *Under Two Ensigns*. New Delhi: Lancer International (1989), p. 1.
74 Ibid, pp. 1–2.
75 'Shrug Off the Cold War, This Is a New World.' New Delhi: Ministry of External Affairs, Government of India, 7 November 2003. Accessed 17 January 2015. www.mea.gov.in/articles-in-indian media.htm?
76 Government of India. 'Freedom to Use the Seas: India's Maritime Military Strategy.' Integrated Headquarters, Ministry of Defence (Navy), New Delhi, 2007.
77 Ibid, p. iii
78 Government of India. *Indian Maritime Doctrine*. Integrated Headquarters, Ministry of Defence (Navy), New Delhi, 2009.
79 Scott, David. 'India's Role in the South China Sea: Geopolitics and Geo-economics in Play.' *India Review*, 12, 2 (2013), 51–69.
80 Baruah, Darshana M., 'India's economic interest in the South China Sea.' 2013 Accessed 18 June 2015, www.orfonline.org/research/indias-economic-interest-in-the-south-china-sea/.
81 Bajpaee, C. 'Reaffirming India's role in the South China Sea.' *Geopolitics*, New Delhi, August 2013.
82 'Annual Report 2011–2012.' Government of India, Ministry of External Affairs.
83 Mathai, Ranjan. 'Security Dimensions of India's Foreign Policy.' New Delhi: Ministry of External Affairs, Government of India, 23 November 2011. Accessed 18 June 2015. www.mea.gov.in/Speeches Statements.htm? +Indias+Foreign+Policy

84 'Oil Exploration in South China Sea.' New Delhi: Ministry of External Affairs, Government of India, May 17, 2012. Accessed 13 January 2014. www.mea.gov.in/bilateral-documents.htm?dtl/19717/Q4532+Oil+Exploration+in+South+China+Sea
85 Pardesi, Manjeet S. 'Is India a Great Power? Understanding Great Power Status in Contemporary International Relations.' *Asian Security*, 11, No. 1 (2015), 1–30.
86 Raja Mohan, C. 'India and the Balance of Power: Will the West Engage?' *Foreign Affairs*, 1 July 2006. Accessed 31 January 2014. www.foreignaffairs.com/articles/asia/2006-07-01/india-and-balance-power
87 See endnote 79.
88 Brewster, David. 'India's Strategic Partnership with Vietnam: The Search for a Diamond on the South China Sea?' *Asian Security,* 5, No. 1 (January, 2009), 22–44.
89 Dueck, Colin. *The Obama Doctrine: American Grand Strategy Today*. New York: Oxford University Press, 2015.

INDEX

Page numbers in **bold** refer to tables; *italics* refer to figures; n refers to endnotes, footnotes.

Abe Initiative 194
acceptability *17–18*
accessibility *17–18*, *20*, 36, 45, 48; Act East policy (2014–) 3, 12n4–12n5, 59, 125–199, 207, 231, 237, 274, 276; ASEAN-India energy cooperation 180–199; energy cooperation with Southeast Asia 127–138; energy dimension 7, 139–156; India's energy trade with Southeast Asia 157–179
Act Far East policy 240, 242, 246n72
Adani Green Energy Ltd **187**, 188
Advisory Board on Energy (India, 1983–) 43
affordability *17–18*, *20*, 36, 99
Afghanistan 206, 253, 256, 275; energy cooperation with PRC 223–224, 228n43
Africa 6, 8, 9, 23, 28, 56, 154, 170, 217, 218, 249; Chinese and Indian energy security 254, 260n20–260n24
Agenda: 2030 of UN Sustainable Development Goals 15
agricultural sector: end-use demand for energy CAGR 73; energy intensity (India 2015–2017) **85**
agriculture 96, 100, **186**; energy efficiency 88
air conditioning 90, **91**
air pollution 68, 241
air quality 43, 67, **120**, 188
air turbine fuel (ATF) 57
Aiyar, M.S. 6–7, 127–128, 137n3–137n4
aluminium: energy efficiency **86**
America First Energy Plan 38
Amoco oil company 134, 265
Andhra Pradesh 88, 255
Angola 2, 223, 249, 254, 255, 267
Arunachal Pradesh 3, 136
ASEAN 3, 11, 42, 59, 128, 136, 208, 212, 213, 216n50–216n51, 277; basic statistics 4; developmental divide 211, 215n29; economic relations with India 143–147; energy cooperation 188–194; energy cooperation with India 7–8, 180–199; energy cooperation with India (policy implications) 196–197; energy cooperation with India (prospects) 194–196; energy cooperation programme with neighbouring countries 193–194; energy at transnational level 129–130, 137n8–137n12; FDI (inward) **146**; hydrocarbon reserves 140; India's Act East policy (energy dimension) 7, 139–156; Indian investment 185, **186**; opportunities for energy trade with India 167–168; renewable energy 135; renewable energy targets *192*, 192–193; security divide 211; trade balance with India (2008–2017) **144**; trade with India (1995–2016) *144*
ASEAN Centre for Energy (ACE, 1999–) 129, 137n8, *190*, 192, 193, 199n28, 199n30
ASEAN Community Vision 2025 189

ASEAN Council for Petroleum (ASCOPE, 1976–) 188, 189
ASEAN Defence Ministers Meeting-Plus 140
ASEAN Economic Community (AEC) 189, 204
ASEAN Emergency Petroleum Sharing Scheme (AEPSS) 188
ASEAN Energy Cooperation Agreement (AECA, 1986–) 188
ASEAN Energy Efficiency and Conservation Sub-Sector Network (EE&C-SSN) 190
ASEAN Energy Mix 191
ASEAN financial crisis (1997–1998) 199n29
ASEAN Forum on Coal (AFOC) 190
ASEAN Fund for Science and Technology 7, 130
ASEAN Ministers of Energy Meeting (AMEM): (2011) 191; (2014) 189
ASEAN Petroleum Security Agreement (APSA, 1986–) 188
ASEAN Plan of Action for Energy Cooperation (APAEC) 116, 123n22, 129, 177n24; third (2010–2015) 188–189, 191, 199n21; fourth (2016–2025) 188–192, 199n20–199n21
ASEAN Power Grid (APG) 116, 168, 177n24, 189, *190*, 193, 194
ASEAN Regional Energy Policy and Planning (REPP) 191
ASEAN Regional Forum 140
ASEAN Renewable Energy Sub-Sector Network (RE-SSN) 191
ASEAN Vision 2020, 129, 199n21
ASEAN+3 (China, Japan, SK) 129, 193, 194, 199n29
ASEAN-China Free Trade Agreement (FTA) 204
ASEAN-IEA MoU (2011) 191
ASEAN-India New and Renewable Energy Initiative 130
ASEAN-India Plan of Action (2004–) 129, 137n9; (2010–2015) 129; (2016–2020) 7, 130
ASEAN-IRENA MoU (2018) 193
ASEAN-PRC strategic energy partnership agreement (2002) 220
Asia-Pacific region 1, 3, 257, 273, 274, 277–278; energy consumption (2007–2017) **69**; energy consumption (country by country, 2007–2017) **70**; energy consumption (growth rate, 2017) *70*; energy cooperation 111–117; low-carbon energy security for India 5–6, 99–124; net energy imports (2010–2013) **112**
Asian Century 7, 128
Asian Development Bank (ADB) 117, 203, 206, 210, 213n2, 238
Asian Infrastructure Investment Bank (AIIB) 10, 117, 218, 259
Asian integration 212–213
Asian Renewable Energy Hub (AREH) 115
Asian Super Grid 239
Assam 136, 151, 183
Atomic Energy of Vietnam 150
Aung San Suu Kyi 251
Australia 55, 56, 58, 65n17, 103, 111, **112**, 188, 189, 194, 204, 207, 222, 242, 262, 277
Australian dollar (AUD) **117**
availability *17–18*, *20*, 36, 99
avoided capacity **91**, 96

Baluchistan Liberation Army 252
Bangladesh 3, 6, 7, 26, 71, 111, 112, 127, 131, 152, 154, 175, 183, 197, 208, 223; bilateral electricity trade with India 168; bilateral energy cooperation with India 134, 135, 137n20; coal and gas reserves 182; coal-mining obstacles 174; electric power consumption per capita (2014) *162*; electricity access (percentage of population, 2016) *162*; electricity trade with India 158; energy connectivity 148; energy cooperation agreement with India (2013) 184; energy mix *159*; environmental concerns 174; existing energy cooperation with India 163–166, 166(box), 167; exports and imports of fuel by India (2018) 163, **163**, 176n16; India's export and import of fuel (2006–2018) *164*, 165; natural gas resources 183; net energy importer (2014) *160*; net energy imports as percentage of energy use (2000–2014) *161*; power imports from India 184; trade-deficit-with-India problem 152, 165, 177n20
Bangladesh-China-India-Myanmar *see* BCIM
Bangladesh-India Friendship Power Company 184
Bangladesh electricity grid: connected with Indian grid 194
Bangladesh Power Development Board (BPDB) 166(box), 176n16, 184

Barapukuria (Bangladesh) coal-based power plant 223
Baruah, D.M. 275, 281n80
Batra, A. xiv, xxviii, 7, 157–179
batteries 57, 62, 66n37
Bay of Bengal 26, 151, 251
Bay of Bengal Economic Community (envisaged) 197, 199n34
Bay of Bengal Initiative for Multi-Sectoral Technical and Economic *see* BIMSTEC
BCIM (Bangladesh-China-India-Myanmar) 256, 257; dropped from BRI (2019) 248
BCIM Economic Corridor (BCIMEC) 170, 178n34, 205–206, *207*, 209, 210; JSG 206, 214n9, 248
BCIM Regional Forum 205–206, 214n8
Behrens, A. 17, 29n8
Belt and Road Initiative *see* BRI
Bhardwaj, P. xxviii, 29n20
Bhardwaj, S.K. xiv, 1–12, 15–31, 262–282
Bhattarai, B. 223, 228n37
Bheramara (Bangladesh) 184
Bhutan 112, 131, 152, 197; bilateral electricity trade with India 168; bilateral energy cooperation with India 135; electricity exports to India 183; electricity trade with India 158, 184; energy connectivity 148; export of power to India 188; HEP potential 182; hydropower project (Indian assistance) 184
Bhutan, Bangladesh, India and Nepal (BBIN) 60, 66n30, 133, 168, 177n22–177n23; opportunities for energy trade with India 167–168
BIMSTEC (Bay of Bengal Initiative for Multi-Sectoral Technical and Economic, 1997–) 26–27, 129, 136, 197, 206–207, 214n16–214n17; energy at transnational level 129, 131–133, 137n13–137n17; renewable energy 135; sub-regional electricity transmission grid idea (2003–) 134–135, 138n22–138n23
BIMSTEC Energy Centre (Bangalore) 132
BIMSTEC MoU on Grid Interconnection 131
BIMSTEC Plan of Action for Energy Cooperation (2005) 131
BIMSTEC summits: 2004 (Myanmar) 131; 2018 (Kathmandu) 131–132, 134
biodiesel **120**
Biodiesel Blending Programme 56
bioenergy 80, **101**
biofuels 57, 88, **120**; alternatives to hydrocarbons 56–57, 65n21–65n22
biomass 25, 44, 57, 76, 89, 91, 135, 159, 182; BIMSTEC 131; installed capacity 93
biowastes 104–105, 123n13
Bloomberg New Energy Finance 36, 49n18
Bo'ao Forum for Asia (2015) 248
Bohi, D.R. 17, 29n12
Bolivia 62, 66n37
Borton, J. 264–265, 279n17
Brazil 2, 94
BRI (Belt and Road Initiative, 2013–) 9, 23, 27, 152, 170, 175, 177n26, 178n34, 212, 213, 219, 223, 228n36, 238; energy security strategy 249–254, 259–260; and GMS 208–210; India-China energy cooperation and competition 10, 248–261; Indian opposition 8, 248, 253; main vehicle 209; opportunities 255
BRI (challenges for China) 257–258, 261n29–261n32; geopolitical factors 257; ghost of debt trap 258; localisation drive 258; socio-cultural factors 257
BRI Action Plan 252
brick industry, energy efficiency **86**, 87
BRICS 23, 257
British Petroleum (BP) 134, 149, 217, 226n3–226n5; *Energy Outlook* 24–25, 30n43, 53, 64n4; *World Energy Statistical Yearbook* 254, 260n23
Brunei [Negara Brunei Darussalam] 129, **144**, 148, 177n24, 191, 221, 269–270, 276, 277; important source of India's crude oil 184; SCS littoral state 262
Budhi Gandaki project (Nepal) 223, 228n35–228n38
buildings sector **122**; energy efficiency 88–89
Bureau of Energy Efficiency (BEE) 86, 88–91
Burke, A. 19, 29n19
Busbarat, P. 210, 215n24
Buzan, B. 23, 30n30, 212–213, 216n40–216n44

CAIT Climate Data Explorer 80, 97n29
Cambodia 130; *see also* CLMV countries
Canada 7, 42, 58, 129, 130
carbon dioxide emissions 5, 12n6, 68, 95, 100, 118; CAAGR (India, 2000–2040) 107; coal 'single largest source' (India, 2016) 107, **108**; energy-related (various scenarios, 2000–2040) *111*; energy-related CAAGR (various countries and regions, 2000–2040) *109*; energy-related (India, 2000–2040) **108**; energy-related (Indian growth rate) 105–107; India

(1990–2015) *81*; India (2016) **72**; India and world (1990–2015) *82*; policy scenarios **119–120**; per unit of TPES (India, 1990–2015) *82*; *see also* GHG
carbon emission intensity of GDP 105, *107*
carbon taxes 6, 96
Cebu Declaration on Energy Security 194
cement 73; energy efficiency **86**, 87–88
Census of India (2011) 105, 123n15
Central Asia (CA) 170, 175, 178n34, 206, 218, 252–253, 257, 258; India's options 255–256
Central Small Leading Group on Energy (中央能源工作领导小组, 2006–) 219
Chabahar Port 256
challenges to energy trade 168–175; China factor 168–172; environmental and humanitarian concerns 174–175; investment 172–173; market structures and sector reforms 173–174; standards (lack of harmonisation) 174
Chashma series of projects 224
Chauhan, P. xv, xxviii, 7, 138n28, 157–179
Checchi, A. 17, 29n8
chemicals 74, 86
Chennai informal summit (2019) 128
Cherp, A. 16–17, 29n6
China 1, 2, 6, 7, 22, 23, 24, 26, 41, 42, 60, 79, 80, 105, 107, 127, 140, 174, 175, 189, 193, 207; competition with India 111, 133, 136, 138n28; cooperation with India in energy sector 128; crude oil imports *via* SCS 267; economic growth 9; economic growth projection 72; energy consumption (2007–2017) **70**, 71; energy context 217–229; energy demand 9; energy forecasts (1995–2020) **218**; energy security 218; energy supplies (switch to overland routes) 219, 226n9; FDI in ASEAN **146**; fuel imports (region-wise dependence, 2018) *171*; fuel imports from selected Southeast Asia countries (2018) *171*; import dependence **218**; intense competition with India 151–152, 154; interest in Indian Ocean 'commercial' 8; investment in energy projects in Southeast Asia 220–221; leading producer and importer of coal in world 103; net energy imports (1999–2014) 168, *169*; net importer of oil (1993–) 217–218, 233; oil and natural gas (import sources) 249; oil and natural gas reserves (2016) 259n1; oil stakes in 30 countries 218–219; over-dependence on Middle East oil 169; playing off Iran against USA 256, 261n28; 'poses major challenge to India' 242; resource vulnerability 233; SCS littoral state 262; swap arrangements sought by India 148; trade with ASEAN 4, 143, *145*
China-ASEAN Free Trade Agreement 208
China-ASEAN Summit (2014) 210
China Central Asia EC 248; energy security 252–253, 260n12–260n19
China-Central-West Asia Economic Corridor (CCWAEC) 170, 178n34
China: energy cooperation with Southeast and South Asia 9, 217–229
China factor 168–172, 177–178
China-India: possibilities for energy cooperation amidst competition 254–257, 260n25
China-Indochina Peninsula EC 248
China-Japan-Korea Free Trade Zone 257
China: Ministry of Foreign Affairs 251
China-Mongolia-Russia Economic Corridor (CMREC) 170, 178n34, 239, 248
China-Myanmar Economic Corridor (CMEC) 8, 152, 219, 248, 250–252, 260n5–260n11
China-Myanmar oil and gas pipeline 251, 255
China National Offshore Oil Corporation (CNOOC) 221, 222, 250
China National Petroleum Corporation 223–224, 254; CNPC AktobeMunaiGas (CNPC AMG) 253
China-Pakistan Economic Corridor (CPEC) 8, 152, 170, 178n34, 178n36, 219, 224, 228n45, 252, 253, 258, 260n13; flagship BRI project 248
China Petroleum Pipeline Bureau (CPP) 255
Chinese Communist Party: 16th Congress 218; 18th Congress (2013) 219
Chinese diplomacy: 'immediate neighbourhood' 208; 'middle range neighbourhood' 208–209; 'wider neighbourhood' 209
Chinese National Offshore Oil Company 265
Chinese shadow (over India) 11–12
Chinese unilateralism 11
Cho, J.R. 21, 29n22
choke points 8, 9, 220, 249, 257
CITIC 251
city gas distribution (CGD) 184

clean coal technologies (CCTs) 190
clean energy 92–95, 96, 197; definition 84; *see also* renewable energy
climate change 6, 19, 26, 43, 46, 95, 96, 163
climate change activists 4, 5, 52
climate change mitigation 96; energy efficiency 5, 67–98; energy transitions 5, 67–98
CLMV countries 129, 185, 194, 203–204, 208, 211, 221; economic growth 204, *206*, 208; hydropower 133; regional power grid with China (prospective) 220, 226n13
coal 4, 5, 15, 21, 22, 32, 34, 38, 52, 53, 55, 68, 73, 75, 79, 80, 82, 87, 117–118, 136, 147, 220, 231; ASEAN 190; BIMSTEC 131; CAGR (2007–2017) 76; carbon dioxide emissions (CAAGR, India, 2000–2040) 109; compound average annual growth rate (CAAGR), India 100; contribution to total primary energy supply (India, 2010, 2016) 76, **77**; dominant fuel source (India) 24; eclipse (UK) 37; import dependence 25, 100; India 'second-largest producer' 40–41; India second-largest producer and importer in world 103; Indian imports 54, 64n13, 65n14; Indian production (2018) 54, 64n12; Indonesian exports to India 152–153, 154; industrial energy use 86; supply and demand (India, 2016–2017) **103**; trends in international trade (India, 2016–2017) 76, **78**
coal balance (India, 2016–2017, provisional) **103**
coal demand (India) 103, **103**; Indian scenario (2016–2040) 24
coal imports 54, 78, 152–153, 154, 163, 188
cobalt 61, 62
Code of Conduct (COC) 278
Colombo 184, 224, 225
compound average annual growth rate (CAAGR) 117–118; net import of coal (India) 103
Comprehensive Asia Development Plan (CADP, 2010–) 206, 207, 214n15
Comprehensive and Progressive Trans-Pacific Partnership (CPTPP) 139
compressed natural gas (CNG) 184
Comtec Solar System 221
concentrating solar power (CSP), installation costs falling **116**, 116
continental shelf 133, 150, 222, 271–272
cooking techniques (rural upgrading) 91
Copenhagen Accord (2009) 71
copper 61, 62, 237, 238
COVID-19 pandemic 1–2, 41, 48, 49n19, 68, 72
cross-border electricity trade (CBET) 6, 103, 111–117, 118; ASEAN-India 197
cross-border grid links 59–60, 188; India-Bangladesh 184, 198n13
Cross-Border Trade of Electricity Guidelines (2016, 2018) 26, 31n46
Cross-Border Trade of Electricity Regulations (2019) 26, 31n47
crude oil: BIMSTEC 131; CAGR 74; consumption (2007–2017) 74; import dependence 100; supply and demand (India, 2016–2017) **104**; trends in international trade (India, 2016–2017) 76, **78**
crude oil and oil products: contribution to total primary energy supply (India, 2010, 2016) 76, **77**
crude oil prices 10, 11, 258; volatility 104, 128
crude oil production, CAGR (2007–2017) 76
current account deficit 4, 105
Current Policies Scenario (CPS) 109, *110–111*, **119**, **121**

Dadwal, S.R. xviii–xix, 5, 52–66, 250, 260n6
Daewoo (SK) 134, 151, 251
Dalby, S. 19, 29n17
dams 174–175, 179n49, 221, 222, 223, 227n24, 228n38
De, P. xv, 7–8, 180–199
decentralised renewable energy (DRE) 37, 38–39, 45, 46–47
decision-making units (DMU) 23–24
Declaration of Code of Conduct (DOC) 278
Deen Dayal Upadhyaya Gram Jyoti Yojana scheme (DDUGJY) 91, **121**
Deepak, B.R. xv, 10, 248–261
deep-sea mining 61–62, 66n33–66n36
Delhi Declaration (2018) 180, 198n1
developed countries 10, 33–34, 259
developing countries 33–34, 37
Development of North-East Region (DoNER) 128
Dhaka Declaration (2005) 157
Dicke, Vera 266, 279n24
diesel 80, 100, 104, 118, 151, 154, 166 (box), 241

digitalisation of energy 37–38
direct reduced iron (DRI) 87
Djibouti 28; PRC naval base 219
DoNER (Development of North-East region): separate department (2001) 3; upgraded to Ministry (2004) 3
Dongfang gas fields 222
Druk Green Power Corporation Ltd (DGPC) 184

East Asia 139–140, 141, 208; economic relations with India 142–143
East Asia Summits (EAS) 140, 194, 206
Eastern Economic Forum (EEF) 239, 240, 242
Ebinger, C.K. 18, 29n16
economic corridors 204–207, 209, 210, 214n7–214n9, 219, 249–250
economic development 19, 143
economic growth 5, 7, 24, 25, 35, 52–53, 63, 67, 82, 99, 100, 102, 148, 157, 230, 232, 233; decoupling from carbon emissions 105; increased demand for energy 6; sustainable 21; projection (India) 72
economic reforms (1991) 163
Economic Research Institute for ASEAN and East Asia (ERIA) 206
ecosystem 19, 38
Ecuador 223, 255
Efficiency Scenario 86, 88, **89**, **90**
Efficient Lighting Programme **121**
Egenhofer, C. 17, 29n8
electoral politics 41, 46
electric vehicles (EVs) 25, 53, 60, 61, 62, 118
electrical appliances 90–91, **91**, 92
electricity 22, 26, 31n46–31n50, 33, 35, 41, 42, 43, **72**, 73, 87, 88, 93, 153, **186–187**; BIMSTEC grids 131; CAGR 74; India net exporter (2016–2017) 112, **113**; renewable sources (cost) **116**; sector-wise consumption (2016–2017) 74, *75*; trends in international trade (India, 2016–2017) 76, **78**
Electricity Act (2003) 95, 174
Electricity Act (Bangladesh) 174
electricity consumption per capita (various countries, 2016) 105, **106**
electricity demand 40, 72
electricity generation 5, 57, 102, 105, 118, 197
electricity generation capacity 40
electricity imports 76; CAGR 78
electricity prices 103
electricity production: CAGR (2007–2017) 76
electricity supply 21, 104
Energy Balance of India for 2016–2017 (CSO, 2018) 99, 112, 123n3
energy and climate change (India) 80–84
Energy Conservation Act 86
Energy Conservation Building Code (ECBC, 2007) 89, **121–122**
Energy Conservation Building Code for Residential Buildings (ECBC-R, 2018–) 91–92
energy consumption and emission intensity of GDP: India 105, **106**; various countries **106**
energy demand: end-use sectors (2010–2016) 76; India 73–75
energy demand projection, CAGR 72
energy diplomacy 134, 219, 236, 255
energy economy (India), future 78–80
energy efficiency 41, 60, 105; clean energy transitions 5, 67–98; climate change mitigation 5, 67–98; and conservation (ASEAN) 190–191; definition 67; implementation barriers 92; sectoral patterns 84
energy elasticity of GDP ratio 148
energy import dependence 53, 76–78; definition 76
energy indicators (India) 72–73
Energy Information Agency (EIA) 221, 227n28
energy intensity 95; bell-shaped curve 84; India and world (1990–2030 projection) 84, **85**
energy intensity of GDP 105, *107*
energy mix 9, 48, 63, 67, 71, 80, 84, **181**, 193, 224, 234
energy perspective: geopolitics of SCS 10–11, 262–282
energy poverty 32, 38–39, 40, 43, 45
energy prices 22, 23, 24, 32, 39, 40, 63; volatility 102, 111, 148
energy at regional [transnational] level 129–133
energy sector: import of energy resources 160–161; modern energy use and accessibility 161–163; reform 25; resource endowments, rising demand, single source dependence 159–160; trends 72–78, 159–163
energy security 9, 132, 172, 189, 231; basic aspects *20*; concepts 16–17; definitions 17, 99, 192; dimensions 21–22; eastward engagement 10; era of global energy transition 5, 32–51; interlinkage with sustainability indicators *17*; perspectives

18; policy framework 18–21; top priority 153–154; *see also* India's energy security
energy security (challenges remaining) 60–64; import dependence (new kind) 61–62; road ahead 63–64
energy security (Indian policy initiatives) 54–60; alternatives to hydrocarbons 56–60; biofuels 56–57; challenges and strategy 5, 52–66; cross-border power grids 59–60; domestic oil and gas sector 54–55; external oil and gas sector 55–56; green energy 57–58; hydropower 59, 66n28; nuclear energy 58
energy security discourse 1–4, 8, 22–24
Energy Security Forum 193
energy security indicators *18*
energy security policy: challenges and strategy for energy-secure India 52–66; debates in India 4–6, 13–124; energy efficiency and clean energy transitions 5, 67–98; energy security (India) during global energy transition 32–51; energy security contours 15–31; low-carbon energy security 99–124
energy self-sufficiency, 'more visionary than practical' 148
energy supply mix 75–76
energy supply: CAGR 75; geopolitics 27–28
energy system transition 19, *20*
energy trade: purchasing from least-cost source 160; rationale 159–163
energy transition 42; climate change mitigation 5, 67–98; definition 34–35
Energy Transition Commission 33–34, 48n2
energy transition era (global) 5, 32–51
energy trilemma 36, 49n20
energy uses 67
ENI East Africa 254
environment 15, *17*, 36, 95, 174–175
Essar Group 147, 225
Ethanol Blended Petrol Programme 56
Europe 8, 23, 170, 209
European Commission 17, 29n11
European Union 1, 71, 80, 141, 184, 189, 190, 254; coal-importer 41; energy consumption *68–69*
exchange rate fluctuations 258
Exclusive Economic Zones (EEZs) 270, 271, 277
Exxon Mobil 55

Fang, Y. 270, 279n33
Faster Adoption and Manufacturing of Hybrid and Electric Vehicles (FAME-2) 60
feed-in-tariffs (FiT) 6, 71, 95
Fernandes, G. 275
fertiliser sector 73–74, 86, 87, 105
final energy consumption: projections (2013–2040) **79**
First Solar (USA) 44
fisheries 264–265
floods 174, 175, 211
food 86, 211
Foreign Direct Investment (FDI) 4, 163, 173, 185, 204, 218, 237
foreign exchange earnings 165
fossil fuels 5, 21, 25, 32, 53; continued expansion in developing countries 34; depletion 26
Framework Agreement on Atomic Energy (India-Vietnam, 2016) 150, 155n5–155n6
France 22, 39, 46, 58, 94
Fravel, M.T. 273, 281n59
freedom of navigation 222, 271, 276, 277
Fukushima accident (2011) 150, 231

Galwan (Sino-Indian clashes, 2020) 253, 256, 259
Gas Authority of India Limited (GAIL) 134, 185, **186**, 251–252
Gazifikatsiya Rossii (Gasification of Russia) 235
Gazprom 65n18, 236, 245n45
generation-based incentives (GBIs) 6, 71, 93
geoeconomics 4, 7, 8, 54, 140, 154
geopolitics 7, 21, 22, 23, 36, 42, 48, 54, 115, 154, 232, 235, 240–241, 257; energy supply routes 27–28; SCS 149–150; SCS (energy perspective) 10–11, 262–282
geothermal energy 196; contribution to total primary energy supply (India, 2010, 2016) 76, **77**
Germany 7, 22, 37, 39, 129, 130, 217
Gezhouba Group Corporation 223, 224
GHG (greenhouse gas) 6, 71, 89, 90; alternative IEA scenarios (India 2013–2040) **83**; per capita (India, 2040) 83; key contributing sectors (India, 2005–2013) **83**; major emitting countries (2010) **81**; target **120**; *see also* carbon dioxide emissions
GHG Platform India database 80
Gilboy, G.J. 273, 281n62
Global Carbon Project 5, 52, 71
Global Centre for Nuclear Energy Partnership (India) 150
global energy consumption *68*; trends (2007–2017) *69*; global energy

consumption: regions of world (2007–2017) **69**; regions of world (growth rates, 2017) *70*
global energy market: Indian re-positioning 41–48
global energy transition 33–39; India's energy security 39–41
globalisation *17*, 84
GMS (Greater Mekong Subregion) 8, 203, 213n2, 227n26; and BRI 208–210; economic corridors 204, *205*, 205
GMS Cross-Border Transport Agreement (CBTA) 204, 214n4–214n5
GMS Economic Cooperation Programme (1992–) 203–204, 214n3–214n5
GMS Ministerial Conference (eighth, 1998) 204
GMS North-South Corridor 207
GMS triennial summit (2002–) 204, 208, 209
Gong, Q. 259, 261n33
Gray, C. 273, 281n63
Greater Mekong Subregion *see* GMS
Greece 39, 218
green energy 57–58
grid connectivity 102, 112, 148, 151, 155n10
Guidelines for Import and Export of Cross-Border Electricity: (BBIN, 2016) 168, 177n23; (BBIN, 2018) 168, 177n22
Gujarat 88, 255
GVK Power & Infrastructure Ltd **186**, 188
Gwadar (Pakistan) 170, 224, 252

Hainan 222, 248
Hambantota port 224, 228n46
Hasina, Ms 168
Hatgyi dam (Myanmar) 174, 175, 221
Hayton, B. 271, 280n53
Heads of ASEAN Public Utilities Authorities (HAPUA) 188, 189
Heginbotham, E. 273, 281n62
high speed diesel (HSD) 182, **183**
high-voltage DC (HVDC) cables 116, **117**
Himalayan region 112, 123n16
Hiranuma Initiative (2002) 193–194
Holbigs, H. 266, 279n24
Holsti, K.J. 269, 279n29
housing 71, 91, 96
Hu Jintao 178n32, 219, 223
hydro hegemony 211, 215n33
Hydrocarbon Exploration Licensing Policy (HELP, 2016–) 55
hydrocarbon reserves, energy connectivity 148
Hydrocarbon Vision 2030 for North East India 59, 183
hydrocarbons 5, 32; BIMSTEC 131; global market 42; India 'leading consumer' 32; MGC countries 133
hydroelectric power (HEP) 112, 182, 184, 220, 221, 223–224, 227n27
hydrogen 102, 115, 123n18, 160
hydropower 25, 26, 44, 53, 57, 76, **77**, 93, **101**, 136, 168, 173, 183, 194; alternative to hydrocarbons 59; BIMSTEC 131; energy connectivity 148; MGC countries 133
hydropower generation 211

IEA (International Energy Agency) 35, 40–41, 49n15, 50n33, 72, 78, *81*, 82, 83, 86, 87, 88, 95, 99, 168, 172–173, 189, 233, 241, 243
IEA: *India's Energy Outlook* (2015) 68, 96n1
IEA: *Southeast Asia Energy Outlook 2017* (2017) 159, 176n8
IEA: *World Energy Outlook 2018* (2018) 100, 109, 114, 115, 117, 123n6–123n8
import dependence 71, 94, 99, 102, 109, 110, 157, **218**; coal 25, 100; energy 53, 76–78, 231, 234; natural gas 6, 96; new kind 61–62; oil 6, 25, 54–55, 96, 100, 104–105, 188; primary energy sources 118
import-substitution strategy 176n15
income per capita 105, 112
independent power producers (IPPs) 160, 173
India: acquisition of oil and gas fields overseas 163; basic statistics 143; coal resources 182; commitments under SDG#7, 195, *196*; economic growth 2; economic relations with ASEAN 143–147; economic relations with East Asia 142–143; electric power consumption per capita (2014) *162*; electricity access (percentage of population, 2016) *162*, 176n12; energy consumption (2007–2017) **70**, 71; energy cooperation with ASEAN 7–8, 180–199; energy cooperation with Southeast Asia 148–153; energy-deficit country **112**; energy economy in global order 68–71; energy investments in Southeast Asia **146**; energy mix *159*; energy scenario 24–26, 53–54; energy security (challenges and strategy) 5, 52–66; energy trade with South Asian countries 181–184; energy trade with Southeast Asia 157–179, 184–188;

energy trends and forecasts 158(box); exports and imports to selected ASEAN countries (2013–2017) **145**; exports of high-speed diesel (2010–2020) 184, **185**; fourth-highest carbon-emitter 52–53, 71; fuel imports (region-wise dependence, 2018) *171*; fuel imports from selected Southeast Asia countries (2018) *171*; import-dependence (energy) 40, 41–42, 48; major exporter of refined petroleum products 184; major importer of coal 184; net energy importer (2014) *160*; net energy imports as percentage of energy use (2000–2014) *161*; prospects for electricity import and export (to 2047) *114*; re-positioning in global energy market 41–48; strategic oil reserves 48; third-largest crude oil importer in world (2018) 2; third-largest energy consumer 52; trade and investment in Southeast Asia (2010–2017) 144, **146**; vulnerability to global energy price shocks 102
India-Africa Forum Summits (IAFS) 254
India-Bangladesh Friendship Pipeline 166(box)
India-China (geopolitics of energy cooperation) 9–11, 201–282; BRI 248–261; China, Southeast Asia and South Asia 217–229; China's energy context 217–229; deconstruction of regions 203–216; India's energy security (Northeast Asia dimension) 230–247; SCS (energy perspective) 262–282; subregional cooperation (emerging role) 203–216
India: Department of Atomic Energy (DAE) 58
India: energy cooperation with Southeast Asia 127–138; bilateral level 133–136; regional level 129–133
India Energy Outlook (IEO) *81*, 82, 83, 86, 87, 88, 95
India Vision Case 78–80, **79**, **83**
India's energy security (Northeast Asia dimension) 9–10, 230–247
India's energy security contours 4–5, 15–31
India's energy security in era of global energy transition 5, 32–51
India-Indonesia Energy Forum 152
India-Myanmar-Thailand Trilateral Highway 207
Indian Air Force (IAF): biofuel trials 57, 65n23
Indian FDI in ASEAN (2012–2016) **147**
Indian Maritime Doctrine (2009) 275
Indian Navy 276
Indian Ocean 170, 207, 274
Indian Ocean Region (IOR): India-US naval cooperation 227n31; strategic importance 8
Indian Ocean Rim Association (IORA) 23
Indian Oil Corporation (IOC) 151, 167(box), 197, 252; LPG terminal in Myanmar (planned) 183
Indian Renewable Energy Development Agency (IREDA) 44
Indo-German Energy Forum (IGEF) 86, 88, 89, 90
Indo-Pacific Economic Corridor 206, 207, 214n10–214n13
Indo-Pacific region 8, 9, 10, 11, 212–213, 214n20, 216n48–216n51, 222, 240, 248, 259, 267, 275–278
Indo-Pacific Strategy (IPS) 23, 27
Indonesia 6, 7, 27, 71, 103, 111, **112**, 115, 127, 128, 129, 136, 138n27, 158, 172, 196, 213, 220, 257, 271; coal production scenario 159; electric power consumption per capita (2014) *162*; electricity access (percentage of population, 2016) *162*; energy cooperation with India 152–153, 154–155, 155n13, 156n16; energy mix *159*; existing energy cooperation with India 167(box); exports and imports of fuel by India (2018) **163**; fisheries 265; fuel exports to China and India (2018 comparison) *171*; GDP forecast (2050) 220; important source of India's crude oil 184; India's export and import of fuel (2006–2018) 165, *165*; Indian energy investments **146**, 147; Indian firms investing in energy sector (2018–2019) **186**; net energy exporter (2014) *160*; net energy imports as percentage of energy use (2000–2014) *161*; SCS littoral state 262; source of coal for India 188
Indonesia: Ministry of Energy and Mineral Resources 152, 167(box)
industrial sector 104, **122**; end-use demand for energy CAGR 73; energy demand (India, 2040 projection) 86; energy intensity (India 2015–2017) **85**; energy savings (2040 projection) 86
infrastructure 8, 40, 116, 172
installed power generation capacity 63, 66n38
institutional connectivity 142, 148
Integrated Energy Policy (IEP, 2006) 39, 95
Inter-State Transmission System (ISTS) 93

International Atomic Energy Agency (IAEA) 58, 65n26, 189
International Centre for Integrated Mountain Development (ICIMOD) 216n39
International Civil Aviation Organisation 88
international cooperation 18, 82
International Energy Forum (IEF) 172
International Monetary Fund (IMF) 52, 64n1
International Renewable Energy Agency (IRENA) 33, 48n1, 115, 189, 193
International Seabed Authority (ISA) 62, 66n34
International Solar Alliance (ISA) 46, 94, 180, 181, 195, 199n33, 241, 247n78
International Solar Energy Initiative 225
investment 109, 111, 115, 116, 117, 118, 124n24, 130, 140, 141, 143, 218, 219; challenge to energy trade 172–173
Iran 2, 23, 27, 42, 249, 252, 254, 255, 267
Iran-Pakistan-India (IPI) pipeline 3, 256
Iraq 2, 27, 249, 267
iron 62, 237
iron and steel sector 86, **86**, 87, 92

Jaishankar, S. 127, 132
Jakarta 115, 142, 167(box)
Japan 2, 4, 7, 41, 42, 128, 130, 140, 150, 169, 172, 189, 190, 193–194, 204, 206, 207, 217, 221–222, 257, 262, 277; crude oil imports *via* SCS 267; energy situation and resource security challenges 233–234; import dependence (energy) 231; investment in Southeast Asia 143–144, **146**; SCS disputes 274; trade with ASEAN (2017) 143
Japan Centre for Economic Research 72
Japan Oil, Gas and Metals National Corporation 238
Jaybee Energy Pvt Ltd **186**, 188
Jewell, J. 16–17, 29n6
Jiang Zemin 219
Johnson, J. 274, 281n67
joint ventures 10, 184, 185, **186–187**, 225, 242
Joint Working Groups 135, 152–153
Jubilant Oil and Gas Private Limited 147, 185
just [fair] transition 35, 49n13
just energy 38, 43–44, 47

Kaplan, R.D. 27, 31n52, 272, 273, 279n14, 281n60
Karen state 174, 175, 221
Kashgar 170, 252
Kashmir 253, 256
Kazakhstan 58, 170, 223, 248, 253, 255, 256, 260n15–260n16
Kerner, R. 230–231
Kerry, J. 206, 214n10
Khulna Power Plant 183
Klein, A. 271, 280n43
Kohli, D. xvi, 5, 67–98
Kondapalli, S. xvi, 9, 217–229, 272, 280n54
Korea Gas Corporation 151
Kovind, R.N. (President of India) 150, 155n7
Kra Canal Project 170, 220
Kulekhani hydroelectricity project (Nepal) 223, 228n39
Kumarasamy, D. xvi, 7–8, 180–199
Kunming 206, 250
Kuwait 2, 27, 267
Kyaukpyu Special Economic Zone (SEZ) 251
Kyaw, U Htin 166
Kyrgyz Republic 258

Ladakh 253, 256
Lancang-Mekong Cooperation (LMC, 2016–) 210–211, 215; pillars 210
Laos (Lao PDR) 220; debt trap 258
Laos-Thailand-Malaysia-Singapore Power Integration Project 193
LEDs 91, **121–122**, 167(box)
Letpadaung copper mines 221
Li Keqiang 206, 217, 219, 225n1
Li Peng 219
Liao, J.C. 220–221, 226n7, 227n21
Liebreich, Michael 36, 49n18
lighting 90, **90–91**, 96
lignite: CAGR (2007–2017) 76
Lincuna, L. 274
lithium 61, 62, 66n37
LMC Fund 210
LNG (liquefied natural gas) 22, 27, 155n12, 168, 189, 220, 231, 236, 252; construction of terminals 53–54, 64n11; import dependency (India) 25; imports (by India) 163; India world's fourth-largest importer 241; prices 55; storage facilities 154
LNG contracts 55, 65n16–65n17
Lombok Strait 170
Look East policy 3, 6–7, 127–128, 131, 133, 139, 207, 240; dimensions 140–141
low-carbon energy security 5–6, 99–124; drivers 105–109, *110*

low-carbon growth path 8, 180, 197
LPG (liquefied petroleum gas) 59, 74, 80, 90, 91, 104, **121**, 151, 238; storage facilities 252

Macclesfield Bank 262, 269, 271
Mackenzie report 35
Mackinder, H.J. 263–264, 278n9
macroeconomic stability 102, 105
Madan, T. 18, 29n15
Mae Sot (Thailand) 207
Mahan, A.T. 8
Mahathir Mohamad 258
Maitri project (Bangladesh) 184
Make in India policy 208, 241
Malacca Dilemma 169, 178n32, 207, 251
Malacca Straits 8, 27, 169–170, 219, 220, 257, 275
Malaysia 2, 6, 7, 27, 60, **72**, 73, 111, **112**, 128, 129, 130, 140, 158, 221, 258; deregulation 173; electric power consumption per capita (2014) *162*; electricity access (percentage of population, 2016) *162*; energy cooperation with India 153, 156n17; energy mix *159*; existing energy cooperation with India 167(box); exports and imports of fuel by India (2018) **163**; fuel exports to China and India (2018 comparison) *171*; gas production scenario 159; GDP forecast (2050) 220; important source of India's crude oil 184; India's export and import of fuel (2006–2018) 165, *165*; Indian investment in energy sector (2018–2019) **186**; net energy exporter (2014) *160*; net energy imports as percentage of energy use (2000–2014) *161*; SCS littoral state 262
Malik, A.R. 252, 260n13
Mandalay 206, 251
Mangdechhu Hydro Electric Project 184
Manipur 112
manufacturing 41, **186–187**, 241
maritime highways 1, 8
maritime security 11, 131
Maritime Silk Road (MSR) 8, 170, 248, 250
maritime sovereignty claims 270–271, 280n35–280n44
Marrakech (Morocco) 46, 94
Mathai, R. 276, 281n83
Md. Obaidur Rahaman xviii, 10–11, 262–282
Medcalf, R. 213, 216n45
Meghalayam 136
Mehra, M.K. xvi, 5, 67–98
Mekong River Commission (1995–) 211
Mekong-Ganga Cooperation (MGC, 2000–) 23, 136, 212, 215n35, 216n39; energy at transnational level 129, 133
Mekong-India Economic Corridor 206, 207
Memorandum on Strengthening Oil and Gas Cooperation (China-India, 2006) 255
microgrids 37, 44
Middle East 1, 6, 23, 27, 249, 267, 269
Mineral Resources Authority of Mongolia 238
Minerals Law (Mongolia, 2006, amended 2017) 237
mini-grids 44, 45, 47
mining **186**
Ministry of Earth Sciences 62
Ministry of Energy Resources 43
Ministry of External Affairs 7, 128, 133
Ministry of New and Renewable Energy (MNRE, 2006–) 43, 93, 98n56–98n59, 194
Ministry of Petroleum and Natural Gas xxvii, 6–7, 152, 167(box)
Ministry of Power 180
Ministry of Renewable Energy 135
Ministry of Statistics and Programme Implementation (MoSPI) 73, *74*, *75*, 97n16
Mizoram 194, 252
Modi, N. 10, 54, 65n22, 128, 139, 141, 153, 167(box), 213, 216n52, 240, 241; foreign policy 256; vision for India's energy future (2016) 239, 246n68
Mollman, S. 272, 280n56
Mongolia 3, 9–10, 58, 103, 170, 178n34–178n35, 231, 242; coal resources 238, 239, 245n55; debt trap 258; energy scenario and potentiality 237–239, 245–246; mining sector 'one of key drivers of export revenue' 237, 245n51; oilfields 238
Mongolia: Ministry of Mining 238
Mongolia Extractive Industries Transparency Initiative 238
Moreh (India) 207
Motihari-Amlekhgunj petroleum product pipeline (India-Nepal, 2019) 183, 198n12
Mozambique 8, 254, 260n21
Mukherjee, S. xvii, 5–6, 99–124

Muni, S.D. xvii, xxvii, xxviii, 6–7, 127–138
Myanmar 3, 6, 7, 10, 26, 111, **112**, 127, 128, 129, 131, 158, 182, 194, 197, 211, 220, 223, 225, 255, 258; bilateral energy cooperation with India 134, 135, 136, 138n25, 138n30; civil war zones 174–175; electric power consumption per capita (2014) *162*; electricity access (percentage of population, 2016) *162*; energy connectivity 148; energy cooperation with India 149, 151–152, 154–155, 155n8–155n12; energy cooperation with PRC 221; energy mix *159*; environmental concerns (dam construction) 174–175; existing energy cooperation with India 166(box); exports and imports of fuel by India (2018) **163**; fuel exports to China and India (2018 comparison) *171*; GMS 214n4; hydropower potential 184; identifiable pipeline routes with India 134, 137n19; India's export and import of fuel (2006–2018) *164*; Indian energy investments **146**, 147; Indian firms investing in energy sector (2018–2019) 185, **186**; net energy exporter (2014) *160*; net energy imports as percentage of energy use (2000–2014) *161*; oil and gas reserves 151; renewable energy cooperation with India 135; swap arrangements sought by India 148
Myanmar: Ministry of Energy 185
Myanmar Oil and Gas Enterprise 251
Myitsone dam project (aborted) 251

Nabar-Shwebo-Ohntaw power transmission line 221
Naidu, G.V.C. xvii–xviii, 7, 139–156
National Action Plan on Climate Change (NAPCC) 6, 71, 94, 96
National Biodiesel Mission 56
National Clean Energy Fund (NCEF) **119**
National Data Repository (NDR) 55, 65n15
National Democratic Alliance (NDA) 63
National Development and Reform Commission (NDRC, PRC) 248
National Energy Plan 2030 (Japan, 2017–) 234
National Energy Policy (NEP, 2017) 39–40, 49n28
national grid 44, 45, 63
National Institute of Oceanography (NIO) in Goa 62
National Institution for Transforming India (NITI) Aayog 43, 44, 50n37, 50n43, 72, *114*
National Mineral Policy (NMP, 2019) 61, 66n32
National Mission for Enhanced Energy Efficiency (NMEEE) 96, **119**, **121–122**
National Renewable Energy Centre (NREC) 178n35
national security 11, 16, 148; energy security 'subset' of 18
National Solar Mission (NSM) 94, **121**, 195
National Thermal Power Corporation (NTPC) 45, 50n47, 184
Nationally-Determined Contributions (NDC) 33–34, 82, 95, **120**, 163
Natuna gas field 189, 220, 222, 262, 270
natural gas 3, 4, 15, 21, 22, 24, 28, 38, 40, 41, 42, 43, 68, 73, 75, 80, 88, 93, 103, 118, 149, 154, 160, **186–187**, 194, 223, 236; BIMSTEC 131; contribution to total primary energy supply (India, 2010, 2016) 76, **77**; geopolitics (SCS) 263–269; import dependence 6, 25, 96, 100; Indian consumption (2016–2017) 105; Indian production (2018–2019) 53, 64n10; Myanmar 151–152; northeastern India 26; sector-wise use (India, 2016–2017) *74*; share of global energy supply (2019) 231; trends in international trade (India, 2016–2017) 76, **78**
natural gas exploration 185
natural gas fields 165, 176n17, 177n18
natural gas imports, CAGR 78
natural gas output (India) 25
natural gas pipelines 3, 7, 170, 183, 194, 250–251
natural gas power generation 33
natural gas prices 115
natural gas production, CAGR (2007–2017) 76
natural resources exploration **147**
Nehru, J. 274
Nepal 3, 12n3, 112, 131, 132, 152, 184, 197, 225, 258; bilateral energy cooperation with India 134–135, 138n21; Chinese investment in energy projects 223; dependence on imported diesel from India 183; electricity trade with India 158, 168; energy connectivity 148; HEP potential 182; power imports from India 183, 188
Nepal Oil Corporation (NOC) 183
New Delhi 130, 132, 254
New Eurasia Land Bridge 248

New Exploration Licensing Policy (NELP) 55
New Policies Scenario (NPS) 78–80, **79**, **83**, 86, 88, 95, **101**, *102*, **108**, *109*, 109, *110–111*, **120**, 172
New Silk Road 206, 214n11
Nguyen Tan Dung 167(box)
Nguyen, A.T. 21–22, 30n24
nickel 61, 62
Nigeria 2, 254, 255
non-tariff barriers 26, 158
North East India: Hydrocarbon Vision 2030, 151
North Eastern Electric Power Corporation Ltd (NEEPCO) 45–46, 50n47
North Korea 23, 231, 232
Northeast Asia 2, 3, 269; energy outlook 232–234, 243–244; energy security challenges 233; escalating rivalries 233; India's energy engagements 239–241, 246–247; one-fifth of world economy 232; role in India's energy security 9–10, 230–247
Northeast Asian Super Grid 234
Northeastern region (India) 6, 7, 59, 128–129, 131, 136, 142, 152, 184–185, 208, 256, 257
NTPC Vidyut Vyapar Nigam (India) 166(box), 176n16
nuclear energy 2, 10, 22, 25, 40, 53, 57, 76, **77**, **101**, 135, 150, 154, 193, 223, 224, 231; alternative to hydrocarbons 58; ASEAN 191–192; Indian cooperation deals with Japan and SK 240
Numaligarh Refinery Ltd (NRL) xxviii, 151, 183

OAO Rosneft (Russia) 44
Observer Research Foundation 132, 137n16
OECD 53, *68–69*, 79
off-grid system 37, 44, 45, 47, 94
Oggaard, L. 273, 281n65
oil 15, 24–25, 27, 28, 34, 40, 41, 53, 68, 79, 82, 103, 109, 117–118, 188, 236; CAAGR (India) **101**, 102; Chinese demand 9; geopolitics (SCS) 263–269; import dependence 6, 25, 54–55, 96, 188; Indian production 54; world's leading fuel (2019) 231
oil buyers' cooperation 11, 172, 175
oil exploration and production (E&P) 55, 127–128
oil and gas sector (India): domestic 54–55; external 55–56
oil imports: Indian scenario (2016–2040) 24
Oil India Limited **146**, 147, 185, **186**
Oil and Natural Gas Corporation Videsh Limited (OVL) 56, 133–134, **146–147**, 148, 149–150, 151, 154, 155n3–155n4, 155n8–155n9, 167(box), 223, 251, 252, 260n9, 275; exploration for hydrocarbons in SCS 10; investments in ASEAN countries 185, **186–187**; oil and gas exploration in SCS 225, 229n48
oil prices: Asian premium 172, 178n40
Oiwa, T. xviii, xxvii, 9, 203–216
Oman 2, 27, 249
OPEC 23, 27, 31n54, 172, 178n40, 217; oil demand peak (2040 prediction) 36, 49n19
Open Acreage Licensing Policy (OALP) 55
Orissa 252

Pakistan 6, 7, 127, 133, 158, 206, 252, 253, 256; coal and gas reserves 182; debt trap 258; energy cooperation with PRC 224; energy security concerns 170, 178n36; relations with India 175
Panikkar, K.M. 263, 278n8
Pant, G. xviii, 5, 32–51
paper and pulp, energy efficiency **86**
Papua New Guinea 7, 128
Paracel Islands 222, 262, 266, 267, 269–270, 271, 272
Parbatipur (Bangladesh) 183
Pardesi, M.S. 276, 282n85
Paris Agreement (2015–) 1, 5, 25, 32, 33, 37, 39, 43, 47, 53, 57, 60, 71, 84, 94, **120**, 163
particulate matter (PM) 68
peace and stability (East Asia, 1979–) 142–143
peak oil 36, 38, 42
Peng, N. 251, 252, 260n5
People's Liberation Army (PLA) 28, 222
Perform, Achieve, Trade (PAT, 2012–) 6, 71, 86–87, 92, **121–122**
Permanent Court of Arbitration 221, 225
Persian Gulf 252, 275
Petro-Canada 255
Petro Engineering Pvt Ltd 185
Petro LNG Ltd 151
Petro Matad 238, 245n57
petrochemicals 74, **103**, 238, 253
PetroChina 250, 251, 254
petrol (gasoline) 57, 74, 80, 118, 238
petroleum products 75, 76, 100, 118, 154, 238; Indian demand 104–105; refined (India net exporter) 104; sectoral consumptions (India, 2016–2017) *74*;

supply and demand (India, 2016–2017) **104**; trends in international trade (India, 2016–2017) **78**
petroleum refinery capacity (India) 104
Petronas (Malaysia) 167(box)
Petronet LNG 252
PetroVietnam (PVN) 149, 150, 167(box), 225, 275
Philippines 71, 130, 196, 221, 262, 265, 266, 270, 271; GDP forecast (2050) 220
pipelines 3, 7, 22, 54, 127, 128, 134, 137n19, 138n21, 147, 151, 152, 154, 172, 183, 197, 221, 224, 252; crude oil 250–251, 253, 256; natural gas 59, 253, 256; undersea 222
Planning Commission (India) 43
Policy Guidelines for Private Participation in Power Sector (Bangladesh, 2008) 174
Policy for Repowering of Wind Power Projects 93
political economy 43–44, 47
political will 10, 133, 136
pollution 6, 19, 52, 60, 63, 67, 118, **119**
population growth 25, 26, 52, 72, 97n11
post-Cold War 139, 140, 274–275
poverty 2, 53, 63, 157
Powell, L. 132, 137n16
Power for All scheme 63, 71, 96
Power Finance Corporation (PFC) 44
Power Integration Project (Bangladesh-China-Myanmar, 2018) 170–171
Power of Siberia gas pipeline 236, 239, 245n44
Power Pricing Framework (Bangladesh) 174
Power Purchase Agreement (PPA) 184
power sector **119–120**; consumption of primary energy 100; present and future demand by fuel (2016–2040) *110*; single largest source of energy-related carbon emissions 109; single largest user of coal (India) 109
Pradhan, D. xxvii, 7, 11, 128, 136, 151, 155n2, 238, 246n60
Pradhan Mantri Ujjwala Yojana 91, **121**
Pradhan Mantri Urja Ganga project 256
Pratas Islands 262, 269, 271
pressurised heavy water reactors (PHWR) 58
PricewaterhouseCoopers 220, 226n16
primary energy (structure of India's demand) 100–105; coal 103; petroleum products 104–105
primary energy mix, India (projection to 2047) **16**
primary energy supply, projections (2013–2040) **79**
private sector 46, 59, 61, 130, 132, 173, 196
privatisation 160, 219
production sharing contracts (PSCs) 151, 185
prosumers 22, 37
PTC India Ltd 184
public sector companies (PSCs) 238
Punj Lloyd 147

Qatar 2, 27, 55, 56, 65n16, 65n19
Quadrilateral Security Dialogue 11, 23, 213, 216n47, 222, 225
quality of life 67

rail links 88, **120**, 237, 252, 258
Raja Mohan, C. 276, 282n86
Rao, N. 275
Rapp-Hooper, M. 262, 271, 273, 278n6, 280n43
rare earth metals 59, 61, 62, 237
Reed Bank 265
refrigeration 90, **90–91**
regasification terminals (RGT) 129, 168, 172, 189–190
Regime of Islands (UNCLOS) 271
Regional Comprehensive Economic Partnership (RCEP) 139, 140, 208, 214n20, 257
regional security complex (RSC) 212, 216n41
regulators 45, 174
Reliance Industries Limited (RIL) xxv, 147, 252
remote areas 38, 44, 63
renewable energy (RE) 5, 6, 10, 22, 24, 25, 32, 33, 35, 39, 40, 43, 48, 53, 76, 80, 92–95, 109, 130, 180, **181**, 220, 257; ASEAN 191, *192*, 192–193; India 'emerging player in global market' 42; India's world ranking 241; Indian capacity (2018) 93; Indian investment 7; installation barriers 95; installed capacity 71; investment requirements (India) 44–46; 'only to fill energy deficit' 41; price 60
renewable purchase obligations (RPOs) 6, 46, 71, 93, 95
research and development (R&D) 46, 56, 63, 95, 152, 153, 154, 196, 197
residential sector 89–90, **90**, 100
resource diplomacy 232
rivers *209*
roads 206–207
Rosatom 236
Rosenberg, D. 264, 279n16

Rosneft 236, 240
rule of law 221–222, 225
rupee exchange rate 58, 102, 104
rural areas 38, 63, 89, 105, 112
rural electrification 47, 51n54, 90, 91, **121**, 129, 195; MGC countries 133
Russia-India-China (RIC) trilateral framework 242
Russian Far East 9–10, 231, 232, 240, 242; energy potential 234–237, 244–245
Russian Federation 1, 2, 3, 23, 28, 58, 103, 127, 128, 150, 175, 189, 217, 233, 238, 249, 253, 256, 262; contribution of energy flows to GDP 235; energy statistics 234–235; Indian oil exploration 56; LNG contracts with India 55–56, 65n17–65n18; swap arrangements sought by India 148
Russian Federation (Ministry of Energy): *Energy Strategy of Russia* (2010) 235–236
Russian Imperial Energy 255

SAARC (South Asian Association for Regional Cooperation) 26–27, 133, 141, 197, 208
SAARC Energy Ring 157
SAARC Framework Agreement on Energy Cooperation (Electricity) (2014) 26, 31n48, 117, 124n23, 157
SAGAR project xxv, 11
Sakhalin 127, 236, 240
Salween River 215n35, 221
Sampur solar power plant (SL) 184
sanduan zhicheng (three-terminal support) 251
sanzu dingli (three-legged cooperation) 251
Saubhagya scheme 63, 157
Saudi Arabia 2, 27, 42, 43, 178n40, 249, 267
Scarborough Shoal 266, 269, 270, 279n23
Scott, D. 276, 281n79
sea lines of communications (SLOCs) 269
Seafloor Massive Sulphides (SMS) 62
security establishment 7, 128
Sedawyagi hydropower project 184
Shanghai Cooperation Organisation (SCO) 23, 208, 257
Shi Ze 257, 261n29–261n30
Shwe Gas Pipeline Scheme 221
Siliguri (WB) 183
Silk Road Economic Belt (SREB) 8, 248
Silk Road initiative (2013–2014) 218
Singapore 27, 42, 115, 140, 142, 184, 196, 250, 269; Indian energy investments **146**, **186–187**; SCS littoral state 262
Singh, M. 127, 255, 275, 276
single source dependence 159–160
SINOPEC 250
Sittwe (Myanmar) 151, 183, 220
small hydropower 93
small and medium enterprises (SMEs) 92, 96, **121–122**; energy efficiency **86**
Smart Cities Mission 71, 88, 89, 96, 122
software, semiconductors, sensors, solar, storage (five S's) 37, 49n21
solar energy 5, 25, 43, 44, 45, 46, 57–58, 76, 115, 118, 136, 170, 196, 220, 224–225; alliances 135; BIMSTEC 131; CAGR (India, 2005–2018) 94; generation capacity (2018) 58; installation barriers 95; potential 102
Solar Energy Centre 194
solar panels 37, 60–61
solar photovoltaic (PV) power 47, 173; falling cost **116**, 116; installed capacity 93
Soni, S.K. xix, xxviii, 9–10, 230–247
South Africa 153, 184, 188, 254
South Asia: energy cooperation with China 222–224, 227–228; energy resource potential (2012 source) **182**; land bridge to Southeast Asia 204–208, 214; renewable energy potential (2012 source) **182**; solar energy 182
South Asian Association for Regional Cooperation *see* SAARC
South Asian Energy Centre (SEC) 157
South China Sea (SCS) 3, 27, 149, 170, 223, 225, 249; China's claim to sovereignty 149–150; estimated hydrocarbon production (2011) **265**; estimated proved hydrocarbon reserves (2011) **266**; exporters and importers of crude oil via *268*; geographical significance 264–266, *267*; geopolitics (energy perspective) 10–11, 262–282; geopolitics of oil and natural gas 263–269; imports of crude oil through (country by country; source dated 2018) *169*; Indian interests 274–277, 281–282; major actors 273–274, 281; oil and gas exploration 148; strategic significance 266–269
South China Sea dispute 211, 221–222, 227n29–227n30, 269–273; maritime sovereignty claims 270–271, 280n35–280n44; naval and military activities 10–11; nine-dash line 270, 271–273, 280–281; territorial rights 269–270
South Korea (SK) 2, 7, 42, 58, 128, 129, 140, 150, 172, 189, 190, 193; crude oil imports

via SCS 267; energy situation 234; import dependence (energy) 231, 234
Southeast Asia 2, 3, 71, 96, 111, 154, 170; energy cooperation with China 220–221, 226–227; energy cooperation with India 127–138, 148–149, 163–167; energy trade with India 157–179; foreign exchange earnings 162; individual countries (bilateral cooperation with India) 149–153; land bridge to South Asia 204–208, 214; natural gas (huge proven reserves) 148–149; oil production scenario 159; SCS disputes with PRC 221–222, 227n29–227n30
Soviet Union 134, 154
Spratly Islands 262, 266–272 *passim*
Spykman, N.J. 263, 278n7
Sri Lanka (SL) 71, 131, 182, 197, 225; debt trap 258; energy cooperation with PRC 224, 228n46–228n47; LNG 183–184
standards and labelling (S&L) measures 90–91, 92, 96, **122**
State Council of China: Energy Commission (2008–) 219, 226n8
State Electricity Regulatory Commissions 95
state governments 47, 95
Statoil (Norway) 134
steel 73, 86, 87; energy efficiency 86
Storey, I. 270, 280n36
Strait of Bab el-Mandeb 28
Straits of Hormuz 8, 27
strategic petroleum reserves (SPRs) 56, 65n20
subregion: definition (ADB) 203
subregional cooperation 203–216
subsidies 6, 25, 63, 71, 96, 104, 158, 163
Suez Canal 27–28
SUMED Pipeline 27
Sunda Strait 170
supercomplexes 212, 216n40
Super-Efficient Equipment Programme 90–91
super-regions 213, 216n43, 216n53
supply and demand 4, 21, 99, 173
supply and demand mismatch 157, 159, 163
sustainable development 19, *20*, 210
Sustainable Development Goals (SDGs) 7–8, 181; SDG#7, 99, 123n2, **181**, 181, *195–196*, 198n4
Sustainable Development Scenario (SDS) 109–110, *110–111*, **120**
Synohydro 221
Syria 254, 255
Taiwan 219, 222, 249, 262, 270, 272
Tajikistan 170; debt trap 258
Tamanti multipurpose project 168, 184
Tasang dam 174, 175, 179n49, 221, 227n24
Tata Power Company 147, 185, **186**, 188
Tehri Hydro Development Corporation (THDC) 45, 50n47
Thailand 111, **112**, 112, 130, 132, 143, 158, 174, 196, 197, 220, 258; electric power consumption per capita (2014) *162*; electricity access (percentage of population, 2016) *162*; exports and imports of fuel by India (2018) **163**; fisheries 265; fuel exports to China and India (2018 comparison) *171*; GDP forecast (2050) 220; GMS 204, 214n4; important source of India's crude oil 184; India's export and import of fuel (2006–2018) 165, *166*; Indian energy investments **146–147**; move towards market-determined pricing of electricity 173, 179n46
Thailand: Look West approach 131
The Energy Resource Institute (TERI) 86, 88, 89, 90
thermal power: energy efficiency 86–87
Three Gorges Dam Company 224
Three Gorges International Corporation 223
Tiananmen Square incident (1989) 208
Tibet *209*, 211, 212, 215n34, 224
Toman, M.A. 17, 29n12
total primary energy demand (TPED) 109, 117–118; CAAGR projections (countries and regions 2000–2040) *102*; Indian scenarios (2000–2040) *110*; policy scenarios **119–120**; source-wise projection (2000–2014) **101**; statistics and projections (India) 100
total primary energy supply (TPES) **77**; per capita (India) 105, **106**; carbon dioxide emission intensity 105; GDP ratio **72**, 73; various countries (2016) **72**
Tran Dai Quang 135, 150, 155n5
Trans-ASEAN Gas Pipeline (2002–) 129, 168, 189–190, 199n23
Trans-Asia Railway (TAR; Kunming to Singapore) 204, 250
Trans-Pacific Partnership 273
transformation process 33, 35, 37–39
transition in India's energy economy, role of energy efficiency and clean energy 84–95
transmission and distribution (T&D) 173, 184

transport sector 24–25, 40, 53, 88, 104, 118, **119–120**; carbon dioxide emissions from oil 109; consumption of primary energy 100; end-use demand for energy CAGR 73; energy intensity (India 2015–2017) **85**
Tri-Nation Highway (India-Myanmar-Thailand) 142
Trina Solar (China) 44
Trincomalee oil storage tank farm 183
Tripura 136, 194
Trump, D.J. 38, 42, 49n24
Turkmenistan 253; gas pipeline to China 249
Turkmenistan-Afghanistan-Pakistan-India Pipeline (TAPI) 3, 256

UAE 2, 27, 43, 184, 267
UJALA xxvi, 91
UN Commission on Continental Shelf 271–272
UN Convention on Law of Sea (UNCLOS, 1982) 66n34, 270–271, 272, 274, 277
UN Economic and Social Commission for Asia and Pacific 204
UN Environment Programme 191
UN Framework Classification for Fossil Energy (UNFC) 46
UN Sustainable Development agenda **120**
United States (USA) 1, 2, 22, 38, 42, 43, 45, 56, 58, 71, 80, 128, 150, 153, 169, 177n30, 189, 191, 203, 207, 213, 216n53, 219, 221–222, 225, 231, 249, 254, 259, 262–263, 274, 277–278; pivot to Asia doctrine 273, 276; trade via SCS 267; trade war with China 23
United States-India Strategic Partnership 206, 214n10
United States: State Department 272
uranium 10, 58, 65n26, 136, 234, 235, 237, 238, 246n61–246n62, 240, 242
urban areas 44, 46, 48, 63, 118, 173
urbanisation 2, 6, 40, 72, 112, 157
Uzbekistan 58, 66n27, 170, 253

Vajpayee, B. 275
Venezuela 2, 154, 255
Vietnam 3, 6, 10, 12n9, 71, **72**, 73, 111, **112**, 127, 129, 130, 143, 211, 265, 266; coal production scenario 159; EEZ 275; electric power consumption per capita (2014) *162*; electricity access (percentage of population, 2016) *162*; energy cooperation with India 133–134, 135, 138n24, 138n26, 138n29, 148, 149–150, 154–155, 155n3–155n7, 167(box), 277; energy mix *159*; exports and imports of fuel by India (2018) **163**; fisheries 265; fuel exports to China and India (2018 comparison) *171*; GDP forecast (2050) 220; India's export and import of fuel (2006–2018) *164*, 165; Indian firms investing in energy sector (2018–2019) 185, **186**; net energy exporter (2014) *160*; net energy imports as percentage of energy use (2000–2014) *161*; oil extraction 133; Paracel Islands dispute 269–270; relations with PRC 222; renewable energy cooperation with India 135; SCS littoral state 262
Vision Statement to Provide Electricity to All by 2020 (Bangladesh) 174

Wæver, O. 212, 216n40–216n44
Wang Yi 251
water **186–187**, 211, 212, 215n33, 250
water quality 67, 188
wave energies: BIMSTEC 131
Wen Jiabao 219, 255
West Asia 8, 9, 56, 170, 178n34, 188, 217, 218; conflict situation 219
West Bengal 88, 183, 184, 252
West Philippine Sea 262
West Seti dam (Nepal) 223
Western Australia 115, 123n19
wind power 25, 35, 43, 44, 57, 76, 102, 115, 118, 135, 170, 173, 182; BIMSTEC 131; installation barriers 95; installed capacity 93; installed capacity (India fifth in world) 61; offshore and onshore 93, **116**
World Bank 43, 46, 50n48, 117
World Economic Forum 37, 49n22
World Energy Council 36, 49n16, 49n20
World Energy Outlook (2018) 105
WOS **186–187**
Wuhan informal summit (2018) 128

Xi Jinping 128, 219, 248, 273
Xinjiang 224, 239, 250, 252, 253, 256

Yangon 151, 251
Yergin, D. 17, 29n4
Yeywa hydropower project (Myanmar) 184
Yuan Xibin 251
Yunnan 142, 152, 170, 204, 210, 222, 250, 251, 256

Zhu Rongji 219
zou chuqu ('going out') policy 218, 226n7

For Product Safety Concerns and Information please contact our EU representative GPSR@taylorandfrancis.com
Taylor & Francis Verlag GmbH, Kaufingerstraße 24, 80331 München, Germany

www.ingramcontent.com/pod-product-compliance
Lightning Source LLC
LaVergne TN
LVHW021119300926
849160LV00010B/781
* 9 7 8 0 3 6 7 7 6 0 0 0 7 *